International Organizations and the Law

Delving into the law and meaning of international organizations, this book addresses the laws relating to international organizations, their undertakings, and the ways in which specific international organizations function and interact with one another.

Assuming little background knowledge of international law, the book brings together key issues in international law and the history of international organizations in a cohesive manner, providing readers with a clear understanding of international organizations' law in context. It addresses topics such as:

- organization functions and structure
- membership and membership powers
- the rights of international organizations
- dispute settlement in international organizations
- termination of an international organization

Written in an accessible and engaging way, this book is ideal reading for students new to the Law of International Organizations and as a reference for those active in fields impacted by international organizations.

Dr. Alexandra R. Harrington is Lead Counsel for Peace, Justice and Accountability at the Centre for International Sustainable Development Law and an adjunct professor at Albany Law School.

International Organizations and the Law

Alexandra R. Harrington

Routledge
Taylor & Francis Group

LONDON AND NEW YORK

First published 2018
by Routledge
2 Park Square, Milton Park, Abingdon, Oxon OX14 4RN

and by Routledge
711 Third Avenue, New York, NY 10017

Routledge is an imprint of the Taylor & Francis Group, an informa business

© 2018 A. Harrington

British Library Cataloguing-in-Publication Data
A catalogue record for this book is available from the British Library

Library of Congress Cataloging-in-Publication Data
Names: Harrington, Alexandra R., author.
Title: International organizations and the law / Alexandra R. Harrington.
Description: New York, NY : Routledge, 2018. | Includes bibliographical
    references and index.
Identifiers: LCCN 2017058003 | ISBN 9780815375302 (hbk) |
    ISBN 9780815375319 (pbk) | ISBN 9781351240123 (epub) |
    ISBN 9781351240116 (mobipocket)
Subjects: LCSH: International organizations. | International
    agencies—Law and legislation.
Classification: LCC KZ4850 .H37 2018 | DDC 341.2—dc23
LC record available at https://lccn.loc.gov/2017058003

ISBN: 978-0-8153-7530-2 (hbk)
ISBN: 978-0-8153-7531-9 (pbk)
ISBN: 978-1-3512-4014-7 (ebk)

Typeset in Joanna
by Apex CoVantage, LLC

Outline contents

Detailed contents

Acknowledgments

This book has been years in the making, and throughout those years I have accumulated debts of gratitude for which words barely seem sufficient. My attempts to do so here are made with apologies to any who might not be specifically named – please know that you have not been overlooked.

The students in my classes at Albany Law School inspired me to write this book and continuously encouraged me with their questions about the subject matter and about all things international. Teaching is a privilege afforded to the lucky few and my students remind me that on a daily basis – from the bottom of my heart, thank you. Specific mention must be made to Nicole Camuti, Robert Sohm, Ashley McDonough, Justin Reyes, Anthony Cove, Claudia Cadenillas, Patrick Duprey and Maxwell Radley.

I am lucky to have a group of friends and family who have encouraged me, pushed me and challenged me, particularly Rex Ruthman, Dr. Elisabeth Ruthman, Molly and Helmut Philipp, Dr. and Mrs. William O'Dwyer, Mr. Norman Mokhiber and Ms. Mia Ebert, Professor Carol Whittaker, Professor Frederic Megret, Dr. Amar Khoday, Dr. Maureen Duffy, Professor Danshera Cords, Professor David Pratt, Professor Marie-Claire Cordonier Segger, Dr. Markus Gehring, Professor Konstantia Koutouki, Dr. Gabrielle Dumas-McBath, Dr. Timi Agenaba-Jeanty, Ms. Maria del Pilar Vanegas Guzman, Professor Pam Armstrong, Professor Debbie Mann, and Dean Alicia Ouellette. Special thanks to the Harrington, McNerney, Manley, and Inkhamfong families for the constant support and laughter throughout the writing of this book.

The editorial staff at Routledge and Taylor & Francis made this book possible and for that I cannot possibly express the extent of my gratitude. Special thanks to Siobhan Poole, Chloe James, Hannah Lovelock, Alex Buckley, Jashnie Jabson and the indubitable Liz Dittner for all their efforts.

In many ways, this book began with when I was a six-year old girl watching a piece about the North Atlantic Treaty Organization on television news with my parents. I was curious about the idea of an international organization, what it could do, what would happen if its members quarreled, and a litany of other issues. Rather than changing the channel or the topic, my parents wryly answered these questions. In that moment, my perpetual fascination with international organizations was created. It is also emblematic of the support and encouragement I have been fortunate to receive from my parents, Dr. George and Mrs. Barbara Harrington – I am more grateful to them than I could possibly express.

My husband and champion, Onchan Inkhamfong, has endured many rushed dinners and missed evenings during the conception and writing of this book and for this and many other things I can only offer a lifetime of thank-yous. And, last but not least, a special acknowledgment must be made to Churchill, my four-legged source of levity who spent many hours diligently guarding my desk while this book was completed.

Abbreviations

ADB	Asian Development Bank
AfDB	African Development Bank
ASEAN	Association of Southeast Asian Nations
AU	African Union
CAT	Committee Against Torture
CDB	Caribbean Development Bank
CDM	Clean Development Mechanism
CEDAW	Committee on the Elimination of all Forms of Discrimination Against Women
CERD	Committee on the Elimination of Racial Discrimination
CESCR	Committee on Economic, Social and Cultural Rights
CMW	Committee on Migrant Workers
CRC	Committee on the Rights of the Child
CRPD	Committee on the Rights of Persons with Disability
EBRD	European Bank for Reconstruction and Development
ECB	European Central Bank
ECCC	Extraordinary Chambers in the Courts of Cambodia
ECOSOC	Economic and Social Council
EIB	European Investment Bank
ESCB	European System of Central Banks
EU	European Union
EUFOR	European Union Force
FAO	Food and Agriculture Organization
GATT	General Agreement on Trade and Tariffs
HRC	Human Rights Committee
IADB	Inter-American Development Bank
IBRD	International Bank for Reconstruction and Development
ICAO	International Civil Aviation Organization
ICC	International Criminal Court
ICCPR	International Covenant on Civil and Political Rights
ICJ	International Court of Justice
ICSID	International Centre for Settlement of Investment Disputes
ICTR	International Criminal Tribunal for Rwanda
ICTY	International Criminal Tribunal for the former Yugoslavia
IDA	International Development Association
ICESCR	International Covenant on Economic, Social and Cultural Rights
IFC	International Finance Corporation
ILO	International Labour Organization
IMF	International Monetary Fund
IMO	International Maritime Organization
MICT	International Residual Mechanism for Criminal Tribunals
MIGA	Multi-lateral Investment Guarantee Agency

NATO	North Atlantic Treaty Organization
NIB	Nordic Investment Bank
OAS	Organization of American States
OAU	Organization for African Unity
OPCW	Organization for the Prohibition of Chemical Weapons
PCIJ	Permanent Court of International Justice
UN	United Nations
UNDP	United Nations Development Programme
UNEP	United Nations Environment Programme
UNESCO	United Nations Education, Scientific and Cultural Organization
UNFCCC	United Nations Framework Convention on Climate Change
UNGA	United Nations General Assembly
UNHCR	United Nations High Commissioner for Refugees
UNSC	United Nations Security Council
VCLT	Vienna Convention on the Law of Treaties
VCLTS/IO	Vienna Convention on the Law of Treaties between States and International Organizations or between International Organizations
WHO	World Health Organization
WIPO	World Intellectual Property Organization
WTO	World Trade Organization

Chapter 1

Introduction

What is an international organization? This is a deceptively difficult question to answer. The initial answers seem rather obvious – it is an organization made up of different States or it is an organization that operates in more than one State or an organization having international areas of focus, or perhaps all three. And these answers are correct as far as they go; however, they only scratch the surface of what an international organization is, the laws and rules that govern it, and how it exists within the international community.

This book is meant as a comprehensive tool for those wishing to learn about the laws that create and govern international organizations and how international organizations function within this system of governance. Since international organizations are not natural creatures but instead must be created through laws and agreements, the book explains the meaning of international organizations generally and also the terms and activities of specific international organizations. The goal of this book is to explain the intricacies of international organizations at the theoretical and law and rules-based level and to allow for application of these lessons to international organizations that cut across the spectrum of political and legal policy orientations and functions.

Throughout the process of reading this book, the reader will learn the specific laws and rules that relate to and govern international organizations. Beyond this, the reader will learn how these laws and rules are applied in a variety of contexts. The first part of the book examines the laws and rules that apply to international organizations generally. The second part of the book provides an in-depth, thematic discussion of specific organizations, comparing and contrasting them so that the reader will walk away from the book with knowledge of the key international organizations that shape the world as well as the laws and rules that govern them generally. The ideology behind this method of analysis and pedagogy is that, given the plethora of international organizations existing in the international system at present and their varied functions, assessing the true nature of these organizations and how laws apply to them is a two-step process. This book asserts that only by understanding the general framework of the law of international organizations can these organizations themselves be understood and analyzed as independent entities and in the context of other international organizations.

It is hoped that the book will be helpful to readers at all levels – this is the purpose of writing the book! As a student of international organizations, the book will be helpful in promoting an understanding of the structure of international organizations and what international organizations mean for international law and national law. As a student of international law, the book will be helpful in promoting an understanding of how international law is implemented and the role of international organizations in developing the future of international law. Regardless the field of study, the reader will find the book helpful and, it is hoped, engaging.

As noted above, the book is divided into two parts. In Part I, this book sets out the essential elements of international organizations. Accordingly, Chapter 2 begins with a discussion of the history behind the rise of international organizations, starting with early attempts to create largely issue-based coalitions of States in the 1800s and the increased switch to international awareness – if not always focus – until World War I. The chapter then examines the role that World War I itself played in the creation of international organizations and in their acceptance, notably the League of Nations and associated entities such as the International Labor Organization and the Permanent Court of International Justice. Following the decline of the League of Nations, Chapter 2 charts the path toward World War II and the impact that the war had on planning for internationalism in the envisioned post-war period. This is then followed by a discussion of the post-war years in actuality, a time when the United Nations was created and a slew of other international organizations followed.

Chapter 2 then turns to the Charter of the United Nations – the crucible for international organizations law and functioning since 1945 – and sets out the important terms and requirements for State inclusion and participation. This includes the essential organs of the United Nations that are often taken for granted in current international law systems but were groundbreaking at the time of their creation. Finally, the chapter examines the Vienna Convention on the Law of Treaties and the Vienna Convention on the Law of Treaties between States and International Organizations or between International Organizations because they have exerted and continue to exert vital interpretive roles in the functioning of the United Nations and its organs.

From this discussion of the history and fundamental texts of international organizations as a function of international law, the book then moves on in Chapter 3 to a discussion of the issue of membership of international organizations. Often, membership might appear a trivial or even self-evident matter for an international organization – after all, the name does suggest that members will themselves be international and public international law suggests that they will be largely State-focused. However, as the chapter highlights, membership is quite an important issue, one that touches the very heart of how the organization conceives of and identifies itself. After all, the parameters of membership and such basic issues as what States can be full members impacts the benefits that the international organization is established to convey and affects everything from voting rights to the daily functioning of the organization. Membership can also be seen as a validation of a State's legitimacy as an actor in the international community and as part of the community of States that has an interest in a particular subject area – such as the International Maritime Organization or the Organisation for the Prohibition of Chemical Weapons.

Closely connected to the issue of membership is the issue of voting within an international organization, an issue examined in Chapter 4. Regardless of the setting, whether national or international, voting and voting rights play an integral part in defining and shaping society and its activities in the short and long term. Extension of the franchise and voting rights to members of an international organization is another aspect of recognizing its legitimacy and membership in the legal and societal structure created through the foundational text of the international organization. Another aspect of voting rights that correlates to legitimacy is the type and number of votes allotted to member States. Depending on the organization, members may share in equal numbers and values of votes – for example, in the United Nations General Assembly – or they may have voting shares that are dependent on their contributions to the international organization – for example, in the International Monetary Fund. Each of these voting forms impacts on organizational governance and on the valuing of member States and the issues of importance to them.

Chapter 5 then discusses the legal tenets involved in the function and structure of international organizations. Any discussion of function and structure must take into account more than the law which implements them, and accordingly this chapter starts with a review of the roles that State power, politics, and civil society actors play in shaping an international organization's functions and structures. Following this, the chapter examines the concept of organizational function to determine its sources and legal impacts on the Member States, international law and the international community. The chapter reviews organizations with general purpose functions, such as the United Nations, as well as those with specific purpose functions, such as the World Health Organization and the Food and Agriculture Organization. The articulation of intended functions is, perhaps obviously, an essential existential element for any international organization. Beyond this, however, the chapter examines the methods by which these functions are put into practice and their legal impact, including situations where an organization exceeds the scope of its authorized functions. Additionally, Chapter 5 examines the structures used by international organizations to facilitate governance, decision-making and decision implementation. Due to their increasing importance for international organizations' operations and funding, this includes a review of oversight bodies used for the organization overall and for specific organization activities, such as lending or disaster aid and assistance.

The discussion of oversight mechanisms in Chapter 5 leads into a discussion in Chapter 6 of using methods of punishment, suspension and, at the most severe, expulsion of Member States to ensure compliance with international organization laws and rules. This discussion stresses the importance of accountability at the Member State and international organization level and also highlights the additional concerns that are often implicated in these situations. These concerns include the human rights impacts and economic impacts of a decision to rebuke a Member State to some degree since a rebuke can often result in devastating consequences to the most vulnerable members of society in the targeted State. Under the heading of general punishment of Member States by an international organization, the chapter addresses methods that have become frequently used, ranging from sanctions to public rebukes or "naming and shaming" to restrictions on the Member State's activities within the organization and, often, its ability to receive funding from the organization. Following from this, Chapter 6 discusses the use of suspension of a Member State, including the legal requirements for this to occur and for the suspension to be cured, where appropriate. Finally, the chapter addresses the rarely used possibility of expelling a Member State from an international organization. For a number of reasons, this is regarded as an extreme measure in international law and the law of international organizations, and typically all possible measures must be exhausted before this occurs. However, procedures do exist for the expulsion of Member States and the impacts of this on the legal structure of the international organization can be significant, thus it is essential that they are understood.

The existence and function of international organizations must necessarily go beyond the terms of the organization's foundational text since, in order to function, the organization must interact with people, corporations, and host States. Chapter 7 examines the concepts of standard diplomatic rights accorded to certain actors and the rights accorded to international organizations and those associated with them. The purpose of this comparison is to make clear the similarities and differences in rights and obligations accorded to diplomatic and international organizations-based actors. In some situations these rights overlap; however, in many situations they do not, or they stem from different sources and can be abrogated in different ways. It is essential for any student of international organizations or international law to understand the terms of these rights and their differences.

Chapter 7 dovetails with Chapter 8, which addresses the legal concepts and standard terms involved in headquarters agreements and host State agreements between an international organization and a State in which it seeks to base its operations. At the outset, the chapter discusses the necessity of these agreements, highlighting the fact that international organizations have a different legal status from diplomatic entities, corporations, or individuals and thus require alternative arrangements to determine their rights and obligations relative to any host State. This is certainly true for the host State of the international organization's headquarters – where, it is presumed, there will be a long-term presence – and is equally true for the host State of an international organization's satellite or other office, including locations of peacekeeping or other military or policing operations conducted under the auspices of an international organization. Accordingly, Chapter 8 reviews the standard rights and protections guaranteed in headquarters and host State agreements and provides influential examples of these agreements in practice.

In addition to headquarters and host State agreements, international organizations have the ability to assist in the negotiation of international instruments under their auspices. Chapter 9 examines this ability from the perspective of international law, beginning with the parameters of international organization involvement and influence from the legal and political perspectives. The chapter then examines the methods through which international instruments, primarily treaties and agreements, are negotiated and promulgated through an international organization's structure and the effect that these instruments have on Member States. As is evident, while Member States might be zealous in the creation of an international instrument under the auspices of an international organization, that instrument must still be subject to the ratification procedures prescribed by national law before it can become binding on the Member State. Additionally, even when the international organization is heavily supportive of the new instrument, the decision of a Member State not to sign and/or ratify the instrument will in no way impair its status as a member of the international organization. Finally, Chapter 9 reviews the use of protocols and amendments to existing international instruments in the international system and their impacts on international organization structure.

Disputes and their settlement form the crux of legal and societal systems from the village to international levels. This is certainly no different in the context of international organizations, which interact with multiple constituencies and consequently face multiple sources of conflict. Chapter 10 addresses the issue of dispute settlement in international organizations, providing general principles and specific examples of how principles of dispute settlement have been applied by various forms of organizations. As an initial matter, the chapter discusses instances in which immunity applies to bar certain types of dispute from being brought against international organizations or requires that such disputes be brought in internal organizational settings rather than through a domestic court system. A primary example of this is in the employment context, in which a number of international organizations reserve the right to have disputes settled through an internal grievance procedure as a term of employment.

While the general premise behind international organizations is that they promote peaceful dialogue between States, disputes between Member States can and do still occur. Chapter 10 explores the methods by which these disputes are handled in different types of organization, starting with the United Nations system and then examining regional organizations, financial and banking organizations, and the World Trade Organization. Throughout this discussion, similarities and differences in methods of using an international organization as an arbiter in cases of dispute settlement between Member States become apparent. In addition to disputes between Member States, it is equally possible for a Member State to have a dispute with an international organization, and indeed there have been notable examples of these throughout the history of modern international law. Chapter 10 reviews the methods used to address these disputes through the frameworks of the United Nations system, regional organizations, and financial and banking organizations to highlight similarities and differences between the organizations and between situations where the disputes are between member States. Finally, Chapter 10 examines situations in which the dispute is between international organizations in order to establish how these disputes are handled and where they might be heard.

Although it is generally not encouraged, and is indeed uncommon, Member States may decide to withdraw from international organizations and international organizations may decide to temporarily or permanently cease operations. These situations raise complex issues that are discussed in Chapter 11. The chapter initially examines situations in which these decisions might arise, including those involving changes to the international system that gave rise to the organization, economic or political changes within a Member State, or political or legal disagreements between a Member State and the organization. It then discusses the impact on the international organization of Member State withdrawal, from a legal and structural perspective. Following this, the chapter examines the differences between an international organization suspending its operations and terminating its operations from a conceptual standpoint and a legal standpoint. Chapter 11 further examines the issues involved in the termination of an international organization. Although the Member States might decide to terminate an international organization with relative ease, the work of wrapping up the organization – similarly to the work of wrapping up a corporation – is far more complex, particularly in terms of settling debts and distributing any remaining organizational assets. Termination of an international organization can also have an impact on the administration of some international treaties and agreements, requiring additional planning and decision-making by the States Parties to those instruments.

Chapter 11 brings Part 1 full circle, beginning with the definition and creation of an international organization and ending with methods of terminating the organization. From this point, the book moves on to Part 2, which delves into the structure and functioning of specific international organizations, through the lens of topic areas in which they focus and operate.

Part 2 opens in Chapter 12 with a discussion of the United Nations system of key entities. As a preliminary matter, the chapter reviews the system of governance originally envisioned for the United Nations and consisting of the United Nations General Assembly, the United Nations Security Council, the United Nations Secretariat, and the United Nations Trusteeship Council. Over time, these entities have changed significantly, particularly in the context of an expanded UN Secretariat that has been tasked with a number of functions not foreseeable in 1945 and a UN Trusteeship Council that ceased operations when the last Trusteeship territory became independent in 1993, yet continues to exist as an entity. Chapter 12 further assesses the functioning and roles of two additional entities that were provided for in the Charter of the United Nations – the Economic and Social Council (ECOSOC) and the International Court of Justice (ICJ). These entities have evolved over time through legal frameworks that were flexible enough to provide for this without requiring significant reworking. In addition, Chapter 12 examines the structure and function of the UN Educational, Scientific and Cultural Organization (UNESCO). Although not specifically provided for in the Charter, UNESCO is an essential element of the UN system, hence its inclusion in Chapter 12.

The same World War II and post-World War II legal, political and societal environment that gave rise to the United Nations gave rise to the concepts of internationalized criminal law manifested in the trials at Nuremburg and Tokyo. In the years that followed, atrocities continued to occur and the international community struggled with the question of how best to address them. Chapter 13 examines the legal structures and functions of international criminal courts from a wide perspective. This includes specific conflict-based criminal courts, notably the International Criminal Tribunal for the former Yugoslavia and the International Criminal Tribunal for Rwanda, as well as hybridized criminal courts in Cambodia and Sierra Leone. While the work of some of these courts is in the process of winding down as at the time of writing, they are still important to discuss because they represent innovations in the concept and constructs of international criminal law and justice and also in the ways in which international organizations' principles can be applied to such entities. Finally, Chapter 13 examines the International Criminal Court (ICC), the first sustained international court for the prosecution of *jus cogens*-based crimes, specifically genocide, war crimes, crimes against humanity and the crime of aggression. The ICC is a unique entity with a similarly unique system of governance, one that is persistently challenged by Member States, especially those threatening to leave the ICC based on its prosecutorial decisions. From an apolitical perspective, the ICC represents an innovation and one of the newer forms of international organization.

Chapter 14 highlights regional organizations in the international system, discussing the largest and most influential of these organizations in order to demonstrate the role of regionalism in adapting standard tenets of international organizations to the needs of particular constituencies. The three purely regional organizations discussed in Chapter 14 are the Organization of American States (OAS), the oldest of such organizations and indeed one of the oldest continuous organizations in the international sphere; the Association of South East Asian Nations (ASEAN), which brings a consensus-based focus to its legal instruments as well as its policy creation and implementation; and the African Union (AU), formerly the Organization for African Unity, which successfully reinvented itself legally and functionally and now has an expanded area in which it works. In addition, Chapter 14 examines the laws and functions of the European Union (EU). Technically, the EU is a supranational entity rather than a pure regional organization; however, it is included in this chapter to offer a contrasting view of a system that aims to bring together States in a region in a more binding manner. This is important to discuss at a time when there is a push for creating greater unity within entities such as the AU and ASEAN. At the same time, the EU offers an evolving study of the potential for a Member State to withdraw from an organization, the ways in which this might be achieved, and the potential impacts a withdrawal will have on the organization and the withdrawing State. The withdrawal of the United Kingdom from the

EU (Brexit) casts a shadow over this section of Chapter 14 and it must be highlighted that the information relating to it is current as at the time of writing.

At the heart of the EU, and to a lesser extent the other regional organizations discussed, was the desire to create an economic union that would foster peace in the region by binding the Member States through law and economic interdependence. It is appropriate, then, that Chapter 15 transition to a discussion of trade, finance and banking organizations. The chapter begins by emphasizing the contrasts between trade agreements and international organizations that address financial and related issues so as to avoid the potential for confusion. It first discusses the World Trade Organization (WTO), the pinnacle of trade organizations that has, since it was formalized as a standing organization in 1993, attracted States from myriad legal, political, and economic systems. The WTO's membership requirements are among the most stringent of any international organization, with an applicant usually requiring ten years to bring its legal and economic systems in line with the requirements to become a member. Chapter 15's discussion focuses on the membership process as well as on the legal structure and functions of the WTO generally and highlights the ways in which it is evolving from strictly trade to include in its ambit issues such as anti-corruption and aid.

Following this, Chapter 15 examines the legal structures and functions of the International Monetary Fund (IMF), an organization characterized by the role of Member States that are considered shareholders and that is often criticized for its lending practices. By examining the legal system at the heart of the IMF, the chapter's goal is to provide clarity on the basic terms of an organization that is rarely analyzed with a dispassionate eye. Chapter 15 then unpacks and discusses the organizations that together comprise the World Bank – the International Bank for Reconstruction and Development (IBRD), the International Development Association (IDA), the International Finance Corporation (IFC), the Multilateral Investment Guarantee Association (MIGA), and the International Centre for the Settlement of Investment Disputes (ICSID). Each of these organizations has a specialized area of focus and allows for differing levels of engagement with public and private actors, although each uses a relatively similar foundational text. Within this context, the chapter examines the meaning of the terms of the foundational text to the individual organizations comprising the World Bank in order to evaluate the ways in which similar legal structures are used in very different situations and purposes.

In addition, Chapter 15 examines regional banking organizations to compare and contrast the legal structures and functions used, notably in terms of oversight and accountability mechanisms. There is a plethora of such organizations, and, accordingly, the chapter seeks to discuss a number of them – ranging from large to small entities – in order to provide a holistic view of their laws and governance. In addition to standard features of structure and function, oversight and accountability mechanisms are of particular importance because they are emerging as a genre of governance and regulation and reflect the priorities and concerns of regional and sub-regional areas. Further, although they carry the shared moniker of banking entities, the organizations profiled carry out vastly different activities involving a number of constituencies and lending activities. The organizations examined in Chapter 15 include the Inter-American Development Bank, the European Central Bank, the European Bank for Reconstruction and Development, the European Investment Bank, the Asian Development Bank, the African Development Bank, the Caribbean Development Bank, and the Nordic Investment Bank.

Chapter 16 of the book shifts the focus from trade and finance to sector and industry-specific international organizations. As a primary issue, the chapter notes the many ways in which these organizations have the potential to directly set national regulatory policies and practices as well as those at the international level – indeed, this is a theme across the majority of the organizations discussed. Chapter 16 begins by discussing the World Health Organization (WHO), a UN specialized agency that has a long history throughout which it has consistently sought to shift the focus of its legal and policy work to respond to the changing public health needs of the international community. While many of these activities have, perhaps unsurprisingly, resulted in significant debate and disagreement between the Member States, the International Health Regulations (IHRs) represent a regulatory undertaking of the WHO that is nearly universally accepted and implemented across Member States. Another UN specialized agency, which works closely with the WHO, is the Food and Agriculture Organization (FAO). Chapter 16 examines the ways in which its legal structure and functions interact with the WHO and are put into effect on the ground and among Member States with frequently disparate concerns regarding food and the preservation of agriculture. However, the FAO promulgates the Codex Alimentarius, a universally accepted set of practices and regulations for food and crop classifications and standardizations among member States. The International Labor Organization (ILO) – which was a product of the World War I period – exists as a significant actor in international labor regulations and many areas of legal and social policy in which labor is implicated. As Chapter 16 highlights, it is a truly unusual organization in that it uses a tripartite representation system to include not only Member States as representatives but also industry and labor representatives from each Member State to ensure that the needs of all key elements of the labor cycle are included in the promulgation of laws and policies under the ILO's rubric. As is highlighted in Chapter 16, there are many overlaps in labor concerns between the ILO and the International Maritime Organization (IMO), although the IMO's jurisdiction relates solely to issues involving maritime workers and the maritime industry. As a result of the specialized nature of its work, the IMO promulgates rules and regulations on maritime trade safety – ranging from environmental safety to worker safety – that are accepted similarly to the IHRs and the Codex. International air travel involving civilians is essential to the economic welfare of many States and is overseen at the international level by the International Civil Aviation Organization (ICAO), discussed in Chapter 16. Similar to the IMO, ICAO promulgates rules and regulations that are widely accepted by Member States due to their scientific and industry-based origins, reflecting the ultimate needs of the industry and public safety in a way that more politically motivated activities could not. Finally, Chapter 16 examines the World Intellectual Property Organization (WIPO), which provides a forum for the creation of rules and regulations regarding intellectual property concerns that are increasingly internationally focused.

As a matter of public international law and sovereignty, military control and military activities are among the most jealously guarded of State functions. Of course, this was historically tempered somewhat by the reality of the alliance system that resulted in World War I and, increasingly, by the reality of the need for cooperation among aligned States that existed during the Cold War. In the post-Cold War era, the need for military alliances and organizations has not abated and this need has only expanded to include policing entities in the face of increasingly internationalized and interconnected criminal networks. Chapter 17 focuses on military and policing organizations at the purely international level and at the regional level. It begins with a discussion of the Organization for the Prohibition of Chemical Weapons (OPCW), which was created under the auspices of the Chemical Weapons Convention and which functions as the Secretariat and oversight body for the Convention's implementation. The OPCW was selected for discussion because it is a regulatory entity for the weaponry of conflict and is a contrast to the entities that follow in this chapter, which engage in conflict operations. The chapter then shifts focus to the North Atlantic Treaty Organization, formed to provide for protection and collective self-defense in the event of an attack on Western States during the Cold War. In the aftermath of the Cold War, NATO could have terminated its operations since the threat it was created to counter was finished. However, NATO members decided instead to significantly expand its areas of operation and its membership base, providing an example of how to handle such a situation from the organizational perspective. Chapter 17 further examines international and regional organizations that are involved in international peacekeeping operations – namely the UN, NATO, the EU, and the AU – in order to provide insights into the legal and regulatory structures and functions used for the implementation of peacekeeping mandates. The chapter closes with a discussion of two key policing entities – INTERPOL and EUROPOL – which serve police coordinating and advisory roles for their jurisdictions without the legal authorization to carry out the direct police function themselves.

Chapter 18 examines human rights organizations and bodies at the international and regional levels. The chapter opens with a discussion of the bodies created through the fundamental international human rights law treaties – the Human Rights Committee; the Committee on Economic, Social and Cultural Rights; the Committee on the Rights of the Child; the Committee Against Torture; the Committee on the Elimination of All Forms of Discrimination Against Women; the Committee on the Elimination of Racial Discrimination; the Committee on Migrant Workers,; and the Committee on the Rights of Persons with Disabilities. These bodies represent key actors in the international human rights system, and in international law generally, as well as functioning as quasi secretariats for the implementation of the correlative treaties. As such, they are governed by set legal structures and functions although they seek to implement different treaties with often overlapping provisions. Following this, the chapter examines the UN High Commissioner for Refugees, an entity that encompasses far more than the individual occupying the Commissionership at any given moment. Instead, this is a UN specialized agency that oversees numerous aspects of law and policy surrounding refugees and other migrants, such as internally displaced persons. Finally, Chapter 18 examines the different regional organizations and systems existing for the adjudication and recognition of human rights. In this context, there are three highly important systems – the Inter-American Human Rights System (comprised of the Inter-American Commission on Human Rights and the Inter-American Court of Human Rights), the European Court of Human Rights, and the African Court of Human and Peoples' Rights – all of which will be discussed. It should be noted that ASEAN has not yet created a similar system.

Chapter 19 focuses on the ever-evolving area of environmental organizations and, necessarily, international environmental law and associated tenets such as sustainable development law. It begins by examining the organizational structure created by the United Nations Framework Convention on Climate Change (UNFCCC) and its associated implementing entities, such as the Kyoto Protocol and the 2015 Paris Agreement. Included in this are the organizational elements of the Clean Development Mechanism and Joint Implementation, both of which were created under the Kyoto Protocol. Together, these organizations represent a continuously evolving system of governance and implementation mechanisms that build on the original legal structure and functions of the UNFCCC. Chapter 19 further examines the United Nations Environment Programme (UNEP), which has an organizational and legal structure distinct from the UNFCCC although much of its work complements the UNFCCC and its subsequently associated entities. As a purely international organization that does not serve the secretariat function for a treaty, other than its foundational treaty, UNEP offers a somewhat different perspective on how organizations can be used in the environmental context. The same rationale guides the inclusion of the United Nations Development Programme (UNDP) in Chapter 19. While UNDP's mandate exceeds environment per se it is essentially intertwined with environmental issues, UNEP, and the UNFCCC, and its inclusion completes the image of environmental organizations.

Finally, Chapter 20 serves as a conclusion to the book, highlighting essential themes and elements in the law of international organizations in both theory and practice. The chapter suggests areas of commonality across topic divides and the ways in which these commonalities serve to foster a coordinated system of international organizations.

Chapter 2

History, the United Nations Charter and Vienna Conventions

The following chapter functions as a source of background on the history leading up to the creation of modern constructs of international organizations. This is, necessarily, an essential element for understanding the laws that govern international organizations, the ways in which these organizations are used nationally and internationally, and the ways in which they may evolve to face the future needs and challenges of the international community. This state of fluidity is in keeping with the history of international organizations and with the intent of those who created such influential organizations as the United Nations.[1] For the framers of the foundational texts of such organizations, larger goals – for example international peace and security – informed the need for the organization itself. Against this background, the importance of international organizations themselves, and as a genre of international law and politics, to continuously evolve so as to meet the changing needs of the world community becomes apparent.

After opening with a discussion of the history of international organizations, the chapter then examines the Charter of the United Nations (UN Charter) in terms of overall meaning and specific provisions. Although the United Nations system is analyzed in Chapter 12, the UN Charter is discussed here because it has created a framework for the norms and terms used in virtually all subsequent foundational texts for international organizations. As such, attempting to study the essential laws of international organizations without a firm grounding in the UN Charter rings hollow.

Finally, the chapter discusses two essential treaties for the interpretation of the foundational texts – and indeed any texts or instruments – of international organizations: the Vienna Convention on the Law of Treaties (VCLT) and the Vienna Convention on the Law of Treaties between States and International Organizations or between International Organizations (VCLTS/IO). While these treaties are often considered to represent gap-fillers in the event of ambiguity or silence in relevant instruments, they also serve an important role in the ways in which legitimate frameworks for international organizations are fashioned and can potentially be refashioned in the future.

Historical background

Growth of international attempts to focus State response to certain issue areas throughout the 1800s

The history of international relations and international law focused – and still focuses – on the State itself. From Biblical examples onward, interactions between entities exercising what would today be classified as State functions were driven largely by conflict, commerce and economy, and/or areas of shared needs and interests.[2] Indeed, the earliest examples of international treaties center on trade, although their durability was questionable.[3] Against this backdrop, coalitions of States formed for primarily defensive purposes, and these coalitions were often fleeting, with former allies becoming enemies in the space of a short period of time.[4] In such a setting, it is perhaps unsurprising that international organizations did not emerge.

In the private sphere, examples of alliances in trade and industry that became so entrenched as to function as quasi-international organizations did exist, for example the Hanseatic League of merchants throughout Northern Europe.[5] These represented powerful entities that often fulfilled functions we now ascribe to States – such as the regulation of trade and those who could enter into it – and yet were not acting on behalf of a State or other public entity.[6] Such alliances were more akin to issue-specific international organizations in some ways; however, they served a constituency that was limited and were not subject to the same strictures of domestic and international law that define the construct of international organizations which developed in later centuries.[7]

At certain periods, notably during the negotiations leading to the Peace of Westphalia in 1648, powerful States in Europe created space for lengthy rounds of negotiations for an encompassing peace agreement that was meant to end several decades-long conflicts.[8] However, these negotiations were not held in a concerted fashion, lacked the centrality which has come to signify a core function of international organizations, and did not result in the creation of any form of entity to monitor the implementation of the agreements or to resolve future disputes over their implementation.[9] Rather, the negotiations had a specific result – the generation of the Peace of Westphalia that has come to define statecraft ever since – and terminated once this was achieved.

It was not until the 1800s that States began to coalesce around certain issues to the point of creating quasi-international organizations in order to address them.[10] This was often the result of pressures from private citizens and social campaigners who had access to better sources of information regarding international practices and increasingly called on their governments to address cross-boundary issues such as infectious disease and pandemic outbreaks.[11] While this represented a significant step toward the creation of a community in which international organizations could be crafted and survive with some semblance of durability, it still was not sufficient to give rise to an international organization system *per se*. The combination of power shifts in Europe and the Americas, increased capacity for weapons that caused catastrophic damage, and increased social awareness through media and communications was rapidly bringing about a climate in which this could occur. At the same time, international law as a genre was able to assert a more visible and dominant role both diplomatically and commercially, generating new norms and structures.

World War I and its aftermath – setting the stage

World War I, the war that would invariably change modern warfare and would give rise to the first attempt at a concerted international organization as such, was caused by myriad tensions and intrigues which in 1914 brought Austro-Hungarian Archduke (and intended successor to the throne) Franz Ferdinand and his wife, Sophie, together with the bullets from Serbian nationalist Gavrilo Princip's gun on a sunny summer day in Sarajevo.[12] This was a conflict that soon escalated to embroil Europe and Europe's colonial holdings as well as the Ottoman Empire. It was also a war which most believed would end quickly and decisively, although most were proven wrong and the war lasted for over four bloody years which saw the elevation of trench warfare to a miserable art form and the introduction of horrendously painful and scaring chemicals to the battlefield.[13]

The war might have ended with the 11 November 1918 Armistice; however, the crafting of a post-war international system had only just begun.[14] For much of the war, it was anticipated that hostilities would end with a victor and the use of victor's justice, including in the division of the territories and States of the vanquished and a re-imposition of the legal status quo.[15] Prominent voices across the victorious coalition of France, the United Kingdom, the United States, and dozens of less influential States ensured that this would not be the case, however.

Over the course of more than six months in 1919, the terms of the peace settlements were laboriously – and acrimoniously – determined at the Paris Peace Conference.[16] The negotiations reflected the legal, political and economic concerns of States that had experienced the war from different perspectives and at varying levels of geographical involvement, and also reflected differing beliefs on how to ensure that this type of conflict could be prevented in the future.[17] When the negotiations were concluded and the resultant Treaty of Versailles was signed, a new era of international law was ushered in.[18] This era was led by the creation of the League of Nations, a dedicated international organization with its own rules and procedures for protecting and promoting peace and allowing for the diplomatic resolution of disputes.[19]

The League of Nations and related organizations
Treaty of Versailles/Covenant of the League of Nations

The League of Nations represented a vast departure from the international coalitions which had previously served to bring States together. Under the terms of the Treaty of Versailles, the League was intended to "promote international co-operation and to achieve international peace and security"[20] by generating an environment in which diplomatic methods would be used to address conflicts and potential conflicts.[21] In the event of an act of aggression against a Member State, other League members were required to take action in support of the territorial and political independence of the State under attack. This represented a step toward future iterations of collective self-defense requirements used by international organizations, although not as strict in its terminology.[22] Additionally, Member States were given the ability to refer a matter to the governing bodies when it posed a threat to "international peace or the good understanding between nations upon which peace depends."[23] Sanctions appear in connection with the unlawful use of force under the terms of the Treaty, as, should this occur, Member States were required to cease diplomatic and financial activities and ties with the belligerent State and to prevent their nationals from undertaking personal interactions with nations of the belligerent State.[24] Such belligerent activities were also grounds for suspension or removal from the League.[25]

The requirements for membership of the League were quite nebulous, as the only terms were that signatory States to the Treaty of Versailles were eligible automatically and that other States – including former colonies or dominion territories – were eligible. The latter entities could become members provided they received a 2/3 majority vote, made "effective guarantees of its sincere intention to observe its international obligations, and shall accept such regulations as may be prescribed by the League in regard to its military, naval and air forces and armaments."[26] Withdrawal from the League was deceptively straightforward, requiring simply a two-year period between notification of a Member State's intention to withdraw and effective withdrawal.[27] As will become evident, this timeframe was not respected in practice.

Three organs were established as the governing organs of the League – the Assembly, the Council and the Secretariat.[28] The Assembly was to be comprised of representatives from each Member State and was to address "any matter within the sphere of action of the League or affecting the peace of the world."[29] The Council was comprised of a more limited membership, namely representatives from the Principal Allied and Associated Powers – the key victorious States in the war – and four other States that would periodically be elected.[30] Acting in conjunction with the Assembly, it was possible for the Council to enlarge its size or to designate additional States that would serve as permanent Council members.[31] It also had the ability to invite States involved in an issue but not represented on the Council to attend meetings on the topic.[32] Unlike future iterations of international organizations, the Council was given the same jurisdiction as the Assembly.[33] The Secretariat was established to serve under the direction of the Secretary General, who would be selected by the Council and the Assembly and would oversee the work of the Secretariat staff.[34]

In terms of voting abilities, each Member State was to have one vote in the Assembly[35] and each State on the Council was to have one vote as well.[36] As a general matter, both the Assembly and the Council were required to use a unanimous voting system subject to the express terms of the Treaty of Versailles providing to the contrary.[37] For example, procedural issues and the formation of committees were to require a simple majority vote,[38] as was the designation of a Secretary General.[39]

Privileges and immunities were established for those representing Member States at the League and League officials "when engaged on the business of the League." It is important to note that these privileges and immunities were expressly classified as diplomatic – a distinction that became increasingly important over time and that continues to serve a role in present day constructs of privileges and immunities.[40] In conjunction with this, the Treaty of Versailles expressly stated that all "buildings and other property occupied by the League or its officials or by Representatives attending its meetings shall be inviolable."[41]

The terms of the Treaty of Versailles and the Covenant of the League of Nations require that States submit their disputes to arbitration under the auspices of the League and not use force to settle them.[42] A caveat existed where the matter was still not settled within three months after the conclusion of the arbitration, although the overall focus is on the use of peaceful means to settle disputes between States.[43] In connection with the resolution of disputes, the Treaty provided for the creation of a court of arbitration and the Permanent Court of International Justice, which was to be given specific definition and detail by the Council.[44] The Treaty also allowed a dispute to be submitted to the Council in the event that the parties decided not to submit the issue to the court of arbitration.[45] Additionally, the Treaty and Covenant specified that already-existing offices created to assist in the enforcement of international treaties would be transferred to the general auspices of the League for administration.[46]

One of the unique and most important terms of the Treaty and the Covenant from the point of view of international law, national and domestic politics, and the international community generally, was the establishment of the mandate system for former colonies and territories of the vanquished States.[47] These were territories not considered able to exercise the requirements of an independent State either in terms of internal functions, such as the protection of ethnic minorities, or external functions, such as participation in the international community at the same level as other States. Using the theory that the victorious States were holders of a "sacred trust of civilization," the Treaty and Covenant implemented the mandate system through which designated victorious States would administer these territories – which were classified by the levels of their abilities for self-governance at the time of the Treaty – in order to prepare them for independence.[48] To monitor this new form of territorial and governmental legal system, the Treaty and Covenant established a standing commission that was to receive reports from the mandate administering States and provide advice on their activities.[49]

Permanent Court of International Justice

The first mention of the Permanent Court of International Justice (PCIJ) was in the Treaty and Covenant, which allowed for its creation under the auspices of the Council but provided very little other guidance.[50] In the years following, the Council appointed a group of international and national law experts to craft the parameters of the PCIJ. This was a particularly arduous task given the need to reconcile differing legal systems as well as tenets of international law and the balance of State sovereignty.

Ultimately, the group of experts crafted – and the League members accepted – a statute establishing the PCIJ as a 15-member entity to be elected by the League members.[51] Part of the unofficial selection criteria for the PCIJ included those from the primary legal traditions and cultures at the global level.[52] In order to be elected to a judicial position in the PCIJ, candidates were selected by qualifications first, with nationality becoming a factor – in theory – in order to ensure that no State had more than one judge seated in a session.[53] Reflecting many aspects of the League's voting requirements, filling seats on the PCIJ bench required an absolute majority of both the Assembly and Council.[54]

In addition to the judiciary, the Statute of the PCIJ established the office of the Registrar, which was tasked with reporting functions to the Secretary General of the League as well as internal functions relating to the operation of the Court as a system.[55] The appointment of the Registrar, along with oversight of Court functioning, was to be conducted by a President, who himself was elected by the members of the PCIJ.[56] To assist in these functions and ensure continuity, the PCIJ members also elected a Vice President.[57] Included in the PCIJ structure was a specialized chamber for labor-related cases,[58] and for cases relating to the provisions of the Treaty addressing Ports, Waterways and Railways.[59] The PCIJ was also provided discretionary abilities to create additional chambers to hear summary cases as deemed appropriate.[60] Specifically excluded from the PCIJ system was an appellate chamber, making the decision of the PCIJ the ultimate source of law between the parties to the dispute unless the Court was convinced of the necessity to reopen the issues raised.[61]

The PCIJ was empowered to hear cases involving League Member States or other States as deemed appropriate by the League Council.[62] The Court's jurisdiction was over cases referred to it by the parties themselves as well as cases arising under treaties and international instruments that establish the PCIJ as having the ability to hear issues arising under their terms.[63] Additionally, it was possible for Member States to declare that they would recognize the PCIJ's jurisdiction over certain matters *ipso facto*.[64]

International Labour Organization

The Treaty of Versailles also gave life to the International Labour Organization (ILO), which was part of the movement toward international regulation of pressing societal issues as well as governmental issues.[65] To connect the issue of labor to that of peace, the Treaty noted that "conditions of labor exist involving such injustice, hardship and privation to large numbers of people as to produce unrest so great that the peace and harmony of the world are imperiled."[66] Unlike the PCIJ, which required several years of negotiation before it became an official organization, the ILO held its first meeting at the end of 1919.[67]

Much of the ILO's Constitution – its foundational text – remains unchanged today and will be discussed in greater detail in Chapter 16. The ILO as a permanent organizational entity was to be comprised of the General Conference of Representatives of the Members along with the International Labour Office, which is controlled under the auspices of the Governing Body.[68] Perhaps one of the most innovative design features of the Treaty of Versailles was its faceting of the tripartite system of representation in the ILO. Under this system, Member States are allotted a representative, and there is also a representative from the employment side and the workers' side in each Member State.[69]

The Governing Body, which oversees the International Labour Office, is an elected group of 24 representatives, 12 of them from Member States, six from representatives of employers and six from representatives of workers.[70] The election of representatives to the Governing Body was – and continues to be – strictly controlled in order to ensure that the highest-level States of "chief industrial importance" are present and involved.[71] The International Labour Office was itself tasked with the functions of a secretariat, as well as with gathering and disseminating information on labor conditions and issues and industrial practices.[72]

The decline of the League of Nations

Shortly after the Treaty of Versailles came into effect, it became apparent that there would be reluctance on the part of the United States to ratify the terms of the Treaty and join the League. In addition, the United States' reluctance to join the newly created international entities under the Treaty extended to the PCIJ, and that the reservations to signing proposed by the US would be contrary to the spirit and meaning of the court.[73]

In the realm of mandate administration, the system became increasingly difficult to implement and manage throughout the interwar period. From conflicting understandings of the legal parameters of mandates on the part of all involved to increasing disrespect of the mandates by the would-be belligerents in World War II to the lack of an adequately composed and empowered oversight body within the League system, the problems faced were myriad and ever increasing.[74] At the same time, the League itself began to falter from a legal and political standpoint, as its members were reluctant to enforce the essential terms of the Treaty of Versailles – such as the early version of collective self defense – while key actors such as the United States were missing from internal organization discussions and policies.[75] In addition, rising economic issues within the League's Member States made it difficult for them to honor their international obligations to the extent envisioned in the Treaty.[76]

Combined, this resulted in a weakened organization in practice that was unable to give effect to many of its legal obligations when called upon to do so. One of the most glaring examples of this came from the Italian annexation of Ethiopia, then a recognized State within the international community, and the limited ability of the League to respond, which was, ultimately, limited to diplomatic protests.[77] Prior to this, Japan withdrew from the League in 1933, following a critical report on its practices and presence in Manchuria.[78] Not only did this result in the loss of a foundational member of the League, it also undermined the concept of the mandate system since Japan took with it a small, former German territory it had been given the mandate to.[79] At the same time, the increased German attempts to retake its former colonies and European territories, and the League's inability to resolve this issue in an effective manner, resulted in Germany flouting the League and withdrawing as well.[80] The message that was becoming clear by the mid-1930s was that the League was unable to fulfill the terms of the Treaty and Covenant, rendering it ineffective in practice although novel and impactful in theory.

It was during this period that the idea of immunity for international organizations – a topic that recurs throughout this book – was recognized in the form of an agreement between the League of Nations and the government of Switzerland.[81] This was supplemental to the terms of the Treaty of Versailles in which employees of the League of Nations were granted immunity for their actions in connection to their organizational functions.[82] Overall, it was during this time that the debate over the immunity of the organization versus the immunity enjoyed by the organization's employees and agents took hold, and continued to inform the post-World War II negotiations that led to the creation of the United Nations and other international organizations.[83]

World War II – background and how international organizations as such functioned during it

By the time World War II erupted in Europe during 1939, the League of Nations was already functionally adrift, losing its ability to act as a representative of the international community and its territorial constructs. Indeed, these constructs were increasingly changed and undermined by the Axis powers, which tended to view it as an anachronistic attempt to prevent them from achieving greater control.

During the war, all attempts at separating out the mandate States and providing them with preferential status were ended, and mandate territories became as much a part of the war efforts as colonies. Further, these territories were equally targets of the warring powers and were often the site of conflict and conquest for the duration of the war.

With the onset of hostilities, the League's functions ground to a halt, as did the functions of other international organizations such as the Permanent Court of International Justice and the International Labor Organization. In their stead, the essential international actors became primarily non-governmental organizations such as the International Committee of the Red Cross, which attempted to provide assistance to civilians and military personnel. While it would be conceivable that the inter-war experience could have undermined the value in which international organizations were held in legal and political circles, the opposite was in fact the case and, by the end of the conflict, it became apparent that the future would be defined by an international community under the sway of international organizations that attempted to tie the States of the world together for the common good.

Post-World War II environment leading to the San Francisco Convention

In the post-World War II environment, there was a concern among the drafters of the San Francisco Convention that too stringently defining the essential aspects of the United Nations, such as the express powers of the United Nations Security Council, could be detrimental to those organs and to the United Nations as a whole.[84]

It was against this backdrop that members of the international community met in San Francisco during 1945 with a view toward creating one overarching international organization that would shape the future world and attempt to promote peace and security. Convened through the good offices of the United States, and particularly the former First Lady Eleanor Roosevelt, this conference ultimately led to the creation of the United Nations organization and a renewed focus on international peace and security as the guidepost for the post-war world.

Charter of the United Nations – contents and meaning

Preamble – what has this meant for the United Nations over time?

It is an axiom in international law that the preamble to any treaty or instrument is an expression of the parties' understandings and beliefs which inform the need for and/or creation of the instrument. It is equally axiomatic that the preamble terms are not in themselves binding law on the States Parties, although they can be used as interpretive aids and provide insights into the parties' intent. In this sense, the preamble is explanatory and typically aspirational.

The preamble to the UN Charter is highly reflective of the experiences of World War II and the global belief that the levels of inhumanity and suffering inflicted should never again occur. To this end, the preamble specifically states that one of the goals in creating the United Nations is "to save succeeding generations from the scourge of war, which twice in our lifetime has brought untold sorrow to mankind."[85] It sets out the essential existence of international norms reflecting human rights concerns and the importance of international law,[86] and provides for equality of rights regardless of the size of the State in which a right-holder lives.[87] These moved the UN Charter on from the lessons of the past to an open view for the future of the organization, one which has allowed it to grow and expand as the needs of the international community have changed.[88]

One of the guiding purposes of the United Nations – the maintenance of international peace and security – is first articulated in the preamble as a method through which to ensure that the organization promotes its core values.[89] As discussed below, when used in other contexts the maintenance of international peace and security has been used as a justification for the use of force as well as for humanitarian purposes. Regardless of the context in which it is used, this term's adaptability and the history behind it have allowed the United Nations to move beyond a limited-scope entity, such as the League of Nations, to become the dominant organizational actor in the international community.

Purposes and goals

Article 1 of the UN Charter sets out the essential purposes of the organization, namely – and as established in the preamble – maintaining international peace and security,[90] developing friendly relations between Member States,[91] the use of cooperation to address issues that face the world community (especially those involving groups that have historically faced discrimination),[92] and generally facilitating good relations between Member States.[93] The Article 1 provisions relating to international peace and security are broad in that they provide for the option of collective action "for the prevention and removal of threats to the peace, and for suppression of acts of aggression or other breaches of the peace,"[94] as well as using force for mediation and alternative dispute resolution methods to address issues that exist or that may exist and result in conflict.[95]

The terms of Article 1, and particularly Article 1(1) relating to maintaining international peace and security, have been used throughout the course of UN history to sanction collective military force, for example in the 2003 invasion of Iraq by coalition forces (comprised of forces from the United States, United Kingdom, France, Canada, and forces from Western Europe, Eastern Europe, Central Asia, Asia and Australasia), and also as a source of justification of the use of UN peacekeeping operations. In addition, the dispute settlement functions outlined in Article 1 have been used by the United Nations to assist in international negotiations and peace processes, including the recent verification mission through which the UN was called on to certify the implementation of disarmament and other provisions of the 2016 Peace Accords between the Colombian government and the Revolutionary Armed Forces of Colombia (FARC).

Member State responsibilities and retained sovereignty rights

Article 2 provides the essential principles that are to guide the conduct of Member States and the organization overall, emphasizing the importance of sovereign equality for each Member State[96] while at the same time highlighting the importance of good faith in Member State agreement to the UN Charter terms and the need to settle disputes peacefully rather than resort to war.[97]

Article 2 also requires that members assist the UN in its undertakings, shifting Member State obligations from merely passive agreements to active requirements.[98] This is particularly important in the sphere of justice, respect for law, and respect for the UN.[99]

At the same time, Article 2 begins and ends with statements that preserve not only the concept of State sovereignty but also the ability of a State to act undisturbed within the parameters of its own borders.[100] This represents the fundamental primacy of the State as sovereign in international law and reflects the inherent tension between sovereignty and the need to devolve some element of it in order for an international organization to function. Such tensions are in no way unique to the UN structure, as will be seen throughout this book, particularly in the context of international organizations relating to military and police operations and banking operations.[101]

Who can become a member and how?

Membership in the United Nations is governed by Chapter II of the UN Charter.[102] As is the case with most international organizations, Article 3 makes it clear that the States that were originally part of the UN Charter negotiation in San Francisco and its subsequent ratification automatically became UN Member States.[103] In addition, membership is open to "peace loving States" which accept the UN Charter's obligations and which the United Nations as a whole believes are willing and able to carry out the obligations of the Charter.[104]

Throughout the history of the UN, admission as a Member State has become a highly contentious and politicized issue, one which has divided close allies and powerful States. In the years immediately following the creation of the UN, the issue of whether to seat representatives from the People's Republic of China or from Taiwan became increasingly divisive. After years of debate, it was decided that the seat of the Chinese Member State was in fact in mainland China, and thus represented by the People's Republic of China.[105] Perhaps the most contentious of all membership questions at the UN has historically been that of Palestine.[106] Questions as to the ability of the Palestinian Territories to form the territory of a State and the ability of various Palestinian governments, notably those with ties to identified terrorist organizations, have typically dominated the debate over the potential for Palestinian membership in the UN.[107] In 2011, Palestine made an official application for membership, although due to political pressure from States such as the US it was not fully acted upon.[108] However, as will be discussed in other chapters, this has not prevented Palestine from becoming a member of other international organizations.[109]

How does the United Nations as a whole decide whether a State is willing and able to carry out the obligations of the Charter? The answer is a three-step process that has been often replicated by other international organizations.[110] First, the would-be Member State must present its membership application to the Secretary General, who is responsible for shepherding the application to the appropriate institutional aspects of the UN.[111] Second, the formal application for membership is made by the State (or entity claiming to be a State[112]) to the United Nations Security Council (UNSC).[113] The UNSC evaluates the application and the applicant entity's abilities and then decides whether to recommend the State to the United Nations General Assembly (UNGA) for a vote.[114]

It has generally been established that the recommendation must be positive in order to go before the UNGA, although there were some early questions regarding this.[115] Provided that a positive recommendation is made, the issue of membership then goes before the UNGA for a vote on admission.[116] If this vote is successful then the entity becomes a Member State and is able to participate in UN activities and groups.[117] If the admission vote is unsuccessful, the entity is not barred from reapplying in the future, although this would presumably raise serious questions about the viability of the application unless the problems which resulted in a negative membership vote were cured.

Just as the UNSC and the UNGA give membership rights they can also suspend them in the event a Member State is found to be acting in violation of its obligations under the UN Charter.[118] To do this, the UNSC must first recommend the suspension and then the UNGA must approve it through a vote.[119] Once the suspension goes into effect it can be lifted by approval of the UNSC.[120] It is also possible for a State to be expelled from the United Nations by a positive vote of the UNGA following the recommendation of the UNSC.[121]

Basic structure of the United Nations

The UN Charter establishes several key organs of the United Nations – the UNGA, UNSC, International Court of Justice (ICJ), the Trusteeship Council[122] and the Economic and Social Council (ECOSOC).[123] The ICJ, Trusteeship Council and ECOSOC are discussed in depth in Chapter 12, but it is important to note that the UN Charter itself envisioned that the work of the organization would require multiple organs. This has provided a durability of function that allows for continued organizational relevance over the course of decades.

As well as these articulated organs, Article 7 of the UN Charter makes further allowances for the creation of additional UN organs and sub-organs as deemed appropriate, and throughout the course of its history the organization has made good use of this ability.[124] From the perspective of understanding the United Nations structure this is important. It is also important for understanding the practices of other international organizations which both establish key organs and allow the organization's members to create additional entities as needed.[125] This framework allows for organizational growth and change as appropriate, making international organizations durable and flexible enough to survive changes in international law and the needs of the international community.

Further, it must be noted that, in the UN Charter and in subsequent UN practice from the beginning onward, the UN has been empowered to recognize and work with regional organizations.[126] While the UN Charter specifically notes that the UN and regional organizations are empowered to coordinate for the purposes of promoting international peace and security, the door was left open for such coordination in other areas deemed appropriate as well.[127]

United Nations General Assembly

The UN Charter establishes the UNGA as the plenary level organ of the UN, in which all Member States have one seat and one vote, regardless of power or size.[128] The UNGA is able to issue non-binding legal declarations on issues ranging from procedure to substance. It can also discuss matters that relate to the powers and functions of the UN generally, issue recommendations to Member States and the UNSC for action or in relation to certain issues, and refer matters to the UNSC.[129] One of the essential topic areas in which the UNGA is empowered to make recommendations to the UNSC is in relation to issues of international peace and security.[130] Similarly, the UNGA may refer international peace and security-related issues to the UNSC.[131]

On several occasions when the UNSC has been unwilling or politically unable to act regarding situations that arguably constituted threats to international peace and security, the UNGA stepped in to fill the void and take action.[132] In a recent example of this, regarding certain Israeli construction activities in the Palestinian Territories, the ICJ endorsed the UNGA's actions as within its powers and purview.[133]

In addition, the UNGA has the ability to undertake studies in order to generate information relating to the promotion of political cooperation,[134] the development of international law,[135] and the promotion of "international co-operation in the economic, social, cultural, educational, and health fields, and assisting in the realization of human rights and fundamental freedoms for all without distinction as to race, sex, language, or religion."[136] The UNGA is also tasked with the receipt and review of annual reports from the UNSC and other subsidiary organs of the United Nations that are created.[137] Over time, this has become a significant task since the number of organs in existence has expanded, along with the scope of their work. With approval from the UNSC, the UNGA is the organ tasked with officially suspending membership of, or expelling a State.[138]

Perhaps most importantly, the UNGA is given the power to approve the UN budget.[139] This includes the budget for the organizations specifically created in the UN Charter and the budgets of UN specialized agencies,[140] such as the World Health Organization. In connection with the budgetary function, the UNGA also has the ability to exempt from suspension of its voting abilities a Member State that is over two years in arrears on its dues payments.[141] Should the UNGA not issue an exemption, the Member State's voting privileges would be suspended until the debt is cured.[142]

United Nations Security Council

The UN Charter establishes the UNSC as the highest-level organ of the UN, with 15 members, of which five — the United States, the United Kingdom, France, the Russian Federation and the People's Republic of China — are permanent members and the other 10 are non-permanent, rotating members.[143] The non-permanent members of the UNSC are elected for their terms of office by the UNGA.[144] In electing the non-permanent members, the UNGA is intended to consider the geographical composition of the UNSC and the commitment of a potential non-permanent member to international peace and security.[145] In this way, the UN Charter intends for the UNSC to be representative of the needs of its Member States and in terms of ability to uphold and respect the essential tenets of the organization.

There have been repeated attempts to reform the UNSC in order to reflect a number of possible global realities, ranging from the current power distribution in the international community (rather than that of the post-war period) to the needs of the developing world.[146] To date, however, these attempts have been fruitless and the terms of the UN Charter regarding membership of the UNSC have remained unchanged.

The UNSC is tasked with "the primary responsibility for the maintenance of international peace and security," hence its designation as the highest-level organ in the United Nations system.[147] It is for this reason that matters brought before the UNSC tend to be extremely grave and/ or represent immediate threats to the stability of the international community. For example, decisions on authorizing the use of force against a Member State — or, increasingly, against a terrorist organization — or sanctions against a Member State's political/governmental regime are issues reserved for the jurisdiction of the UNSC.[148]

Since its inception, the UNSC's areas of competence and activity have expanded and become more encompassing of the issues facing the international community at a given time.[149] This is not without some controversy, however, with critics from different genres and schools of thought arguing that the UNSC has overstepped its intended bounds under the terms of the UN Charter.[150]

While nine votes are needed to form a majority at the UNSC, the veto of a measure by any of the five permanent members will defeat it.[151] In the event that a permanent member abstains from voting on a measure, this does not count as a veto and the measure may still be approved provided it meets the other procedural requirements.[152] The ability to abstain has been a frequently employed tool for highly contentious issues in which a permanent member wishes not to take a side[153] and in instances where the measure at issue involves a permanent member.[154]

The UNSC has the ability to create organs as it deems fit[155] and also has the ability to act as a mediator in the course of dispute resolution between Member States.[156] The latter ability includes the ability to investigate matters independently in order to determine the gravity of the issues involved and the threat to the international community.[157] In limited circumstances, the UNSC has the ability to evaluate, mediate, or order other measures to be taken in respect of matters that involve at least one non-member State.[158] The caveat to this is that the non-Member State must agree to be bound by the obligation to use pacific means of dispute settlement.[159] Where the issues involved are largely related to law, it is expected that the UNSC will refer the matter to the ICJ,[160] and in practice this happens on a regular basis.

In addition, and in promotion of fairness and the sharing of information, it may allow a Member State that does not sit on the UNSC but is involved in a matter that is before the UNSC – such as a conflict or a request for a peacekeeping mission – to attend the meeting at which the matter will be discussed and to participate in the discussions.[161] The Member State would not be permitted to vote, however.[162] Similar allowances exist where the matter before the UNSC involves a State that is not a United Nations Member State.[163]

United Nations Secretariat

In order to function on a daily basis, the UN Charter establishes a Secretariat that will handle the general management of the United Nations and function as the administrative side of the organization.[164] The Secretariat is headed by the Secretary-General, who is appointed by the UNGA on the recommendation of the UNSC.[165] In recent practice, the post of Secretary-General has rotated between the continents in order to ensure geographic representation of all membership constituencies at some point in time.

The Secretary-General oversees the other United Nations organs and officers,[166] and is required to represent the Secretariat at meetings of these organs. The UNSC, UNGA and ECOSOC have the ability to delegate responsibilities to the Secretary-General and the Secretariat,[167] and throughout the UN's history this has happened with increasing frequency. This has resulted in an expanded role and prominence for the Secretariat overall. Where the Secretary-General believes there is an issue constituting a threat to international peace and security, he is authorized to refer it the UNSC for further action.[168]

The Secretary-General and all UN officers are required to act in conformity with organizational rules and standards on conduct.[169] It should be noted that the United Nations has created the United Nations Administrative Tribunal to hear legal claims and complaints from employees rather than allowing these matters to be tried in local courts.[170] The intricacies of this practice will be discussed more in Chapter 12.

Vienna Conventions

Vienna Convention on the Law of Treaties

The Vienna Convention on the Law of Treaties (VCLT) was established to create uniformity in the international system through guidelines regarding treaties and their application.[171] As noted in the preamble, treaties and their interpretation have been the source of disputes between States and within the international community for years, and these disputes are a threat to international peace and security, hence the need to create uniformity in their interpretation.[172]

The VCLT applies to treaties between States and to treaties that create international organizations.[173] In terms of international organizations, the VCLT applies to the foundational treaties of the organization as well as to treaties that are subsequently promulgated through the organization.[174] As in many national legal systems, the VCLT does not apply retroactively, and in questions of application it is essential to examine whether 1) the treaty at issue was promulgated before or after the VCLT was promulgated, and 2) the signatories to the treaty were parties to the VCLT at the time of the treaty's promulgation.[175] These are basic analytical questions for any national legal system and translate directly to the international legal context, as is often the case.

The VCLT creates a series of criteria that cover the ability of a State representative or international organization representative to function as such for the purposes of creating a binding treaty.[176] In order for a person to have this capability, 1) such representative must have the appropriate credentials – largely a matter of diplomatic recognition, and 2) the State/international organization in question must have a manifested intent that he/she act as their representative.[177] As a matter of logic, there are certain high-level actors – such as recognized heads of State, foreign ministers, heads of diplomatic missions to the State involved in the treaty negotiation, and those with official credentials to a treaty-creating conference or meeting from a government to attend and act on its behalf – who do not need to have any further confirmation of their abilities.[178] This is, perhaps, self-evident yet is also important in order to avoid potential diplomatic incidents and impolitic questioning of authority.

Why does this matter? After all, it seems rather obvious that the people who are at the negotiating table for the involved States or international organizations would have the ability to bind their employers. However, there have been instances where lower-level State employees, such as low-level embassy staff, have claimed to have the ability to agree with diplomats on important matters even when they were not authorized by their employers to do this.[179] The goal of the VCLT rules regarding the legitimacy of representatives is to ensure that there are clear-cut rules for such situations.[180] It should be noted that where a State subsequently acts to ratify the unauthorized actor's actions – overtly or by acting as if it is bound by the terms of the treaty involved – that State would be estopped from denying that there was an agreement.[181]

When the terms of a treaty have been negotiated and agreed, the work is typically not finished. Unless the treaty is self-executing, it will have to return to the legislatures of each Member State for ratification or other forms of agreement in order for the State to be bound by its terms. If ratification does not occur, the State is not bound even if it was a signatory State to the treaty.[182] If ratification does occur, the State must then deposit a properly ratified and executed copy of the treaty with the treaty-designated agent, usually the United Nations Secretary-General's office.

Under the VCLT and in international law generally, a key principle for all treaties – and, as a corollary, treaty interpretation – is *pacta sunt servanda* (agreements must be kept).[183] Another key principle for treaty implementation is that, when a State Party becomes bound by a treaty, this treaty is binding for all of the territory under the State Party's control.[184] Why does this matter? Often States administer irregular territorial areas that are not fully incorporated into their jurisdiction, so it is important to clarify how far the State Party's obligations extend.

Like any piece of domestic legislation, treaties are often subject to questions in interpretation. In addition to *pacta sunt servanda* and the full territorial boundary rules regarding the application of treaties, what are other rules of interpretation? As in domestic rules of interpretation, words used in treaties are given their ordinary meaning unless there is evidence to support a particular specialized meaning.[185] If the meaning of certain treaty terms is obscure, or if applying a standard meaning of the term would result in an absurd outcome overall, then it is possible to look to surrounding documents to determine the meaning of the terms.[186] Such documents include the *travaux préparatoires* and any other significant public Statements regarding the treaty terms and negotiations.[187]

For many reasons, it may become necessary to amend or change the terms of a treaty, although negotiating an amendment can be rather difficult because it opens up the entire treaty to potential revision. A treaty will usually contain basic information about whether and how it might be amended.[188] Indeed, the vast majority of treaties creating international organizations do allow for amendment to some degree. As long as this is allowed, the amendment will be negotiated and then must be ratified by the States Parties.[189] In the event a State Party does not ratify the amendment, it remains bound to the terms of the original treaty text.[190]

Another way in which a treaty may be updated to address a particular issue is through the adoption of a separate protocol to the treaty. For example, when the Convention on the Rights of the Child (CRC) was first promulgated it contained some general references to child soldiers.[191] Later, however, the issue of child soldiers became far more nuanced and prominent and, as a result, a protocol focusing solely on the issue of child soldiers was adopted.[192] In this way, the CRC was updated without having to fully open the original treaty text to the potential for changes outside the scope of the limited issue of child soldiers.

Treaties may be terminated or invalidated depending on their provisions. Many treaties will contain provisions regarding their termination, which can occur at the will of the States Parties.[193] If provided for in the treaty, termination may occur where some States Parties withdraw from the treaty and, as a result, there are fewer States Parties left than the required number of States Parties to make the treaty effective in the first place.[194]

There are several reasons for which a treaty may be invalidated. These are: 1) a legitimate error among the drafters of the treaty itself; 2) fraud among the parties in the negotiation of the treaty; 3) corruption on the part of a State representative or international organization representative involved in the treaty negotiation process; 4) coercion on the part of a State representative or international organization representative involved in the treaty negotiation process; and 5) the treaty conflicts with or contains terms that violate *jus cogens* norms.[195] Additionally, depending on how the treaty is crafted, it is possible for the breach of a treaty's terms by some States Parties to allow all States Parties to terminate their obligations under the treaty.[196]

A change in circumstances may allow a State to withdraw from a treaty regime or may be used as another reason to terminate the treaty regime.[197] This provision is reflected in both general and topic-specific treaties, particularly those which create international organizations, as will be discussed throughout this book. An additional option exists to the termination of a treaty – the suspension of the treaty or of its terms.[198] Suspension can occur either through the mechanisms set out in the treaty terms themselves or through the agreement of the States Parties.[199] This is important to remember in the context of treaties creating international organizations because it triggers an additional issue of how organizational operations are to be handled during the period of suspension.

Vienna Convention on the Law of Treaties between States and International Organizations or between International Organizations

Many of the terms of the Vienna Convention on the Law of Treaties between States and International Organizations or between International Organizations (VCLTS/IO) are the same as the VCLT and are simply extensions to international organizations.[200] And it must be noted that the VCLTS/IO has not, as of the time of writing, been adopted by sufficient States for ratification. It is included in this chapter, however, to demonstrate the areas in which the drafters believed there was need for a separate instrument that related solely to operations involving international organizations.

What is perhaps most noticeable is the VCLTS/IO's highlighting of the different legal capacities enjoyed by international organizations in comparison to States. This is essential to such fundamental aspects of the operation of international organizations as their capacity to enter into treaties only if they are granted this ability in their foundational documents or subsequent documents.[201]

Conclusions

As has been discussed and will continue to be evident throughout the remainder of this book, the crafters of the UN created more than one organization – they created a template for future organizations of all specializations and locations. However, very few international instruments can be entirely perfect, especially those which are intended to stand the test of time in a changing political, legal and societal climate. With this in mind, it is essential to understand the Vienna Conventions and how they impact constructions and interpretations of fundamental international organizations documents such as the foundational texts.

This chapter has contained many lessons, some quite obvious, some rather nuanced, that are intended as takeaways themselves and as framing for the remainder of this book. In essence, they form the bedrock principles of most international organizations and will carry through both sections in order to demonstrate their broad-based application. This chapter, as each chapter after it, will conclude with four key lessons regarding international law, international organizations and the materials covered in order to provide a concise summary.

In this chapter, perhaps the most important lesson is how the parameters of the UN – and thus of many international organizations that followed – were established and the process through which it emerged from a concept to a concrete entity. In the purely UN context, the Charter can be seen as a method of ensuring specificity and durability at once. It provides for specificity in its procedural requirements and in the most fundamental of its values – international peace and security. At the same time, it allows the Member States and organs of the UN as a whole flexibility in the decision-making process – for example, by providing a budgetary function for the UN General Assembly but not creating strict requirement for budgetary levels or practices – that results in a tendency toward organizational durability. It is in this balance of rigidity and pliability that the UN Charter is able to construct an organization that is durable and meaningful for its constituency and the international community as a whole.

A corollary to this is the ability of the UN Charter to promote stability within organs and sub-organs, thus providing a framework for other international organizations to use when constructing their governance systems. The governance systems used by subsequent international organizations – even those with UN affiliations – do in many instances vary slightly from the established UN pattern of governance. These variances reflect the identity and work of the organization rather than a wholesale repudiation of the UN Charter-based system and are geared toward ensuring the functionality and meaningful quality of the organization.

Outside of this, the UN Charter system for governance is a durable system that has not been altered over the course of decades and drastic changes to the political and legal environments in which it operates. In this way, it is dependable at the institutional level and promotes stability within the organization and international law generally by providing a guaranteed system of rules and relationships between organs. In a modern international system that seeks to promote stability and minimize chaos this is an essential feature.

Within a system that seeks to generate stability and reduce the chance of chaos – breeding conflict – the Vienna Conventions are essential to discuss from the outset since they provide further rules that can be used as fallback positions. The Vienna Conventions reach further than the UN Charter as a matter of law and have the potential to impact all international organizations as well as the treaties they assist in promulgating. As such, they act as guides that can be turned to in order to combat uncertainty and promote uniformity in the international system. They are vital to understand from the outset of any study of international organizations because they form part of the board on which the game of creating and implementing a foundational text plays out.

Finally, it is essential to note the importance of commonality of language and experience in creating and implementing an international organization. In a global context with differing cultures, legal systems and traditions, motivations and political regimes pose considerable obstacles to the creation of a meaningful and respected international organization, whether it be general or specific purpose. Against such a backdrop, the availability of a common system, such as that created in the UN Charter, is essential to forming an organization with an opportunity to crystalize around issues and laws rather than suffering from an inadequate framework in which to conclude even the most basic policy discussion. This is as true in today's globalized culture as it was in the devastation of the immediate post-World War II era, demonstrating the necessity and viability of a strong framework and set of fallback rules to the generation of any international organization. These lessons will be reinforced and deepened countless times throughout the following chapters of this book.

Notes

1 For an attempted definition of an international organization see International Law Association, Study Group on the Responsibility of International Organizations (2012); but see Joel P. Trachtman, The Economic Structure of the Law of International Organizations, 15 Chicago Journal of International Law 162 (2014–2015).

2 See Alexandra R. Harrington, Anomalies of Territory (2015) (doctoral thesis on file with McGill University and the Library & Archives Canada).

3 See id.

4 See id.

5 See id.

6 See id.; William Thomas Worster, Relative International Legal Personality of Non-State Actors, 42 Brooklyn J Int'l Law 207 (2016).

7 See Harrington, supra note 2. Worster, supra note 6.

8 Malcolm N. Shaw, International Law 7th edn (Cambridge University Press 2014) 931.

9 Id.

10 See Jurisdiction of the European Commission of the Danube between Galatz and Braila, Permanent Court of International Justice, Series B – No 14, Advisory Opinions (Dec. 8, 1927) (discussing the history of the creation and extension of the European Commission of the Danube, beginning in the 1800s); Interpretation of the Agreement of 25 March 1951 between the WHO and Egypt, Advisory Opinion, ICJ 1980, p 73, 77 (describing the evolution of the Board of Health in Egypt from a national entity to and increasingly internationally focused entity that worked on issues such as quarantines, international sanitation, and public hygiene).

11 See id.; Shaw, supra note 8, 931–932.

12 See generally Margaret MacMillan, The War that Ended Peace: The Road to 1914 (Random House 2013) (setting out important political, legal and societal steps which led to World War I); Philipp Blom, The Vertigo Years: Europe, 1900–1914 (Basic Books 2008); Charles Emmerson, 1913: In Search of the World Before the Great War (Bodley Head 2013).

13 See Geoffrey Wawro, A Mad Catastrophe: The Outbreak of World War I and the Collapse of the Habsburg Empire (Basic Books 2014); Christopher Clark, The Sleepwalkers: How Europe Went to War in 1914 (Allen Lane 2012).

14 See Margaret MacMillan, Paris 1919: Six Months That Changes the World (Random House 2003).

15 See generally David Fromkin, A Peace to End All Peace (Henry Holt 1989).

16 See MacMillan, supra note 14.

17 See id.

18 See id.; Treaty of Versailles (1919).

19 Treaty of Versailles at pt 1, art 1.

20 Id.

21 See id.

22 Treaty of Versailles at arts 10–11. Perhaps this is understandable given that the Treaty of Versailles concluded a war that was in part the product of an intense system of political alliances.

23 Id. at art 11.

24 Id. at art 16.

25 Id.

26 Id. at art 1.

27 Id.

28 Id. at art 2.

29 Id. at art 3.

30 Id. at art 4.
31 Id. at art 4.
32 Id.
33 Id.
34 Id. at art 6.
35 Id. at art 3.
36 Id. at art 4.
37 Id. at art 5.
38 Id.
39 Id. at art 6.
40 Id. at art 7.
41 Id.
42 Id. at arts 12, 13.
43 Id. at art 12.
44 Id. at art 14.
45 Id. at art 15.
46 Id. at art 24.
47 Id. at art 22; Michael D. Callahan, *A Sacred Trust: The League of Nations and Africa, 1929–1946* (Sussex Academic Press 2004).
48 Treaty of Versailles at art 22; Callahan (2004), *supra* note 47.
49 Id.
50 Treaty of Versailles at art 14.
51 PCIJ Statute (1920) at arts 2–4.
52 Id. at art 9.
53 Id. at art 4.
54 Id. at art 10.
55 Id. at art 18.
56 Id. at art 21.
57 Id.
58 Id. at art 26.
59 Id. at art 27.
60 Id. at art 29.
61 Id. at arts 59–61.
62 Id. at arts 32–33.
63 Id. at art 36.
64 Id.
65 *See* ILO Constitution (1919) preamble.
66 Treaty of Versailles at pt XIII sect 1.
67 International Labor Organization, *ILO between the two world wars*, http://www.ilo.org/legacy/english/lib/century/, last accessed 21 December 2017. In a telling effort to foster international dialogue and unity surrounding labor issues, the first official act of the inaugural ILO meeting was to admit both Germany and Austria as full ILO members. Id.
68 Treaty of Versailles at art 388.
69 Id. at art 389. Indeed, even though other international organizations have heavily involved these and associated sectors in their planning and legislative processes, for example the International Maritime Organization, the system of providing them with this level of access and participation is a durable and unique feature of the ILO.
70 Treaty of Versailles at art 393.
71 Id.
72 Id. at art 396.
73 *See* Minutes of the Conference of State Signatories of the Protocol of the Statute of the Permanent Court of International Justice, First Session, 10–15 (1 September 1926).
74 *See generally* Callahan (2004), *supra* note 47.
75 *See id.*
76 *See id.* at 33–34, 64.
77 Harrington, *supra* note 2.
78 W.G. Beasley, *Japanese Imperialism 1894–1945* (Oxford University Press 1987) 200.
79 *See* Callahan (2004), *supra* note 47 at 44. It should be noted that, in this instance, Japan continued to file the appropriate reports and act as part of the mandate oversight committee although no longer part of the League. Far from recognizing a retained power by the League, this was interpreted at the time as demonstrating the powerlessness of the League to discipline States that acted contrary to League rules and accepted international law. *See id.*
80 Callahan (2004), *supra* note 47, ch 3.
81 Niels Blokker, *International Organizations: the Untouchables?*, 10 International Organizations Law Review 259, 262 (2013).

82 *See generally* Treaty of Versailles.

83 Blokker, *supra* note 81, at 266–267 (explaining that "the overall conclusion of the interbellum period was that the regime of diplomatic privileges and immunities could not simply be transposed onto international organizations and their staff, due to fundamental differences in the nature and function of embassies and international organizations, and of diplomats and the staff of international organizations . . . Therefore, new rules had to be drafted . . . they were firmly based on the relevant law, practice, and thinking of the 1920s and 1930s.").

84 Maurizio Arcari, *Limits to Security Council Powers Under the UN Charter and Issues of Charter Interpretation*, 32 Polish Yearbook of International Law 239, 247.

85 UN Charter preamble.

86 *Id.*

87 *Id.*

88 *Id.*

89 *Id.*

90 UN Charter at art 1(1).

91 *Id.* at art 1(2).

92 *Id.* at art 1(3).

93 *Id.* at art 1.

94 *Id.* at art 1(1); *see also* Shaw, *International Law* (2014), *supra* note 8, at 875.

95 UN Charter at art 1(1).

96 *Id.* at art 2(1).

97 *Id.* at art 2.

98 *Id.*

99 *See generally id.* at art 2. In relation to respect for the organization, *see* art 2(4) ("All Members shall refrain in their international relations from the threat or use of force against the territorial integrity or political independence of any State, or in any other manner inconsistent with the Purposes of the United Nations.") and Article 2(5) ("All Members shall give the United Nations every assistance in any action it takes in accordance with the present Charter, and shall refrain from giving assistance to any State against which the United Nations is taking preventive or enforcement action.").

100 UN Charter.

101 *See infra* ch 12.

102 UN Charter at arts 3, 4.

103 *Id.* at art 3.

104 *Id.* at art 4.

105 *See* Repertoire of the Practice of the Security Council, p 5 (1952–1955).

106 United Nations, 2011 Highlights of Security Council Practice 12 (2012).

107 *Id.*

108 *Id.*

109 *Id.*

110 This process was set out in 1946 and has remained largely the same since then. *See* Repertoire of the Practice of the Security Council p 243 (1946).

111 Repertoire of the Practice of the Security Council, p 260 (2000); Repertoire of the Practice of the Security Council pp 89–90 (1964–1965).

112 Recognition as a member of the United Nations is regarded as the imprimatur of Statehood, and thus entities which have not formally been recognized by the entire international community as States are able to apply for membership.

113 UN Charter.

114 *Id.*

115 Jans Klabbers, *An Introduction to International Institutional Law* 96–98 (2010); *Competence of the General Assembly for the Admission of a State to the United Nations*, 1950 ICJ Reports 4.

116 UN Charter at art 4.

117 *Id.*

118 *Id.* at art 5.

119 *Id.*

120 *Id.*

121 *Id.* at art 6.

122 The Trusteeship Council was established in order to oversee and facilitate the decolonization process in which the areas to be decolonized were placed under the authority of certain States in trust until they were able to become viable States in the international system. The Trusteeship Council's work has been suspended at present since the last trust territory was made a State within the international system in the 1990s. However, the Trusteeship Council still exists as a UN organ whose work has been suspended. *See* United Nations, Trusteeship Council, http://www.un.org/en/mainbodies/trusteeship/, last accessed 22 December 2017.

123 UN Charter at art 7.

124 *Id.* at art 7.

125 *Id.*

126 *Id.* at art 52.

127 *Id.*; Repertoire of the Practice of the Security Council, p 164 (1952–1955).

128 UN Charter at art 9; Shaw (2014), *supra* note 8, at 879–880.

129 UN Charter at arts 10, 11; Shaw (2014), *supra* note 8, at 881.

130 UN Charter at art 11(1) ("The General Assembly may consider the general principles of co-operation in the maintenance of international peace and security, including the principles governing disarmament and the regulation of armaments, and may make recommendations with regard to such principles to the Members or to the Security Council or to both.").

131 *Id.* at art 11(2) ("The General Assembly may discuss any questions relating to the maintenance of international peace and security brought before it by any Member of the United Nations, or by the Security Council, or by a State which is not a Member of the United Nations in accordance with Article 35, paragraph 2, and, except as provided in Article 12, may make recommendations with regard to any such questions to the State or States concerned or to the Security Council or to both. Any such question on which action is necessary shall be referred to the Security Council by the General Assembly either before or after discussion."), art 11(3) ("The General Assembly may call the attention of the Security Council to situations which are likely to endanger international peace and security."); Shaw (2014) *supra* note 8, at 881.

132 This occurred in terms of peacekeeping when the UNGA decided to authorize and empower the Secretary General to organize and deploy the United Nations Emergency Force, an operation that was primarily focused on the Middle East. See United Nations Peacekeeping, *What Peacekeeping Does*, http://www.un.org/en/peacekeeping/missions/past/unef1backgr2.html, last accessed 22 December 2017. More recently, this occurred when the UNGA took up the issue of Israeli construction of a security wall in the Palestinian Territories. *See Legal Consequences of the Construction of a Wall in the Occupied Palestinian Territory*, Advisory Opinion, ICJ Reports 2002, p 126.

133 See *Legal Consequences of the Construction of a Wall in the Occupied Palestinian Territory*, Advisory Opinion, ICJ Reports 2002, pp 126, 151–152.

134 UN Charter at art 13(a); see also Miguel de Serpa Soares, UN70: *Contributions of the United Nations to the Development of International Law*, 40 Fletcher Forum of World Affairs 99, 101 (2016).

135 UN Charter at art 13(a).

136 *Id.* at art 13(b).

137 *Id.* at art 15.

138 *Id.* at art 17. This has, indeed, been used by the ICJ to highlight the importance of the UNGA in the governance of the United Nations structure *per se*. *Certain Expenses of the United Nations (Article 17, paragraph 2, of the Charter)*, Advisory Opinion of 20 July, 1962, ICJ Reports 1962, pp 151, 163.

139 UN Charter at art 17. It should be noted that there have been attempts to circumscribe the budgetary decision-making abilities of the UNGA; however, they have been ineffective and the ICJ has reiterated that the UNGA has wide latitude in its decisions. *See Certain Expenses of the United Nations (Article 17, paragraph 2, of the Charter)*, *supra* note 138; Shaw (2014), *supra* note 8, at 881, 923–925.

140 UN Charter at art 17(3). Far from being an automatic stamp of approval, the UNGA has used its budgetary function as a method of restricting activities it does not support and endorsing activities it does. See International Law Association, *United Nations Reform Through Practice: Report of the International Law Association Study Group on United Nations Reform* (2011) at 11 (discussing the instance of the UNGA using the budgetary function to severely restrict the International Criminal Tribunal for the former Yugoslavia's capacities as a means of showing disfavor for the ICTY as an institution); Shaw (2014), *supra* note 8, at 881.

141 UN Charter at art 19. The standard to determine whether the exemption should be given is where "the failure to pay is due to conditions beyond the control of the Member." *Id.*

142 *Id.* at art 19.

143 *Id.* at art 23.

144 *Id.* at art 23(1). The terms of office for non-permanent members are two years. *Id.* at 23(2); Shaw (2014), *supra* note 8, at 877.

145 UN Charter at art 23(1).

146 For a discussion of this, see Shaw (2014), *supra* note 8, at 877–878. It should be noted that scholars have identified ways in which the non-permanent member States – including developing States – have the ability to use the UNSC structure to promote the role of law and similar legal doctrines that benefit States at all stages of development. See Alejandro Rodiles, *Non-Permanent Members of the United Nations Security Council and the Promotion of the International Rule of Law*, 5 Goettingen Journal of International Law 333 (2013).

147 UN Charter at art 24.

148 *See infra* ch 12.

149 *See* Arcari, *supra* note 84, 239–242 (discussing, in particular, the expansion of the UNSC's activities in the realm of international criminal law and the creation of criminal tribunals); International Law Association, *United Nations Reform Through Practice: Report of the International Law Association Study Group on United Nations Reform* (2011) p 2; Miguel de Serpa Soares, UN70: *Contributions of the United Nations to the Development of International Law*, 40 Fletcher Forum of World Affairs 99, 101 (2016).

150 Arcari, *supra* note 84.

151 UN Charter at art 27; Shaw, *supra* note 8, 877.

152 UN Charter art 27; Shaw, *supra* note 8, at 877.
153 Shaw, *supra* note 8.
154 *Id.*, at 877 (2014); Repertoire of the Practice of the Security Council p 139 (2000).
155 UN Charter at art 29; Shaw, *supra* note 8, at 878.
156 UN Charter at art 32, ch VI.
157 *Id.* at art 34.
158 *Id.* at art 35(2).
159 *Id.*
160 *Id.* at art 36(3).
161 *Id.* at art 31.
162 *Id.*
163 *Id.* at art 32.
164 *Id.* at ch. XV; Shaw (2014), *supra* note 8, at 882.
165 UN Charter at art 97; Shaw (2014), *supra* note 8, at 882.
166 UN Charter at art 98; Shaw (2014), *supra* note 8, at 875.
167 UN Charter at art 98; see also Danesh Sarooshi, *The Role of the United Nations Secretary-General in United Nations Peace-Keeping Operations*, 20 Australian Yearbook of International Law 279 (1999); Shaw (2014), *supra* note 8, 882.
168 UN Charter at art 99; Shaw (2014), *supra* note 8, at 883–884.
169 UN Charter at art 100.
170 *See infra* ch 12.
171 Vienna Convention on the Law of Treaties preamble (1969).
172 *Id.*
173 *Id.* at art 1. The latter is easy to overlook, however the foundational texts for international organizations are in fact treaties between multiple States rather than with an international organization.
174 Vienna Convention on the Law of Treaties at art 5.
175 *Id.* at art 4.
176 *Id.* at art 7.
177 Vienna Convention on the Law of Treaties.
178 *Id.* at art 7.
179 Vienna Convention on the Law of Treaties.
180 *Id.*
181 *Id.* at art 8.
182 *Id.*
183 *Id.* at art 26.
184 *Id.* at art 29.
185 *Id.* at art 31.
186 *Id.* at art 32.
187 Vienna Convention on the Law of Treaties.
188 *Id.* at art 32.
189 *Id.*
190 *Id.*
191 *See* Convention on the Rights of the Child (1989).
192 *See* Optional Protocol to the Convention on the Rights of the Child on the Involvement of Children in Armed Conflict (2002).
193 Vienna Convention on the Law of Treaties at arts 42, 54.
194 *Id.* at art 55.
195 *Id.* at arts 46–53.
196 *Id.* at art 60.
197 *Id.* at art 62.
198 *Id.* at art 58.
199 *Id.* at art 58.
200 *See generally* Vienna Convention on the Law of Treaties between States and International Organizations or between International Organizations (1986).
201 *See id.* at art. 5.

Chapter 3

Membership and membership powers

Membership in an entity typically indicates that the entity carries with it rewards and benefits. This is certainly true in the context of international organizations, as rewards of some form are usually the incentive for a State to join an international organization in the first place. After all, it would seem rather odd for a State to join an international organization that would expressly cause it harm or be contrary to its established values. Of course, there are some exceptions, for example in the situation where joining the World Trade Organization causes a State to introduce market reforms that harm the interests of businesses which were formerly protected by State regulations. Even in this situation, however, the harm is to a specific segment of society rather than the entire State and should be transitory.

Defining who will be a Member State of an international organization is essentially a step in defining the parameters and interests of the international organization itself. Membership requirements and allowances demonstrate the commitment of the organization to its goals and purposes and determine how the organization will function in the long and short term. The reasons for membership inclusion or exclusion can be highly rational or seemingly irrational depending on the policy issues involved and the aims to be advanced by the organization.

This chapter sets out the international law standards for membership of international organizations, emphasizing areas in which these standards are used to unify would-be Member States as a group and to create – or at the very least acknowledge – differences between States. Further, the chapter discusses the ways in which international organization membership can be used by a State to validate its legitimacy in specific sectors – for example, with business and industry where a State is a member of the World Trade Organization – or in general – for example, as a validation of Statehood itself where a State is admitted to the United Nations.

Why do States join international organizations?

As some authors have noted, the ability of such a broad segment of the international community to join general purpose organizations gives their voices a place that they might otherwise not have.[1] The same can be argued even in smaller regional or topic-specific organizations, since the rules and regulations of these organizations also promote equality in participation and voting ability in ways that realpolitik and diplomacy often cannot replicate.

At the same time, there are arguably several layers of legal benefit to a State's joining an international organization. At the most international level, the inclusion of a State in an organization's regime allows it a vehicle to provide insights on potential iterations of international law that stem from the processes generated by international organizations. For example, having the ability to influence the way in which an environmental law treaty is crafted through the auspices of the UN Framework Convention on Climate Change presents States with the opportunity to mold international law as an active participant rather than a passive recipient.

Membership status in international organizations also allows States the opportunity to evaluate the future of international legal regimes and determine how they should evolve. They are also afforded the opportunity to determine the ways in which other States are applying – or not – the terms of international laws, providing insights into what aspects of international laws need refining and what aspects most benefit international and domestic society.

Domestically, membership in international organizations provides States with the ability to review their legal regimes, learn from the mistakes and best practices of others, and generally adapt their laws to internationally accepted norms within the confines of an entity that is geared toward promoting the generation of international laws and norms. Particularly in terms of topics that are potentially divisive, controversial or sensitive, having the ability to negotiate a State's obligations in a more neutral environment and learn from practices in similarly situated States can be essential to domestic legal reforms. These legal benefits often can translate into tangible assistance such as access to benefits and technology transfers.

Admission criteria

Statehood – the essential criterion

International organizations are, as a rule, composed of Member States only.[2] This means that while other international organizations may be afforded a lesser membership status or civil society organizations may be afforded recognition for the purposes of attending meetings, the only entities entitled to full membership are States. An exception to this formula comes from the International Labour Organization, discussed at length in Chapter 16.

Perhaps it is thus obvious to say that membership in an international organization requires recognition as a State. As those familiar with international law will recognize, there are four standard factors used to determine statehood claims (the so-called Montevideo factors): defined territory, permanent population, effective government, and international capacity.[3] Some scholars assert the existence of other factors, although the Montevideo factors form the essential criteria to date.[4] Although these criteria have existed for nearly a century, their application over time has not been uniform, and especially to the extent that members of the international community – including international organizations – are willing to grant recognition of a claimed State.

Each international organization is different, however, and so it is possible that an entity, such as the Palestinian Authority, will be recognized as a State by Interpol and seated as a member although the UN does not recognize it as a State.[5] While Palestine is the most often occurring example in the post-World War II context, this issue is not new and not limited to the Palestinian context. Indeed, following the Treaty of Versailles and the creation of international organizations such as the League of Nations and the International Labour Organization, these issues were not infrequent, notably in the context of whether areas under international control, for example the Free City of Danzig, could become Member States.[6]

In a typical international organization, membership can happen at two stages. The first stage is when the international organization is originally created by States and the second is when States are admitted as members after the organization has been established. The States that create the international organization effect this by ratifying the foundation treaty and are commonly referred to as "original members".[7] Original member status is important in terms of deciding whether to admit future Member States and often leads to preferential placement on committees and similar administrative preferences, but typically does not convey significantly preferential treatment in terms of rights and obligations over new Member States.[8]

The foundational text of an international organization will contain provisions that articulate the process for seeking membership, including membership criteria.[9] It is possible for the international organization to promulgate rules or regulations regarding the technical details of membership application and admission, such as where to deliver the application, however the international organization must abide by the terms of the foundational text unless there is an amendment in the future.[10] In the context of membership criteria, it is important to differentiate between general purpose international organizations, specific purpose international organizations, and regional organizations, because criteria for each will vary to reflect the organization's constituencies and goals.

General purpose organizations

In general purpose organizations, such as the UN, membership is by definition open to a broad swathe of States and State-claiming entities and centers on whether the entity seeking admission is recognizable – and recognized by the organization – as a State and whether it will honor fundamental organizational tenets.[11] For example, in the context of the UN this requires the ability and commitment to promote international peace and security.[12]

Specific purpose organizations

Specific purpose organizations, such as the World Health Organization and the International Monetary Fund, have a more focused set of admissions requirements that examine a State's abilities and interests in terms of their areas of operation and governance.[13] In addition, many of these organizations require that a State be a member of the United Nations in order to successfully be admitted as a Member States.[14] Conversely, this requirement means that a State's membership in one of these organizations would be imperiled in the event it withdrew from or was expelled by the United Nations.[15]

Since specific purpose organizations are geared toward the promotion of certain activities or topic areas, it is perhaps unsurprising that they may – and often do – include requirements relating to these activities and topics in their membership criteria.[16] As the needs and realities of these organizations may change and evolve over time, membership criteria may be amended in accordance with procedures established in the foundational text.

Regional organizations

At first the membership criteria for regional organizations seem rather obvious – States within a designated region or geographic area. However, it must be remembered that not all States within a region join the regional organization when it is founded, if they join it at all. Thus, the terms of membership admission are still important to examine.

There is perhaps no better example of the potential for limitations in regionally centered organization admission than the European Union (EU). From a relatively small and contained regional entity at the time of its founding, the EU has grown to 27 members, including Eastern European States that are frequently at a different level of development from the original Western European members.[17] Throughout the history of EU expansion there has been a constant debate over the wisdom of expansion, particularly in terms of maintaining the cultural identity of the EU.[18] The EU has established membership admission requirements that are very similar to those of the World Trade Organization in terms of the applicant State's being required to bring its laws and policies into conformity with the laws and policies of the EU prior to admission.[19] Within the EU negotiation process it must be noted that simply bringing a State's laws into compliance with EU requirements is not necessarily enough and that a formal vote by the Member States is necessary. In this setting, any form of issue may arise and hinder the admission of a State.

Another organization that began life as a small regional organization is the North Atlantic Treaty Organization (NATO). NATO is a military alliance that initially was composed of Western European States, the United States and Canada, and was created in order to counter the influence and threats posed by the Union of Soviet Socialist Republics to continental Europe and the safety of the United States and Canada.[20] As such, NATO was intended to be limited in scope in order to ensure the protection of its members.[21] This is reflective of the purpose and goals of the organization.

After the end of the Cold War, NATO continued to function and today focuses on issues from terrorism to trafficking to peacekeeping to piracy,[22] and recently admitted Member States have predominantly been from Eastern Europe, altering the initial vision of NATO in terms of membership and geographic jurisdiction.[23] In order to accomplish this, it was necessary for there to be changes to the NATO foundational text. This represented an amendment that demonstrates the durability of an international organization even if it is a specific purpose or regionally focused organization.

Additionally, many regional organizations allow for full or lesser membership to be achieved by States that are not part of the geographic area of the region, particularly where they have a presence in or significant relationship with the region.[24] Although these forms of membership often have a different status – such as a lack of the franchise – they still allow non-regional members to participate in organizational settings such as meetings and conferences of the parties.[25]

Admission status

In addition to full member status there are often other forms of memberships available in international organizations for States – or entities that do not qualify as States – that might not otherwise meet the criteria for full membership.

Associate members

One such status is associate membership, which is accorded to States that have more limited overall legal rights, for example the territory of Guam, which has its own personality but is also under the territorial control of the United States.[26] In organizations other than the World Trade Organization, designation as an associate member can indicate that the State is in the process of becoming a full member.[27] Standard practice in international organizations is to allow States to use this designation for as long as they are in the process of seeking to become full Member States.

A related status is that of partial members, which are States that might belong to an organ of the international organization, such as the United Nations Educational, Scientific and Cultural Organization (UNESCO) or the United Nations Development Programme (UNDP), but are not members of the international organization itself.[28]

Observer States

Another form of membership status is observer membership or observer status, which typically allows a State to send representatives to organization meetings and often provide policy papers or otherwise voice an opinion regarding the issues facing the international organization.[29] However, observer States will typically not be afforded a vote in the international organization, cannot offer motions, declarations or other binding materials, and do not pay dues to the organization.[30] Observer status is most often used for States or entities seeking to be States which either do not have the full recognition of the international community, such as the Palestinian Authority,[31] or which are unable to enter into full-fledged membership owing to their governing domestic laws, such as the Holy See.[32] It should be noted that the rights of States with observer status will vary not only from organization to organization but also within an organization itself.

In addition, regional (and supranational) organizations, namely the European Union, have the ability to be observers in some systems, such as the UN, although their constituent States are also active Member States of the organization.[33] When this occurs, there can be different responsibilities placed on the Member States by the international organization and the supranational entity. Continuing with the example of the European Union and the UN, EU Member States are required to report certain actions before the UNSC to EU organs and also to defend the EU at the UNSC.[34] As an entity, the UN has granted the EU extensive powers of place and participation in committee meetings and conferences, and the EU has responded by making statements that present a unified front of members.[35]

Outside of this, in the World Trade Organization (WTO) context, observer States except the Holy See are States that are in the process of applying for full membership but have not yet achieved it.[36] In the WTO, observer States are allowed 10 years to fulfill the requirements for full membership and successfully be admitted.[37]

Another form of membership is that of international organizations in other international organizations. In this situation, the member international organization will typically not exercise the same voting powers or other rights as Member States but is able to participate in the deliberations of the organization as a whole.[38]

Conclusions

Membership in any entity – be it a playground sports team or an international organization – is fundamental to generating an identity for the entity itself. Without members, there would be no international organization in practice regardless of how eloquently written the foundational text might be. Membership in an international organization helps to fix the parameters of the organization by determining how the organization comes together – as a willing community or as grudging participants – which in turn impacts the perceived legitimacy of the organization. If, for example, the organization has very few willing members but those members are powerful in the international community and coerce other States to join this will alter the perception of organizational legitimacy from within and without. The organization will appear to exist for the benefit of a few members and will not be given the space to speak as a legitimate voice in the international community that it might have had if members were eager to join volitionally.

At the same time, the ability of States to join international institutions across a spectrum of time and events demonstrates the flexibility of international organizations as institutions. Regardless of the exact terms used in their foundational texts, the ways in which the international community has construed such texts tends toward the ability of international organizations to use open membership rather than closing themselves off to anyone but the original members. This provides a space for new States and States that are newly capable of joining or interested in joining, demonstrating the durability of organizational tenets over time and regimes. While some international organizations might provide preferential treatment for original members, this is usually in a limited scope and the true benefit to the State tends to be in not having to go through a membership application process. Outside of this, new members are generally given the same status and sense of place as other members, offering an institutional setting in which – at least in theory – there is greater parity between States than in other aspects of the international community.

Membership in an international organization serves as a means of validation for the organization and the Member State. At the organizational level, that new States seek to become members and that existing members wish to retain their membership are indicia of legitimacy for the organization. At the State level, the ability to join an international organization can be seen as a source of legitimacy, particularly in instances of an entity with contested statehood or a newly recognized State in the international community. Granting membership to a State recognizes that, in the eyes of the international organization, it constitutes a valid State in the international system and that it is capable of meeting the membership requirements, which can at times be onerous, and of upholding and advancing the purposes of the organization itself. In some instances, such as the UN and the International Monetary Fund, membership can also be used to pave the way to joining other international organizations for which these forms of membership is a threshold requirement. Again, this is a way of establishing validity and reinforcing a State's existence as a legitimate actor in the international community.

As a corollary, membership in most international organizations demonstrates their flexibility. The admission of new members in itself indicates the flexibility within the organization and its intended place as an actor in the international community. For example, when the North Atlantic Treaty Organization was created, many States in Eastern Europe were regarded as being potential threats to its members since they functioned as Soviet satellite States. Today, due to changes in political, legal and societal status and changes to NATO's foundational texts, many of these same Eastern European States are NATO members or work in close cooperation with the organization. Beyond this, the use of alternate membership status such as observer status and associate member status allows for the presentation of views from and involvement of additional voices within the international community. This provides for a better informed organizational structure in terms of the ability to render decisions and act. It also recognizes the realities of politics and law in the international system and seeks to accommodate them while still ensuring that there is a proper structure through traditional, full membership status. In this way, international organizations are able to bend with the realities of the international community rather than breaking due to rigidity of structure and application.

Notes

1 See Miguel de Serpa Soares, UN70: Contributions of the United Nations to the Development of International Law, 40 Fletcher Forum of World Affairs 99, 101 (2016).
2 For a discussion of what constitutes a non-State actor in international law, see International Law Association, Johannesburg Conference Report, Non-State Actors (2016); see also William Thomas Worster, Relative International Legal Personality of Non-State Actors, 42 Brooklyn Journal of International Law 207 (2016).
3 Montevideo Convention on the Rights and Duties of States (1933).
4 See James Crawford, The Creation of States in International Law (Oxford University Press, 2007).
5 See Interpol, The State of Palestine and the Solomon Islands become INTERPOL member countries, https://www.interpol.int/News-and-media/News/2017/N2017-121 (27 September 2017), last accessed 27 December 2017.
6 See Free City of Danzig and International Labour Organization, Permanent Court of International Justice, Advisory Opinion, Series B – No 18 (August 26, 1930).
7 Jan Klabbers, An Introduction to International Institutional Law 2nd edn (Cambridge University Press 2010), 93.
8 Id. at 93.
9 For example, based on the terms of the UN Charter, the International Court of Justice established that the admissions criteria for the United Nations is as follows: the State "must (1) be a State; (2) be peace-loving; (3) accept the obligations of the Charter; (4) be able to carry out these obligations; and (5) be willing to do so." Admission of a State to the United Nations (Charter, Art. 4), Advisory Opinion, ICJ Reports 1948, p.57.
10 Admission of a State to the United Nations, supra note 9 at 62 (noting that, in the context of membership in the United Nations, the requirements enumerated in the foundational text "would lose [] significance and weight, if other conditions, unconnected with those laid down, could be demanded").
11 See de Serpa Soares, supra note 1, 101 (noting that this requirement is not dependent on other factors, such as size, and that as a result the number of United Nations member States has dramatically increased throughout its history).
12 See id.
13 See infra ch 15.
14 See infra ch 12.
15 See infra ch 12.
16 See Constitution of the Maritime Safety Committee of the Inter-Governmental Maritime Consultative Organization, Advisory Opinion of 8 June 1960, ICJ Reports 1960, p 150 (determining the meaning and appropriate application of terminology relating to organizational committee structure membership as well as general organizational membership).
17 European Union, Countries, http://europa.eu/about-eu/countries/index_en.htm, last accessed 27 December 2017.
18 European Union, Joining the EU, http://europa.eu/about-eu/countries/joining-eu/index_en.htm, last accessed 16 January 2018.
19 European Union, Joining the EU, http://europa.eu/about-eu/countries/joining-eu/index_en.htm.
20 North Atlantic Treaty Organization, Discover NATO, http://www.nato.int/cps/en/natolive/what_is_nato.htm, last accessed 27 December 2017.
21 See id.
22 See id.
23 See North Atlantic Treaty Organization, NATO Member Countries, http://www.nato.int/cps/en/natohq/nato_countries.htm, last accessed 27 December 2017.
24 See infra ch 14.
25 See infra ch 14.
26 Klabbers, supra note 8 at 99–100.
27 Id. at 99.
28 Id. at 100.
29 See United Nations, Permanent Observers, http://www.un.org/en/sections/member-states/about-permanent-observers/index.html.
30 See id.
31 See id.
32 See id.

33 *See* Natividad Ferdandez Sola, *The European Union as a Regional Organization Within the Meaning of the UN Charter*, 32 Polish Yearbook of International Law 259, 260 (2012); Edith Drieskens, *Beyond Chapter VIII: Limits and Opportunities for Regional Representation at the UN Security Council*, 7 International Organizations Law Review 149 (2010).

34 *See* Fernandez Sola, *supra* note 33 at 260; TEU at 34.

35 Fernandez Sola, *supra* note 33 at 261; Drieskens, *supra* note 33.

36 *See* World Trade Organization, Members and Observers, http://wto.org/english/thewto_e/whatis_e/tif_e/org6_e.htm, last accessed 22 December 2017.

37 World Trade Organization, Members and Observers, *supra* note 36.

38 *See id.*

Chapter 4

Voting rights and allotments

Throughout time and legal systems, individual voting rights have been the source of repression and/or freedom. Indeed, voting rights have come to symbolize essential aspects of human rights and fundamentally guaranteed rights for all peoples. At the same time, activists have sought to increase voting rights for larger sections of the population in order to ensure that greater segments of the population were able to vote and participate in the electoral process.

Far from solely national achievements, voting rights are guaranteed in a number of international law instruments[1] in addition to national constitutions and legislative acts. For individuals, voting is an expression of political and personal beliefs and concerns, allowing each voter to feel connected to society and to ensure that he/she is a part of it. For national and international society, voting is an expression of its values and priorities.

Why is the issue of voting rights of such importance for States at the international organizations level? Similar to individuals, voting rights for States in international organizations relate to issues of inclusion and exclusion in the immediate and in the future. The immediate impact is perhaps obvious – the ability to vote determines which States hold what positions of authority and power in the international organizations, how organization assets are appropriated, what entities will be recognized as States by the organization, and, in some situations, when the use of force is to be permitted.

In the future, the ability to vote empowers every State to give voice to the interests of its constituency and to raise issues that are of importance to the State, no matter how large that State is, at the international level.[2] This also allows the State to vote for policies that will shape future funding and areas of support, including for projects of importance to the State and its allies.

Enfranchisement in international organizations

Voting rights within an international organization are decided through the foundational texts of that international organization. Although, as discussed in Chapter 3, there are sometimes benefits to the status of an original Member State, these benefits typically do not extend to voting rights outside of the decision to admit a State and thus grant it the right to vote within the organization system. This is another reason that membership is such an important status for States – from within an organization they can better control and influence its policies and practices, while it is very difficult to do so from without.

As also discussed in Chapter 3, full membership status conveys a variety of rights, including the right to vote within an international organization; however, other statuses such as associate membership and observer membership, do not. This is the case even if a State is classified as an observer or associate member because it has not completely perfected its application for full membership in the international organization.

Most international organizations allow Member States to vote on issues that affect them or that they bring to the organization. However, in some instances, for example permanent members of the United Nations Security Council, it is traditional that permanent members abstain in votes on matters that directly affect them.[3]

Voting allotment in international organizations

In short, votes are allotted in any way that the foundational text deems appropriate. And as a matter of practice there is no requirement that voting allocations be the same for all policy issues within an international organization. For example, in terms of membership decisions, the Association of South East Asian Nations (ASEAN) Charter requires that there be consensus, meaning that all

Member States must agree to admit a State in order for it to gain membership.[4] In contrast, the United Nations requires that a 2/3 majority of the United Nations General Assembly Member States vote in favor membership in order for a State to be admitted.[5]

Differences in the number of votes needed for measures to be approved by an international organization vary by organization organ and topic of the measure at issue. Many international organizations require a more substantial majority of votes – or even unanimity – for issues of greater importance to, and potentially having greater impact on, the organization and its functions.[6] In itself, this represents a statement as to the importance of issues to organizations and also the culture of the organizations themselves.

When examining voting practices, it cannot be too frequently emphasized that the definition of accepted practices is solely the province of the specific international organization itself. An excellent example of this is how an international organization defines the concept of a "qualified majority" for voting purposes. A simple majority is indeed quite simple – the majority of members.[7] A qualified majority, however, is more than the simple majority but can be anything more than that and can vary within the international organization itself. Whereas, for example, the United Nations General Assembly requires a 2/3 majority vote for membership and budgetary decisions, the UN Security Council requires that measures be passed by a 3/5 majority.[8]

Abstentions from voting are also handled according to the foundational text of the international organization and the practice can vary even within the same international organization organ. For example, the abstention of any permanent member of the UN Security Council will not negate a majority vote of the Security Council, while a negative vote by any of the permanent members will result in a veto.[9] However, neither the abstention of a non-permanent member nor a negative vote by a non-permanent member is sufficient to trigger a veto.[10]

While some international organizations, such as the United Nations, the International Maritime Organization and the World Health Organization, allow all States equality in terms of the weight of their votes, other organizations such as the World Bank Group[11] and the International Monetary Fund use weighted systems of voting that take into account the investment of States in the banking system created.

Conclusions

In any society, suffrage is essential as a measure of validation and recognition of those who exercise it as those who are vested in the community and are able to decide upon its future. This is not limited to the domestic sphere, and indeed suffrage within an international organization is a vital indication of a State's place within the organizational structure. For example, even though the inclusion of associate members and observer States in an international organization's membership scheme is an important aspect of their validation, they are typically not afforded voting rights or capabilities under the organization's foundational text.

In the context of an international organization, suffrage indicates the connection between the State, the subject matter of the organization and the organizational structure itself, a connection that is of fundamental significance to determining the identity of the organization and the powers of the State. This relationship is also reflective of the priorities within an international organization, particularly when voting powers are not equal but are instead tied to something such as the number of shares a State subscribes to in an international banking organization. Here, the prioritization within the organization is similar to that of corporate entities in most jurisdictions, in that votes are tied to the amount a State has invested rather than the State's identity as a sovereign entity. This is seen as a reflection of the amount of interest a State has in the operations of the organization – especially in its financial soundness – and the amount of risk undertaken by a State. Regardless of the justification, such a system is an overt expression of organizational priorities and values regarding Member States.

This ties in to another essential lesson of this chapter – the ways in which voting power and suffrage can be seen as reflective of a State's power within the international community. In this instance, there is no hard evidence to attach a discrepancy in voting power to, as there is in the instance where votes are ties to shares or other investments in the international organization. Rather, votes are tied to perceived or real beliefs as to the powers of States at a certain time. Perhaps the best example of this comes from the veto power available to the five permanent members of the UN Security Council. At the time the UN Charter was written, these were the five major powers identified as being the principal victors in World War II. Thus, they were believed to be the strongest States in the international community at the time and were rewarded with the ability to control measures impacting international peace and security through the UN Security Council. Although each of these States has remained a powerful actor in the international community since that point, power balances have shifted over time and there are currently many arguments suggesting the need for reform to reflect the new powers on the world stage. However, the UN Security Council's voting system has remained intact and reinforced the idea of voting power and gravity being tied to certain organizational principals.

Further, suffrage and voting in an international organization context connect directly to the organization's culture. This can be seen as an extension of State power perceptions but also goes further to determine how much the organization values aspects of its foundational charter. The NATO example has previously been discussed in the context of membership but it is important to note that not only did it change its admissions process to allow Eastern European States to become members, it also vested them with the same voting rights as other States. In this context there was no waiting period to exercise votes and a member is regarded as a member regardless of the context or location. Similar patterns can be seen in the EU and the WTO, where members are required to undergo extensive membership processes as part of the organizational culture but, once accepted, are given membership and suffrage right parity.

Notes

1 *See, e.g.*, Universal Declaration of Human Rights at art 21; International Convention on Civil and Political Rights at art 25.
2 This is endemic in the majority of international organizations' foundational texts, which provide for parity between the States in the plenary organ at the very least.
3 *See* UN Charter at ch V (1945).
4 *See* ASEAN Charter at art 6(3) (2008).
5 UN Charter at art 18.
6 *See* e.g. ASEAN Charter at art 6; Constitution of the World Health Organization (1946) at art 60; North Atlantic Treaty (1949) at art 4.
7 *See* e.g. UNESCO Constitution (1945) at art 8(a).
8 UN Charter at art 27.
9 *Id.*
10 *Id.*
11 Composed of the International Bank for Reconstruction and Development, the International Development Association, the International Finance Corporation, the Multilateral Investment Guarantee Agency and the International Center for Settlement of International Disputes.

Chapter 5

Organization functions and structure

As discussed in Chapter 2, there are essential models for the foundational texts of international organizations, largely those using the UN Charter. There are many advantages to this, including predictability, ease of understanding and implementing terms and requirements, and a structured system of governance. However, there are some areas in which it is not practical – or desirable – for an international organization's foundational text to completely model itself on the UN Charter or any other foundational text.

One of these areas is the enunciation of the organization's intended functions. Functions, along with purpose, are the guiding forces behind any international organization and inform Member States, organizational actors, and the international community of what the organization intends to do and how it intends to do it. As such, it is vital that these portions of a foundational text be tailored specifically to the international organization at issue.

The structure of an international organization provides the framework through which the organization's functions may be accomplished. Unlike functions, structures are often modeled on the UN Charter and other foundational texts in order to provide for a relatable system of governance that features an established history. At the same time, organizations can – and often do – incorporate specific elements of their functions and identities into their structures in order to make them meaningful and productive for their particular constituencies.

Organization functions

What is their source?

The functions of an international organization should not be confused with the purpose or goals of an international organization, although they are of necessity connected. The purpose or goals of an international organization relate to the overarching statement of why the organization has been created, which is articulated in the foundational text.[1] As with so many important elements of international organizations, the functions of the organization will vary according to the terms of the foundational text and can be almost anything other than illegal activities and/or a violation of established international law or jus *cogens* norms.[2]

What is their legal impact?

Deciding on a purpose or set of goals for an international organization does not, however, mean that the purpose or goals will automatically be achieved or fully respected in the short or long term. Indeed, the articulation of goals without more generates very little in the way of actionable law for the organization, its members and its staff. In order to ensure this, the Member States must decide on the organization's functions and how they will be carried out.

These decisions must take into account important questions such as whether the members of the international organization intend to meet frequently or only at scheduled times,[3] whether the members intend the organization to be hands-on in the implementation of its purpose and goals or whether they intend it to play a more abstract role,[4] and whether the Member States intend that the organization provide technical standards and guidelines in the relevant policy areas,[5] such as the World Health Organization or the Food and Agriculture Organization.

Although seemingly mundane, these functions allow for the fluid operation of the international organization and render it able to meet the needs for which it was created. In this way, it is similar to any corporation or other group – the framework rules allow it to be effective and responsive to the needs of its constituency.

Once these functions are established, the Member States will then have to decide how to implement them. It is in this context that the structure of the international organization emerges as an essential tool in organizational design and policy implementation. Should an international organization exceed the scope of its articulated functions it may endorse the actions through a decision of the appropriate organs or, otherwise, repudiate the actions and take internal measures for sanctions.

Organization structure

With the functions of the international organization established, the next question to address is how these functions will be carried out. For example, it is impractical to expect that every administrative decision from staffing to office supplies be decided by a vote of all Member States. Convening a vote for every bureaucratic and administrative issue would be impossible and would create institutional gridlock, as well as needless expense for the organization and the Member States.

In order to allow the international organization to fully function and to govern itself, the foundational text of the organization will establish organs – and sometimes sub-organs – to carry out the designated work of the organization. These organs and sub-organs take the abstract and often aspirational concepts that underlie the foundational texts of international organizations and provide a practical mechanism through which they can be implemented and, hopefully, achieved. At the same time, most international organizations use a bi-cameral structure of governing bodies in which there is the equivalent of an upper and lower house. These are the binding entities of the organization, tasked with varying degrees of decision-making and policy promulgation.

Highest-level organs

Regardless the international organization, there will be one organ that is identified as being the highest-level organ for the purposes of decision-making. This is necessary, as without a final source of authority there would be the potential for dysfunction – if not anarchy – within the organizational system.

Typical functions

Highest-level organs have a number of names depending on the organization at issue. However, what is common to them all is that they represent the elite decision-making body, one in which a select group of members hold voting rights and specialized powers. Sometimes membership in these organs is semi-fixed, as in the case of the mixture of permanent and non-permanent members of the United Nations Security Council.[6] In other instances, membership rotates depending on a number of criteria that reflect the principles and purposes of the organization.[7]

These organs serve as the arbiters of the most essential matters facing their organizations. They act to decide the more existential aspects of their organizations and to ensure that the functions of the organization accord with the purposes of the organization, as well as the overall tenor of the foundational text.[8] It is intended that their decisions have gravity within the organization and within the international community, for example decisions authorizing the use of force or the imposition of sanctions against a Member State.

Typical powers

Highest-level organs will typically have the power to issue decisions that affect the entire constituency of organization Member States and relate to the most important and grave questions facing that constituency. These issues can range from the suitability of a State for membership in the organization to the approval of the use of force to the deployment of peacekeeping troops to the conclusion of agreements with other organizations.

The highest-level organ in an international organization will typically have the ability to address disputes involving Member States and/or the organization and may be tasked with using its offices to solve these disputes.[9] These organs are also responsible for receiving reports from certain sub-organs, and may discuss the most pressing matters before the organization.[10] They may receive requests for opinions from the secondary organs or other organs and may, at their discretion, issue such opinions.[11]

Any discussion of these organs would not be complete without acknowledging the gravitas carried by their statements and decisions. Even simple statements of recognition or condemnation carry weight within their constituencies, be they issue-oriented constituencies or the global community. Thus, the power of these organs to convey messages by speaking without further action must be recognized and remembered.

Secondary organs

Although they carry the designation of secondary organs, these entities are in fact the site of collaboration and decision-making by the entirety of an international organization's Member States. Secondary organs function as plenary bodies, allowing every Member State a voice and a vote – albeit sometimes not in equal measure – on matters before it. The ability to convene Member States in plenary is in itself an accomplishment, and these meetings are often the site of important policy debates and statements. The secondary organs also allow for coalitions of Member States – for example, the Small Island Developing States at the United Nations General Assembly – to act with one voice and gain influence and solidarity as a result.

Typical functions

The secondary organs in international organizations are generally vested with a number of functions that involve handling issues that are less pressing and grave than those brought to the highest-level organs. This in no way should denigrate the importance of their functions, as many essential organizational decisions are made by these organs and as a result they have the opportunity to hear information on a far greater number of issues facing the international community.

In the majority of cases, secondary organs function to decide the operational details of the international organization. They also provide a plenary venue in which the entirety of the Member States have the opportunity to meet, debate, and generate new norms and policies.

Typical powers

Perhaps the most consistently important power allotted to the majority of secondary organs is the ability to approve the organizational budget.[12] This has immediate effects not only on the organization itself but more specifically on those involved in and benefiting from its operations and services. For example, a failure to approve the budget of the UN could result in the cessation of peacekeeping operations around the world and in the termination of research work being undertaken under the organization's auspices. It would also throw the general capacity of the organization into question. Similarly, approving a budget means approving the membership fees apportioned to each Member State. This is a powerful tool.

Secondary organs have a number of different powers in order to carry out their functions. They typically share in the process of membership decisions,[13] provide a venue for discussion and debate which generates a record that can be used by the highest level organ for information,[14] receive reports from sub-organs and actors,[15] and have the power to generate or give voice to new norms in international law through the issuance of non-binding instruments such as declarations.[16] A quintessential example of this is the United Nations Declaration on the Rights of Indigenous Peoples (UNDRIP), issued by the United Nations General Assembly after the majority of Member

States voted in favor of it.[17] The UNDRIP is not a treaty and is not legally binding; however, it has become an essential tool for many practitioners and scholars and is reflective of new norms for the rights of indigenous communities across the world.[18]

Administration – the Secretariat

The UN Charter established more than the bi-cameral governance system for international organizations. It also created a separate entity to handle the quotidian functions and work of the international organizations, the Secretariat, and placed it under the control of a separate officer, the Secretary General. This system has become entrenched within the UN and allows the organization to maintain a presence in States that were not contemplated as existing when the UN Charter was crafted and for purposes that were well beyond foreseeability in 1945. At the same time, the durability of this system has been proven again and again with its incorporation into the foundational texts of the vast majority of international organizations in existence today.

Typical functions

In a typical administrative system, such as the UN, the Secretary General has many functions, a number of them diplomatic, and so there will be a series of Under-Secretaries General to handle specific issues and portfolios.[19] From there on down the ladder of bureaucracy there are additional layers which often are segregated by function. For example, there is a specific sub-organ that handles peacekeeping issues ranging from deployment order implementation to procurement.[20] All of these layers have been created to allow the work of the UN to continue without having to involve the Member States in basic issues of the daily running of an organization. In this sense, international organizations are similar to corporations – one would not expect the members of a corporate board of directors to decide which brand of toner to order for the copier or to hire a new employee.

The same system has been replicated throughout international organizations, with the work of implementing organizational policy being carried out by the secretariat whether that policy be military, diplomatic, cultural, political, or societal. It is perhaps obvious that the scope of the work performed by secretariats – and their size – will depend on factors such as the purpose and function of the international organization. For example, the functions of the World Health Organization's Secretariat are broad and its portfolio continues to expand,[21] while the function of the Secretariat for the Organization for the Prohibition of Chemical Weapons is more centralized in function and has a limited scope.[22]

Some functions are fairly universal across secretariats. These functions tend to cluster around preparation for organization meetings,[23] facilitating the review and transmission of reports from Member States,[24] coordinating responses to these reports where appropriate,[25] liaising with members of civil society on matters such as the receipt of information,[26] and liaising with the secretariats of other international organizations as appropriate.[27] Other functions may include the daily operation of peacekeeping and policing forces,[28] coordinating and implementing projects on behalf of the organization,[29] liaising with Member States on issues such as the disbursement of funds from the organization,[30] and conducting scientific studies.[31]

Typical powers and limitations

Of course, this is not to say that the members of the secretariat (collectively all of those under the umbrella of the Secretary General) are allowed to act in areas that are designated as being within the control of the governing entities. For example, a UN Deputy Under-Secretary could not decide to accept a State's bid for membership in the United Nations because that is a decision that must be taken by the UN Security Council and the UN General Assembly.

At a more practical level, international organizations regulate the work and conduct of their secretariats through the promulgation of rules and regulations that enunciate the powers of various officers and the limitation on these offices.[32] In a multinational environment, where various legal traditions come in constant contact with one another, differences in expectations and allowed work practices are arguably inevitable. It is for this reason that rules and regulations, such as codes of conduct and organizational rules of procedure, play an important role establishing the powers and limitations of an organization's secretariat.[33]

Additionally, it must be remembered that the secretariat functions with the guidance of the organization's governing bodies and that these bodies may expand or contract its powers. Modern practice has tended toward expanding the powers and functions of the secretariat rather than attempting to contract them; however, it is possible since this remains in the majority of foundational texts.

Additional organs/committees/subcommittees

In addition to the UN governing entities and the Secretariat, there is also a variety of other UN organs that have come into existence over the course of the organization's history and in response to the changing needs of the international community. Some of these, such as the Economic and Social Council (ECOSOC) and the International Court of Justice, were directly provided for in the UN Charter,[34] while others, such as the UN Development Programme[35] and the United Nations Environment Programme,[36] were created later as the result of decisions by the UN governing bodies. Recall that this was possible because of the open language in the UN Charter that provided for the establishment of other organs.[37] Without this language and organizational competency it is unclear whether new organs could have been established and vested with extensive powers and decision-making abilities.

The UN is not the only international organization to use this form of governance and bureaucratic body structure to achieve its goals. This is a common practice regardless whether the international organization is general or specific purpose or whether it is global or regional in nature. Indeed, many other international organizations have adopted the same nomenclature as that used by the UN to demarcate organs and have drawn parallels in terms of organ roles and responsibilities.[38] In certain specialized entities that focus on finance, particularly banks which require members to take out subscriptions to the organization, the terminology is somewhat different in order to reflect the varied interests held by Member States; the effects, however, are the same.[39]

It should also be noted that the ability to create new organs and sub-organs under the auspices of the international organization is not limited to the United Nations context either. For example, the Organization of American States has created a highly-regarded and nuanced human rights system, comprised of the Inter-American Commission on Human Rights and the Inter-American Court of Human Rights – since the enactment of its foundational text. Another example can be found in the context of the European Union, where a number of bodies have been established to handle the plethora of subject areas in which it works. Further, international trade and finance organizations, such as the World Trade Organization, continuously generate new sub-organs to meet the changing needs and complexities of their constituencies. This can be seen in some of the WTO's newer entities, such as Aid for Trade and Trade Policy Reviews, discussed in Chapter 15.

Oversight bodies

Accountability is an essential requirement of any international organization, particularly from the administrative entity tasked with implementing the daily operations of the organization. The governance organs of an international organization may have the ability to oversee one another and may be referred to the International Court of Justice by a Member State or another international organization.[40] However, the same level of scrutiny is typically unavailable in issues regarding the organization's secretariat and general administrative decisions.

In order to address this gap, many international organizations have created oversight bodies in some form. Chapter 10 is devoted to the mechanisms of dispute settlement employed by a wide variety of international organizations across the expanse of subject areas and functions. However, disputes between Member States themselves and between Member States and the organization represent only one form of oversight. Throughout the evolution of international organizations, a number of other mechanisms have emerged to review compliance with rules and regulations, as well as the overall organizational mission.

One such entity is a standing oversight body, such as an ombudsman, which is dedicated to conducting operational reviews and may hear complaints from employees, contractors or other actors regarding certain organizational functions. Examples of this include the European Union, where the European Ombudsman is authorized to receive and review complaints from citizens of Member States regarding compliance with European Union laws and rules at the organizational and Member State levels.[41]

Another method of oversight centers on complaints by employees regarding the terms of their employment – for example, the failure to achieve a promotion, or what is regarded as improper termination of employment.[42] Depending on the context, in many situations these claims could be adjudicated in national courts under the domestic law of the State in which the employee was based or the employee's home State. However, international organizations as a rule prefer not to submit themselves to domestic jurisdiction, particularly for matters relating to internal organization functions and decisions. As a result, international organizations have established internal mechanisms, such as the United Nations Dispute and Appeals Tribunals and the World Bank Administrative Tribunal, to hear and adjudicate these issues.[43] Some have gone further and have also created an appellate system.[44] This system has been largely respected by domestic courts, although on occasion there have been courts willing to challenge the appropriateness of this system and the ability of an international organization to compel its usage.

Additionally, issues have arisen regarding citizens of Member States who are acting on behalf of an international organization and suffer harm from a third party. In these situations, there were initial questions as to whether the organization would have standing and capacity to bring a claim against the third party for harms done to its agents and experts. The landmark ICJ case, *Reparations for Injuries Suffered in the Service of the United Nations*, involving claims stemming from harms done to those acting on behalf of the United Nations, addressed many of these issues.[45] In the *Reparations* case, the ICJ noted that there is a significant onus on the organization using agents – particularly in dangerous areas throughout the world – to ensure their protection and that this included making claims on their behalf.[46]

Further, the ICJ stressed that it was the obligation of the international organization involved to ensure the safety and security of its agents, and others sent on missions, in an unbiased way so that these individuals would not feel dependent for their survival on any State or organization and, thus, potentially produce biased outcomes.[47] In this context, the ICJ has specifically held that the international organization's responsibilities and ability to bring a claim for harms to an agent or other acting on its behalf exists and is legitimate regardless whether the third party is a Member State of the organization itself.[48] In subsequent cases, the ICJ has allowed for a wide interpretation of experts acting on behalf of the United Nations to include those acting as rapporteurs under the auspices of subsidiary organs of the United Nations, such as those associated with international human rights body committees.[49]

Oversight issues in the organizational context are brought not only by employees and officers of the organization but also by contractors or the general public that is impacted by organizational operations and decisions. A primary example of this comes from the banking organization context, where citizens groups and others affected by lending decisions that support the construction or implementation of certain projects have complained about the procedural defects of these decisions and their practical impacts. In response, these organizations have established review panels and similar bodies that are tasked with assessing whether the bank's decisions to fund an activity – and its continued oversight requirements for the activity – were properly followed.

For example, the Inter-American Development Bank created the Independent Consultation and Investigation Mechanism to evaluate claims regarding the appropriateness of its funding decisions and whether the activities of supported projects are in violation of the terms of institutional policies.[50] Similarly, the World Bank Group uses Inspection Panels to examine its lending operations, with a focus on the impacts they have on non-State entities in order to ensure that these entities are not suffering prohibited or inappropriate harms as a result of World Bank practices.[51]

The overarching goal of such oversight mechanisms is to provide a balance between organizational priorities and operations and the needs and interests of those affected most by these policies. The existence of oversight mechanisms is not meant as a vehicle for undoing the work of the organization, but rather for ensuring that the organization complies with its own rules and requirements in rendering and implementing decisions.

Conclusions

As essential legal principles, it is vital to remember that every international organization needs to have articulated functions and purposes to give meaning and legitimacy to the organization as a whole. It would be nonsensical to create an international organization and not vest it with functions and purposes, since this would generate an empty shell of an entity. These functions and purposes can be somewhat vague and can leave open spaces for the organization to expand, contract, change course or otherwise evolve throughout time and necessity; however, they need to exist.

Similarly, it is essential that the structure of the organization be articulated, since this speaks to the values of the organization itself. The way in which an organization structures its governance mechanisms and oversight bodies is telling for the sense of legal and political environments to be incorporated and encouraged, while limitations on these indicates that the organization's powers will often be circumscribed. Further, the relationship between the governance structures themselves is extremely important to understanding the values and cultures involved in an organization. For example, the ability of the International Court of Justice to settle disputes involving certain international organizations is essential to the determination of how an international organization values the settlement of disputes.

Although functions of an international organization necessarily vary, uniformity in structure – if not always nomenclature – is a key aspect of generating norms and rules that relate to the law of international organizations and the place of international organizations in international law. This is important to place international organizations within a legal system for the purposes of regulation and also incorporation of their practices into the laws and rules of Member States. At the same time, uniformity in structure generates a relatable set of parameters for an international organization and for the community of international organizations, allowing institutional actors and the international community to judge the activities and outcomes of their undertakings. By crafting expectations of international organizations that are based on their structure and its application of designated functions, organizations are held accountable to their constituencies, and Member States are similarly held accountable to their constituencies, for their activities and priorities within the organizational context.

Within the context of an international organization, oversight and oversight bodies can be seen as a method of generating and reinforcing legitimacy. The will and ability to self-police through governance structures demonstrate the culture of the organization and its Member States, at the same time circumscribing the parameters of oversight within organizational parameters rather than allowing it to go to local court systems. In this way, organizational structures can be seen as either helping or hindering the goals of their creators depending on the way in which they are constructed and allowed to operate. Structure can thus be seen as essential to organizational accountability, provided the will to utilize them properly also exists within the institution and among its actors.

Notes

1 For instance, one of the main purposes of the United Nations is the maintenance of international peace and security.

2 See International Law Association, *Study Group on the Responsibility of International Organizations, Sofia Conference* (2012) 10 (noting that "international organizations are characterized by considerable diversity, including different mandates, structures, operating philosophies, and activities. Depending on the powers and competences conferred upon them by their members, international organizations will be able to act on the international plane, for instance, by concluding treaties, or by being subjected to the law of responsibility for a breach of their international obligations.").

3 See, e.g., UN Charter (1945) art 20 (establishing guidelines for UN General Assembly meetings); Articles of Agreement of the International Monetary Fund (2016) art XII(8).

4 See, e.g., UN Charter, *supra* note 3 at arts 68–72 (relating to the functions and relationships to be undertaken by ECOSOC); IBRD Articles of Agreement (1944) art IV.

5 See, e.g., Constitution of the United Nations Food and Agriculture Organization (1945) art I; Convention on the International Maritime Organization (1948); World Health Organization Constitution (1946) ch II.

6 See UN Charter, *supra* note 3 at ch V.

7 See, e.g., International Civil Aviation Organization Constitution (1944) art 50 (requiring that the Assembly take into account and ensure representation for the "States of chief importance to air transport" when electing members of the Council); IMO Convention, *supra* note 5.

8 See, e.g., UN Charter, *supra* note 3 at ch V; Constitutive Act of the African Union (2000); Convention on the Prohibition of the Development, Production, Stockpiling and Use of Chemical Weapons and on Their Destruction (1994); Agreement Establishing the Asian Development Bank (1965).

9 See, e.g., UN Charter, *supra* note 3 at ch. V (1945); *infra* ch 10.

10 See, e.g., Constitutive Act of the African Union, *supra* note 8 at art XIII; Charter of ASEAN (2007) art 7; WHO Constitution, *supra* note 5 at art 24; Constitution of the Food and Agriculture Organization of the United Nations (1945) art V; ILO Constitution (1944) art 7.

11 See, e.g., ASEAN Charter, *supra* note 10 at art 7; Articles of Agreement of the International Monetary Fund (1944) art XII(2); WHO Constitution, *supra* note 5 at art 24; FAO Constitution, *supra* note 10 at art V; ILO Constitution, *supra* note 10 at art 7.

12 See, e.g., UN Charter, *supra* note 3 at ch IV; Asian Development Bank Charter (1966) arts 31, 34; Convention Establishing the World Intellectual Property Organization (1967) art 6.

13 See, e.g., UN Charter, *supra* note 3 at ch IV; ADB Charter, *supra* note 12 at arts 31, 34; Convention Establishing the World Intellectual Property Organization (1967) art 6.

14 See, e.g., UN Charter, *supra* note 3 at ch IV; ADB Charter, *supra* note 12 at arts 31, 34; WIPO Convention, *supra* note 13 at art 6.

15 See, e.g., UN Charter, *supra* note 3 at ch IV; ADB Charter, *supra* note 12 at arts 31, 34; WIPO Convention, *supra* note 13 at art 6.

16 See, e.g., UN Charter, *supra* note 3 at ch IV; UNESCO Constitution (1945); IDA Articles of Agreement (1960) art VI; WIPO Convention, *supra* note 13 at art 6.

17 See United Nations Declaration on the Rights of Indigenous Peoples (2007).

18 See *id.*

19 UN Charter, *supra* note 3 at arts 97–99.

20 United Nations, United Nations Peacekeeping, http://www.un.org/en/peacekeeping/, last accessed 2 January 2018.

21 See generally WHO Constitution, *supra* note 5.

22 See Convention on Chemical Weapons, *supra* note 8.

23 See, e.g., UN Charter, *supra* note 3 at ch VII; ICSID Convention (1966) arts 9, 10; WHO Constitution, *supra* note 5; FAO Constitution, *supra* note 10.

24 See, e.g., UN Charter, *supra* note 3 at ch VII; Charter of the Organization of American States (1967); WHO Constitution, *supra* note 5; FAO Constitution, *supra* note 10.

25 See, e.g., UN Charter, *supra* note 3 at ch VII; OAS Charter, *supra* note 24; WHO Constitution, *supra* note 5; FAO Constitution, *supra* note 10.

26 *See, e.g.,* UN Charter, *supra note* 3 at ch VII; OAS Charter, *supra note* 24; WHO Constitution, *supra note* 5; FAO Constitution, *supra note* 10.

27 *See, e.g.,* UN Charter, *supra note* 3 at ch VII; OAS Charter, *supra note* 24; WHO Constitution, *supra note* 5; FAO Constitution, *supra note* 10.

28 *See* United Nations, United Nations Department of Peacekeeping Operations, https://peacekeeping.un.org/en/department-of-peacekeeping-operations, last accessed 2 January 2018.

29 *See generally* OAS Charter, *supra note* 24; WHO Constitution, *supra note* 5; FAO Constitution, *supra note* 10.

30 *See, e.g.,* Agreement Establishing the European Bank for Reconstruction and Development (1990).

31 *See, e.g.,* WHO Constitution, *supra note* 5; FAO Constitution, *supra note* 10.

32 *See, e.g.,* UN Charter, *supra note* 3 ch VII; OAS Charter, *supra note* 24; WHO Constitution, *supra note* 5; FAO Constitution, *supra note* 10.

33 *See, e.g.,* UN Charter, *supra note* 3 ch VII; OAS Charter, *supra note* 24; WHO Constitution, *supra note* 5; FAO Constitution, *supra note* 10.

34 UN Charter, *supra note* 3 at art 7.

35 United Nations Development Programme, About Us, http://www.undp.org/content/undp/en/home/operations/about_us.html, last accessed 2 January 2018.

36 United Nations Environment Programme, About UNEP, http://staging.unep.org/Documents.Multilingual/Default.asp?DocumentID=43, last accessed 2 January 2018.

37 UN Charter, *supra note* 3 at art 7(2).

38 *See, e.g.,* OAS Charter, *supra note* 24; AU Charter, *supra note* 10; WHO Charter, *supra note* 5.

39 *See, e.g.,* IMF Articles of Agreement, *supra note* 11; EBRD Articles of Agreement, *supra note* 31; ADB Articles of Agreement, *supra note* 12; Agreement between Denmark, Estonia, Finland, Iceland, Latvia, Lithuania, Norway and Sweden concerning the Nordic Investment Bank (1975); Agreement establishing the African Development Bank (2011).

40 *See, e.g.,* WHO Charter, *supra note* 5; ILO Charter, *supra note* 10.

41 *See infra* ch 14.

42 *See* Yaraslau Kryvoi, *The Law Applied by International Administrative Tribunals: From Autonomy to Hierarchy,* 47 George Washington International Law Review 267 (2015).

43 It should be noted that, based on the division of competencies and the statute creating the United Nations Administrative Tribunal, it was to serve as a stand-alone entity and is largely outside the direct review of the United Nations General Assembly. *See Effect of awards of compensation made by the U.N. Administrative Tribunal,* Advisory Opinion of July 13th, 1954, ICJ Reports 1954, p 47; Tamara A. Shockley, *The Evolution of a New International System of Justice in the United Nations: The First Sessions of the United Nations Appeals Tribunal,* 13 San Diego International Law Journal 521 (2012) (discussing the overhaul of the United Nations Administrative Tribunal system into the United Nations Appeals Tribunal system); Paolo Vargiu, *From Advisory Opinions to Binding Decisions: The New Appeal Mechanism of the UN System of Administration of Justice,* 7 International Organizations Law Review 261 (2010); Malcolm N. Shaw, *International Law* 7th edn, 947–948 (Cambridge University Press, 2014); United Nations Security Council, Administration of Justice at the United Nations, S/RES/62/228 (2008).

44 *See* United Nations Security Council, Administration of Justice at the United Nations, S/RES/62/228 (2008).

45 *Reparations for Injuries Suffered in the Service of the United Nations,* Advisory Opinion, ICJ Reports 1949, p 174; *see also* Shaw, *supra note* 43, 939–940.

46 *Reparations for Injuries Suffered in the Service of the United Nations* 183 ("Both to ensure the efficient and independent performance of these missions and to afford effective support to its agents, the Organization must provide them with adequate protection."). In the same opinion, the ICJ found that there was a duty on the part of the United Nations to provide "every assistance" to its agents and others acting on its behalf. Id.

47 Id. at 183.

48 Id. at 185.

49 *See Difference Relating to Immunity from Legal Process of a Special Rapporteur of the Commission on Human Rights,* Advisory Opinion, ICJ Reports 1999, p 62.

50 For an in-depth discussion, *see* Alexandra R. Harrington and Valentina Duran, *Principles of inter-generational equity, public participation and good governance in the Inter-American Development Bank's oversight mechanism,* in Marie-Claire Cordonier Segger and H.E. Judge C.G. Weeramantry, eds, *Sustainable Development Principles in the Decisions of International Courts and Tribunals* (2017).

51 *See* Sabine Schlemmer-Schulte, *Sustainable development priorities in World Bank Inspection Panel decisions,* in Cordonier Segger and Weeramantry (2017), *supra note* 50.

Chapter 6

Punishment, suspension and expulsion of errant Member States

Punishment of Member States

Member States of an international organization typically have an interest in complying with the rules and policies of the organization. After all, it would seem illogical to join an organization and not comply with its rules. However, there are instances in which Member States fail to comply with the rules and policies of the international organization. The reasons for this are myriad. When it occurs, there are a number of options available for these organizations and their Member States to impose in order to attempt to ensure compliance and/or cease the conduct that has caused problems.

It should be noted that some international organizations, such as the African Union, provide that one of the core functions of the General Assembly equivalent is to monitor the implementation by Member States of organization rules and policies.[1] Others task the secretariat with this function.[2]

As a general matter, international organizations tend to act in ways that are conciliatory or attempt to address the issues involved rather than acting in a retributive way. This raises the complex question of the value of imposing punishments on an errant Member State in an attempt to cure the wrong while at the same time ensuring that the Member State remains a part of the organization versus expelling the Member State from the organization for conduct that violates its tenets.

Typical punishment options

A number of punishment options exist throughout the realm of international organizations. In international organizations, as in national legal systems, punishment is reflective of the priorities of the community and the balance of restorative and retributive justice constructs. International organizations are also bound by the strictures of international law requirements and by the collective will of the Member States, which may be influenced by political, economic, or other factors as well as law and justice.

It is perhaps for this reason that the range of punishments available is so broad, encompassing everything from a public acknowledgment of allegations of wrongdoing to the imposition of sanctions against a Member State – or those associated with it – to the expulsion of an errant member.

Sanctions

Sanctions come in many forms and serve many functions, from punishing a regime to punishing individuals who are associated with particular conduct that is seen as egregious. Throughout the course of international organizations' functioning, sanctions have been used in attempts to halt conduct that is deemed to violate international law, including human rights practices involving a State's own citizens.

For example, the UN Security Council has authorized a number of economic and political sanctions against errant Member States.[3] In the years following the First Gulf War, the UN imposed many forms of sanctions against Iraq and the leaders of the Saddam Hussein regime.[4] However, there was a slight break in the sanction regime to allow Iraq to trade limited quantities of oil for food intended to feed its population – while this program was riddled with problems and accusations of graft and corruption, it was an example of a form of punishment taken against an errant member.[5] As a side note, there is a common question as to whether such sanctions are effective against the conduct of the targeted Member State or whether instead they disproportionately harm the vulnerable populations of that Member State.[6]

The UN is not the only international organization to use sanctions as a method of punishment for errant members. For example, the African Union imposes sanctions on Member States that are in arrears on payment of membership dues – these sanctions include the inability of the Member State's representatives to speak at meetings, to vote on issues before the organization, and the inability of the Member State's representatives to stand for organizational office.[7] Further, if a Member State of the African Union fails to implement the organizations rules and policies, it may be subject to other forms of sanctions, including economic sanctions.[8]

Forms of sanctions used

A traditionalist view of sanctions tended to focus on imposition against a particular government or State that, in the view of an international organization's constituency, had fallen afoul of acceptable laws and norms and was unwilling to compromise over its policies.[9] These forms of sanction are still in use and often are the continuation of years – if not decades – of sanction regimes.[10] However, recent practice in some organizations – including the United Nations and European Union – is to target not only a State with sanctions but also to target individuals who are part of the regime, have lent it support, or are otherwise implicated in its survival and practices.[11]

Further, sanctions against goods or services from the regime – recently, for example, agricultural products such as cheese from the Russian Federation – are another innovation in the realm of sanction use.[12] These seek to impact the State in a different way from standard sanctions by targeting entire swaths of industry or those who benefit from them, as well as the consumer in the affected State directly.

Duration

Subject to the rules of the particular international organization, there is no set requirement for the duration of or limitation on sanctions. In settings such as the UN and the EU, sanctions will be for set periods of time and, when they are close to expiration, the appropriate organ will review the issue with the option of extending the sanctions as deemed necessary. In some instances, such as the Republic of South Africa under the apartheid system, sanctions may continue for decades. Thus, provided these decisions comply with international law requirements and the regulations of the applicable international organization, the decision as to duration of sanctions can be seen as political.

Limitations

Limitations on sanctions will be dependent on their compliance with legality, as described below, and also on their compliance with organizational terms and requirements. Further, limitations will focus on the will of the international community and the effectiveness – or potential for effectiveness – of the sanctions in achieving the desired policy or legal change.

Considerations in legality and effectiveness

Within the context of sanctions, it should be noted that, particularly when used against individuals rather than States *per se*, significant issues have been raised, such as errors in due process and human rights violations against those targeted.[13] In addition, some have raised concerns that in many international organizations – notably the United Nations – only one organ is empowered to impose, alter and remove sanctions of all forms.[14] Attempts to create specialized oversight bodies within the international organization have been used to remedy these complaints, although many States and commentators do not believe them to be adequate.[15]

Public rebukes/shaming

There are nominally lighter penalties than sanctions, such as public condemnation of a Member State for certain actions, most often those that violate accepted human rights practices or otherwise undermine the goals of the international organization. In these instances, there are numerous venues of impact for the public shaming to touch on, such as economic interactions with other States or private funders, diplomatic interactions with States, military interactions with other States and international organizations, and the empowerment of domestic groups seeking to assert their rights.[16]

As with sanctions, shaming and public rebukes can be carried out against individuals, such as those associated with a current or former regime, with the ability to highlight culpability and stigmatize the individual in multiple facets of life and function.[17] Different States and individuals respond to shaming in a variety of ways, as can be expected in any punishment situation.[18]

Restrictions on funding or other organization activities in Member States

Use of restrictions as tools

Within the organizational context, there are several aspects of restrictions available. These will recur throughout the discussion of membership in particular international organizations in the second section of this book and are important to note because they represent areas of uniformity between many Member States.

Depending on the issue involved, a Member State may be temporarily suspended from activities in the international organization. This typically involves an embargo on participation in meetings, voting abilities and the ability to receive organizational funding or other support, and generally will extend until the issue involved is remedied by the Member State. In some instances, a Member State has a year to cure the issue, after which it is subject to termination by vote of the other Member States. However, depending on the cause of the issue and will of the other Member States, this termination requirement can be waived.

Suspension of Member States

Additionally, some international organizations that focus on consensus-based decision-making, such as ASEAN, will require that issues of non-compliance with organization rules and policies be sent for mediation or other forms of in-house adjudication.[19]

Violations of the international organization's rules and policies are not the only reasons for which a Member State's functions and abilities may be suspended. A key reason for the suspension of certain membership privileges, particularly voting privileges, is the non-payment of membership dues or other financial obligations of the Member State toward the international organization.

In the context of the UN, a Member State that is in arrears on payment of assessed membership dues for the equivalent of two years can have its voting privileges suspended until the dues are paid or the UN General Assembly decides that the Member State cannot control its failure to pay dues.[20] Decisions on suspension for financial or any other reasons require a 2/3 majority vote by the UN General Assembly.[21]

Similarly, UN-associated international organizations, such as the World Health Organization and the International Labour Organization, allow the General Assembly equivalent to suspend voting or other privileges of membership in the event that a Member State does not comply with its requirement to pay assessed financial dues.[22] Where these provisions are included in the foundational text there is often a procedure under which the appropriate governing body of the international organization can vote to lift the suspension of the Member State once the dues have been paid.[23] Other UN-associated international organizations use the same exception to the arrears requirement where the Member State is proved to be unable to control its failure to pay dues.[24] Additionally, in the event that a UN Member State is suspended by the UN, that Member State can often also be suspended from a UN-associated international organization if the UN requests the suspension.[25]

Other international organizations, particularly regional organizations, will suspend the ability of a Member State to act as part of the organization if an undemocratic, unconstitutional or illegitimate government has come to power in that Member State.[26]

Expulsion of Member States

Expulsion, perhaps not surprisingly, is the most extreme way in which an international organization might handle an errant Member State. Indeed, even where a Member State is blatantly in violation of the rules and policies of the international organization, there is a school of thought that it is still a better practice to keep the Member State in the organization system so that it can be watched and monitored. This theory works on the principle that it is better to include an outlying member than to have that member operating completely without the supervision of the organization community. Of course, the converse argument is that by allowing a Member State to flagrantly break the rules and still remain a member this diminishes the prestige of the international organization and the importance of its rules and policies.

There is no right or wrong theory to the issue of expulsion, and certainly a great deal would depend on the specifics of the international organization, the Member States, and the circumstances. Of particular note should be the rules and policies that are being violated – for example, whether they are procedural issues or substantive aspects of the international organization's identity.

Some foundational texts make express reference to the possibility of expulsion of a Member State. In this situation, the ability to expel a Member State is unquestioned and the only issue becomes following the appropriate procedural requirements. For example, as with suspensions, the UN General Assembly must approve the expulsion of a Member State through a 2/3 majority vote.[27] Further, the foundational texts of UN-associated international organizations often provide that a Member State's membership in the associated organization will be terminated if the Member State's UN membership is terminated for any reason.[28]

Similarly, various banking and financial institutions have related provisions, although many of them are key to membership in the International Monetary Fund or another financial entity.[29] Even when this happens, the terminated Member State remains responsible for the payment or repayment of amounts owed to the financial institution.[30]

However, a larger problem exists where there is no specific mention of the ability to expel a Member State in the foundational text. In this situation, it is far from clear whether the international organization would have the ability to do so.

Conclusions

When an international organization is being formed, it is generally hoped that measures such as punishment and expulsion will not be necessary. However, to protect the organization and its members, the vast majority of foundational texts provide for these measures. When crafting them, there is a necessary balance between the interests of the organization, those of the Member State at issue, those of the core of Member States that comprise the organization, and the constituencies that might be harmed by such decisions. It is clear that these are not decisions to be taken lightly and that international organizations will seek to implement a number of softer measures, such as temporary suspension or written rebukes, rather than diving directly into extreme punishments such as expulsion or the imposition of a sanction regime.

This is no mean feat, as generating a balance among such a complex web of actors requires compromise and conciliation on all sides. The same is true in the specialized realm of sanctions, where there are significant sovereignty issues to be weighed against the interests of the international community and, often, the rights of those living within the Member State. Such exercises place international organizations in a delicate position as a matter of diplomacy but in a strong position as a matter of organizational legitimacy.

The ability vested in most international organizations to impose such powerful punishments serves as a deterrent factor. In addition, the ability to impose measures that have such deep ramifications on the political, legal, economic and societal levels demonstrates a profound statement on the power of international organizations as actors in the international community. This statement provides another indication of legitimacy for the international organization which possesses the ability to punish and sanction Member States, and the ability to use lesser options further manifests the flexibility of these organizations in the internal and external spheres.

As a final point, the methods of expulsion of a Member State utilized by an international organization demonstrate the seriousness and value of membership *per se* by requiring that significant substantive and procedural steps are met prior to a decision. This is an important demonstration of the methods through which organizational structure can be used to reinforce the value of membership and remove it from serving as a tool that can be easily terminated at the whim of another Member State. Instead, establishing a high threshold for expulsion from an international organization ensures – to the extent possible – that membership will not be used as a tool for coercion or threats.

Notes

1 Constitutive Act of the African Union (2000) art 9.
2 ASEAN Charter (2007) art 27.
3 *See* Grant L. Willis, *Security Council Targeted Sanctions, Due Process, and the 1267 Ombudsman*, 42 Georgetown Journal of International Law 673 (2011); Malcolm N. Shaw, *International Law* 7th edn, 901 (2014).
4 *See* Willis (2011), *supra* note 3.
5 *See id.*
6 *See id.*
7 Constitutive Act of the African Union, *supra* note 1 at art 23(1).
8 *Id.* at art. 23(2).
9 *See* Devika Hovell, *Due Process in the United Nations*, 110 American Journal of International Law 1, 8–9 (2016); Willis (2011), *supra* note 3; Shaw, *supra* note 3 at 901–907. United Nations, 2011 Highlights of Security Council Practice 12 (2012).
10 Repertoire of the Practice of the Security Council, p. 249 (2000); United Nations, 2011 Highlights of Security Council Practice, *supra* note 9 at 12.
11 *See* Hovell, *supra* note 9 at 8–9; Willis, *supra* note 3; Irene Couzigou, *The United Nations Security Council Sanctions and International Human Rights*, 10 Vienna Journal of International & Comparative Law 277 (2016); Shaw, *supra* note 3 at 907–910; United Nations, 2011 Highlights of Security Council Practice, *supra* note 9 at 12.
12 *See* Hovell, *supra* note 9 at 9.
13 For a discussion of the due process claims involved, *see* Hovell, *supra* note 9; Couzigou, *supra* note 11.
14 *See* Hovell, *supra* note 9 at 9.
15 Hovell, *supra* note 9 at 9–10; Willis, *supra* note 3.
16 *See* Sandeep Gopalan & Roslyn Fuller, *Enforcing International Law: States, IOs, and Courts as Shaming Reference Groups*, 39 Brooklyn Journal of International Law 73, 87–88 (2014) (explaining that "for a State with a strong sense of identity and attendant conceptions of national pride, the imposition of a shame sanction triggers internal consequences . . . [i]n other circumstances, whether it is because a State does not have a strong sense of identity and national pride, or because a State that possesses these attributes denies wrongdoing, shaming has largely external consequences.").
17 *See id.* at 79.
18 *See id.* at 89.
19 ASEAN Charter, *supra* note 2 at art 5(3) (2007).
20 UN Charter (1945) art 19. For example, if a Member State is suffering from severe economic hardship due to a natural disaster, the UN General Assembly would likely hold this to be a situation beyond the Member State's control.
21 *Id.* at art 18.
22 *See* Constitution of the World Health Organization (1945) art 7; International Labor Organization Constitution (1944) art 13(4); UNESCO Constitution (1945) art 4(8)(b).

23 *See* WHO Constitution, *supra* note 22 at art 7.

24 ILO Constitution, *supra* note 22 at art 13(4); UNESCO Constitution, *supra* note 22 at art 4(8)(c).

25 UNESCO Constitution, *supra* note 22 at art 2(4).

26 *See* Constitutive Act of the African Union, *supra* note 1 at art 30; Charter of the Organization of American States (1967) art 9 (providing that the requirement can be lifted or waived if the OAS General Assembly agrees).

27 UN Charter, *supra* note 20 at art 18.

28 *See* UNESCO Constitution, *supra* note 22 at art 2(5).

29 International Bank for Reconstruction and Development Articles of Agreement (1944) art V sect 3; International Development Association Articles of Agreement (1960) art VII sect 3; International Financial Corporation Articles of Agreement (2012) art V.

30 IBRD Articles of Agreement, *supra* note 29 at art V sect 4; IDA Articles of Agreement, *supra* note 29 at art VII sect 4; IFC Articles of Agreement, *supra* note 29 at art V; Multilateral Investment Guarantee Agency Convention (2010) art 53.

Chapter 7

Diplomatic rights versus international organization rights

In the international context, it is essential to understand the application of privileges and immunities to the diplomatic and consular realm as well as the realm of international organizations. This is so because, while the same policy considerations inform the similarities in these rights, there are also significant areas where the diplomatic and organizational worlds do not overlap and, thus, the rights afforded to each form of entity vary. Even within the realm of diplomatic rights there are differences in status (for example, full diplomatic mission rights versus consular rights), and within international organization rights there are differences (for example, the rights of the organization's Secretary General versus the rights of the organization's hired expert for a particular topic).

This chapter begins with a discussion of diplomatic rights and then proceeds into international organization rights. Finally, it directly compares and contrasts these forms of rights to highlight the key differences and similarities.

Legal and political sources behind rights and immunities for international actors

Some provisions of diplomatic law have existed for centuries – if not longer – and the fact that they have been enshrined in recent Conventions seems almost secondary to their existence. These provisions are the ones with which many tend to be familiar, even if only from television and the movies, such as diplomatic immunity and the inviolability of an embassy overseas.

Although much of the law and practice surrounding diplomatic rights is essentially customary international law, the majority of it was codified through two international Conventions that went into effect in the 1960s. The first of these Conventions was the Vienna Convention on Diplomatic Relations (Diplomatic Convention) and the second was the Vienna Convention on Consular Relations (Consular Relations Convention). As might be gathered from the fact that there are two Conventions on the issue, there is an inherent difference in status – and rights afforded to – diplomatic missions and consular offices.

This difference can be found in the opening articles of each Convention, where the responsibilities of diplomatic missions and consular offices are elucidated. Diplomatic missions, most notably embassies, have primarily high-level diplomatic and political functions, such as facilitating treaty negotiations, officially representing the sending State, providing protections for citizens of the sending State, and facilitating diplomatic and practical relations between the host State and the sending State.[1] In contrast, consular offices have many additional elucidated functions; however, they are far more bureaucratic than the higher-level functions of diplomatic offices.[2] Some of the functions of the offices are the same; however, many are an outgrowth of core diplomatic functions, for example providing practical assistance in developing economic ties between States,[3] and some are quintessentially bureaucratic, such as issuing passports and visas, registering births and deaths of nationals overseas, assisting nationals with legal and other representation within the host State, and facilitating the transmission of judgments from the sending State to the host State.[4] As the differences in functions might suggest, the level of privileges and immunities needed for diplomatic offices and consulates are different owing to the delicacy of the functions attributed to each form of entity, thus occasioning the differences in rights afforded.

Further, it must be noted that States will often enact domestic legislation enunciating the extent of privileges and immunities to be granted to international organizations within their jurisdiction.[5] These pieces of legislation are, of course, to be understood in conjunction with the treaty obligations undertaken by the State, whether in the form of a multilateral Convention, such as the foundational texts of the international organization, or a bi-lateral headquarters or host State agreement.

Diplomatic rights

Personal rights

It must be emphasized that in both situations, particularly in the consular setting, there is to be an attempt not to hire or otherwise engage a national of the host State.[6] Further, under both Conventions the host States retain the ability to deem a member of the diplomatic or consular staff to be *persona non grata* and then cause him/her to be removed or terminated by the sending State.[7]

In terms of taxation, members of the diplomatic mission and, by extension, the sending State itself, are exempt from taxation.[8] There are lesser exemptions from host-State taxation for consular officials and employees than for officials and employees at diplomatic missions.[9]

Property rights

Under both Conventions, an agreement must be made between the host State and the sending State in terms of the establishment of a diplomatic/consular office.[10] Additionally, the host State must be informed of the identities of the ambassadors and other high-ranking diplomatic and consular officers who will be sent – this includes a requirement that the officer's credentials be accepted by the host State.[11]

Reasonable limitations on the size of a diplomatic or consular office can be imposed by the host State.[12] Once the sending State has established either form of office, there is a requirement that the host State be allowed to impose some limits on the use of additional space by the sending State.[13] Not only is a diplomatic mission inviolable by the host State or any other State, the host State has an obligation to provide protection of the diplomatic mission, including from domestic threats.[14] The Diplomatic Convention also specifically provides that "the premises of the mission, their furnishings and other property thereon and the means of transport of the mission shall be immune from search, requisition, attachment or execution."[15]

Although diplomatic missions, such as embassies, are afforded the status of blanket inviolability, the same is not true for consular offices. According to the Consular Relations Convention, there is limited inviolability for consular offices.[16] As with diplomatic missions, the host State is under a special obligation to provide assistance and protection to consular offices,[17] for example police protection in the event of a protest in front of the consular office. There is a more limited protection for the property of the consular office as opposed to the diplomatic mission in that, although both are to be shielded from requisition by the host State for explicit use by the host State, consular property can be expropriated in some circumstances.[18] In the event that expropriation occurs, the host State must compensate the sending State for the loss and also must ensure that the expropriation does not interfere with the official functioning of the consular office.[19]

The archives of a diplomatic mission, meaning the official documents stored in and possessed by the mission, are protected and cannot be invaded or requisitioned by the host State.[20] Similarly, diplomatic correspondence, including the contents of the "diplomatic pouch," is inviolable for diplomatic missions because of the fundamentally essential aspects of diplomatic communications.[21] While many of the same protections apply to consular communications and the consular pouch, the host State is able to order the opening of the consular pouch – albeit in the present of a sending State representative – in the event that the host State suspects the pouch is being used to transport things other than official correspondence.[22]

Limitations

Perhaps the most fundamental limitation to diplomatic rights and immunities is the simple potential for them to be waived by the national government or the appropriate ambassadorial official.

This can be done in any instance and for any charge, from jaywalking to murder to espionage, based on the discretion of the State and its designated representatives. Waiver is, perhaps understandably, quite rare.

Additionally, in the diplomatic and international organizations settings it is essential to examine the type of immunity held, as the general immunity granted to an ambassador and his family members is quite different in scope from the functional immunity granted to lower-ranking staff at an embassy or consulate. Further, it must be remembered that these forms of immunity are granted only to those attached with a diplomatic function and that citizens of another State are subject to the full laws and rules of the host State.

International organization rights

The diplomatic rights discussed above are informed by the idea of respect for State sovereignty and also by the concept of reciprocity of rights afforded by States. There is, accordingly, a certain amount of gravity that attaches to diplomatic rights because these rights relate to sovereignty and respect for other States in the international system. This distinction is also essential when examining international organization rights, since international organizations by their nature do not possess the same degree of sovereignty as States and are not regarded as having the same standing within the international system. However, the work of international organizations is similar in many ways to the diplomatic work undertaken by States, such as assisting dispute settlement and facilitating relationships between Member States. This means that some forms of protection are necessary in order to ensure that the legitimacy of international organizations, their employees and those affiliated with them is preserved and protected.

International organization rights stem, first and foremost, from the foundational text of the organization itself. Part of the foundational text will typically address the privileges and immunities to be afforded to offices and officers of the international organization within the States that host them. The statements in the foundational text provide the backdrop for the establishment of headquarters agreements, which will be discussed and compared in detail in Chapter 8.

In addition to the terms of the foundational texts there is established treaty law on the topic. Shortly after the UN Charter was adopted, the Convention on Privileges and Immunities of the United Nations (UN Convention) was promulgated. The terms of the UN Convention were solely intended to establish the rights of the United Nations and those working for it, although many of them have been adopted by other international organizations to serve as models if not wholesale.[23]

Personal rights

Under the terms of the UNESCO agreement with the French Government, through which France became the seat of UNESCO's headquarters, representatives of the organization and those from Member States are to be afforded privileges and immunities commensurate with those of diplomatic personnel from foreign States.[24] The full scope of the immunities provided is dependent on the equivalence of the UNESCO representative/Member State representative and the staff level of diplomatic personnel.[25] The dependents of UNESCO representatives/Member States are afforded the same level of privileges and immunities.[26] It is possible for these immunities to be waived and the agreement specifies that the privileges and immunities afforded under it are for functional rather than personal or blanket purposes.[27]

In order for the International Criminal Court (ICC) to function as an organization and as a court system, immunities for those ranging from Member State representatives to employees and organizational representatives to experts and witnesses are essential. For the prosecutor, registrar, their deputies, and judges, these immunities are similar to those who head diplomatic missions and extend to their families.[28] Those who are associated with the ICC as counsel and deputy counsel are to be afforded functional immunity and allowed to pass through the Dutch territory without interruption or seizure in order to participate in proceedings at The Hague.[29] Witnesses and victims for ICC proceedings are to be afforded the necessary immunities to allow their participation in the proceedings.[30] In the same vein, experts who are participating in ICC proceedings are provided functional immunities during the course of their functions.[31] As is standard, it is possible for immunities based on ICC connections to be waived by the appropriate ICC-based body, although this would necessarily be a rare occurrence in order not to undermine the open and impartial functions of the ICC as a judicial entity.[32]

Property rights

Generally, the property of an international organization that is located in a host State is provided immunity from confiscation and taxation by the local authorities. This is quite similar to the protections granted to diplomatic property and demonstrates the overall recognition that it is essential for either a diplomatic entity or international organization to have unfettered access to property in order to carry out its basic functions. Property in this context includes not only standard goods and chattels such as furniture and cars but also archives and other information held as records.[33]

The UN Convention starts off with an explicit statement of the juridical status of the United Nations, explaining that the United Nations has the ability to contract, to "acquire and dispose of" property, and "to institute legal proceedings."[34] In terms of communications protections, the UN Convention provides that communications of the United Nations will be afforded the same status as those of diplomatic communications – meaning that they too will be considered inviolable.[35]

Also, under the ICC's privileges and immunities agreement, its property is inviolable, and – arguably of more importance – the archives and documents of the ICC are themselves inviolable.[36] As an international court designed to try those accused of some of the worst crimes possible as a matter of criminal law, these provisions are essential to the secure functioning of the Court because of the sensitive nature of the documents housed by the Court relating to victims as well as to the accused.

Immunities

The UN Convention also provides classifications for instances in which United Nations personnel in a host State are covered by immunity as long as they are acting in their official capacity.[37] A key element of the UN Convention protections for its personnel is the ability of these personnel to have freedom of speech within the host State, provided that they are acting in an official capacity, even where the speech might not be popular with the host State regime.[38] At first this might seem rather trivial; however, it is indeed quite important, as without this protection personnel could face imprisonment or other severe punishment for undertaking these functions. This could realistically create a scenario in which personnel are forced to decide between executing their functions and facing punishment from the host State or providing inaccurate or incomplete information in the course of their duties.

Property, including currency and other financial assets, of the UN is given immune status from taxation or other interference by the host State, and the inviolability of the UN offices and archives is established.[39]

In addition to UN officials and employees, the UN Convention also covers the privileges and immunities to be afforded to those who serve as experts for the United Nations.[40] Those who serve as experts are usually not full-time UN staff members but have been retained for a specific purpose, such as election lawyers hired to consult on and oversee the electoral process in a particular State.[41] These experts receive qualified privileges and immunities for the purpose of actions undertaken as part of their commission as experts.[42] Such protections also extend to immunity from arrest or interference with personal property while serving as an expert, as well as protection from suits stemming from official functions.[43] This protection has been interpreted by the International Court of Justice as applying even against the expert's home State[44] – more than esoteric, in some cases this protection is essential to allowing an expert to provide information about practices in his home State without threat of suffering retributive harm from the State.

In addition, national courts have extended this immunity to military personnel on United Nations peacekeeping missions, even when these peacekeepers were citizens of the State in question.[45] A key example comes from the Netherlands, which agonized through the horrors of the Yugoslavian conflict in which Dutch peacekeepers could do little to prevent egregious mass killings due to the parameters of their rules of engagement. One of the primary arguments asserted in favor of extending privileges and immunities was that the troops were acting as agents of the United Nations even though they were still under the structure of the Dutch military and, as such, their actions were part of the functional immunity enjoyed by the organization.[46] The court in question took the matter further, holding that almost absolute immunity was necessary for the proper functioning of the international organization.[47] The overall idea of immunity in these situations is quite controversial, especially where the activities giving rise to the claims against an organization involve explicit or tacit violations of *jus cogens* norms or are contrary to the public good which such forces are sent to preserve and protect.[48]

Shortly after the UN Convention was promulgated, a similar Convention was promulgated for privileges and immunities for United Nations-associated international organizations, such as the World Health Organization and the International Labour Organization.[49] The terms of this Convention are essentially the same as the UN Convention.[50] However, other non-UN-associated international organizations are not covered by this Convention and, thus, have established their own forms of privileges and immunities. Within the foundational texts of these organizations, the influences of the UN Convention are apparent.

The organizations which are most divergent in form if not in substance from the UN Convention are the regional organizations; however, even these organizations essentially adopt the same privileges and immunities for themselves and their actors. Some international organizations, such as the North Atlantic Treaty Organization (NATO), rely on the headquarters agreements they enter into with host States to set out the essentials of privileges and immunities rather than setting out these rights in their foundational texts.[51]

Conclusions

It is perhaps axiomatic to say that diplomatic protections such as those discussed in this chapter are necessary to ensure the functioning of the diplomatic relations system. Indeed, before it was ever subject to treaty obligations, the customary international law practices of inviolability for embassies and the person of an ambassador were ingrained in international relations. However, international organizations are not diplomatic missions, do not represent a particular State, and thus require their own constructs of privileges and immunities.

Indeed, international organizations require their own foundational texts because they are artificial constructs as a matter of law. In this way, an analogy between an international organization and a corporation is entirely apt – both are legal creations and both require permission to operate in the State where their headquarters are located and in all other States to which they intend to send officers. It is for this reason that the privileges and immunities of an international organization must be articulated and agreed upon by all parties. This takes on notable significance when the international organization in question is involved with sensitive information or activities that could cause danger to lives should it be improperly disclosed.

Privileges and immunities for international organizations are more than a statement of protections and rights. In a situation where an international organization must establish itself and its operations within the larger international community, privileges and immunities recognize the legitimacy of the particular organization. They allow the organization to function as a recognized juridical entity within a host State or, more generally, within the territory of that Member State, and provide a basis for the organization to assert legal existence.

Finally, privileges and immunities for international organizations can be seen as designating benchmarks for their capacities and the scope of their activities. As the organization's activities expand or contract and as it begins its work in additional States, the ways in which it can enjoy and act upon its privileges and immunities can be seen as indicators of its growth.

Notes

1 Vienna Convention on Diplomatic Relations (1961) art 3.
2 Vienna Convention on Consular Relations (1963) art 5.
3 Id.
4 Id.
5 *See* Aaron I. Young, Note: *Deconstructing International Organization Immunity*, 44 Georgetown Journal of International Law 311 (2013) (discussing these practices in the United States); Michael Singer, *Jurisdictional Immunity of International Organizations: Human Rights and Functional Necessity Concerns*, 36 Virginia Journal of International Law 53 (1995) (noting the potential for conflicts where a State is a Member State of an international organization and called upon to address a complaint regarding in the international organization in the domestic court system); Richard J. Oparil, *Immunity of International Organizations in United States Courts: Absolute or Restrictive?*, 24 Vanderbilt Journal of Transnational Law 689 (1991) (providing a history of the different legislative schemes applicable to international organizations in the United States); Daniel D. Bradlow, *Using a Shield as a Sword: Are International Organizations Abusing Their Immunity?*, 31 Temple International and Comparative Law Journal 45 (2017).
6 *See* Vienna Convention on Diplomatic Relations, *supra* note 1 at art 8; Vienna Convention on Consular Relations, *supra* note 2 at art 22.
7 Vienna Convention on Diplomatic Relations, *supra* note 1 at art 9; Vienna Convention on Consular Relations, *supra* note 2 at art 23.
8 Vienna Convention on Diplomatic Relations, *supra* note 1 at art 23.
9 Vienna Convention on Consular Relations, *supra* note 2 at art 32.
10 Vienna Convention on Diplomatic Relations, *supra* note 1 at art 2.
11 Vienna Convention on Consular Relations, *supra* note 2 at arts 10, 11; Vienna Convention on Diplomatic Relations, *supra* note 1 at art 4.
12 Vienna Convention on Diplomatic Relations, *supra* note 1 at art 11.
13 Id. at art 12.
14 Id. at art 22.
15 Id. at art 22(3).
16 Vienna Convention on Consular Relations, *supra* note 2 at art 31. There is an implicit assumption of permission from the appropriate consular authority where assistance from the host State is needed for security purposes, such as firefighting or disaster relief. Id. Of course, in this instance the host State would enter the consular premises solely for the purpose of assistance and not to undermine the work or sovereignty of the consular mission.
17 Id. at art 31.
18 Id.
19 Id.
20 Vienna Convention on Diplomatic Relations, *supra* note 1 at art 24.
21 Id. at art 27.
22 Vienna Convention on Consular Relations, *supra* note 2 at art 35.
23 Convention on the Privileges and Immunities of the United Nations (1946) preamble.
24 Agreement between the Government of the French Republic and the United Nations Educational, Scientific and Cultural Organization regarding the Headquarters of UNESCO and the Privileges and Immunities of the Organization on French Territory (1994) art 18.
25 Id. at art 18(1).
26 Id. at art 18(2).
27 Id. at art 21.
28 Agreement on the Privileges and Immunities of the International Criminal Court (2002) arts 15, 16.
29 Id. at art 18.
30 Id. at arts 19, 20.

31 *Id.* at art 21.

32 *Id.* at arts 25, 26.

33 *See* Convention on the Privileges and Immunities of the United Nations (1946) preamble.

34 *Id.* at art 1.

35 *Id.* at art 3.

36 Agreement on the Privileges and Immunities of the ICC, *supra* note 28 at arts 6, 7.

37 Convention on the Privileges and Immunities of the United Nations, *supra* note 33 at art 4; Malcolm N. Shaw, *International Law* 7th edn, 955–963 (2014).

38 Convention on the Privileges and Immunities of the United Nations, *supra* note 33 at art 4.

39 *Id.* at art 2.

40 *See generally id.*

41 *Id.* at art 5.

42 *Id.*

43 *Id.*

44 *See Applicability of Article VI, Section 22, of the Convention on the Privileges and Immunities of the United Nations (Mazilu)*, 1989 ICJ Reports 177 (advisory opinion); *Difference Relating to Immunity from Legal Process of a Special Rapporteur of the Commission on Human Rights, Advisory Opinion*, ICJ Reports 1999, p. 62.

45 *See* Mothers of Srebrenica case; *see also* Otto Spijkers, *The Immunity of the United Nations in Relation to the Genocide in Srebrenica in the Eyes of the Dutch District Court*, 13 J of International Peacekeeping (2009) 197–219. Interestingly, this was a case in which there was no formal appearance by the United Nations before the court even for the purposes of lodging the allegations over immunity. Instead, this was done directly by the Dutch Government acting in its capacity as a United Nations Member State. *Id.*

46 Spijkers, *supra* note 45 at 203 (noting that "one need not look at the particular acts objected to in order to determine whether they are necessary to fulfill the purposes of the Organization . . . one must assess the negative consequences the denial of immunity would have for the proper functioning of the UN.").

47 *Id.* at 206.

48 *Id.*; Alexandra R. Harrington, *Prostituting Peace: The Impact of Sending State's Legal Regimes on U.N. Peacekeeper Behavior and Suggestions to Protect the Populations Peacekeepers Guard*, 17 Florida State U. College of Law J. Trans. L. & Pol'y 217 (2008); Alexandra R. Harrington, *A Tale of Three Nations?: The role of United Nations peacekeepers and missions on the concept of nation-State, nationalism, and ownership of the State in Lebanon, the Democratic Republic of the Congo, and Kosovo*, 21 Conn. J. Int'l L. 213 (2006); Alexandra R. Harrington, *Victims of Peace: Current Abuse Allegations against UN Peacekeepers and the Role of Law in Preventing Them in the Future*, 12 ILSA J. Int'l & Comp. L. (2005); *see also* Jasna Hasanbasic, *Liability in Peacekeeping Missions: A Civil Cause of Action for the Mothers of Srebrenica against the Dutch Government and the United Nations*, 29 Emory International Law Review 415 (2014).

49 *See generally* Convention on Privileges and Immunities of the Specialized Agencies (1947).

50 *See generally id.*

51 *See, e.g.*, North Atlantic Treaty (1949).

Chapter 8

Headquarters agreements of international organizations

Against the backdrop of diplomatic and organizational rights from Chapter 7, this chapter examines the concept and contents of headquarters agreements between various international organizations and host States. Privileges and immunities are general in many ways and provide for more blanket allowances of rights to international organizations and those affiliated with them. Headquarters agreements, however, carve out more specific allowances for international organizations operations and rights within the scope of the international organization's functioning and needs. At the same time, they seek to ensure that the host State's interests are not imperiled as a result of the presence and activities of the particular international organization.

Philosophy behind headquarters agreements and property protections

Once international organizations have been created and have set out the appropriate privileges and immunities in their foundational texts, they exist as a matter of law. And yet, as a legally created entity, an international organization cannot simply conclude that it likes the weather in New Zealand and decide to base its operations there. Instead, it must enter into negotiations with the government of New Zealand to arrange the terms under which it will operate within the State. The end result of these negotiations – if successful – is a headquarters agreement that sets out the rights, obligations and guarantees made by the State and the international organization regarding its presence in New Zealand.

After the headquarters agreement is finalized, the international organization can then commence its operations in New Zealand pursuant to the terms of the agreement. From that point onward, the international organization's headquarters location will be recognized as New Zealand, although this does not prevent it from establishing additional subsidiary or satellite offices, field offices, or other relationships for its work to take place in other States. Any such offices will, however, have a different status since they will not be headquarters sites and will require negotiation of further host State agreements with the States in which the international organization seeks to operate.

Headquarters agreements

As with the majority of international organizations' foundational texts, no two organizations are alike. This is reflected in the terms of headquarters agreements between the international organization and the host State, as there are standard terms for these agreements and yet each one is characterized by the particularities of the organization involved.

Perhaps the most representative example of a headquarters agreement for an international organization is that for the UN Headquarters compound, located on the East Side of Manhattan. Indeed, the looming UN office building is a key part of the New York City skyline and yet the entire area that comprises the UN headquarters area is not technically under the sovereignty of the United States. Instead, under the terms of the UN Headquarters Agreement, sovereignty over the area is suspended so that the UN, its officers and employees can operate within the area free from local or federal intrusion.

The UN Headquarters Agreement, first and foremost, designates the areas that are to be considered part of the UN area.[1] Under the terms of the UN Headquarters Agreement, the United States guarantees that it will ensure the protection of UN property within the headquarters area unless the UN states that the property is no longer to be considered United Nations territory.[2]

Perhaps the most controversial terms of the UN Headquarters Agreement relate to the transportation of those who have official business at the UN, work with the United Nations or who have been expressly invited to appear at the United Nations.[3] The terms of the UN Headquarters Agreement require the United States to allow and facilitate transportation of these persons to and from the UN headquarters district.[4] At first, this may seem innocuous and indeed logical – there is no airport within the UN headquarters area, nor is there a port facility, so there must be a way for visitors to access the UN even if this involves traveling through sovereign United States territory. However, in application these terms have been highly problematic because they have been interpreted to require the United States at times to admit those classified as terrorists or enemies of the State under national policy and give them safe passage to and from the United Nations headquarters district.[5] Additionally, the UN Headquarters Agreement exempts UN officials and associates from traditional United States visa and residency requirements, with some exceptions, notably where a person poses a health risk.[6] This is only somewhat less controversial.

In the event of a disagreement between the United States and the United Nations over the United Nations Headquarters Agreement, the issue first goes to an arbitration panel and then, if necessary, to the International Court of Justice.[7] In this way, disputes between the parties are kept away from the United States legal system.

The scope of personal privileges and immunities for the United Nations Educational, Scientific and Cultural Organization (UNESCO) representatives/Member States while at the UNESCO headquarters in France is discussed in Chapter 12. The Headquarters Agreement provides the terms of UNESCO's legal personality in France,[8] and recognizes that, while French laws and regulations will generally apply to the headquarters area, UNESCO will have the ability to craft regulations for its own functioning and that these must be upheld.[9]

Under the terms of the headquarters agreement, the UNESCO headquarters area is inviolable and special organizational permission must be granted to any French agent prior to his/her entry onto the premises.[10] However, the agreement is specific in that UNESCO is required not to allow its headquarters area to be used as a safe haven for wanted criminals and/or those fleeing from prosecution.[11] The French Government is required to allow and facilitate access to the headquarters area by those who are representatives of Member States, who are part of official delegations from Member States, who are serving as experts for any UNESCO organ, who represent other affiliated international organizations and non-governmental organizations, who have been invited to UNESCO, and their families.[12] All these categories of representative are still required to comply with, and be subject to, the French rules and regulations on health.[13]

UNESCO's Executive Board members, when in France for official duties, are afforded the same privileges and immunities as equally ranked diplomats from foreign States.[14] The immediate family members of those sitting on the Executive Board are to receive the same privileges and immunities, as are the designated alternates for each member.[15] Within the scope of his/her functions, the Chair of the Executive Board is regarded as having similar diplomatic status to that of a diplomatic mission head.[16] Outside of France, the Executive Board members are to receive the same privileges and immunities as accorded under the Convention on the Privileges and Immunities of Specialized Agencies.[17]

Interpol headquarters are also located in France and the Interpol Headquarters Agreement states that France grants recognition of the legal personality of Interpol, including its ability to contract, acquire property, and be involved in judicial proceedings.[18] Interpol agrees that French law will apply within the headquarters area, although Interpol itself has the reserved right to create regulations and other rules needed for the functioning of the organization.[19]

Standard organizational privileges and immunities protections are established for Interpol communications, archives, and limitations on taxation,[20] as are protections of Interpol property.[21] Visa requirements for those who are affiliated with Interpol are to be waived by France, although there is again an exception for public health purposes.[22] Those who are in France on official Interpol business are protected from arrest and detention by French authorities, immune from service of process for their official acts in connection with Interpol, and are to be covered by protections for diplomatic papers.[23]

Further, the Interpol Headquarters Agreement establishes that claims against Interpol by individuals or disagreements between Interpol and the French Government are to be settled through arbitration rather than the court system.[24]

The International Criminal Court (ICC) is headquartered in the Netherlands.[25] Under the authorization from the United Nations General Assembly, the Netherlands is to specifically recognize and enforce the legal personality of the ICC and all that this entails.[26] Included in the ICC Headquarters Agreement are protections for basic freedoms of assembly, discussion and publication, which are essential for the functioning of any court.[27] In order to facilitate proceedings before the ICC, the Netherlands is required to ensure that visas and other papers be granted to those taking part in the proceedings.[28]

Perhaps unsurprisingly, the premises of the ICC are to be inviolable except in instances of emergency or requests for assistance from the ICC[29] – this is especially important when one considers the gravity, and often politically unpopular nature, undertakings by the ICC. Standard organizational privileges and immunities are to be applied to the ICC, including communications facilitation and exemption from taxation.[30] Of particular importance for the proper functioning of the ICC as a court is the guarantee of immunity from prosecution for those involved in ICC proceedings, such as the Prosecutor, who must present cases alleging extremely egregious conduct against well-known and often influential political and other figures.[31] Similarly, the UN General Assembly insisted that those who appear before the ICC as witnesses be guaranteed immunity to protect them and to ensure that they and their families do not suffer more due to testimony before the ICC.[32]

As an organization, the International Monetary Fund (IMF) enjoys the customary privileges and immunities afforded to the majority of international organizations, including the recognition of its legal identity and existence.[33] Generally, IMF staff members, officers and Member State representatives are afforded functional immunities and immunity for the purposes of immigration requirements.[34]

The International Bank for Reconstruction and Development (IBRD) is accorded standard privileges and immunities associated with an international organization, and its staff members, as well as those representing Member States and IBRD organs, are provided functional immunity under the Articles of Agreement.[35] The International Centre for the Settlement of Investment Disputes (ICSID) is subject to standard privileges and immunities as an organization, and its officers, leadership, Administrative Council members, and Panel members enjoy functional immunity.[36] Similar immunities from prosecution are available for those participating in the dispute settlement process, but only in the context of their official duties and travel in the host State for the purposes of executing their official functions.[37]

As a separate organization that is affiliated with the United Nations, the World Health Organization (WHO) is subject to the standard privileges and immunities afforded to international organizations, and those individuals affiliated with it receive functional immunity.[38] As a general rule, the International Maritime Organization (IMO) enjoys the standard privileges and immunities granted to international organizations, and those affiliated with the IMO receive functional immunity.[39] In keeping with typical international organization terms, especially those with a UN affiliation, privileges and immunities extend to its work and premises throughout Member States and those associated with the organization in some capacity receive functional immunity.[40] The World Intellectual Property Organization (WIPO) is to enjoy the standard privileges and immunities afforded to international organizations in its Member States and those who are affiliated with WIPO are to be afforded functional immunity in these areas as well.[41] The Organization for the Prohibition of Chemical Weapons (OPCW) enjoys standard privileges and immunities throughout the States in which it operates and those who are associated with the OPCW in an official capacity enjoy functional immunity, which is important given the sensitive portfolio carried by the organization.[42]

The headquarters of the Organization of American States (OAS) is located in Washington, DC.[43] Under the terms of the OAS Headquarters Agreement, the OAS has recognized legal personality and capacity within the United States.[44] Included among the allowances are that the OAS has the ability to hold property, including currency reserves, free from US interference or taxation.[45]

In terms of legal process, the OAS is immune unless this immunity is waived by the appropriate official.[46] The OAS is authorized to issue travel documents to those doing its work or affiliated with it, and the US is obliged to respect these documents and allow passage for those carrying them.[47] Specific immunities are established for OAS officials and experts so long as they are acting within the scope of their official capacity.[48] Unlike other organizations, there is an opening for the OAS to use the local and federal United States court systems for some disputes, although all other disputes are subject to arbitration according to specific terms.[49]

When the Inter-American Development Bank (IADB) was designed, the standard privileges and immunities were granted to the organization, with functional immunities granted to its staff members, governance members, and similar personnel.[50] The Asian Development Bank (ADB) enjoys the standard privileges and immunities afforded to international and regional organizations, and those employed by or affiliated with it enjoy functional immunity.[51] While the Nordic Investment Bank (NIB) avails itself of the standard privileges and immunities for international organizations in many ways, it does allow itself to be sued in competent courts of national jurisdiction in the Member States.[52] Employees of the NIB, those who serve a governance function within the NIB structure, and others associated with the NIB are, however, subject to functional immunity for their official actions.[53]

The general law to be applied within the premises of the Special Court for Sierra Leone was that of Sierra Leone, but the Special Court also had the ability to promulgate and enforce rules and regulations provided they were not in conflict with applicable law.[54] Under the terms of the Agreement, the same system of privileges and immunities as used in the Extraordinary Chambers in the Courts of Cambodia (ECCC) was adopted for international personnel at the Special Court – and their families – and Sierra Leonean personnel at the Special Court.[55] Similarly, victims, witnesses and experts were provided the same forms of protection and security guarantees while at the Special Court and in Sierra Leone for the purposes of giving testimony or evidence.[56] Due to the volatile security situation in Sierra Leone at the time of the Agreement, security for the Special Court's premises was made the responsibility of the existing UN Mission on Sierra Leone.[57]

Special categories of protections – air rights, access to media and communications, access to mail

While protections for the international organization's territorial area are extremely important in terms of keeping out interference from the host State, it is equally important that the international organization's ability to communicate outward to the international community be preserved and protected. It is for this reason that headquarters agreements tend to include provisions relating to the international organization's access to communications methods, access to media and unmolested access to mail.

For example, the United Nations is to be allowed to communicate freely inside and outside the United Nations headquarters district, including free and unrestricted use of radio and other media.[58] Additionally, the United States is to ensure that the United Nations headquarters district has access to essential infrastructural support, such as electricity and water.[59]

UNESCO is to be provided access to basic utilities, transportation methods, fire assistance, and standardized removal of snow, based on the specific requests of the Director General.[60] However, the Headquarters Agreement makes it quite clear that these services are to be provided for a fee set by the French administration and that they are not to be granted free of charge to UNESCO unless the Government so decides.[61]

Additionally, should there be an interruption in the provision of these services, notably as a result of force majeure, the French Government agrees to provide UNESCO with priority in their repair and restoration.[62] It is notable that, while UNESCO is to receive priority, it is not afforded primacy of place in service restoration as is the case for the UN. This agreement is also of note because it demonstrates the flexibility of international organizations' law for even the most basic issues such as weather and climate.

Similar terms apply for the provision of services to the ICC's headquarters area.[63] The ICC is also to have the full ability to use all available means of communication without interruption from the Dutch State, including the ability to publish freely.[64] The latter allowance is perhaps the most important for the ICC, given its function as a judgment-issuing body that frequently generates opinions which are controversial.

The standard protections for communication are provided in the OAS Headquarters Agreement, and the headquarters area itself is deemed to be inviolable unless outside authorities are expressly requested to enter the premises.[65] Again, the US is required to protect the OAS headquarters from outside danger or intrusion, and may enter the premises in times of disaster.[66] All standard protections for property, freedom from domestic taxation, and communications apply in the African Union context.[67] Further, officials of the African Union and those associated with the organization are granted immunity for actions taken or statements made in their official capacities.[68]

Protections in times of emergency/strife

The majority focus of headquarters agreements is on the ability of the international organization to function as a legal entity within the host State. In this context, the special status of international organizations tends to be emphasized in terms of the ability of the organization to function without interference from the host State. And yet it is equally important to emphasize the terms of these agreements that relate to mechanisms for protecting international organizations areas from domestic strike in the host State and threats targeted at the international organization.

Importantly, the United Nations Headquarters Agreement provides that the UN is responsible for the enforcement and application of law within the headquarters district.[69] While it is possible for the UN to make local and federal United States law applicable within the UN headquarters, this is solely within the discretion of the UN to the extent that these laws do not conflict with the regulations established by the UN.[70] There is a specific exception for local United States fire regulations, which the UN agrees to abide by due to safety and security concerns.[71] Further, United States local and national law enforcement agencies are required to ensure the "tranquility" of the headquarters district – for example, to ensure that protesters outside the UN do not harm the UN or its officials – and to assist the UN in these matters if requested.[72]

As with diplomatic and consular offices, the UN headquarters district is deemed inviolable by any United States authority unless invited in by the Secretary General.[73] There is, however, a requirement that the UN headquarters district not be used to harbor individuals who are seeking to avoid arrest or prosecution by the United States or whom the United States is under an obligation to extradite to another State.[74] While the UN may expel any person who violates the terms of its regulations or allowable United States laws, it does not have the ability to prosecute and would have to turn the person over to United States authorities for prosecution.[75]

In some cases, issues have arisen when a State or regime that is opposed by the host State either sends a representative to an international organization meeting or establishes a diplomatic mission under the auspices of the headquarters or host State agreement. A particularly prominent example of this occurred when the United States sought to bar the continued existence of the Palestinian Liberation Organization (PLO) diplomatic offices – recognized as legitimate political actors and representatives by the UN – in New York City despite their being arguably covered under the terms of the Headquarters Agreement.[76] The UN sought to use the arbitration clauses in the Headquarters Agreement; the United States refused, however, stating that it was acting outside the scope of the Agreement.[77] In the *Applicability of the Obligation to Arbitrate* case, the International Court of Justice (ICJ) determined that the Headquarters Agreement was implicated regardless the intentions of the United States and that the arbitration clause was triggered.[78] Ultimately, the PLO mission was allowed to remain in the United States.

The UNESCO Headquarters Agreement requires the French Government to both provide direct protections for the UNESCO headquarters area and to maintain law and order in the general area surrounding it.[79] Included in this is the ability of the UNESCO Director General to specifically request assistance from the French Government.[80]

Within the ICC's structure, the Registrar's consent is required for the Dutch authorities to enter the headquarters premises.[81] As is typical the applicable law throughout the headquarters territory remains Dutch law although generally the ICC has the ability to operate through its own regulations.[82] However, the ICC is not permitted to enforce rules or regulations within the headquarters when they are contrary to Dutch law.[83] In a somewhat unusual requirement, under the ICC Headquarters Agreement designated personnel – for example, security officers – are permitted to carry firearms in the Headquarters area even if this allowance is contrary to standard Dutch law.[84]

This allowance is perhaps best understood when recalling the controversy generated by the ICC's cases and the threats that are often issued against victims and witnesses who are willing to testify. Further, the ICC Headquarters Agreement contains a number of provisions regarding the protection of ICC staff, judges, prosecutors, defense counsel, witnesses, victims, experts, defendants and others who are passing through Dutch territory in order to appear at the ICC's premises.[85] The Agreement also provides for arrangements under which convicted defendants may be held in Dutch prisons during the course of their prison terms.[86]

The inviolability terms of the African Union Headquarters Agreement are extensive and apply to the residences of African Union officials as well as strictly to the headquarters area.[87] However, the local authorities are permitted to enter either type of premises when there is an emergency unless there is an express statement to the contrary.[88] These immunities and protections also apply to aircraft and vessels that are owned by or operated under the auspices of the African Union.[89] Additionally, there is a requirement that the host State allow for transportation for officials and invitees to and from the African Union headquarters.[90] In terms of dispute settlement, the African Union Headquarters Agreement requires that negotiation and/or arbitration be used rather than resort to a court system.[91]

Withdrawal

The ability of an international organization or a host State to terminate a headquarters or host State agreement is an impactful one. Indeed, as the ICJ has noted, there is a significant practice of not including detailed provisions for this possibility within the terms of the main agreement itself, rendering the eventuality of this occurrence potentially difficult if not dangerous.[92]

In the *Interpretation of the Agreement of 25 March 1951 between the WHO and Egypt, Advisory Opinion* case, the ICJ was called upon to decide the validity of the procedures through which the WHO voted to move its Egyptian regional headquarters to another location.[93] It noted the importance of maintaining privileges and immunities for WHO officials during the process of wrapping up its activities and the necessity of working with the Egyptian Government effectively during this time to ensure a complete and coordinated series of activities.[94] Any undertaking between the parties to effect a transfer would, according to the ICJ, need to be governed first and foremost by the use of good faith in dealings.[95] This opinion has served as the guiding source of terminology and allowances under subsequent headquarters agreements.

Conclusions

Headquarters agreements require the balance of several legal and policy areas, each of which is essential and which is telling for understanding how to implement the personality of an international organization. First, an international organization must look inward to appraise its own specialized needs in order to determine the appropriate balance of powers and protections to seek and to omit from the headquarters agreement. For example, the needs of an organization such as the ICC will be far different from the needs of the UN overall. Seeking the same privileges and immunities for each organization would be illogical and would not necessarily provide the necessary protections.

Second, international organizations and host States together must balance international law-based concepts of State sovereignty with those of privileges and immunities for international organizations. The vehicle of a headquarters agreement ensures rights and benefits for some parties but it does so at the cost of sovereignty rights for the State and/or organizational powers, depending on the topic at issue. There is no set formula for this balance, and each negotiation will result in a different outcome based on the weight given to various issues.

This balancing also affects the roles played by international organizations in the host State and the headquarters area, as well as the identity of the international organization itself. The greater leeway and place granted to an international organization, the more it tends to become part of the domestic community.

A further aspect of headquarters agreements is the role of legitimacy in their drafting and enforcement. The act of negotiating a headquarters agreement with a potential host State in itself is a tacit acceptance of the organization's legitimacy by the host State. This, in turn, can impact the ways in which other States view the international organization in terms of legality and legitimacy. Since the majority of headquarters agreements do not contain designated termination dates, their continuation is indicative of the host State's belief that the international organization continues to exercise valid functions and is a legitimate entity as a matter of international law.

Notes

1 Agreement Between the United Nations and the United States Regarding the Headquarters of the United Nations (1947) art 1.
2 Id. at art 2 sect 3.
3 Id. at art 4 sect 11.
4 Id. at art 4 sect 11.
5 A primary example of this was the invitation extended by the UN to Yasser Arafat, then president of the Palestine Liberation Organization, whom the US classified as a terrorist, to speak at the opening session of the United Nations General Assembly.
6 Agreement Between the United Nations and the United States Regarding the Headquarters of the United Nations, *supra* note 1 at art 4 sect 13.
7 Id. at art 8 sect 21.
8 Agreement between the Government of the French Republic and the United Nations Educational, Scientific and Cultural Organization regarding the Headquarters of UNESCO and the Privileges and Immunities of the Organization on French Territory (1994) art 1.
9 Id. at art 5.
10 Id. at art 6.
11 Id. at art 6(3).
12 Id. at art 9.
13 Id. at art 9(7).
14 The Executive Board of UNESCO (2016) 12.
15 Id.
16 Id.
17 Id.
18 Agreement Between the International Criminal Police Organization – INTERPOL – and the Government of the French Republic Regarding Interpol's Headquarters in France (1982) art 2.

19 Id. at art 3.
20 Id. at arts 7, 8, 10.
21 Id. at arts 6, 11.
22 Id. at art 14.
23 Id. at art 15.
24 Id. at art 24.
25 Basic Principles Governing a Headquarters Agreement to be Negotiated Between the Court and the Host Country (2002) preamble.
26 Id. at art 6.
27 Id. at art 4.
28 Id. at art 31.
29 Id. at arts 8–12.
30 Id. at arts 13–16.
31 Id. at arts 18–25.
32 Id. at arts 26–30.
33 See Articles of Agreement for the International Fund (1944) art IX.
34 Id. at art IX (8).
35 See International Bank for Reconstruction and Development, Articles of Agreement (2012) art VII.
36 See ICSID Convention (1965) sect 5.
37 Id. at art 22 (1965).
38 World Health Organization Constitution (1948) ch XV.
39 International Maritime Organization Convention (1958) pt XVI.
40 Convention on International Civil Aviation (2006) art 60.
41 Convention Establishing the World Intellectual Property Organization (1979) art 12.
42 Convention on the Prohibition of the Development, Production, Stockpiling, and Use of Chemical Weapons and On Their Destruction (1996) arts 48–51.
43 See Headquarters Agreement Between the Organization of American States and the Government of the United States of America (1992).
44 Id. at art II.
45 Id. at arts III, IV.
46 Id. at art IV.
47 Id. at art VI.
48 Id. at arts XIII, XIV, XV.
49 Id. at art VII.
50 See Agreement Establishing the Inter-American Development Bank (1995) art XI.
51 Agreement Establishing the Asian Development Bank (1965) ch VIII.
52 Agreement between Denmark, Estonia, Finland, Iceland, Latvia, Lithuania, Norway and Sweden concerning the Nordic Investment Bank (2005) art 5–14.
53 Id. at arts 10–11.
54 See Headquarters Agreement between the Republic of Sierra Leone and the Special Court for Sierra Leone (2003) art 4.
55 Agreement between the United Nations and the Government of Sierra Leone on the Establishment of a Special Court for Sierra Leone (2002) arts 12, 13; Headquarters Agreement between the Republic of Sierra Leone and the Special Court for Sierra Leone, supra note 54 at arts 14, 15.
56 Agreement between the United Nations and the Government of Sierra Leone on the Establishment of a Special Court for Sierra Leone, supra note 55 at arts 14–16; Headquarters Agreement between the Republic of Sierra Leone and the Special Court for Sierra Leone, supra note 54 at art 19.
57 Agreement between the United Nations and the Government of Sierra Leone on the Establishment of a Special Court for Sierra Leone, supra note 55 at art 16.
58 Id. at art 2 sect 4.
59 Id. at art 7 sect 17.
60 Agreement between the Government of the French Republic and the United Nations Educational, Scientific and Cultural Organization regarding the Headquarters of UNESCO and the Privileges and Immunities of the Organization on French Territory (1994) art 8.
61 Id. at art 8(2).
62 Id. at art 8(3).
63 Basic Principles Governing a Headquarters Agreement to be Negotiated Between the Court and the Host Country, supra note 25 at art 9.
64 Id. at art 13.
65 Id. at arts VII, XIX.
66 Id. at art IX.
67 Id. at arts 5, 10.
68 Id. at art 14.

69 *Id.* at art 3 sect 7.

70 *Id.* at art 3 sects 7, 8.

71 *Id.* at art 3 sect 8.

72 *Id.* at art 5 sect 16.

73 *Id.* at art 3 sect 9.

74 *Id.*

75 *Id.* at art 3 sect 10.

76 See *Applicability of the Obligation to Arbitrate under Section 21 of the United Nations Headquarters Agreement of 26 June 1947, Advisory Opinion,* ICJ Reports 1988, p 12.

77 *See generally id.*

78 *Id.* at 34.

79 Agreement between the Government of the French Republic and the United Nations Educational, Scientific and Cultural Organization regarding the Headquarters of UNESCO and the Privileges and Immunities of the Organization on French Territory, *supra* note 60 at art 7.

80 *Id.* at art 7(2).

81 Basic Principles Governing a Headquarters Agreement to be Negotiated Between the Court and the Host Country, *supra* note 25 at art 6.

82 *Id.* at art 8.

83 *Id.* at art 8(3).

84 *Id.* at art 8(5).

85 *Id.* at arts 43, 44.

86 *Id.* at art 49.

87 *Id.* at art 6.

88 *Id.*

89 *Id.*

90 *Id.*

91 *Id.* at art 25.

92 *Interpretation of the Agreement of 25 March 1951 between the WHO and Egypt, Advisory Opinion,* ICJ 1980, pp 73, 94.

93 *Id.* at p 89.

94 *Id.* at p 94.

95 *Id.* at p 96 (stating that "the paramount consideration both for the Organization and for the host State in every case must be their clear obligation to co-operate in good faith to promote the objectives and purposes of the Organization as expressed in its Constitution").

Chapter 9

Promulgation of international instruments under the auspices of international organizations

International organizations are created through foundational texts that function as treaties in their own right. Beyond this, however, international organizations are vested with the ability to act as negotiating entities or umbrellas for future treaties, Conventions, and less binding forms of international instrument. While the organization itself might not have the ability to sign and ratify an international instrument, its place as a negotiating venue and subsequent enforcement entity for these instruments is essential.

Organizational ability to promulgate international instruments

One of the core functions of most international organizations is to create policy in the areas of specialty or sub-specialty in which it works. The creation of policy is achieved in many different ways, from deciding that an international organization should work in a policy field – such as extending the scope of the World Health Organization's work to include the avian flu when this issue first came onto the scene as a threat to public health[1] – to deciding to create a sub-organ or affiliated entity to work in a particular area – such as the many international organizations founded under the auspices of the United Nations – to entering into partnerships with non-organization entities in order to further the policy goals of the organization – such as the alliance between the United Nations Children's Fund (UNICEF),[2] a UN-affiliated organization which seeks to protect and assist children across the globe, and Save the Children, a private charity.

In addition, international organizations often create policy through the promulgation of specialized treaties and Conventions under their auspices. As has been noted, the exact policy and procedure through which the promulgation of these treaties and Conventions is possible will vary by the terms of the foundational text. However, even when the foundational text is silent on the issue of treaty or Convention promulgation, the prevalent school of thought is that an international organization will still have the ability to do so since this was not explicitly prohibited by the foundational text.[3]

Methods of promulgating international instruments

Foundational texts govern the exact methods through which each international organization may serve as a venue for the creation and implementation of binding and non-binding international instruments. The former includes treaties and Conventions while the latter includes declarations and resolutions of the organization and its organs and sub-organs. As will be discussed in this and subsequent chapters, more binding forms of international law are negotiated in other forums.

Non-binding international instruments, though of lesser legal value, are still valuable to discuss for the entirety of this system. Any international organization has the ability, at least in theory, to issue non-binding instruments that are intended to serve as guidelines or statements of the will of their constituencies. This ability can be used by organs in international organizations which might otherwise not have the capacity to create treaty regimes.

For example, the United Nations General Assembly has quite limited abilities when it comes to promulgating binding international instruments. The typical form of instrument that the UN General Assembly will issue is a declaration or resolution – such as the Declaration on the Rights of Indigenous Peoples – which is essentially a policy statement on the part of the world community, with the exception of those States that vote against the measure or abstain from voting on the measure.[4] As a matter of law, these declarations are not automatically binding, although they can constitute a source of international law and norms for the international community. If a Member State decides to incorporate the terms of a declaration into its domestic law, this is fine; however, it is under no obligation to do so.

In another example, a recommendation in the context of the International Labour Organization (ILO) is very similar to that of a declaration in the UN General Assembly context – it is agreed to by the ILO Conference but constitutes a lesser set of obligations than a Convention and is transmitted to the Member States as a recommendation for legislative action or change rather than as a wide-ranging convention.[5] Thus, although there is a reporting requirement for disclosure of whether the recommendations have been taken, there is no specific ratification issue.[6]

Binding quality of these instruments on Member States

Ratification processes required

What is important to remember is that, although these treaties and Conventions must be approved by the applicable international organization through its established voting requirements, this is not the end of the story. Instead, each Member State must then take the treaty or Convention back to the Member State and submit it to the standard ratification process for any international instrument before that specific Member State can be bound by its terms. Thus, one cannot simply look at the voting record of States within an international organization and assume that they are all bound by a newly promulgated Convention merely because they voted for it within the confines of the international organization. Further, Member States which do not ratify a treaty or Convention at the domestic level are still members of the international organization that promulgated the treaty or Convention; however, they typically will not take part in activities relating to the treaty or Convention, such as Conferences of the Parties.

An example of this is the International Labor Organization functions, which on a unique, two-tier system through which it adopts either Conventions or recommendations.[7] In order for a Convention to be promulgated, it must receive a 2/3 majority vote within the Conference – the equivalent of the UN General Assembly[8] – and is then forwarded on to the individual Member States for ratification in accordance with their constitutional requirements and procedures.[9] In the event that the Convention is appropriately ratified at the domestic level, the Member State is then bound by the terms of the Convention as a matter of law and is subject to periodic reporting requirements to the Secretary General of the ILO.[10] Should the Convention fail to be ratified, the Member State is not bound by its terms and is required only to issue periodic reports to the Secretary General of the ILO that express whether the Member State's domestic stance on the issues addressed by the particular Convention have changed.[11]

The ILO's practice of using Conventions and recommendations as a dual level of attempting to achieve policy change and generate international and domestic laws is mirrored in UNESCO's practices. UNESCO uses the same dichotomy between Conventions and recommendations, and also uses a system of declarations – policy statements that do not require ratification of any sort on the domestic level but rather are intended to be used as statements of beliefs and understandings by the international legal community.[12]

Impacts of non-ratification by a Member State

The same practices occur at the regional level. For example, both the Organization of American States (OAS) and the African Union (AU) have promulgated a number of treaties and Conventions under their auspices; however, not all Member States have ratified these treaties and Conventions at the domestic level.[13] Thus, the organization continues to function although its Member States have different levels of commitment to the instruments created by the organization itself.

Use of protocols and amendments in international organization system

There are two additional ways in which an international organization can act to create new law and legal obligations for willing Member States, or even non-Member States in certain instances.

Protocols

A protocol seeks to add to or amplify an existing portion of a treaty or Convention while leaving the body of the original treaty or Convention intact. This means that, in the event a Member State of the underlying treaty or Convention does not ratify the protocol, it is still legally a Member State of the treaty or Convention. There are many reasons that protocols might be used.

In some instances, such as the Kyoto Protocol to the United Nations Framework Convention on Climate Change (UNFCCC), a protocol is used to update the terms of a treaty or Convention through the addition of new or changing factual (often technological) information. The Kyoto Protocol example is one in which the UNFCCC specifically authorized the use of a protocol, and the Conference of the Parties then promulgated a protocol that contained terms and agreements that were the subject of separate negotiations based on scientific evidence and, of course, political interests.[14] As with a standard international treaty or Convention, the terms of a protocol must be ratified by each Member State through the conventional domestic system prior to the Member State's becoming bound by them even though the Member State is already bound by the underlying treaty that the protocol expands.

In other instances, a term contained in the initial treaty or Convention becomes of such importance that it requires amplification, in which case a protocol will also be used. An excellent example of this comes from the issue of child soldiers. The underlying text of the United Nations Convention on the Rights of the Child makes a brief mention of this issue, particularly in terms of the age at which children can enter the armed forces, but does not otherwise address the issue.[15] However, in the years since the Convention on the Rights of the Child was promulgated, child soldiering has become a grave and pressing matter of international law.

As a result, a new protocol "on the involvement of children in armed conflict" was promulgated in 2000 – as the name suggests, child soldiering is the sole focus of the protocol, which builds on the terms of the Convention of the Rights of Child.[16] This protocol is instructive in many ways, not the least of which is that it illustrates a situation in which even States that have not ratified the underlying treaty or Convention may elect to be bound by the protocol. Here, while the United States was active in the creation of the Convention on the Rights of the Child, it has not ratified the Convention owing to several domestic policy-related concerns. However, the United States identified the issue of child soldiering as being so important that it agreed to ratify the protocol regardless.

Amendments

The second method is through the use of amendments to the actual body of the treaty or Convention itself. For the reasons outlined above, protocols are a popular tool because they do not actually alter the terms of the underlying treaty or Convention. Opening a discussion about amending or changing the main text of a treaty or Convention can be a dangerous and time-consuming decision, as it allows issues with the text to come to light. However, there are times when this might be necessary, provided that the foundational text allows for them.

Some foundational texts are quite open regarding the ability of the Member States to propose and enact amendments.[17] Regardless, since the terms of an amendment will change the international obligations of each Member State, the terms of the amendment must go through the standard domestic ratification process in order to be binding on a Member State. In the event that a Member State does not vote for and/or ratify the amendment, it will still be bound by the former treaty or Convention terms.

Conclusions

The creation of any treaty regime or other instrument of international law is a special undertaking in itself as it involves the generation of consensus between States on a particular topic. International organizations play a unique role in creating treaty and Convention-based law by convening Member States in a setting that allows for negotiations and, where possible, the generation of new law that can be overseen by the organization. This demonstrates the power of international organizations and also their flexibility in the realm of international law.

As a corollary, the ability of international organizations to function as entities that create non-binding instruments demonstrates the limitations of organizations since they are unable to enforce these mechanisms. However, they may in fact be the site of continuous dialogue on the topic of the instrument, and can create sub-organs or other entities to monitor the issues contained in the non-binding instrument. This gives international organizations a unique ability to assist in the crafting of non-binding instruments that tend to be responsive to emerging issues in international law, and create sub-organs that can provide for the future development of laws and regulations on the subject matter.

Finally, the ability of an international organization to craft and assist in the crafting of protocols and amendments is indicative of its longevity and flexibility, because it allows the organization to facilitate the future of instruments that were created under its auspices. Taken together, these abilities demonstrate the special, and indeed unique, place of international organizations in the international community as building bridges and acting as catalysts for development.

Notes

1 See World Health Organization, Avian influenza, http://www.who.int/topics/avian_influenza/en/, last accessed 3 January 2018.

2 See UNICEF, Who we are, http://www.unicef.org/about/who/index_introduction.html, last accessed 3 January 2018.

3 See Jan Klabbers, *An Introduction to International Institutional Law* (Cambridge University Press 2010) 255–258.

4 See UN Charter (1945) ch IV.

5 Id.

6 Id.

7 International Labour Organization Constitution (1944) art 19.

8 Id. at art 3.

9 Id. at art 19.

10 Id.

11 Id.

12 UNESCO, General introduction to the standard-setting instruments of UNESCO, http://portal.unesco.org/en/ev.php-URL_ID=23772&URL_DO=DO_TOPIC&URL_SECTION=201.html#name=3, last accessed 3 January 2018.

13 See Organization of American States, Multilateral Treaties, http://www.oas.org/DIL/treaties_signatories_ratifications_member_States.htm, last accessed 3 January 2018; African Union, OAU/AU Treaties, Conventions, Protocols & Charters, http://www.au.int/en/treaties, last accessed 3 January 2018.

14 See United Nations Framework Convention on Climate Change (1992) art 17; Kyoto Protocol to the United Nations Framework Convention on Climate Change (1998).

15 United Nations Convention on the Rights of the Child (1990) art 38.

16 See Optional Protocol to the Convention on the Rights of the Child on the involvement of children in armed conflict (2000).

17 See, e.g., United Nations Framework Convention on Climate Change, supra note 15 at art 16.

Chapter 10

Dispute settlement in international organizations

Disputes and disagreements are a fact of life whether on the playground, in personal lives, diplomatic relations, or relations between the Member States of international organizations. With this in mind, it is perhaps not surprising that the majority of foundational texts for international organizations contain some provisions for the settlement of disputes between Member States.

As this chapter explains, some of these disputes stem from arguments regarding whether a State is acting in compliance with a specific treaty or agreement that was created under the auspices of the international organization – such as the World Trade Organization – while others stem from general assertions that a State is acting against the purpose of the international organization – such as an assertion that a Member State is acting to undermine peace and security, which are the core purposes for which the United Nations (UN) exists. Regardless of their source, the majority of dispute settlement mechanisms seek to settle the dispute at the internal level first. While some international organizations allow for an appeal to an outside entity – most often the International Court of Justice (ICJ) – in the event that the internal dispute settlement mechanism does not work, others have created a complex appeals system within the organization.

Although different international organizations and forms of dispute settlement mechanisms will be discussed throughout this chapter, the one common thread between them all is that they seek to ensure the survival of the international organization at the same time as seeking to ensure that the Member States of the organization have a voice and a mechanism for intervention.

Immunity of international organizations from disputes brought by individuals

In the context of UN peacekeeping operations, as is discussed further in Chapter 17, a number of allegations of misconduct on the part of deployed peacekeepers have been brought over the past decades. These claims range from sexual abuse of the local population, to fathering illegitimate children and abandoning them, to human rights abuses. Under international law tenets and the terms of Status of Forces Agreements used by the UN, such allegations must generally be handled through the national juridical system of the State of which the alleged wrongdoer is a citizen. When claims have been brought by individuals against the UN for the wrongdoing of its peacekeepers or others acting on its behalf, the typical organizational response stresses that these are allegations against which the organization is immune since they are matters of private claims rather than administrative claims for which the UN has an established system.[1] While there are internal procedures to review such claims on a situational basis, they are typically of limited accessibility to individuals and are conducted away from the court systems of any particular State.[2] In the UN setting *per se*, this approach has been endorsed by the ICJ, and, in a separate opinion by Judge Weeramantry, the basis for this opinion was articulated as concern that issues which might have a particular local importance could come to hinder the needs of the international community as represented through UN activities.[3]

These immunities extend to more standard issues of employment disputes which, as discussed above, will typically fall under the jurisdiction of an internal system created by the international organization.[4]

Disputes between Member States in an international organization

Dispute settlement in the United Nations system

In essence, the UN was itself created as a dispute settlement mechanism that arose out of the horrors and lessons of war. When a dispute arises, the UN Charter stipulates that it will be solved peacefully, first through attempts at negotiation or other forms of non-military dispute resolution and then through referral to the UN General Assembly or the UN Security Council if necessary.[5] However, the UN Security Council serves a more central role in the hearing and resolution of disputes, and has the ability to investigate any "dispute or situation" that could threaten international peace and security.[6]

While typically membership in an international organization is essential for a State to avail itself of the organization's dispute settlement mechanism, this is not necessarily the case in the context of the UN. Under the terms of the UN Charter, a non-Member State may still bring a matter to the UN General Assembly or the UN Security Council if the non-Member State agrees to be bound by the terms of the UN Charter for the issue at hand.[7]

Ultimately, either the UN General Assembly or the UN Security Council may suggest methods of dispute resolution to the parties involved. These organs may also refer the case to the ICJ or, in extreme situations, authorize the use of force against a State in order to serve the greater goal of preserving international peace and security.[8] Additionally, it should be noted that any UN-affiliated entity, such as UNESCO or the World Health Organization (WHO), may ask the UN General Assembly to refer a dispute to the ICJ.[9]

The ICJ, as has already been noted, is another UN body that is specifically enumerated in the Charter. The ICJ may hear disputes between States only,[10] although it may receive information regarding the practices of an international organization[11] and it is possible for the foundational text of an international organization to provide that intractable disputes between the organization's Member States may be referred to ICJ settlement.[12] In addition to issuing standard judicial opinions, the ICJ has the ability to issue advisory opinions[13] and has indeed done so in cases that involve disputes between Member States of international organizations.[14]

Dispute settlement in regional organizations

Unlike the UN dispute settlement mechanisms, which typically can be resolved at the ICJ level, regional organizations tend not to be as reliant on an outside judicial entity as the ultimate arbiter of a dispute, although there are instances where it can be used as a court of last resort. Rather, regardless of the region discussed, the focus tends to be on providing multiple layers of alternate dispute resolution-based bodies that can be used to provide insights and incentives for the parties to a dispute. The exception to this is the European Union (EU), but even in that system there is a preference for organization-based resolution of member disputes rather than taking such matters to the ICJ.

Dispute settlement in financial and banking organizations

The majority of key international financial organizations have provisions regarding dispute settlement mechanisms within their foundational texts. While there is some reliance on outside assistance in carrying out the terms of these provisions, as a trend international financial organizations also tend to be insular in resolving these disputes. Perhaps this is understandable, given the complex and unique policy and legal considerations that are involved in the relationships between Member States of international financial organizations and the highly technical subject matter involved.

Dispute settlement in the World Trade Organization

Disputes can, and often do, occur between Member States regarding the proper application of one or more of the WTO treaties and agreements in respect to trade and services activities. Unlike in a traditional domestic contract case between two parties, or even in a free trade agreement, the potential for upheaval in the meaning of these treaties through multiple interpretations was worrisome to the drafters of the WTO Agreement. At the same time, it was necessary to find some method through which to allow the resolution of disputes since they have the potential to undermine the international trading system and the good faith upon which it relies.[15] This method is the Dispute Settlement Body (DSB), which primarily encompasses the Dispute Settlement Mechanism and its associated appellate entity.[16] The DSB operates under the auspices of the General Council and receives assistance from the WTO Secretariat as necessary.[17]

The DSB entails many steps and processes through which disputes might be settled using everything from good offices and negotiations to adversarial system procedures and appellate mechanisms. When a Member State's representative files an initial request for consultations with the DSB, this triggers the beginning of the formal DSB process.[18] Often, the initiation of proceedings at the WTO is enough to bring the States involved together and allow for a diplomatic solution to the issue. In these instances, the DSB is empowered to act in a dispute resolution-focused capacity that involves assisting through the provision of good offices, encouragement of dialogue and conciliation, and the provision of mediation.[19] It is within the discretion of the States Parties to enter into a mutually agreed solution to the dispute at any point during the proceedings.[20] States are not required to enter into this consultative phase in the sense that, if there is a failure on the part of a State to respond to a request for consultation within a certain period of time the other State Party can go directly to the complaint procedure.[21] The DSB became operationalized in 1995, and since that time over 500 complaints have been launched before it.

The next step in the DSB process is the creation of a formal panel to hear the complaint.[22] The creation of a panel must be done through a formalized request from a party to the dispute that also provides the legal grounds for the complaint.[23] These panels consist of recognized experts in fields related to law, economics, trade, and related topics and who are selected as individuals rather than national representatives.[24] Generally, each panel consists of three panelists, although the parties together have the ability to request that the panel instead consist of five panelists.[25] The Director General of the WTO has the responsibility of recommending panelists to the parties, who have the right to confirm or reject them.[26]

The panels receive information from the parties to the dispute, as well as from interested third-party States,[27] and, using this is as the basis for a finding, issue an interim report on the facts and allegations involved.[28] Each party has the opportunity to review and provide comments on the interim report when appropriate.[29] Following this, the panel issues a final report on the complaint, which is reviewed by the DSB prior to final adoption.[30] Should they be pursued, appeals from the panel report are referred to a designated seven-person panel for further findings.[31] These findings too require adoption by the DSB and are generally to be considered as final and binding on all parties.[32] In the event the reports are not complied with, a number of opportunities exist for additional complaints and, ultimately, there are retaliatory measures which the DSB and the WTO General Council can authorize.[33]

It should be noted that attempts to reform the WTO dispute settlement system have been ongoing since the commencement of the Doha negotiation rounds in 2001, however have yet to come to meaningful fruition.[34]

Conclusions

One of the fundamental reasons for the use of international organizations over time has been that they provide a method of containing disputes and attempting to settle them in a quasi-judicial setting rather than through armed conflicts or other acts of aggression between States.

As this chapter has demonstrated, dispute settlement mechanisms exist at all levels of organizations and their governance, and are intended to provide outlets for disagreements between Member States. Rather than functioning through *ad hoc* practices or rules, dispute settlements within the international organizations context have become regulated – and, depending on the context, stand-alone – processes. It is possible to see the goals and concerns of the organization reflected in the terms and processes of international organizations, for example attempts to ensure compliance within the market in the WTO's DSB and attempts to ensure that regional disputes are decided within the principles of the region as they are reflected in the appropriate organization.

Regardless the venue and rules used, dispute settlement mechanisms in international organizations have grown since their inception and now occupy a vital role in the ways that organizations contribute to the international community.

Notes

1 Alexandra R. Harrington, *Prostituting Peace: The Impact of Sending State's Legal Regimes on UN Peacekeeper Behavior and Suggestions to Protect the Populations Peacekeepers Guard*, 17 Florida State U. College of Law J. Trans. L. & Pol'y 217 (2008); Alexandra R. Harrington, *A Tale of Three Nations?: The role of United Nations peacekeepers and missions on the concept of nation-State, nationalism, and ownership of the State in Lebanon, the Democratic Republic of the Congo, and Kosovo*, 21 Conn. J. Int'l L. 213 (2006); Alexandra R. Harrington, *Victims of Peace: Current Abuse Allegations against UN Peacekeepers and the Role of Law in Preventing Them in the Future*, 12 ILSA J. Int'l & Comp. L. (2005); Patrick J. Lewis, *Who Pays for the United Nations' Torts?: Immunity, Attribution and "Appropriate Modes of Settlement*," 39 North Carolina Journal of International Law & Commercial Regulation 259 (2014).

2 Lewis, *supra* note 1 at 272–274.

3 *See Difference Relating to Immunity from Legal Process of Special Rapporteur of Commission on Human Rights*, Advisory Opinion, ICJ Reports 1999, p 62 (separate opinion of Judge Weeramantry).

4 John R. Crook, *Second Circuit Finds Convention on Privileges and Immunities of the United Nations Self-Executing, Upholds Immunity of United Nations and of Former UN Officials*, 104 American Journal of International Law 281 (2010).

5 UN Charter (1945) art 33.

6 *Id.* at art 34.

7 *Id.* at art 35.

8 *Id.* at ch VII.

9 *Id.* at art 96.

10 Statute of the Court of International Justice (1946) art 34.

11 *Id.* at art 34.

12 *Id.*

13 *Id.* at ch IV.

14 *See, e.g., Applicability of Article VI, Section 22, of the Convention on the Privileges and Immunities of the United Nations*, Advisory Opinion, ICJ Reports 1989, p 177.

15 *See* Understanding on Rules and Procedures Governing the Settlement of Disputes (1995) art 3(2) ("The dispute settlement system of the WTO is a central element in providing security and predictability to the multilateral trading system. The Members recognize that it serves to preserve the rights and obligations of Members under the covered agreements, and to clarify the existing provisions of those agreements in accordance with customary rules of interpretation of public international law. Recommendations and rulings of the DSB cannot add to or diminish the rights and obligations provided in the covered agreements.").

16 *Id.* at art 2(1) ("The Dispute Settlement Body is hereby established to administer these rules and procedures and, except as otherwise provided in a covered agreement, the consultation and dispute settlement provisions of the covered agreements. Accordingly, the DSB shall have the authority to establish panels, adopt panel and Appellate Body reports, maintain surveillance of implementation of rulings and recommendations, and authorize suspension of concessions and other obligations under the covered agreements.").

17 *Id.* at art 27.

18 *Id.* at art 4(3).

19 *Id.* at art 5.

20 *Id.* at art 3(6).

21 *Id.* at art 4(3).

22 *Id.* at art 6(1). It should be noted that the possibility of continuing to use conciliation, good offices and mediation is available to the parties even as the formal panel process takes place. *See id.* at art 5(5).

23 *Id.* at art 6(2). Included in this is a formal requirement that the panel act "to examine, in the light of the relevant provisions in (name of the covered agreement(s) cited by the parties to the dispute), the matter referred to the DSB by (name of party) in document . . . and to make such findings as will assist the DSB in making the recommendations or in giving the rulings provided for in that/those agreement(s)." *Id.*

24 *Id.* at art 8.

25 Id. at art 8(5).

26 Id. at art 8(6).

27 In the appropriate circumstances, third-party States are permitted to file statements and other information with the panel through the DSB. *See id.* at art 10. Additionally, in instances where more than one State brings the same complaint against the same Member State, it is possible for the DSB to combine the complaints into one larger proceeding. *See id.* at art 9.

28 *See generally id.* The exact timeframe for the issuance of a report is dependent on many factors, key among them the willingness and ability of the State parties to produce information and filings within the given calendar agreed upon by the parties and the panel. Id. at art 12.

29 Id. at art 15.

30 Id. at arts 15, 16.

31 Id. at art 17.

32 Id. at art 17.

33 Id. at art 22.

34 *See* WTO, Negotiations to improve dispute settlement procedures https://www.wto.org/english/tratop_e/dispu_e/dispu_negs_e.htm, last accessed 4 January 2018.

Chapter 11

Termination of an international organization

Chapter contents

According to the old saying, all good things must come to an end. The ambiguity of this statement is as applicable to the study of international organizations as it is to life in general, especially as the answers are notably lacking in the foundational texts of many international organizations. With this in mind, Chapter 11 examines the available information and practice regarding the end of an international organization as well as Member State withdrawal from an international organization. It is important to understand that such events very rarely happen, and that when international organizations decide to end their operations they will usually carry over to a successor international organization rather than disappear completely.

Why might termination occur?

Situations might occur, especially in sectors such as banking and finance, that cause the continued functioning of an international organization to fall into question. For example, drastic changes to the international financial markets which render the lending operations of an entity such as the International Monetary Fund (IMF) impractical could undermine the ability of the organization to continue for the near future at the very least. In such situations, and depending on the terms of the foundational text, the international organization may have the opportunity to temporarily suspend its operations in order to determine the appropriate course of action in the future.[1] These situations will require votes from within the organization and must be tightly monitored in order to ensure that a decision is ultimately made regarding its future activities.[2]

Should situations change and, for example, the markets become more stable, it would be possible for the suspension to be lifted and the IMF to recommence its operations.[3] Alternatively, it would be possible for the IMF to decide that it would be unable to carry out its functions in the future and that termination would therefore be necessary.[4]

Termination of an international organization is a drastic measure, and it has been demonstrated that organizations can – and do – make changes to their foundational texts in order to address situations that could otherwise necessitate their termination. These issues can take any form, from legal to political to economic to societal and beyond, provided they have some impact on the organization, its functions and its members.

As has been discussed, a key example of this comes from the context of the North Atlantic Treaty Organization (NATO), when the initial threat for which it had been created, the Cold War, ended and the organization was faced with the question how to proceed. In this context, the NATO members decided to allow for an expanded membership and shift in the organization's permitted activities in order to maintain relevance and effectiveness.[5] On the other hand, the Organization of African Unity (OAU) saw the political changes during the 1990s as a harbinger of significant change to its mandate and decided to completely terminate as an entity.[6] Even then, the OAU leadership decided to reconstitute the remaining parts of the organization in the new African Union (AU), which would move on, and has indeed moved on, from where the OAU ended.[7]

The exact legal parameters of termination will be dependent upon an organization's foundational text. As a general matter, termination will require a higher majority vote (i.e. 2/3 or unanimous voting) than standard issues in order to be recognized as valid under the terms of the foundational text and thus international law.[8] Once a termination is triggered, the organization must then determine its assets and liabilities, and ensure that it has paid outstanding liabilities and distribute the remaining organizational assets to the Member States or other appropriate entities.[9]

Regardless the form of termination procedure used, and the ways in which assets and liabilities are distributed, the termination of an international organization does not result in the termination or voiding of international instruments that were negotiated or implemented through the organization, since these exist as separate entities in international law. In these instances, States Parties to the international instrument would still be bound by the terms of the instrument and would have the ability to determine how to proceed for implementation and governance.

Effects of Member State withdrawals

In many international organizations, the issue of withdrawal is unclear because there is no provision within the foundational text for withdrawing as a member. Indeed, in some international organizations, such as the United Nations (UN), there seems to be an assumption that this would not occur once a State is recognized and granted membership because of the gravity of the responsibilities involved in joining the organization.[10] Still, it is possible for a Member State to wish to withdraw, in which case the procedure and requirements would be unclear. For example, would the State, as a sovereign entity, simply be able to make this announcement? Or would some combination of vote-based approval – similar to that used for the admission of Member States – be required on the part of the UN membership as a whole? The answers to these questions are unsettled.[11]

What seems fairly obvious, however, is that in international organizations where membership can be suspended or terminated if the Member State is suspended/terminated from the UN, withdrawal from the UN would trigger withdrawal from the UN-affiliated organization.[12] It is perhaps not surprising that some of the most detailed provisions regarding Member State withdrawal come from this type of organization. When looking at the details of these foundational text provisions, it is very important to note the overall impact of the financial stake that Member States have in these organizations has on the terms of withdrawal – as well as the extent to which Member States are in the debt of these organizations.

In another example, under the terms of the IMF's Articles of Agreement there are two forms of withdrawal – voluntary and compulsory. Voluntary withdrawal is done at the election of the Member State, while compulsory withdrawal is done through the vote of the organization when a Member State fails to comply with its requirements. In either instance, there are still requirements for the withdrawing State. It should also be noted that withdrawal from the IMF for any reason will trigger the cessation of a State's membership in the International Bank for Reconstruction and Development, thus hindering its work within the World Bank Group system.[13]

In addition to international financial organizations, some regional organizations also provide for withdrawal within their foundational texts.

Conclusions

The general lessons from international law and the law of international organizations demonstrates, as illustrated through a number of foundational texts, center on the inherent need for flexibility in organizations. This is demonstrated by the many stages of suspension of organization activity, termination of organization activity and, at its most severe, withdrawal of a Member State. The systems available for each of these actions provide for wide latitude and circumstance-based decision-making, even within the same organization, thus allowing for the reality of these decisions to be accepted as a matter of law. Without this, the possibility for organizational flexibility would not exist and the rigidity in the organizational system would thus arguably result in a greater number of terminated organizations and withdrawn members.

At the same time, the lessons from this chapter demonstrate that there is, necessarily, a limit to the flexibility of international organizations in legal and political constructs. With this in mind, there is necessary guidance on the termination of an organization in order to provide for a stable system of dismantlement rather than a chaotic cessation of activities and attempt at determining future activities.

The ability of a Member State to withdraw from an international organization demonstrates the powers of organizations themselves. This might at first seem counter-intuitive. However, upon reflection, it is clear that there is a level of control exercised over a Member State on the part of any international organization which provides laws and rules for a State's withdrawal. If this were not the case, it would be possible for a State to withdraw easily, cutting into the stability and power of the organization and undermining the ways in which international organizations function.

Additionally, it must be noted that the lessons of this chapter regarding suspension of operations, termination of operations and withdrawal from an international organization legitimize the functions of organizations as acting only when needed by the international community and ceasing to function when no longer necessary. Taken together, what could be viewed as the more negative aspects of the law of international organizations can be viewed as positive statements regarding their flexibility.

Notes

1 *See* IMF Articles of Agreement (1946) art XXVII.
2 *See id.*
3 *See id.*
4 *See id.*
5 *See infra* ch 17.
6 *See infra* ch 14.
7 *See infra* ch 14.
8 *See* IBRD Articles of Agreement (1946); Articles of Agreement of the International Financial Corporation (2012) art V; MIGA Articles of Agreement (2012) arts 54–55; African Development Bank Charter (2011) art 44.
9 *See* IBRD Articles of Agreement, *supra* note 8; Articles of Agreement of the International Financial Corporation, *supra* note 8 at art V; MIGA Articles of Agreement, *supra* note 8 at arts 54–55; African Development Bank Charter, *supra* note 8 at art 44.
10 *See generally* UN Charter (1945).
11 *See id.*
12 *See, e.g.,* UNESCO Constitution (1946).
13 IBRD Articles of Agreement, *supra* note 8 at art VI.

Chapter 12

The United Nations system

Chapter contents

There is perhaps no more logical place to begin discussions of specific international organizations and topic areas than the United Nations (UN) system. As was noted in Chapter 2, the UN itself serves as the framework for a number of international organizations' regimes and has provided structure that is easily adaptable to a number of organizational and legal situations. Even membership, the most quintessential of all elements for organizations, tends to be modeled on the UN's system of full membership of the General Assembly and more limited membership in the Security Council. Thus, the discussion of the UN system serves as the opening chapter to Section 2 of the book. Governance is the starting point due to the vital role it plays in the UN system and the systems which have adopted it.

Governance system of the United Nations

UN Security Council

Under the UN Charter, the UN Security Council (UNSC) is given broad latitude to establish committees, subcommittees, rapporteurships and similar entities as it deems necessary.[1] During the course of its history and through the present day, the UNSC has made use of this authorization to create such entities in order to address both long- and short-term issues facing the international community.[2] Indeed, one of the hallmarks of the importance of this capacity is the ability of the UNSC to respond to rapidly emerging global concerns, such as terrorism or political unrest, through the committee system.[3]

These committees have also been created for long-term durability in order to address issues that are insidious and in many ways perpetual problems, such as corruption throughout various forms of national governments, international organizations and indeed the UN itself.[4] In accord with the evolving practice of sanction use and forms discussed previously, the UNSC has established a number of committees that oversee the implementation of sanction regimes for specific State entities or groups of individuals.[5]

Overall, there has been an attempt to refocus much of the work of the UNSC and its committees to promote transparency in their activities and decision-making processes.[6] In addition to requiring an attitudinal shift for the organization, the introduction of increased transparency has required procedural changes in order to accommodate these practices.[7] Further, throughout the years the UNSC has adopted a more lenient stance toward the involvement of non-Member States in decision-making and resolution votes in at least an informal, consultative capacity.[8] This can be seen as recognizing the potential insights and perspectives of States outside of the 15 UNSC Member States and those directly interested in the matter.

As previously established, one of the key aspects of the UNSC's functions is the ability to authorize and oversee the use of force and also the deployment of peacekeeping operations. More will be said about peacekeeping entities in Chapter 17; however, from the organizational perspective it is important to note here that in 2000 the UNSC formalized a consultative mechanism with States that contribute troops to peacekeeping operations.[9] This mechanism allows for the use of public and private meetings between UNSC members and troop-contributing States in which information is exchanged and consultation on the state of peacekeeping operations – and peacekeeping generally – can occur.[10] These efforts at coordination, consultation and information-sharing have expanded to include the Secretariat.[11] The UNSC committee structure includes entities intended to exist for long durations and those with finite durations or benchmarks.[12]

UN General Assembly

The UN Charter lays out the forms of questions that require a 2/3 majority vote of the UN General Assembly (UNGA) for approval and those requiring a simple majority vote.[13] When voting, the UNGA rules allow for either a show of hands vote or an electronic vote, and generally these votes are unrecorded.[14] However, a Member State does have the ability to request that the vote on any particular issue be recorded.[15] While not required to do so, it is possible for a representative of a Member State to provide a statement or explanation of the Member State's vote during the roll call.[16]

In the discussion of powers granted to the UNGA under the UN Charter it was noted that the UNGA has budgetary powers for the UN *per se*. Consequently, the UNGA is required to enact financial regulations for the entirety of the UN organization.[17] Further, the UNGA has the ability to suggest policy and craft discussions and declarations on a number of policy issues and has repeatedly used this opportunity to advance global environmental and social issues as well as issues of international peace and security.[18]

As with the UNSC, the UNGA has the Charter-based ability to create new committees and sub-committees when they are deemed to be required.[19] These entities are governed by the rules of the UNGA, including the promotion of transparency through holding public meetings unless it is deemed necessary to do otherwise.[20] As of the time of writing, the six-main committees in the UNGA system are: 1) disarmament and international security committee; 2) special political and decolonization committee; 3) economic and financial committee; 4) social, humanitarian and cultural committee; 5) administration and budgetary committee; and 6) legal committee.[21] In addition to their delegated functions, committees themselves are empowered to create sub-committees as appropriate.[22] As in the UNSC, the UNGA has created additional committees that address the emerging needs of the international community as well as the issues that represent its fundamental concerns.[23]

In recent years, the UNGA has begun to craft a system of coordination and cooperation between its officers and those from the UNSC and the Economic and Social Council (ECOSOC).[24] The fundamental goal of this cooperation scheme is to ensure complementarity between the various organs of the UN and their priorities.[25] This was an outgrowth of timely need and also of historical issues in communications between the UNSC and ECOSOC in particular, which was highlighted as causing problems in the implementation of attempts at peace building generally.[26] From 2000 onward, this coordination has been particularly important in the fields of peace-building in Africa, where the various UN organs have determined that it is necessary for the multiple entities to work together to achieve the best outcome.[27]

UN Secretariat

As part of its core functions, the Secretariat – and particularly the Secretary General – is heavily involved in the organization and structure of the UNGA's meetings.[28] This includes not only organizational functions and providing information, but also, critically, serving as an informational bridge between the UNSC and the UNGA regarding efforts to promote and protect international peace and security.[29]

The UNGA has the responsibility of creating the regulations that govern the UN Secretariat.[30] This includes staffing regulations and the regulations relating to all offices and entities that are encompassed within the general heading of the Secretariat. The Secretary General retains the responsibility to implement these regulations and to otherwise govern the Secretariat in accordance with the requirements of the UNGA and, where applicable, the UNSC.

UN Trusteeship Council

The Trusteeship Council was created to oversee the implementation of the Trust system that was intended to assist in the transition of designated trust territories to independent States.[31] When functional, it consisted of Member States designated by the UNGA.[32]

Through an official resolution in the UNSC, the trust agreement for Palau, the last remaining trust territory under UN supervision, was terminated and the work of the UN Trusteeship Council came to an end as such.[33] To reflect this, the UN Trusteeship Council passed amendments to its established procedure that suspended the practice of regular Council meetings.[34]

The official work of the Trusteeship Council was concluded in 1993 with the independence of Palau.[35] However, it continues to exist as an entity within the UN system and has the ability to resume its operations should the appropriate requirements be met.[36] Through its statements, the UNGA has indicated that it would prefer for organizational attention to decolonization to focus on entities that are currently classified as non-self-governing.[37] Some have posited that the Trusteeship Council could be resumed as a fully operational entity to handle certain of the claims regarding purported independence groups.[38] This is largely an academic debate at this point and it remains to be seen whether this would, in practice, be legal under the terms of the UN Charter.

United Nations Economic and Social Council

Background

The United Nations Economic and Social Council (ECOSOC) was established shortly after the UN Charter became effective and has progressed along a path in which it concerns itself with the economic, social and, increasingly, environmental, issues that face the world and also individual communities.[39] According to the UN Charter, ECOSOC is specifically tasked with: 1) undertaking reports and/or studies on subjects within its jurisdiction; 2) offering recommendations to the UNGA or UN specialized agencies on subjects within its jurisdiction; 3) offering draft Conventions on subjects within its jurisdiction to the UNGA; and 4) convening international conferences on topics within its jurisdiction.[40]

Membership and voting

Not all UN Member States sit on ECOSOC, as there are only 54 Member States sitting on ECOSOC at any one time.[41] Rather, the members of ECOSOC are elected to three-year, rotating terms by the UNGA.[42] There are, however, limits to the General Assembly's ability to elect ECOSOC members, as there is a requirement that the members of ECOSOC represent all geographical areas and UN constituencies.[43] Each of the 54 members has an equal vote and ECOSOC uses majority voting to pass resolutions and other measures.[44]

Structure

The ECOSOC governing structure is similar to the main UN structure, using both a meeting of the States and an administrative body – in this case the Bureau – for the implementation of daily policy and practices.[45] Additionally, there is a President of ECOSOC, which between Member States on a yearly basis.[46]

Functions

When ECOSOC meets, it meets with two different focuses. The first is to allow those from the non-UN world – academics, researchers and representatives from non-governmental organizations (NGOs), for example – to present their work and findings.[47] This also provides the representatives at ECOSOC with the ability to question those who are involved in handling important issues of the time, thus giving the representatives a broader understanding of the issues at hand.[48] This is a convenient way for the group of representatives to hear from experts and gain information that might otherwise be difficult to come by or more highly politicized in settings such as the UN General Assembly. The second focus is when the representatives themselves meet during a once-yearly session.[49] It is at this session that ECOSOC establishes its own policy stances and practices, and also issues resolutions. These resolutions do not have the same binding force as treaties or Conventions but do allow ECO-SOC to give a voice to important issues that are within its field of oversight.[50]

Prior to 2015, much of the focus of the ECOSOC members' meeting sessions and preparatory work focused on ways to implement the Millennium Development Goals (MDGs) across multiple segments of policy areas, such as environment and education.[51] Since the MDGs were phased out in 2015 in favor of the Sustainable Development Goals (SDGs), ECOSOC has taken a leading role in their implementation as well.[52]

ECOSOC also uses an extensive series of commissions that focus both on particular policy areas, such as the Commission on the Status of Women and Commission on Crime Prevention and Criminal Justice,[53] and on regional areas and their implementation of ECOSOC policies.[54]

ECOSOC uses experts in multiple ways and divides up such experts into those serving within their governmental capacity and those serving in their individual capacity.[55] The bodies using governmental experts include those responsible for transportation of hazardous goods and their regulations, standards of accounting and reporting, and geographical names.[56] The bodies consisting of experts serving in their individual capacity include those responsible for development policy, public administration, international cooperation on tax issues, and the Permanent Forum on Indigenous Peoples.[57] What emerges is a pattern of using governmental experts for highly technical matters and individual experts for more substantive legal and political issues. Recall that both forms of experts will receive legal protections but they will be somewhat different because of the contrast between individual and governmental representative status.

Finally, a word about the participation of NGOs in ECOSOC. In order to participate in ECOSOC meetings – for example, by providing statements or policy papers to the Members – and also to be qualified for contracts that come from ECOSOC – for example, contracts to research certain issues – an NGO must apply for consultative status.[58] This process involves a thorough evaluation of the applicant NGO, its members, its purposes, its prior work, its funders, whether it receives an excessive amount of money from one government or source, and whether its core functions are in line with those of ECOSOC. Typically, this process takes at least a year.

United Nations Education, Scientific and Cultural Organization (UNESCO)

Background

The United Nations Education, Scientific and Cultural Organization (UNESCO) was one of the earlier created UN-affiliated entities, with its constitution going into effect in 1946.[59] UNESCO was created in the post-World War II environment based on the idea that it was necessary to increase understanding between different cultures and to educate international society overall in order to avoid future conflict.[60] As stated in the preamble to its constitution, the organization was founded "for the purpose of advancing, through the educational and scientific and cultural relations of the peoples of the world, the objectives of international peace and of the common welfare of mankind."[61] Included in the stated purposes and functions of UNESCO are the promotion of the rule of law, the emphasis of human rights concerns and fundamental freedoms, the importance of non-discrimination in all areas of life, and the use of education to promote all these goals.[62]

Membership and voting

UN members are eligible for full membership in UNESCO, as are non-members if they are approved by the appropriate UNESCO bodies.[63] Associate membership status was available to trust territories – prior to their achieving independence – and also to territorial entities that are not fully independent, such as Aruba or the British Virgin Islands.[64] Associate members have the ability to participate in organizational activities but are not eligible to vote in any capacity.[65]

In the event a UN Member State is expelled, it will be expelled as a UNESCO member as well.[66] When a UN Member State is suspended by the UN for any reason, the UN may then request that the Member State be suspended as a UNESCO Member State.[67] A UNESCO Member State may withdraw from the organization at any time; however, the withdrawal will not be effective until 31 December "of the year following that during which the notice was given."[68]

Structure

UNESCO uses a similar power division structure to the UN generally, but with slightly different terminology. The equivalent of the UN General Assembly is the General Conference, the equivalent of the UN Security Council is the Executive Board, and both organizations use a designated Secretariat.[69] The General Conference is comprised of a representative from each of the UNESCO Member States.[70] As in the UNGA, each UNESCO Member State has one vote within the General Conference context.[71] At 58 members, the Executive Board is much larger than the UN Security Council and does not feature any category of membership that carries an absolute veto power.[72]

The General Conference has several pre-determined committees assigned to it, and has the power to create additional commissions or organs within the UNESCO structure as deemed appropriate.[73] The pre-determined committees are the 1) Credential Committee; 2) Nominations Committee; 3) Legal Committee; 4) Headquarters Committee; and 5) Bureau.[74] It also has the power to approve the organization's budget.[75]

The UNESCO Secretariat is governed by a Director General and functions in much the same manner as the UN Secretariat in terms of jurisdiction and bureaucracy.[76] As in the UN, the Director General is jointly approved through a process involving both the General Conference and Executive Board.[77] At meetings of the main UNESCO organs or other organs created under the auspices of the organization, representatives from the UN itself or from other recognized international organizations may be granted permission to attend and participate.[78]

The Executive Board – the highest-level organ in the UNESCO system – is comprised of 58 Member States serving renewable three-year terms.[79] In order to ensure some level of parity of access and representation, for the purposes of elections the entirety of UNESCO's membership is divided into five areas that reflect geography and other factors, such as development status.[80] Once this is completed, the representatives are elected from within these areas based on the number of seats allotted to each sector.[81] The Executive Board's Chairman is elected from this group and is assisted in his/her functions by the UNESCO Bureau.[82] While there are several committees provided for in the Constitution and the Rules, additional committees and commissions may be created on the understanding that they are renewable with each session of the Executive Board.[83]

The Executive Board is required to function with several designated commissions and committees, although it has the jurisdiction to create additional commissions and committees as deemed appropriate.[84] Designated commissions and committees for the Executive Board are the 1) Programme and External Relations Commission; 2) Finance and Administrative Commission; 3) Special Committee; 4) Committee on Conventions and Recommendations; and 5) Committee on Non-Governmental Partners.[85] While membership of the designated committees is open for election, all members of the Executive Board automatically become members of the designated commissions.[86]

In addition to participation in the organization through voting, debates and similar activities during UNESCO organ meetings, Member States have several national requirements.[87] One is to create, as appropriate in the national system, a designated National Cooperating Body/Commission that is meant to act as a conduit of information and suggestions between national governments, national representatives, and UNESCO.[88] Another essential requirement for each Member State is to submit to UNESCO for review annual reports in national activities, such as enactment and enforcement of relevant laws and regulations and support for conferences associated with UNESCO obligations.[89]

Functions

To review, there are three categories of legal instrument issued by UNESCO. Conventions are binding upon the Member States that ratify them; however, a UNESCO Member State will continue as a Member State in the event that it decides not to ratify a Convention.[90] Examples of relatively recent Conventions promulgated by UNESCO include: the International Convention against Doping in Sport; the Convention on the Protection and Promotion of the Diversity of Cultural Expressions; the Convention for the Safeguarding of the Intangible Cultural Heritage; and the Convention on Technical and Vocational Education.[91]

Recommendations are policy suggestions that are enacted by the General Conference and sent to all UNESCO Member States.[92] The Member States are not required to ratify them or even to agree with them but the recommendations do provide guidance, often in areas that are in need of it.[93] Examples of relatively recent recommendation include: Recommendation Concerning the Protection and Promotion of Museums and Collections; Recommendation on Historic Urban Landscape; Recommendation concerning the Status of Higher-Education Teaching Personnel; and Recommendation on the Safeguarding of Traditional Culture and Folklore.[94]

Finally, declarations are statements of belief by the General Conference but do not come with the binding or even strong persuasive authority that Conventions or recommendations carry.[95] Examples of relatively recent declarations include: the Universal Declaration on Bioethics and Human Rights; the UNESCO Declaration concerning the Intentional Destruction of Cultural Heritage; and the Charter on the Preservation of Digital Heritage.[96]

Other than promulgating Conventions, recommendations and declarations, what does UNESCO do? In terms of the education sector, UNESCO works on several levels. At the most fundamental, UNESCO works with local and national governments and international entities to promote childhood and adult literacy.[97] This is the key to all of UNESCO's education-based initiatives, since it is impossible to focus on ensuring educational access for women and girls and those in underserved areas, as well as health education – particularly information on HIV/AIDS – and training of teachers without basic literacy.[98] In order to promote access to jobs across all sectors of society, UNESCO actively promotes increasing access to and the quality of vocational training in communities across the globe.[99]

UNESCO has become active in the natural sciences and environmental policy sector, including the promotion of science and technology – which links very well with the education sector – as well as the promotion of environmental knowledge, biodiversity, bioethics, the preservation of oceans and rivers, and climate change issues.[100] UNESCO conducts and supports research in these fields, as well as linking them to other related fields such as indigenous knowledge and the protection of indigenous communities.[101]

In addition, UNESCO convenes and sponsors conferences on these issues, assisting those who are involved with them in sharing their work and information.[102] UNESCO's work in the fields of environment and sustainable development has been pronounced over the course of its history, especially since the promulgation and attempts at implementation of the MDGs and, subsequently, the SDGs.[103] Under the social and human sciences sector, UNESCO works with issues relating to sports, especially doping in sports, as well as indigenous community protection and knowledge support and training in issues related to bioethics.[104]

Perhaps one of the areas in which UNESCO is best known is in its work with culture, and particularly protecting and preserving tangible and intangible culture and heritage.[105] This policy area is particularly important due to issues such as the illegal taking of cultural property in conflicts, the purposeful destruction of cultural heritage sites as part of internal and international conflicts, and also the idea of preserving intangible knowledge – legends, songs, ceremonies and similar pieces of culture that are not concrete – in the face of modernization, globalization and also communities separating due to migration.[106] UNESCO further works with issues such as how to protect cultural heritage that is now located underwater – or perhaps might be in the future given projections for rising sea levels – and the recovery of illegally taken artworks and pieces of cultural heritage.[107]

In addition, UNESCO works in the area of communications and information in order to promote access to communications and technology within poor and indigenous communities.[108] It also has programs that seek to allow those with disabilities to access technology and to ensure that there are records of historical and present-day acts of atrocities so that they will not be forgotten.

Recent iterations of UNESCO policies and budgets establish the totality of the areas of work and interest for the organization. These include a fundamental assessment of the ways in which UNESCO is and is not working effectively in its policy goals and throughout various regions and States, increasing UNESCO's standing as an individual and collaborative entity within the UN system, focusing heavily on youth and education programing, and promoting interdisciplinarity.[109] However, UNESCO has noted that it faces increased issues in implementing these policies because various members of the organization have not paid their assessed contributions in recent years.[110]

International Court of Justice

Background

The International Court of Justice (ICJ) was originally created in 1945 through the UN Charter.[111] The ICJ is the successor entity to the Permanent Court of International Justice (PCIJ), which was established by the League of Nations at the end of World War I and which is regarded as one of the few League of Nations bodies to have been successful.[112] In fact, much of the PCIJ's jurisprudence is still respected and can be cited today, although, like the jurisprudence of the ICJ, it is not binding on any State other than a party to the particular dispute.

Membership and voting

It has already been established that the ICJ has jurisdiction over States and that all members of the UN are members of the ICJ unless they opt out of ICJ jurisdiction.[113] Under established practice, there are several ways for a case to appear before the ICJ. The UN General Assembly and the UN Security Council have the authority to refer a matter directly to the ICJ.[114] The States involved may consent to the ICJ's jurisdiction over the case.[115] If there is an issue between States in any UN-affiliated organization, this issue may be referred to the ICJ by the UN General Assembly.[116] And, finally, the terms of an international organization's foundational text may specifically provide that disputes between Member States may be subject to the ICJ's jurisdiction.[117] In all situations, it must be remembered that taking a matter to the ICJ is typically a last resort and is an indication that diplomacy and some form of alternate dispute resolution have failed.

Structure

There is a total of 15 sitting ICJ judges at any one time,[118] each of whom serve a nine-year term.[119] These judges are elected based on their "high moral character" and not their individual nationality, provided that they are eligible to serve as judges at the highest level of their national courts.[120] This is a long way of saying that, for example, a judge from the US would have to be eligible to sit on the US Supreme Court in order to sit on the ICJ. Nationality is taken into account in that the ICJ rules specifically bar two judges of the same nationality sitting on the bench at the same time.[121] One must be placed on a list of eligible candidates by a vetting group – the Permanent Court of Arbitration – and then be selected by both the UN General Assembly and the UN Security Council.[122] Interestingly, the election of a judge to the ICJ is one of the few times in which the permanent members of the UN Security Council do not enjoy veto power.[123]

If a case comes to the ICJ – for example, a case between Canada and Mexico – and there is a Mexican judge on the bench but no Canadian judge, the Mexican judge is free to hear the case; however, Canada is also able to appoint a judge to act as a counter-balance.[124] Once the case is concluded, only a simple majority is needed for a decision.[125] The decision of the ICJ is final and binding and there is no body to appeal to from a decision.[126] On rare occasions the ICJ will entertain a rehearing of a case or a particular issue within the case, but this is not a typical occurrence.[127]

Functions

In terms of decisions, it has been established that the ICJ can issue a standard judicial opinion – usually accompanied by concurring and dissenting opinions – or an advisory opinion.[128] Judicial opinions are binding on the parties involved, while advisory opinions seek to answer a question but are not technically binding.[129]

Conclusions

The primary UN organs discussed in this chapter vary considerably in terms of jurisdiction, subject matter and membership. They do, however, share commonalities that are essential to the UN system and to the systems which have emerged from it. Perhaps the most central commonality within the systems is the structure utilized for internal governance. These structures – two quasi-legislative governing bodies and a quasi-executive functioning secretariat – have become a hallmark of the UN system and demonstrate the ability to translate systems to different settings through the law of international organizations.

Within this system, although there are separate organs, many of them share overlapping subject areas. This is most certainly not uncommon within the international law system, as the international community routinely vests the regulation of similar fields in differing bodies. What is striking is the ability of these entities to work together in many instances to begin crafting what can be seen as a form of customary international law for addressing these areas and issues. Further, it is noteworthy that, just as the contents and nuances of such topic areas change over time, the relationships between organs and entities have evolved in order to keep pace.

As a corollary, this can be seen as working with the formalized systems of UN law to create self-serving systems with internal apparatuses and entities that fulfil the governance function for the international community. With changes to the international community occurring frequently and globalization challenging the way in which many aspects of the traditional international law regimes are applied, these commonalities and potentials to evolve with changes are vital for the existence and function of international organizations.

Notes

1 UN Charter (1945) art 41; United Nations, 2011 Highlights of Security Council Practice 14–15 (2012).
2 Repertoire of the Practice of the Security Council 165 (2000); Repertoire of the Practice of the Security Council ch 5, pt I (2007); Repertoire of the Practice of the Security Council, 665/1225 (2008–2009).
3 *See* Repertoire of the Practice of the Security Council, *supra* note 2 at 165 (describing the UNSC's response to the terrorist attacks of September 11, 2001 as including the creation of a new committee on counter-terrorism); Repertoire of the Practice of the Security Council, *supra* note 2 at ch 5, pt I; Repertoire of the Practice of the Security Council, *supra* note 2 at 665/1225; United Nations, 2011 Highlights of Security Council Practice, *supra* note 1 at 14–15.
4 *See* An effective international legal instrument against corruption, UN General Assembly Resolution 22 January 2001, A/RES/55/61.
5 Repertoire of the Practice of the Security Council, *supra* note 2 at 665–666/1225; United Nations, 2011 Highlights of Security Council Practice, *supra* note 1 at 14–15.
6 Repertoire of the Practice of the Security Council, *supra* note 2.

7 Id.; Repertoire of the Practice of the Security Council 75 (1966–1968); Repertoire of the Practice of the Security Council ch 5 (1969–1971); Repertoire of the Practice of the Security Council 51 (1972–1974); Repertoire of the Practice of the Security Council ch 5 (1975–1980); Repertoire of the Practice of the Security Council ch 5 (1981–1984); Repertoire of the Practice of the Security Council ch 5 (1985–1988); Repertoire of the Practice of the Security Council ch 5 (1989–1992); Repertoire of the Practice of the Security Council ch 5 (1993–1995); Repertoire of the Practice of the Security Council ch 5 (1996–1999); Repertoire of the Practice of the Security Council ch IX (2012–2013); Repertoire of the Practice of the Security Council ch IX (2014–2015).

8 Repertoire of the Practice of the Security Council, supra note 2 at 116; Repertoire of the Practice of the Security Council, supra note 7 at 75; Repertoire of the Practice of the Security Council, supra note 7 at ch 5 (1969–1971); Repertoire of the Practice of the Security Council, supra note 7 at 51; Repertoire of the Practice of the Security Council, supra note 7 at ch 5; Repertoire of the Practice of the Security Council, supra note 7 at ch 5; Repertoire of the Practice of the Security Council, supra note 7 at ch 5; Repertoire of the Practice of the Security Council, supra note 7 at ch 5; Repertoire of the Practice of the Security Council, supra note 7 at ch 5; Repertoire of the Practice of the Security Council, supra note 7 at ch IX; Repertoire of the Practice of the Security Council, supra note 7 at ch IX.

9 Repertoire of the Practice of the Security Council, supra note 2 at 8; Repertoire of the Practice of the Security Council, supra note 7 at ch 5.

10 Repertoire of the Practice of the Security Council, supra note 2 at. 8.

11 Id.; United Nations Security Council, S/RES/ 1353 (2001).

12 Repertoire of the Practice of the Security Council, supra note 2 at 165.

13 See also Rules of Procedure of the General Assembly (2016) at 25.

14 See id.

15 See id.

16 See id.

17 Rules of Procedure of the General Assembly, supra note 13 at 42.

18 A/54/3/Rev.1 pp 23–25, ch VI.

19 Rules of Procedure of the General Assembly, supra note 13 at 28.

20 See id. at 17.

21 Id. at 28.

22 Id. at 29.

23 See, e.g., United Nations General Assembly, Measures to eliminate international terrorism, A/RES/51/210 (1997).

24 See Repertoire of the Practice of the Security Council, supra note 7 at 9.

25 Repertoire of the Practice of the Security Council, supra note 7 at ch 6 (2007); Repertoire of the Practice of the Security Council, supra note 7 at 216–221 (1996–1999).

26 Repertoire of the Practice of the Security Council, supra note 7 at ch 6 (1993–1995); Repertoire of the Practice of the Security Council, supra note 7 at 216–221 (1996–1999).

27 Repertoire of the Practice of the Security Council, supra note 7 at ch 5 (2007); Repertoire of the Practice of the Security Council, supra note 7 at 372/1225 (2008–2009); United Nations Security Council, Res. 1654 (2005), S/RES/1654 (2005); Report of the Economic and Social Council for 1999, General Assembly, A/54/3/Rev.1 (1999) p 1.

28 See Rules of Procedure of the General Assembly, supra note 13 at pt VII.

29 Id.

30 Id. at 15.

31 See Repertoire of the Practice of the Security Council, supra note 7 at ch 6, pt III (1989–1992).

32 Rules of Procedure of the General Assembly, supra note 13 at 41.

33 Repertoire of the Practice of the Security Council, supra note 7 at ch 6 (1993–1995).

34 Id. at ch 169.

35 Repertoire of the Practice of the Security Council, supra note 7 at 241.

36 Id.

37 See Report of the Secretary General, Third International Decade for the Eradication of Colonialism, A/70/73 (27 March 2015); Report of the Secretary General, Dissemination of information on decolonization during the period from April 2016 to March 2017, Special Committee on the Situation with regard to the Implementation of the Declaration on the Granting of Independence to Colonial Countries and Peoples, A/AC.109/2017/18 (10 March 2017) 1–2; Report of the Secretary General, Dissemination of information on decolonization during the period from April 2015 to March 2016, Special Committee on the Situation with regard to the Implementation of the Declaration on the Granting of Independence to Colonial Countries and Peoples, A/AC.109/2016/18 (17 March 2016) 1–3; Report of the Secretary General, Dissemination of information on decolonization during the period from April 2014 to March 2017, Special Committee on the Situation with regard to the Implementation of the Declaration on the Granting of Independence to Colonial Countries and Peoples, A/AC.109/2015/18 (16 March 2015) 1–2; Report of the Secretary General, Dissemination of information on decolonization during the period from April 2013 to March 2014, Special Committee on the Situation with regard to the Implementation of the Declaration on the Granting of Independence to Colonial Countries and Peoples, A/AC.109/2014/18 (26 March 2014) 2–4; Report of the Secretary General, Dissemination of information on decolonization during the period

from April 2012 to March 2013, Special Committee on the Situation with regard to the Implementation of the Declaration on the Granting of Independence to Colonial Countries and Peoples, A/AC.109/2013/18 (24 March 2013) 2–4; Report of the Secretary General, Dissemination of information on decolonization during the period from April 2011 to March 2012, Special Committee on the Situation with regard to the Implementation of the Declaration on the Granting of Independence to Colonial Countries and Peoples, A/AC.109/2012/18 (22 March 2012) 1–2; Report of the Secretary General, Dissemination of information on decolonization during the period from April 2010 to March 2011, Special Committee on the Situation with regard to the Implementation of the Declaration on the Granting of Independence to Colonial Countries and Peoples, A/AC.109/2011/18 (23 March 2011) 2–4; Report of the Secretary General, Dissemination of information on decolonization during the period from April 2008 to March 2009, Special Committee on the Situation with regard to the Implementation of the Declaration on the Granting of Independence to Colonial Countries and Peoples, A/AC.109/2009/18 (23 March 2009) 1–2; Report of the Secretary General, Dissemination of information on decolonization during the period from April 2007 to March 2008, Special Committee on the Situation with regard to the Implementation of the Declaration on the Granting of Independence to Colonial Countries and Peoples, A/AC.109/2008/18 (24 March 2008) 1–3; Report of the Secretary General, Dissemination of information on decolonization during the period from April 2006 to March 2007, Special Committee on the Situation with regard to the Implementation of the Declaration on the Granting of Independence to Colonial Countries and Peoples, A/AC.109/2007/184 (2 August 2007) 1–4; Report of the Secretary General, Second International Decade for the Eradication of Colonialism, A/60/71 (5 April 2005); Report of the Secretary General, International Decade for the Eradication of Colonialism, A/55/497 (20 October 2000).

38 *See* Report of the Secretary General, Universal realization of the right of peoples to self-determination, A/61/333 (12 September 2006).

39 About ECOSOC, http://www.un.org/en/ecosoc/about/index.shtml, last accessed 4 January 2018; Report of the Economic and Social Council, General Assembly, A/55/Rev.1 (2000) ch IV; Report of the Economic and Social Council, General Assembly, A/56/Rev.1 (2001) ch VI; Report of the Economic and Social Council, General Assembly, A/57/3/Rev.1 (2002) ch VI; Report of the Economic and Social Council, General Assembly, A/59/3 (2004) ch. VI; Report of the Economic and Social Council, General Assembly, A/60/3 (2005) ch VI; Report of the Economic and Social Council, General Assembly, A/61/3 (2006) chs V, VI; Report of the Economic and Social Council, General Assembly, A/62/3 (2006) chs V, VI; Report of the Economic and Social Council, General Assembly, A/63/3 (2007) chs III, VII; Report of the Economic and Social Council, General Assembly, A/64/3 (2008) chs IV, VII; Report of the Economic and Social Council, General Assembly, A/65/3 (2010) chs IV, V, VI; Report of the Economic and Social Council, General Assembly, A/66/3 (2011) chs IV, V, VI; Report of the Economic and Social Council, General Assembly, A/67/3 (2010) ch. VI, VII; Report of the Economic and Social Council, General Assembly, A/68/3 (2013) chs VIII, IX; Report of the Economic and Social Council, General Assembly, A/69/3 (2014) chs VI, VII; Report of the Economic and Social Council, General Assembly, A/70/3 (2015) chs VII, IX; Report of the Economic and Social Council, General Assembly, A/71/3 (2016) ch IX.

40 UN Charter, *supra* note 1 at art 62.

41 ECOSOC Members, https://www.un.org/ecosoc/en/content/members, last accessed 4 January 2018.

42 Rules of Procedure of the General Assembly, *supra* note 13 at 40.

43 Id.

44 UN Charter, *supra* note 1 at art 67.

45 Rules of Procedure of the Economic and Social Council (2017).

46 Id.

47 Id.

48 Id.

49 Id.

50 Id.

51 Id. The MDGs, as the name suggests, were created at the turn of the millennium in order to focus world efforts on policy areas that need to be improved locally and globally. Specifically, the MDGs were: 1) End Poverty and Hunger; 2) Universal Education; 3) Gender Equality; 4) Child Health; 5) Maternal Health; 6) Combat HIV/AIDS; 7) Environmental Sustainability; 8) Global Partnership. *See* UN Millennium Development Goals, http://www.un.org/millenniumgoals/bkgd.shtml, last accessed 4 January 2018.

52 ECOSOC was also heavily involved in the negotiations leading to the content and terms of the SDGs themselves. The SDGs are far broader and more comprehensive that the MDGs, with over 100 sub-targets for accomplishment by 2030, but their main areas of focus cluster around: "1) End poverty in all its forms everywhere; 2) End hunger, achieve food security and improved nutrition and promote sustainable agriculture; 3) Ensure healthy lives and promote well-being for all at all ages; 4) Ensure inclusive and equitable quality education and promote lifelong learning opportunities for all; 5) Achieve gender equality and empower all women and girls; 6) Ensure availability and sustainable management of water and sanitation for all; 7) Ensure access to affordable, reliable and modern energy for all; 8) Promote sustained, inclusive and sustainable economic growth, full and productive employment and decent work for all; 9) Build resilient infrastructure, promote inclusion and sustainable industrialization and foster innovation; 10) Reduce inequality within and among countries; 11) Make cities and human settlements inclusive, safe, resilient and sustainable; 12) Ensure sustainable consumption and production patterns; 13) Take urgent action to combat climate change and its impacts; 14) Conserve and sustainably use the oceans,

seas and marine resources for sustainable development; 15) Protect, restore and promote sustainable use of terrestrial ecosystems, sustainably manage forests, combat desertification, and halt and reverse land degradation and halt biodiversity loss; 16) Promote peaceful and inclusive societies for sustainable development, provide access to justice for all and build effective, accountable and inclusive institutions at all levels; and 17) Strengthen the means of implementation and revitalize the global partnership for sustainable development." *See* UN Sustainable Development Goals, https://sustainabledevelopment.un.org/topics/sustainabledevelopmentgoals, last accessed 4 January 2018.

53 Rules of Procedure of the Economic and Social Council, *supra* note 45.

54 Id.

55 Id.

56 Id.

57 Id.

58 *See* United Nations Department of Economic and Social Affairs (UNDESA), http://csonet.org/, last accessed 4 January 2018.

59 UNESCO Constitution (1946).

60 Id. Specifically, the UNESCO Convention's preamble states that: "ignorance of each other's ways and lives has been a common cause, throughout the history of mankind, of that suspicion and mistrust between the peoples of the world through which their differences have all too often broken into war . . . That the wide diffusion of culture, and the education of humanity for justice and liberty and peace are indispensable to the dignity of man and constitute a sacred duty which all the nations must fulfill in a spirit of mutual assistance and concern; That a peace based exclusively upon the political and economic arrangements of governments would not be a peace which could secure the unanimous, lasting and sincere support of the peoples of the world, and that the peace must therefore be founded, if it is not to fail, upon the intellectual and moral solidarity of mankind." Id.

61 Id. at preamble.

62 Id. at art I.

63 Id. at art II. It is theoretically possible for a non-UN Member State to join UNESCO, although this requires the Executive Board to provide a formal recommendation of membership. The Executive Board of UNESCO (2016) 14.

64 UNESCO Constitution, *supra* note 59 at art II(3).

65 Rights and Obligations of Associate Members, UNESCO General Conference Res. 41.2.

66 UNESCO Constitution, *supra* note 59 at art II(5).

67 Id. at art II(4).

68 Id. at art II(6).

69 Id. at art III.

70 Id. at art IV(A).

71 Id. at art IV(C).

72 *See* UNESCO Constitution, *supra* note 59.

73 Rules of Procedure of the General Conference ch. VIII (2014).

74 Id. at ch IX.

75 UNESCO Constitution, *supra* note 59 at art IX.

76 *See* Rules of Procedure of the General Conference Rule, *supra* note 73 at 26.

77 UNESCO Constitution, *supra* note 59 at art VI (2).

78 Rules of Procedure of the General Conference Rules, *supra* note 73 at 64–68.

79 Rules of Procedure of the Executive Board Rule 9 (2015); The Executive Board of UNESCO (2016) 9.

80 The Executive Board of UNESCO, *supra* note 79 at 10.

81 Id.

82 Rules of Procedure of the Executive Board Rule, *supra* note 79 at 14.

83 Id. at Rule 16. The permanently existing committees are the 1) Special Committee; 2) Committee on Recommendations and Conventions; and 3) Committee on Non-Governmental Partners. Id.

84 The Executive Board of UNESCO, *supra* note 79 at pt. III.

85 Id. at 19; *see also* Committee on Conventions and Recommendations (2016).

86 The Executive Board of UNESCO, *supra* note 79 at 19.

87 UNESCO Constitution, *supra* note 59 at art VII.

88 Id. at art VII; Charter of National Commissions for UNESCO.

89 UNESCO Constitution, *supra* note 59 at art VIII.

90 Conventions, UNESCO, http://portal.unesco.org/en/ev.php-URL_ID=12025&URL_DO=DO_TOPIC&URL_SECTION=-471.html, last accessed 4 January 2018.

91 *See* id.

92 Recommendations, UNESCO, http://portal.unesco.org/en/ev.php-URL_ID=12026&URL_DO=DO_TOPIC&URL_SECTION=-471.html.

93 Id.

94 Id.

95 Declarations, UNESCO, http://portal.unesco.org/en/ev.php-URL_ID=12027&URL_DO=DO_TOPIC&URL_SECTION=-471.html, last accessed 4 January 2018.

96 Id.
97 Literacy, Education, UNESCO, http://www.unesco.org/new/en/education/themes/education-building-blocks/literacy/, last accessed 4 January 2018.
98 Themes, Education, UNESCO, http://www.unesco.org/new/en/education/, last accessed 4 January 2018.
99 Id.
100 Id.
101 Id.
102 Id.
103 Examples of these activities include: From Green Economies to Green Societies: UNESCO's Commitment to Sustainable Development (2011); *see also* Draft Programme and Budget, First biennium 2018–2019, 39 C/5 vols. I & II (2017).
104 Social and Human Sciences, UNESCO, http://en.unesco.org/themes/learning-live-together, last accessed 4 January 2018.
105 *See* Culture, UNESCO, http://en.unesco.org/themes/protecting-our-heritage-and-fostering-creativity, last accessed 4 January 2018.
106 Id.
107 Id.
108 Communications and information, UNESCO, http://www.unesco.org/new/en/communication-and-information/, last accessed 4 January 2018.
109 *See* 2014–2017 Approved Programme and Budget, 37 C/5 (Paris: UNESCO, 2014) ii–iii; 2014–2021 Medium-Term Strategy, 37 C/4 (Paris: UNESCO, 2014).
110 *See id.* at i.
111 UN Charter, *supra* note 1 at ch. XIV.
112 *See* History, International Court of Justice, http://www.icj-cij.org/en/history, last accessed 4 January 2018.
113 UN Charter, *supra* note 1 at ch. XIV; Malcolm N. Shaw, *International Law* 7th edn, (Cambridge University Press, 2014) 771–773.
114 Shaw, *supra* note 113 at 771–773.
115 ICJ Statute (1945) art 35; Shaw, *supra* note 113 at 771–787.
116 UN Charter, *supra* note 1 at ch. XIV.
117 Id.; Shaw, *supra* note 113 at 771–787.
118 UN Charter, *supra* note 1 at art 3.
119 Id. at art 13; Shaw, *supra* note 113 at 767.
120 UN Charter, *supra* note 1 at art 2; Shaw, *supra* note 113 at 767–771.
121 UN Charter, *supra* note 1 at art 3; Shaw, *supra* note 113 at 767–771.
122 UN Charter, *supra* note 1 at art 4; Shaw, *supra* note 113 at 766–767.
123 UN Charter, *supra* note 1 at art 10.
124 Id. at art 31.
125 Id. at art 55.
126 Id. at art 60.
127 Id. at art 61.
128 ICJ Statute, *supra* note 115 at art 36.
129 Id. at ch IV.

Chapter 13

International criminal courts

The current construct of an international criminal court has its genesis in the Nuremberg and Tokyo trials after World War II. Unlike prior post-war eras and post-war victors, it was decided amongst the Allied powers that those deemed responsible for the mass atrocities during this conflict would be tried in special, international courts applying several different variations on laws that were available at the time.

The Nuremberg and Tokyo trials offer many complex and often not fully resolved issues for international law. They were conducted in the militarized settings of the post-war periods in both cities, and were administered and overseen by judges and staff members representing a number of legal traditions. These trials coalesced around the defendants and the accusations rather than an established court structure within which to work that had significant basis in precedent. As groundbreaking as the Nuremberg and Tokyo trials were, they can also be seen more properly as pathfinding, in that they established a precedent and also provided at least a basic international organizational structure in which to take place.

Although an essential aspect of the Nuremberg and Tokyo trials involved bringing infamy to justice so as to ensure that such crimes would not be repeated, subsequent decades proved this assumption to be sadly mistaken. Indeed, a number of acts of genocide, war crimes, crimes against humanity and crimes of aggression have occurred since these trials, leading to an international quest for a meaningful justice that would have value for the immediately victimized community and the international community as a whole.

With this in mind, a variety of international organizations have created and/or supported the implementation of different attempts at international criminal courts in recent years. This chapter discusses the essential aspects of *ad hoc* criminal courts, hybrid criminal courts and, ultimately, the International Criminal Court as a separate international organization.

Conflict-based criminal courts

Separated by geography and many underlying issues, Rwanda and the former Yugoslavia are united in the horrific and genocidal violence that overtook them in the 1990s. After the violence had largely ceased, and peace agreements had been secured, the UN created special international criminal tribunals for the crimes committed in these States.[1] Both tribunals were used to try individuals for their alleged crimes during the conflicts and involved the use of an international court, comprised of international judges, to try these individuals.[2] These judges were selected in accordance with the procedures that are standard for the International Court of Justice (ICJ) and, later, the International Criminal Court (ICC).[3] Further, these criminal tribunals featured an Office of the Prosecutor and, in many ways, can be seen as setting the framework for the ICC's creation and structure.[4]

Currently, there are few cases pending at the trial chamber level of the International Criminal Tribunal for the former Yugoslavia, while the vast majority of them were successfully prosecuted.[5] The International Criminal Tribunal for Rwanda officially closed in 2015 after handling its assigned caseload and assigning other issues to the appropriate subsequent entity.[6] Regardless their status as historical entities, these tribunals are profoundly necessary to understanding the current and future trends in international tribunals and justice institutions.

International Criminal Tribunal for the former Yugoslavia

Background

In 1993, UN Security Council (UNSC) Resolution 827 took an extraordinary step for the institutionalization of international courts by authorizing the creation of the International Criminal Tribunal for the former Yugoslavia (ICTY).[7] This was a result of UNSC Resolution 808, also from

1993, which voiced growing international concerns at human rights violations taking place during the wars in the former Yugoslavia and tasked the UN Secretary General with generating a report on the topic, including specific suggestions for the establishment of an appropriate tribunal.[8]

The Secretary General's report highlighted another key aspect of coordination within international organizations, particularly the UN system, by referencing the fact that the UN Security Council's activities regarding the former Yugoslavia were informed by the report on the atrocities by the Commission of Experts convened to examine the issue.[9] Although the report ultimately endorsed the creation of a tribunal, it did so with the explicit caveat that this was to be done only for the context of the former Yugoslavia.[10] Importantly for an assessment of the relationship between UN organs when creating an international tribunal, the report suggested that it was necessary for the UNSC to act alone and not refer the issue or the drafting of the instrument needed to create the tribunal to the UN General Assembly (UNGA) because of the "urgency" of the matters involved and the time that would be necessary for a full UNGA debate.[11] As a result, it was suggested that the tribunal be created using the Chapter VII powers of the UNSC.[12] The report explained that "the Security Council would be establishing, as an enforcement measure under Chapter VII, a subsidiary organ with the terms of Article 29 of the Charter, but one of a judicial nature."[13] Further, the report asserted that, if created, a tribunal would be enforcing existing international humanitarian law rather than creating new law or allowing the UNSC to do so.[14] This was also essential to defeating issues and arguments regarding the application of *ex post facto* laws at the international level.

In Resolution 827, the UNSC adopted the Secretary General's report and findings and decided to create an international tribunal solely for alleged violations of international humanitarian law that occurred in the territory of the former Yugoslavia.[15] At the time of its adoption, Resolution 827 stated that the time frame for prosecution of crimes was for those allegedly committed between 1 January 1991 and a time to be determined by the UNSC.[16] The Resolution required all UN Member States to comply with its terms, assist the tribunal and organs that were to be created for it, and support the creation of the seat of the tribunal in the Netherlands.[17]

Jurisdiction

Following enactment of the ICTY statute, a number of States signed formal agreements with the Tribunal regarding the volitional surrender of those sought for prosecution or who had been convicted by the Tribunal and who are found in their territories.[18] These agreements extend to citizens of the signatory State when found in their home States,[19] although the home State has a greater deal of discretion in extradition decisions when the person at issue is sought for conduct that would be considered contempt of court, perjury or otherwise hindering prosecution rather than violations of international humanitarian law.[20] Additional agreements or terms of the larger agreements were promulgated with some States in order to officially allow them to cooperate with the investigation and discovery processes needed to facilitate the ICTY's activities and potential prosecution.[21]

As has become standard practice in international tribunals, the ICTY entered into agreements with several States regarding the housing and enforcement of sentences for those convicted of crimes under its jurisdiction.[22] In some cases, particularly in relation to Germany, a State will make agreements to enforce the prison terms of particular individuals rather than a blanket agreement.[23] In either case, these agreements have allowed the financial and practical burden of hosting prisoners to be shifted from the ICTY's host State to other Member States.[24] It has, arguably, also made the internationalization of enforcement prominent in ways that it was not before and allowed the international community to assume responsibility for punishment as well as prosecution.

Structure

Within the ICTY judicial structure, the judges themselves elected a President to serve for a maximum two-year term.[25] The role of the President was to coordinate the operations of the chambers, coordinate and cooperate with other organs of the ICTY, and oversee the Registry's operations.[26] In addition, the judges elected a Vice-President to fulfill the duties of the President in the event the President was unavailable.[27] Beyond this, a chain of succession was established within the judiciary to determine who would serve as President so as to ensure continuous operation of the Court.[28]

The Registrar was selected by the President after consulting with other members of the judiciary and, subsequently, with the UN Secretary General.[29] While the Registrar held consultative capacities with the other branches of the ICTY structure, his primary function was to serve as the administrative officer for the Court, ensuring that technical aspects of Court functioned properly.[30] These functions were carried out by overseeing the Registry and also the Chambers Legal Support Section.[31]

In addition to the judges, Prosecutor and Registry, there were several other organs within the ICTY system. The Bureau, consisting of the President, Vice-President, and presiding Trial Chambers judges, was a consultative body to address significant issues relating to the ICTY's functions.[32] The Coordination Council, consisting of the President, Prosecutor and Registrar, was tasked with coordinating the functions and operations of the ICTY.[33] In addition, the judges themselves met in plenary sessions to make critical decisions for the Tribunal, such as electing the President and adopting rules or other changes.[34] In recognition of the sensitive – and often dangerous – aspects of providing testimony before the ICTY, its structure included the Victims and Witnesses Section, which was tasked with seeking the appropriate protections for those who would give testimony.[35] In addition, this Section was required to provide victims with counseling, particularly when they had experienced sexual violence.[36]

The Prosecutor oversaw the prosecution staff and the conduct of prosecution for all cases brought before the Tribunal.[37] The Prosecutor's office was empowered to conduct investigations into allegations of criminal activities in the former Yugoslavia and was able to liaise with international organizations and other entities as necessary to gather the necessary facts.[38] The ICTY as a whole was not given powers to effect arrests; however, the Prosecutor was empowered to request the arrest or detainment of a suspect, or the seizure of evidence, from a State.[39] Those accused of crimes by the ICTY had the ability to select their own counsel provided that the counsel applied with the Registrar and met certain criteria relating to education, licensure and character.[40]

As has become standard practice in many international criminal proceedings, the ICTY's structure contained an Appeals Chamber as well as the standard Trial Chamber. The Appeals Chamber was comprised of a separate set of judges and was open to either side in a case provided a legitimate and articulated ground existed.[41]

As is discussed further in the sections below, there was growing concern over the ability of the ICTY to promptly and effectively handle the full complement of cases on its docket given that these ranged from the lowest level offenders to those charged with high-level offenses. The ICTY itself noted that the reasons for this stemmed partly from the political instability and prolonged conflicts in the region, which necessitated its hearing the full measure of cases rather than simply those it asserted the UNSC intended it to hear, namely "the most serious crimes which directly threaten international peace and security."[42] With this in mind, the ICTY suggested several potential solutions and methods of speeding up the prosecutions while maintaining the full extent of justice and fairness required under international law.[43] Ultimately, while the requested procedural changes were made, it was decided to refer lower- and mid-level offenses to various national courts for prosecution.[44] The eventual outgrowth of this was the slow transfer of remaining cases to the International Residual Mechanism for Criminal Tribunals.

Given the intensity of volume faced by the ICTY and concerns over the efficiency of its system, in 2000 the UNSC authorized the creation of a pool of *ad litem* judges and also authorized an increase in the number of judges available for the Appeals Chamber.[45] Concurrently, the UNSC decided to extend the same authorizations to the ICTR.[46] The UNSC's explicit intent was that all new judges in both tribunals should be selected quickly and that, once selected and relocated to the tribunals' seats, they should begin work immediately.[47] In accordance with this, the number of *ad litem* judges was set at six and the number of judges of the Appeals Chamber was increased to seven.[48]

From the outset, the ICTY was plagued with issues that hampered its functionality and progress toward hearings and judgments. Early on, there were problems with the retention of a Prosecutor, resulting in delays for proceedings they were moving toward trials.[49] Additionally, from 1994 onward, problems with the adequacy of funding for the ICTY affected proper and efficient functioning.[50] Further to this, the ICTY's investigative abilities were impacted by the ongoing conflicts in the region,[51] particularly in terms of the ability to conduct thorough investigations and receive cooperation from the necessary parties on the ground.[52] With this in mind, internationally negotiated agreements, notably the Dayton Accords, contained terms meant to assist in the willingness of States in the former Yugoslavia to work with and provide information to the ICTY,[53] although in practice these were quite difficult to implement.[54] Eventually, levels of State cooperation with the ICTY increased and trials were able to move through the judicial system.[55]

The majority of activities formerly associated with or delegated to the ICTY have now been transferred to either national courts or the International Residual Mechanism for Criminal Tribunals (MICT). However, it should be noted that the ICTY will not cease to function as an entity until 2018, completing its final caseload and providing assistance to courts and training programs.[56]

International Criminal Tribunal for Rwanda

Background and jurisdiction

In 1994, the UNSC examined the information generated regarding the Rwandan conflict by a designated Special Rapporteur for Rwanda of the United Nations Commission on Human Rights, the Commission of Experts it had previously convened, and the UN Secretary General, and found evidence of massive violations of international humanitarian law.[57] The UNSC determined that, given the nature of the crimes alleged and the situation on the ground in Rwanda at the time, it was incumbent upon the international community to ensure their prosecution under international humanitarian laws through the creation of an international tribunal.[58]

There were some issues faced in the Rwandan context that were not present in the context of the former Yugoslavia, notably the need to receive permission for international trials from the Rwandan Government.[59] This was not an issue to the same extent as for the ICTY because of the state of flux occurring in the territories of the former Yugoslavia and the issues of new statehood for many elements of the former Yugoslavia. Ultimately, the International Criminal Tribunal for the Prosecution of Persons Responsible for Genocide and Other Serious Violations of International Criminal Law in the Territory of Rwanda and Rwandan Citizens Responsible for Genocide and Other Violations Committed in the Territory of Neighbouring States between 1 January 1994 and 31 December 1994 (ICTR) was created by the UNSC as part of Resolution 955.[60]

Structure

Under the terms of the ICTR Statute, the Court was composed of three main organs, the Chambers (both Trial Chambers and Appeals Chambers), the Prosecutor, and the Registry.[61] The Statute provided for 11 judges, of whom five would be eligible to hear appeals and three would serve in the individual Trial Chambers according to their qualifications and backgrounds.[62] Judges serving on the Trial Chambers were elected by the UNGA, while the members of the ICTY's Appeals Chamber were also to serve as appellate judges in the ICTR.[63] The collective ICTR judges were empowered with the ability to elect the President in the same way that the ICTY functioned.[64] The Presidency also included the Bureau, which held the same functions as the ICTY's Bureau.[65]

Subsequently, the UNSC added an additional Trial Chamber – and, concomitantly, additional judges – to the ICTR's structure in order to increase efficiency and promote justice and fairness.[66] The UNSC later increased the number of appellate judges within the ICTR system[67] and also established *ad litem* judges for the ICTR as it had for the ICTY.[68] In addition to placing the onus on the ICTR to fully complete the tasks of investigation when many suspects were in different jurisdictions and when there were complications in accessing information and evidence, the UNSC issued specific requirements for all UN Member States – especially those bordering Rwanda and thus likely to have necessary information and access to suspects – to cooperate with the ICTR.[69]

The ICTY's Prosecutor was also designated as the Prosecutor for the ICTR.[70] In order to alleviate the potential for an overload of cases between the two courts, the ICTR Statute allowed the Prosecutor to have designated staff, and a Deputy Prosecutor, who focused solely on investigating and conducting prosecutions for the ICTR.[71] The final organ, the Registry, functioned in the same manner as at the ICTY and was also headed by a Registrar who was selected by the ICTR President and approved by the UN Secretary General.[72]

From the outset, the ICTR was plagued by infrastructural problems and issues with securing funding outside of specific grants from specialized donor entities.[73] This became problematic for the Tribunal's ability to function quickly and efficiency and to fulfill its mandate with full cooperation from States and other necessary parties.[74] These issues were compounded by auditors' findings of severe financial irregularities and mismanagement of the Tribunal in 1997 along with institutional problems involving a lack of communication between the Registry and the Prosecutor.[75] As a result, at a relatively early phase in the ICTR's history it underwent a significant reorganization and staff change in order to ensure the proper functioning of the Tribunal and of its financial resources.[76]

One additional issue that hampered the functioning of the Tribunal was the threat to the security and safety of victims and witnesses who were willing to consult with the ICTR's investigations and/or give evidence in the Chambers.[77] Further, as with the ICTY, the ICTR's work in investigation and prosecution was consistently hampered by the reticence of States to provide information and to extradite those accused of crimes.[78] This problem was continual throughout the ICTR's existence, and even the final cases in which transfer to a national court was deemed appropriate were difficult to share with other national systems outside of France and Rwanda itself.[79]

As should be evident, the ICTR was significantly modeled on the ICTY. This includes the UNSC's request that the ICTR begin planning for transfers of lower- and mid-level cases to various national courts rather than keeping them on its docket.[80] Further, the UNSC encouraged the creation and implementation of a plan for the ICTR to finish its operation by 2010.[81] Despite this, by 2009 it became apparent that the ICTR was not in a position to fully and completely terminate its mandate and cease to function by 2010.[82] In the short term, the UNSC's response was to extend the mandate of the permanent judges of the ICTR until the end of December 2010 and to undertake a further study as to the utility of extending the terms of the *ad litem* judges.[83] Later, the decision was made to extend the mandates of the *ad litem* judges until the end of December 2010 and to extend the terms of the appellate judges until the end of 2012.[84]

Efforts to transfer lower- and mid-level cases to national courts began in earnest by 2003, with overtures being made to Rwanda as well as other States for this purpose.[85] From the outset, there was an organizational concern that the legal system and codes in place in Rwanda would not allow for the type of charges and justice that the ICTR was created to enforce.[86] Additional concerns related to the structural ability of the Rwandan court system to try cases transferred from the ICTR since it was already prosecuting a number of cases that related to the acts of genocide committed.[87] As part of the ICTR's functions, it undertook a number of training sessions for members of the Rwandan legal community and civil society that focused on the use of the international humanitarian law standards in national court systems.[88]

The ICTR, through the UN, also made agreements with other States to house and enforce the sentences of those found guilty and sentenced to prison terms by the Court. In some instances, particularly where the arrangement was made with a State that was still in the process of development, the agreement featured provisions through which the ICTR pledged to approach donor States to create a fund for States holding its prisoners and the State was given the opportunity to approach that fund for support.[89] Where, however, such an agreement was made with a developed State, the terms required the State to bear the costs after the prisoner was transferred to its jurisdiction.[90]

International Residual Mechanism for Criminal Tribunals

Background and jurisdiction

By 2003, the UNSC took note of rising concerns from the ICTY itself[91] regarding the Tribunal's ability to successfully prosecute everyone on its docket within an acceptable time frame for the international community, the victims, and the concepts of justice and fairness.[92] As a result, it allowed the ICTY to discuss the possibility of transferring those charged with lower- and some middle-level offenses to various willing national courts in the region for swift trial.[93] At the same time, the UNSC also took note of this as an important step for the ICTR to contemplate for the same reasons as the ICTY.[94]

It has been noted that some of these cases were indeed transferred to national courts, including courts in the State where the alleged crimes had been committed. However, many cases, especially those involving high-level offenses and alleged offenders, still remained to be addressed years after they occurred. At the same time, by 2010 a number of individuals wanted for alleged crimes remained unapprehended, including those wanted for some of the most significant crimes within each of the conflicts.[95]

In order to consolidate the functions of the ICTY and the ICTR, in 2010 the UN Security Council established the International Residual Mechanism for Criminal Tribunals (MICT) as an entity with the power to continue the limited remaining functions of the Tribunals.[96] This included trying the high-ranking leaders in each territory who were alleged to have committed the most serious forms of crimes as well as lower- and mid-level cases where they were unsuccessful in being transferred to or tried by national courts.[97] Additionally, the MICT was given the ability to prosecute those attempting to interfere with investigations and trials.[98] It is notable that the MICT was specifically exempted from the ability to issue any indictments outside of those for the crimes and situations elaborated in the Statute, ensuring that it would not become a perpetual tribunal.[99]

Structure

Given the complexities of each geographical area in which the crimes at issue occurred, the UNSC required there to be two branches of the MICT, one for each Tribunal.[100] In order to effect the aims of the UNSC, and justice generally, the UNSC required all Member States to "cooperate fully" with the new juridical entity in the same way they were obligated to cooperate with the prior Tribunals.[101] Initially, the intended time frame of the MICT was set at four years, with the ability for the UNSC to extend its time frame after an evaluation of its work during this period.[102] The MICT structure for each branch is the same as the ICTY and ICTR in that they rely on separate Chambers – Trial and Appeals – as well as a shared Prosecutor and Registry.[103] Overall, the MICT structure allowed for 25 judges within its system, who were to be nominated by the UNSC after an open call for nominations issued by the Secretary General.[104] The UNSC then forwarded the list of names to the UNGA, which had the final ability to vote on and confirm judges.[105] The President of MICT is chosen by the Secretary General with consultation from the UNSC and the MICT judges.[106] The Prosecutor is selected and functions in the same general manner as those for the ICTY and ICTR, as is the Registry.[107] Indictments may issue from the Prosecutor in the event that an individual inter-feres with an act of prosecution for an alleged crime.[108]

The work of the MICT – and those affiliated with it, as well as those assisting it – is to be subject to the Convention on the Privileges and Immunities of the United Nations in the same manner as the ICTY and ICTR.[109] Somewhat unusually, the Rules of Procedure and Evidence for the MICT carve out another area of immunity for the International Committee of the Red Cross by providing that the Red Cross "shall not be obligated to disclose any information, including documents or other evidence, concerning the performance of its mandate . . . [n]or shall such information acquired by a third party on a confidential basis from the ICRC or by anyone while in the service of the ICRC be subject to disclosure or to witness testimony without the consent of the ICRC."[110] While not a formal immunity *per se*, the MICT's Rules of Procedure and Evidence create a structure through which any party involved in a trial proceeding may request that the Victims and Witnesses Section of the MICT provide protection to individuals functioning as victims and/or witnesses.[111]

In the spirit of continuity, agreements between States and either the ICTY or ICTR for the hous-ing and enforcement of sentences of those found guilty were deemed to transfer to the MICT.[112] Additionally, four new housing and enforcement agreements were concluded with the MICT itself, including two with Germany that were individually focused on specific convicted persons[113] and two that were general agreements, one with Benin[114] and the other with Mali.[115] Further, the MICT signed separate headquarters agreements for each branch of its operations, largely reflecting the same elements and protections as were afforded under the prior headquarters agreements for the ICTY and ICTR.[116]

The MICT's operations in Rwanda began in 2012 with the slow transfer of some cases and information from the ICTR to its offices in Arusha.[117] This required extensive cooperation and knowledge-sharing between the two entities and was overseen by the designated President of both institutions.[118] One of the most pressing, and seamlessly achieved, matters in the transition was the continued protection of victims and witnesses, which had proved difficult in the beginning of the ICTR's history and had become crucial by the time handover occurred.[119] In addition, the MICT assumed the role of oversight entity for the trial proceedings of cases that had been transferred to national courts – a function it continues through the time of writing.[120]

By 2013, the MICT branches were established in both Arusha, for transfer from the ICTR, and The Hague, for transfer from the ICTY.[121] Similar arrangements were made for the transfer of pro-tection obligations for victims and/or witnesses from the ICTY to the MICT, along with the trans-fer of cases and other matters.[122] In 2016, the full liquidation activities by the ICTR were deemed concluded and any remaining liquidation matters were transferred to the MICT.[123] As noted above, the ICTY was given until 2018 to complete these activities before they are to conclude and transfer any remaining matters to the MICT.[124] From that point onward, all Tribunal activity will have been transferred to the MICT.

Hybrid/internationalized criminal courts

The tribunals discussed above are examples of juridical entities that were created by the interna-tional community to hear what were regarded as crimes against not only the immediate victims but also international society as a whole. These entities use international standards of justice and international judges to impose penalties on those found guilty and to exonerate those who were found not guilty.

There is, however, another form of judicial entity that should be discussed: the international-ized court. This is essentially a hybrid court in that it uses the resources of the UN to establish a court in the aftermath of a conflict in a particular State and yet involves domestic law and legal actors in the overall court system. There are two prominent examples of this: the Special Court for Sierra Leone (SCSL), a State in which conflict ended only in 2002, and the Extraordinary Criminal Court for Cambodia (ECCC), where the conflict ended decades ago but the scars are still palpable.

At present, the ECCC is hearing cases, although in the beginning, owing to issues between the international and domestic components of the system, it had a great deal of trouble with establishing its functions and working cohesively.[125] The Special Court for Sierra Leone has concluded its function at the time of writing. Both of these systems borrowed the prosecutorial, trial chamber and appellate chamber structure from the international criminal tribunals and the ICC. They differ, however, in the measure of active engagement they invited from domestic legal actors and domestic society in general. In the case of Sierra Leone, this seems to have worked well; however, the issues that have occurred in Cambodia call into question whether this is always an advisable solution.

Extraordinary Chambers in the Courts of Cambodia

Background

The Extraordinary Chambers in the Courts of Cambodia (ECCC) was first conceived in 1997 although its jurisdiction was linked to crimes committed from 1975 to 1979 under the Khmer Rouge regime that brutalized the State for a brief but intense time.[126] Although the regime ended decades before, it was well established that the effects of its brutality were long-lasting and still served as an impediment to full national reconciliation in Cambodia.[127] This was not assisted by the fact that many who had been in high levels of leadership under the Khmer Rouge were able to live in Cambodian society with seeming impunity, undermining efforts to ensure that society saw justice done for the mass atrocities committed.[128]

In order to counter these issues, and at the request of the Cambodian Government, the UNGA first undertook a study of the possibility and utility of either the creation of a domestic, Cambodian court to try the crimes that had been committed under the Khmer Rouge, the creation of an ad hoc international court for these issues in a manner similar to those used in Rwanda and the former Yugoslavia, or an internationalized system representing a hybrid of these options.[129] The issue was referred to the UN Secretary General, who undertook a study along with a specialized Group of Experts for Cambodia.[130]

While part of the Group's functions involved a purely historical study to create a set of facts for the record, it also considered the various international laws which could be applicable in the Cambodian situation and thus appropriate for inclusion in the jurisdiction of a juridical entity.[131] After a thorough evaluation, the Group recommended the creation of a hybrid system with careful consideration for issues such as where to site the court and how to balance the international and domestic legal intersections and requirements.[132]

In the years that followed, there were abortive attempts to craft a statute and agreement that would allow for the UN to work with the government of Cambodia for the establishment and implementation of an internationalized court system to address these specific crimes.[133] Importantly, even when these negotiations were at their nadir, the concept of having an entity titled the ECCC rather than another international criminal tribunal – this time for Cambodia – remained at the heart of the construction of the court.[134] This is highly indicative of the sense of agency that both Cambodia and the international community felt over the court as an organization and for the understanding that it is possible to craft a court entity that recognizes under national and international law wrongs done on a mass scale. In addition, it should be emphasized that the negotiating and drafting of the ECCC Agreement was conducted by the Secretary General under the auspices and supervision of the UNGA rather than the UNSC. This is a significant organizational shift from the creation of earlier international criminal tribunals, which were conducted solely under the auspices of the UNSC.

Jurisdiction

A final instrument allowing for the creation of the ECCC was agreed to in June 2003 in the Agreement between the United Nations and the Royal Government of Cambodia Concerning the Prosecution Under Cambodian Law of Crimes Committed during the Period of Democratic Kampuchea.[135] From the outset, the Agreement emphasized that the ECCC would be a hybrid in terms of administration and that its purpose was to apply relevant Cambodian law, international humanitarian law, and the international treaty regimes to which Cambodia was a party during the period from 1975 to 1979.[136] Under the terms of Cambodian law, endorsed by the Agreement, the ECCC was to be regarded as a special branch existing within the overall Cambodian domestic legal structure rather than as an entirely separate entity.[137]

Structure

The Agreement established two chambers within the ECCC – the Trial Chamber and the Supreme Court Chamber.[138] The Trial Chamber is empowered to serve the standard functions of a trial court and is comprised of two international and three Cambodian judges.[139] The Supreme Court Chamber is empowered to preside as the appellate body, where appropriate, and the chamber of final instance, and is comprised of three international and four Cambodian judges.[140] Generally, both chambers are encouraged to make decisions in any case unanimously.[141] Should this be impossible to achieve, the Trial Chamber requires at least four votes to form a majority and the Supreme Court Chamber requires at least five votes to form a majority.[142] In order to form an investigating judge situation, it is required that there be a Cambodian judge and an international judge assigned in each instance.[143]

Joint operations also extend to the Office of the Prosecutor, in which there is a requirement for a Cambodian and international prosecutor to conduct investigations and prosecutions together.[144] As part of the joint functioning of the Prosecutor's office, there should be agreement between the two prosecutors as to whether and how to act in furtherance of the investigation.[145] However, should there be a split vote on whether to prosecute, it is generally appropriate for the prosecution to continue unless the applicable organization dispute settlement system is triggered.[146] Should there be a dispute between the prosecutors, or between co-investigating judges, the dispute settlement system allows for the creation of a Pre-Trial Chamber to hear and decide on these issues.[147]

The facilitation of the ECCC's functioning falls under the rubric of the Office of Administration.[148] In keeping with the joint system used in the judicial and prosecutorial aspects of the ECCC, the Office of Administration is headed by a Cambodian Director and an internationally appointed Deputy-Director.[149] Under the Agreement, Cambodia is responsible for providing the physical premises for the ECCC's functions and administration, although details on additional infrastructure such as services are subject to other agreements between the UN and the Government of Cambodia.[150] The bulk of financing necessary for the ECCC is to be provided by the UN through the international community, with the exception of the expenses incurred for Cambodian personnel.[151] Cambodian personnel at the ECCC are entitled to privileges and immunities similar to those of the standard international organizations staff in connection with their offices and official functions.[152] International personnel at the ECCC are entitled to the privileges and immunities granted for themselves and their family members under the Vienna Convention on the Law of Treaties.[153] Witnesses and experts who appear at the ECCC are provided immunity from arrest and prosecution during the course of their functions,[154] and victims and witnesses are to be provided additional personal protections while in Cambodia and fulfilling these activities.[155] The security of those associated with the ECCC in any capacity is subject to a further instrument in which Cambodia and the UN agreed to share these obligations.[156]

In implementation, the ECCC experienced – and continues to experience – issues with functionality, particularly in terms of ensuring the appropriate and requisite standards of justice on the national and international levels in a politically charged atmosphere.[157] Politics has played a particularly important role in stalling the immediate implementation of the Agreement and implementation of an effective ECCC due to changes in the government and in the Cambodian constitution that happened close to the signing of the Agreement itself.[158] Funding for the ECCC has also generated controversy and problems, as it has been difficult to ensure that the parties meet their financial obligations for the ECCC and for the investigative and prosecutorial elements within it.[159]

A key example of this was the 2007 revelation of a significant corruption scheme within the Cambodian portion of the ECCC's administration.[160] This resulted in an audit by the UN and, ultimately, the creation of a special office of the Independent Counselor to address these allegations and to act as the official entity to complain about such issues in the future, shielding would-be whistleblowers from public scrutiny.[161] Additionally, the role of Special Expert for advisement regarding funding and other matters to the United Nations Assistance to the Khmer Rouge Trials was founded as an organization response to the financial issues and as a mechanism to coordinate the international law-based relations with the Government of Cambodia regarding the ECCC's activities.[162] From this initial portfolio, the Special Expert's functions grew to include monitoring and oversight of the ECCC and the Independent Counselor, assistance to the ECCC in questions of its organizational functions and structure, and assistance in ensuring that trials are swiftly completed.[163] Further, a separate steering committee to coordinate oversight of the UN-based activities at the ECCC was established in 2008.[164]

Special Court for Sierra Leone

Background

The civil war in Sierra Leone was intense and bloody, lasting over a decade and seeing unspeakable acts occurring between the sides. The ceasefire and peace agreement for this conflict, referred to as the Lome Peace Agreement, was originally promulgated in 1999, although it would take several years for it to be fully effective.[165] The Lome Peace Agreement contained a number measures to foster accountability for the atrocities committed and to foster reintegration and reconciliation of society as a whole; however, it did not include specific terms relating to a court system to address the acts committed during the civil war.[166] As a result of the violence and durable conflict, the UN was heavily involved in Sierra Leone through efforts such as the deployment of a peacekeeping mission as well as assistance to and encouragement of the peace process and Lome Peace Agreement once signed.[167]

Part of this UN-based assistance included efforts to create a court that would hear and adjudicate allegations of mass atrocities and violations of national and international law.[168] This undertaking was first authorized by the UN Security Council, making it consistent with the organizational approvals given for the ICTY and the ICTR rather than for the ECCC.[169] The UN's goal in supporting the idea of a court was to allow for cases to be heard in Sierra Leone rather than in a secondary State – as had been done for the ICTY and ICTR – and generally that the lessons taught by the previous experiences of the ICTY and ICTR be incorporated into the envisioned court structure.[170]

Jurisdiction

In 2002, the Agreement between the United Nations and the Government of Sierra Leone on the Establishment of a Special Court for Sierra Leone was concluded.[171] The parameters of the Special Court's jurisdiction extended in general to those "persons who bear the greatest responsibility for serious violations of international humanitarian law and Sierra Leonean law committed in the territory of Sierra Leone since 30 November 1996."[172] In contrast to the ECCC, the Sierra Leonean Government explicitly required that the Special Court not be considered part of the standard domestic judicial structure.[173] As in other internationalized court systems, the essential organs of the Special Court were the judiciary, the Prosecutor and the Registry.[174]

Structure

The Agreement allowed for two chambers from the outset, a Trial Chamber and an Appeals Chamber, but also allowed for expansion to a second Trial Chamber if this became necessary for expediency.[175] Five judges were provided for in the Trial Chamber, of whom three were to be designated by the Government of Sierra Leone and two by the UN Secretary General with preference to the input and suggestions of those from the Economic Community of West African States and the Commonwealth.[176] In the Appeals Chamber, the Agreement provided for two judges selected by the Government of Sierra Leone and 3 by the UNSG with similar input from regional organizations and actors.[177] Within the Appeals Chamber, the judges are responsible for electing a presiding judge, who then functions as the President of the Special Court.[178] The role of the President is largely to coordinate the work of the various organs within the Special Court and to supervise the undertakings of the Registry.[179] Additionally, and as in the purely international courts, a Council of Judges – comprised of the presiding judges for each Chamber and the President – exists to assist in the coordination of Special Court activities and to provide advice to the President if requested.[180]

The appointment of the Prosecutor for the Special Court, who is responsible for overseeing investigations as well as court prosecutions, was vested in the UNSG, while the Government of Sierra Leone was given the power to appoint the Deputy Prosecutor.[181] However, the selection criteria for the Prosecutor and Deputy Prosecutor were established as being the same.[182] In keeping with the joint Sierra Leonean and international system, the Office of the Prosecutor's staff was required to be a mix of both aspects of the system.[183] Regardless the nationality, Prosecution staff members dealing with issues involving gender-based violence, particularly sexual assaults, and/or violence involving children, were recommended to have experience in the investigation of such issues prior to their functions at the Special Court.[184]

Appointment of the Registrar was designated as solely a decision for the UNSG.[185] The Registry functioned as the administrative branch of the Special Court, with a particular focus on providing assistance to the victims of the civil war.[186] To that end, a specialized Victims and Witnesses Unit was placed under the rubric of the Registry and intended to ensure protections and security for victims and witnesses and also to ensure that victims and witnesses received assistance and counseling for their experiences, especially in light of their reliving traumas to those at the Special Court.[187]

Costs for the operation of the Special Court were allotted to the international community through the UNSG's fundraising efforts while the premises for the Special Court, along with necessary services and infrastructure, were allotted to the Government of Sierra Leone.[188] To address this allocation of responsibilities, the Agreement provided for the creation of a Management Committee that coordinated the views and priorities of interested States – such as States in the region as well as Sierra Leone – in terms of funding, and "advice and policy direction on all non-judicial aspects of the operation of the Court, including questions of efficiency."[189]

Overall, there was a preference that those convicted by the Special Court serve out their sentences in Sierra Leone rather than being transferred to another State.[190] In the event this was not possible; however, it was agreed that prison sentences could be served in a State that had entered into agreements for the enforcement of sentences with the ICTY and/or the ICTR.[191] The Special Court was also empowered to enter into similar agreements with additional States[192] and did so with Finland,[193] Rwanda,[194] Sweden,[195] and the United Kingdom.[196] In all these agreements the costs of housing and sentence enforcement were transferred to the State once the prisoner had been transferred to their territory by the Special Court.[197]

In 2013, the Special Court officially finished its work, having handled its last cases. The story of the Special Court did not completely end with this, however, as the UN and the Government of

Sierra Leone agreed to the creation of a separate entity, the Residual Special Court for Sierra Leone, which would handle the largely administrative and technical aspects of the Special Court that would need to be continued.[198] Further, the Residual Special Court has a responsibility to ensure that appropriate cases are referred to national court systems for prosecution.[199] While technically the Residual Special Court maintains the same organizational structure as the Special Court, it's powers are quite limited.

International Criminal Court

Background

In the aftermath of World War II, those who were deemed responsible for the atrocities committed by the Nazi regime were tried openly at Nuremberg according to transparent and internationally crafted judicial practices.[200] Similarly, although somewhat less well publicized, those who were deemed responsible for atrocities committed under the aegis of the Japanese Government were also tried at international trials in Tokyo.[201] From these trials came an international belief that there were crimes of such gravity that they harm not only the immediate victims but all mankind and should be prosecuted accordingly.

Jurisdiction

Decades later, in the aftermath of continued acts of genocide and crimes against humanity, the international community created the International Criminal Court.[202] In its foundational text, the ICC was given jurisdiction over four crimes: crimes against humanity, genocide, war crimes and the crime of aggression.[203] However, there was significant disagreement over how to define the crime of aggression and in order to ensure that the ICC existed to prosecute the other enumerated crimes, it was agreed that the ICC's foundational text – the Rome Statute – would be ratified with a provision stating that the crime of aggression would be defined later.[204] Over ten years later, a definition of the crime of aggression was finally agreed upon and ICC Member States are in the process of implementing this amendment, known as the Kampala Amendment to the Rome Statute.[205]

Structure

The ICC structure involves the Court itself as well as the Office of the Prosecutor, an appellate entity and other administrative offices.[206] Unlike the ICJ, in which States are the parties involved in the dispute, the ICC hears cases that involve individual conduct.[207] States play a primary jurisdictional role in ratifying the Rome Statute and accepting the jurisdiction of the ICC over acts that are committed within their jurisdiction.[208]

There are three primary ways in which a charge occurs and all of them require that the Prosecutor take control of the case, investigate and, if appropriate, bring the case before the ICC itself.[209] The first way is for a State Party to the Rome Statute to refer a matter to the Prosecutor – this, of course, requires the matter being referred to have happened within the jurisdiction of a State Party to the Rome Statute.[210] The second way is for the UN Security Council to refer a matter under the Rome Statute – and occurring within the jurisdiction of a State Party to the Rome Statute – to the Prosecutor for investigation.[211] Finally, the Prosecutor herself may start an investigation against a State Party to the Rome Statute where there is, in her view, sufficiently serious evidence to do so.[212] Before a Prosecutor-initiated investigation can go very far it has to demonstrate merit to a Pre-Trial Chamber of the ICC.[213] In addition to the trial and appellate-based system in which the majority of ICC organs operate, the Rome Statute creates the Registry to function in the role of a secretariat.[214]

Notably, the Rome Statute specifically removes the idea of immunity from prosecution based on official status within a governmental entity as a defense against prosecution at the ICC.[215] Similarly, there is no immunity for those who were in military or other command during the commission of the alleged crimes.[216] This waiver of immunity is due to the horrific nature of the crimes that the ICC prosecutes. There is, however, immunity for those who were under 18 years old when the alleged crimes were committed.[217]

There are 18 ICC judges provided for in the Rome Statute, but there are allowances for increasing this number and, given that there are pre-trial and appellate chambers within the ICC system, this would seem logical.[218] These judges may serve for one nine-year term.[219] The eligibility requirements for ICC judges are the same as those used for the ICJ, however they are more subject-specific in that they require a judge to have significant criminal law experience and experience within the criminal justice system of their home State.[220] Further, they must have experience in international law and preferably international human rights law.[221] The list of those nominated is then sent to the Assembly of the States Parties to the Rome Statute – the equivalent of the UN General Assembly – for voting.[222] Although there is no exact geographical or gender allotment of ICC judges, equality of representation in both areas is supposed to be a factor in the voting decisions of States Parties.[223]

In addition to the judicial offices discussed above, the Rome Statute provides for the election of a Prosecutor, who then has a prosecutorial office of lawyers, investigators and other experts work for her.[224] There is, however, independence of office and functions between these branches.[225]

Finally, no discussion of a criminal court would be complete without a discussion of the sanctions it can impose. The ICC has the ability to punish a person found guilty of any of the four crimes with prison time; however, the maximum period of imprisonment that may be ordered is 30 years[226] unless the crimes are so grave that they merit life in prison.[227] The ICC can also assess a monetary penalty against a defendant and/or order forfeiture of certain assets.[228]

In addition to the ICC's juridical activities, the Rome Statute provides for the Trust Fund for Victims (TFV) as a means of facilitating non-juridically based assistance to those who have been identified as victims of the crimes over which the ICC has jurisdiction.[229] Regardless of the reparations decisions that may or may not be issued as a result of a prosecution, the TFV is responsible for implementing and overseeing activities meant to rehabilitate the victims in terms of psychological harms, physical harms, and material harms suffered.[230] The TFV receives its funds from donors – public and private.[231]

The first cases which have advanced to the reparations stage have made assessments of monetary amounts owed as compensation in addition to more holistic approaches to reparations and justice.[232] A key problem faced in the collection of these assessed monetary awards is the claimed financial insolvency of those convicted of crimes under the ICC's jurisdiction. In these instances, the Court has been willing to acknowledge the insolvency but has steadfastly refused to allow this factor to defeat an assessment as to proper compensation amounts due.[233] While the TFV serves to fill part of this gap, it cannot sustainably be expected to provide the bulk of reparations funding. The ICC has recognized the importance of this problem not only to those who have been awarded compensation but also to the inherent ICC structure.[234] As a result, it has begun examining methods of using financial investigations to determine whether the defendant does indeed have assets that can be reached.[235]

The ICC is governed by the Assembly of States Parties, in which all Member States to the Rome Statute are represented.[236] In order to facilitate a continuous and effective dialogue between the President of the ICC, the Prosecutor and the Registrar, ICC regulations require the creation of a Coordination Council that meets monthly or more often as needed.[237] In the context of an evolving juridical system that is constantly undertaking investigations into potential violations of international law, this ability to meet often is important to highlight. Given the evolving nature of international criminal law and ICC functions, the ICC is also required to create the Advisory Committee on Legal Texts.[238] This Committee is composed of representatives from all the chambers and bodies within the ICC structure as well as from the Prosecutor's office, the Registrar, and the practicing legal community.[239]

Within the ICC structure, the Victims and Witnesses Unit functions to provide assistance and protections to both classes of individual.[240] As part of this function, the Victims and Witnesses Unit is empowered to seek protective or other special measures for the individuals it represents.[241] To ensure fairness and equal access to justice, the ICC structure provides for a designated Office of Public Counsel for the Defence as well as Office of Public Counsel for the Victims.[242]

The structure of the Office of the Prosecutor is focused on several committees and divisions in addition to the physical acts of litigation before the ICC. These committees and divisions are: 1) the Executive Committee; 2) the Jurisdiction; Complementarity and Cooperation Division;[243] 3) the Investigation Division;[244] 4) the Prosecution Division;[245] 5) the Services Section;[246] and 6) the Legal Advisory Section.[247] Further, to facilitate in prosecuting the high number of crimes before the ICC that involve sexual violence and/or children, the OTP includes a Gender and Children Unit.[248]

In addition to its own functions and working with national governments to access information and other necessary resources, the ICC maintains strong relationships with other international organizations. As might be expected, perhaps the strongest of these relationships is with the UN, which is able to provide a large amount of access, information, investigative skill, and legal resources to any attempt at fact-gathering and potential prosecutions.[249] Necessarily, the ICC maintains a strong relationship with INTERPOL, which is able to assist in fact-finding and the location of those sought for ICC proceedings.[250] Efforts to create and enforce a strong relationship with regional organizations, particularly with the African Union, have been quite important – if not essential – to the ability of the ICC to generate information, locate potential defendants and witnesses, and inform national governments and citizens about its activities.[251] Cooperation between the ICC and the ICJ is also important to the ICC's structure and presence in the international criminal law and justice community.[252]

For the period from 2014–2017, the TFV established four areas of priority in its activities: 1) reparative justice; 2) "facilitating assistance and reparations"; 3) victims' advocacy within the ICC throughout all stages of the prosecution and reparations processes; and 4) "good governance, accountability, and transparency."[253] Specific issues to be included in these activities include gender concerns and equality, protection for and promotion of children and their rights, environmental protection, peacebuilding, and victims' participation.[254]

Conclusions

In and of themselves, the above-discussed international criminal courts are innovative as organizations and provide alternative theories of how international organizations or hybridized organizations can be used to promote justice. Taken together, the progression from the Nuremberg and Tokyo trials through current international criminal courts demonstrates an evolution of organizational structures to meet the needs and expectations of the international community and the domestic communities they serve. This is illustrative of the flexibility of international organizations that work with or are vehicles for international criminal law and justice throughout time and in response to the legal, societal and historical needs of their constituencies.

Further, the creation and implementation of these courts as organizations – albeit fleeting in some instances – demonstrate the power of efforts to use organizations as a means to balance State sovereignty with the needs of the international community and the victims of the crimes that are at the heart of the allegations. These forms of organization carve a place for victims' assertion of agency over their suffering by giving them an international venue to testify and accuse those who perpetrated unspeakable horrors against them, their families and their communities. In so doing, they redefine the relationship between organization and individual in a way that would not be possible if the law of international organizations were not characterized by flexibility in the quest for legitimacy.

It must be recalled, however, that not all of these organizations use the same structures or possess the same views on how to define and implement systems of prosecution for grave crimes. For example, the ECCC's mandate and the system which grew up around it demonstrate an attempt to keep the organization as something more domestically oriented, while the ICTY clearly manifested an intent to utilize the international community as a means to craft and apply justice. That the law of international organizations can accommodate this spectrum of commonalities and differences without becoming irrelevant or unable to properly function is a testament to its durability over time and challenge.

The evolution of court systems as part of the international organizational framework is, further, illustrative of the ways in which legitimacy in the international community can be conveyed across a swath of organizational forms which seek to accomplish similar results.

Notes

1 About International Criminal Tribunal for Rwanda, http://www.unictr.org/AboutICTR/GeneralInformation/tabid/101/Default.aspx, last accessed 4 January 2018; About the ICTY, http://www.icty.org/, last accessed 4 January 2018.

2 Id.

3 Id.

4 Id.

5 The Cases, ICTY, http://www.icty.org/en/action/cases/4 .

6 See Cases, ICTR, http://www.unictr.org/Cases/tabid/204/Default.aspx, last accessed 4 January 2018. Although it is beyond the scope of this chapter, it should be noted that there are many critics of the ICTR process because it took such a long time to complete that there has been recourse to tribal courts in order to settle issues of culpability, punishment and, ultimately, reconciliation.

7 United Nations Security Council Resolution 827, S/RES/827 (1993).

8 United Nations Security Council Resolution 808, S/RES/808 (1993).

9 Report of the Secretary-General Pursuant to Paragraph 2 of Security Council Resolution 808 (1993), S/25704 (3 May 1993) para 10.

10 Id. at para 12 (clarifying that "[t]he decision does not relate to the establishment of an international criminal jurisdiction in general, nor to the creation of an international criminal court of a permanent nature, issues which are and remain under active consideration by the International Law Commission and the General Assembly.").

11 Id. at para 21.

12 Id. at paras 22–24.

13 Id. at para 28. The report went on to note that "[t]his organ would, of course, have to perform its functions independently of political considerations; it would not be subject to the authority or control of the Security Council with regard to the performance of its judicial functions. As an enforcement measure under Chapter VII, however, the life span of the international tribunal would be linked to the restoration and maintenance of international peace and security in the territory of the former Yugoslavia." Id.

14 Id. at para 29.

15 United Nations Security Council, Resolution 827 (1993), S/RES/827 (1993) paras 1, 2.

16 Id. at paras 1, 2.

17 Id. at paras 4, 6.

18 See Agreement on Surrender of Persons between the Government of the United States and the Tribunal (1994); The Netherlands, Provisions Relating to the Establishment of the International Tribunal for the Prosecution of Persons Responsible for Serious Violations of International Humanitarian Law Committed in the Territory of the former Yugoslavia since 1991 (1994); Confederation of Switzerland, Federal order on cooperation with the International Tribunals for the Prosecution of serious violations of International Humanitarian Law (1995); Sweden, Act relating to the Establishment of an International Tribunal for Trial of Crimes Committed in Former Yugoslavia (1994); Spain, Organisation Act on Co-operation with the International Tribunal for the Prosecution of Persons responsible for serious violations of International Humanitarian Law Committed in the Territory of the Former Yugoslavia (Organisation Act 15/1994 of 1 June 1994); Romania, Law No. 159/ 28 July 1998, regarding the cooperation of the Romanian authorities with the International Criminal Tribunal for the Prosecution of Persons Responsible for Serious Violations of International Humanitarian Law Committed in the Territory of the Former Yugoslavia since 1991 (1998); Republic of Croatia, Constitutional Act on the Cooperation of the Republic

of Croatia with the International Criminal Tribunal (1996); Norway, Bill relating to the Incorporation into Norwegian Law of the UN Security Council Resolution on the Establishment of an International Criminal Tribunal
for the Former Yugoslavia (Law 1994–06.24 38JD/31–1–1995); New Zealand, International War Crimes Tri-
bunal Act 1995; Italy, Provisions on Co-operation with the International Tribunal for the Prosecution of Serious
Violations of International Humanitarian Law Committed in the Territory of the Former Yugoslavia (Decree-Law
No. 544 of 28 December 1993); Hungary, Act XXXIX of 1996on the fulfillment of obligations deriving from the
Statute of the International Tribunal established for punishing the serious violations of international law (1996);
Greece, Law No. 2665, Enforcement of resolutions 827/25 5.1993 and 955.8.11.1994, taken by the Security
Council of the United Nations, by which two International Criminal Courts were established in order to try viola-
tions of the International Humanitarian Law that have taken place within the territories of the former Yugoslavia
and Rwanda (1998); Republic of Germany, Law on Cooperation with the International Tribunal in respect of the
former Yugoslavia (10 April 1995); Denmark, Act on Criminal Proceedings before the International Tribunal for
the Prosecution of Persons Responsible for War Crimes Committed in the Territory of the former Yugoslavia (Act
No. 1099 of 21 December 1994); Republic of Bosnia and Herzegovina, Decree with Force of Law on Extradition
at the Request of the International Tribunal (1995); Belgium, Law on the recognition of the International Criminal Tribunal for the former Yugoslavia and the International Criminal Tribunal for Rwanda and cooperation with
those tribunals (22 March 1996); Austria, Federal Law on Cooperation with the International Tribunals (1996).

19 Agreement on Surrender of Persons between the Government of the United States and the Tribunal, *supra* note 18;
Confederation of Switzerland, Federal order on cooperation with the International Tribunals for the Prosecution
of serious violations of International Humanitarian Law, *supra* note 18; Sweden, Act relating to the Establishment
of an International Tribunal for Trial of Crimes Committed in Former Yugoslavia, *supra* note 18; Spain, Organisation Act on Co-operation with the International Tribunal for the Prosecution of Persons responsible for serious
violations of International Humanitarian Law Committed in the Territory of the Former Yugoslavia (Organisation
Act 15/1994 of 1 June 1994), *supra* note 18; Romania, Law No. 159/ 28 July 1998, regarding the cooperation of
the Romanian authorities with the International Criminal Tribunal for the Prosecution of Persons Responsible for
Serious Violations of International Humanitarian Law Committed in the Territory of the Former Yugoslavia since
1991, *supra* note 18; Republic of Croatia, Constitutional Act on the Cooperation of the Republic of Croatia with
the International Criminal Tribunal, *supra* note 18; Norway, Bill relating to the Incorporation into Norwegian Law
of the UN Security Council Resolution on the Establishment of an International Criminal Tribunal for the Former
Yugoslavia (Law 1994-06.24 38JD/31-1-1995), *supra* note 18; Republic of Germany, Law on Cooperation with
the International Tribunal in respect of the former Yugoslavia (10 April 1995); Republic of France, Law no.
95-1 of 2 January 1995 on adapting French law to the provisions of United Nations Security Council resolution
827 establishing an international tribunal for the prosecution of persons responsible for serious violations of
international humanitarian law committed in the territory of the former Yugoslavia since 1991 (1995); Finland,
Act on the Jurisdiction of the International Tribunal for the Prosecution of Persons Responsible for Crimes Committed in the Territory of the Former Yugoslavia and on Legal Assistance to the International Tribunal (5 January
1994/12); Belgium, Law on the recognition of the International Criminal Tribunal for the former Yugoslavia and
the International Criminal Tribunal for Rwanda and cooperation with those tribunals (22 March 1996); Austria,
Federal Law on Cooperation with the International Tribunals (1996).

20 Agreement on Surrender of Persons between the Government of the United States and the Tribunal, *supra* note
18 at art 1; Confederation of Switzerland, Federal order on cooperation with the International Tribunals for the
Prosecution of serious violations of International Humanitarian Law, *supra* note 18; Sweden, Act relating to the
Establishment of an International Tribunal for Trial of Crimes Committed in Former Yugoslavia, *supra* note 18;
Spain, Organisation Act on Co-operation with the International Tribunal for the Prosecution of Persons responsi-
ble for serious violations of International Humanitarian Law Committed in the Territory of the Former Yugoslavia
(Organisation Act 15/1994 of 1 June 1994), *supra* note 18; Romania, Law No. 159/ 28 July 1998, regarding the
cooperation of the Romanian authorities with the International Criminal Tribunal for the Prosecution of Persons
Responsible for Serious Violations of International Humanitarian Law Committed in the Territory of the Former
Yugoslavia since 1991, *supra* note 18; Republic of Croatia, Constitutional Act on the Cooperation of the Republic
of Croatia with the International Criminal Tribunal, *supra* note 18; Republic of Germany, Law on Cooperation with
the International Tribunal in respect of the former Yugoslavia (10 April 1995), *supra* note 19; Republic of France,
Law no. 95–1 of 2 January 1995 on adapting French law to the provisions of United Nations Security Council
resolution 827 establishing an international tribunal for the prosecution of persons responsible for serious violations of international humanitarian law committed in the territory of the former Yugoslavia since 1991, *supra* note
18; Finland, Act on the Jurisdiction of the International Tribunal for the Prosecution of Persons Responsible for
Crimes Committed in the Territory of the Former Yugoslavia and on Legal Assistance to the International Tribunal
(5 January 1994/12), *supra* note 19; Republic of Bosnia and Herzegovina, Decree with Force of Law on Extradition at the Request of the International Tribunal, *supra* note 18.

21 *See* United Kingdom, Statutory Instrument No. 716, The United Nations (International Tribunal) (Former Yugoslavia) order 1996, *supra* note 18; Sweden, Act relating to the Establishment of an International Tribunal for Trial
of Crimes Committed in Former Yugoslavia, *supra* note 18; Spain, Organisation Act on Co-operation with the
International Tribunal for the Prosecution of Persons responsible for serious violations of International Humanitarian Law Committed in the Territory of the Former Yugoslavia (Organisation Act 15/1994 of 1 June 1994),
supra note 18; Republic of Croatia, Constitutional Act on the Cooperation of the Republic of Croatia with the

International Criminal Tribunal, *supra* note 18; New Zealand, International War Crimes Tribunal Act 1995, *supra* note 18; Finland, Act on the Jurisdiction of the International Tribunal for the Prosecution of Persons Responsible for Crimes Committed in the Territory of the Former Yugoslavia and on Legal Assistance to the International Tribunal (5 January 1994/12), *supra* note 19; Austria, Federal Law on Cooperation with the International Tribunals (1996); Commonwealth of Australia, International War Crimes Tribunals Legislation 1995.

22 *See* Agreement between the United Nations and the Republic of Albania on the Enforcement of Sentences of the International Criminal Tribunal for the Former Yugoslavia (2008); Agreement between the United Nations and the Federal Government of Austria on the Enforcement of Sentence of the International Criminal Tribunal for the Former Yugoslavia (1999); Agreement between the United Nations and the Government of the Kingdom of Belgium on the Enforcement of Sentences of the International Criminal Tribunal for the Former Yugoslavia (2007); Agreement between the United Nations and the Government of the Kingdom of Denmark on the Enforcement of Sentences of the International Criminal Tribunal for the Former Yugoslavia (2002); Agreement between the United Nations and the Government of the Republic of Estonia on the Enforcement of Sentences of the International Criminal Tribunal for the Former Yugoslavia (2002); Agreement between the United Nations and the Government of Finland on the Enforcement of Sentences of the International Criminal Tribunal for the Former Yugoslavia (1997); Agreement between the United Nations and the Government of the French Republic on the Enforcement of Sentences of the International Criminal Tribunal for the Former Yugoslavia (2000); Agreement between the United Nations and the Government of the Italian Republic on the Enforcement of Sentences of the International Criminal Tribunal for the Former Yugoslavia (1997); Agreement between the United Nations and the Government of Norway on the Enforcement of Sentences of the International Criminal Tribunal for the Former Yugoslavia (1998); Agreement between the United Nations and the Government of the Republic of Poland on the Enforcement of Sentences of the International Criminal Tribunal for the Former Yugoslavia (2008); Agreement between the United Nations and the Portuguese Republic on the Enforcement of Sentences of the International Criminal Tribunal for the Former Yugoslavia (2007); Agreement between the United Nations and the Slovak Republic on the Enforcement of Sentences of the International Criminal Tribunal for the Former Yugoslavia (2008); Agreement between the United Nations and the Kingdom of Spain on the Enforcement of Sentences of the International Criminal Tribunal for the Former Yugoslavia (2000); Agreement between the United Nations and the Government of Sweden on the Enforcement of Sentences of the International Criminal Tribunal for the Former Yugoslavia (1999); Agreement between the United Nations and the Government of the Kingdom of Great Britain and Northern Ireland on the Enforcement of Sentences of the International Criminal Tribunal for the Former Yugoslavia (2004); Agreement between the United Nations and Ukraine on the Enforcement of Sentences of the International Criminal Tribunal for the Former Yugoslavia (2007).

23 *See* Agreement between the Government of Germany and the Mechanism for Mr Dordevic (2014); Agreement between the International Criminal Tribunal for the Former Yugoslavia and the Government of the Federal Republic of Germany concerning the conditions under which Mr Stanislav Galic's prison sentence shall be enforced (2008); Agreement with the Government of the Federal Republic of Germany to enforce Mr Dragoljub Kunarac's prison sentence (2002); Agreement with the Government of the Federal Republic of Germany to enforce Mr Dusko Tadic's prison sentence (2000); Agreement with the Government of the Federal Republic of Germany to enforce Mr Johan Tarculovski's prison sentence (2011).

24 *See* Agreement between the United Nations and the Republic of Albania on the Enforcement of Sentences of the International Criminal Tribunal for the Former Yugoslavia, *supra* note 23; Agreement between the United Nations and the Federal Government of Austria on the Enforcement of Sentence of the International Criminal Tribunal for the Former Yugoslavia, *supra* note 23; Agreement between the United Nations and the Government of the Kingdom of Belgium on the Enforcement of Sentences of the International Criminal Tribunal for the Former Yugoslavia, *supra* note 23; Agreement between the United Nations and the Government of the Kingdom of Denmark on the Enforcement of Sentences of the International Criminal Tribunal for the Former Yugoslavia, *supra* note 23; Agreement between the United Nations and the Government of the Republic of Estonia on the Enforcement of Sentences of the International Criminal Tribunal for the Former Yugoslavia, *supra* note 23; Agreement between the United Nations and the Government of Finland on the Enforcement of Sentences of the International Criminal Tribunal for the Former Yugoslavia, *supra* note 23; Agreement between the United Nations and the Government of the French Republic on the Enforcement of Sentences of the International Criminal Tribunal for the Former Yugoslavia, *supra* note 23; Agreement between the United Nations and the Government of the Italian Republic on the Enforcement of Sentences of the International Criminal Tribunal for the Former Yugoslavia, *supra* note 23; Agreement between the United Nations and the Government of Norway on the Enforcement of Sentences of the International Criminal Tribunal for the Former Yugoslavia, *supra* note 23; Agreement between the United Nations and the Portuguese Republic on the Enforcement of Sentences of the International Criminal Tribunal for the Former Yugoslavia, *supra* note 23; Agreement between the United Nations and the Slovak Republic on the Enforcement of Sentences of the International Criminal Tribunal for the Former Yugoslavia, *supra* note 23; Agreement between the United Nations and the Kingdom of Spain on the Enforcement of Sentences of the International Criminal Tribunal for the Former Yugoslavia, *supra* note; Agreement between the United Nations and the Government of Sweden on the Enforcement of Sentences of the International Criminal Tribunal for the Former Yugoslavia, *supra* note 23; Agreement between the United Nations and the Government of the Kingdom of Great Britain and Northern Ireland on the Enforcement of Sentences of the International Criminal Tribunal for the Former Yugoslavia, *supra* note 23;

Agreement between the United Nations and Ukraine on the Enforcement of Sentences of the International Criminal Tribunal for the Former Yugoslavia, *supra* note 23.

25 Rules of Procedure and Evidence, International Tribunal for the Prosecution of Persons Responsible for Serious Violations of International Humanitarian Law Committed in the Territory of the former Yugoslavia since 1991 (hereinafter "ICTY"), Rules 18(A), 24.

26 Id. at Rule 19.

27 Id. at Rule 21.

28 Id. at Rule 22.

29 Id. at Rules 30, 31.

30 Id. at Rule 33.

31 Id. at Rule 33*ter*.

32 Id. at Rule 22.

33 Id. at Rule 23*bis*.

34 Id. at Rule 24.

35 Id. at Rule 34.

36 Id.

37 Id. at ICTY, Rule 37.

38 Id. at Rule 39.

39 Id. at Rule 40. As noted in the section below, these powers included the ability to request extradition or transfer of suspects. *See id.* at Rule 40*bis*.

40 Id. at Rule 44.

41 Id. at Rules 108, 108*bis*.

42 Report on the Judicial of the International Criminal Tribunal for the former Yugoslavia and the Prospects for Referring Certain Cases to National Courts (June 2002) 5.

43 Id.

44 *See* Fifteenth Annual Report of the International Tribunal for the Prosecution of Persons Responsible for Serious Violations of International Humanitarian Law Committed in the Territory of the former Yugoslavia since 1991, A/63/210, S/2008/515 (2008); Sixteenth Annual Report of the International Tribunal for the Prosecution of Persons Responsible for Serious Violations of International Humanitarian Law Committed in the Territory of the former Yugoslavia since 1991, A/64/205, S/2009/394 (2009); Seventeenth Annual Report of the International Tribunal for the Prosecution of Persons Responsible for Serious Violations of International Humanitarian Law Committed in the Territory of the former Yugoslavia since 1991, A/65/205, S/2010/413 (2010) 19; Eighteenth Annual Report of the International Tribunal for the Prosecution of Persons Responsible for Serious Violations of International Humanitarian Law Committed in the Territory of the former Yugoslavia since 1991, A/66/210, S/2011/473 (2011) 16; Nineteenth Annual Report of the International Tribunal for the Prosecution of Persons Responsible for Serious Violations of International Humanitarian Law Committed in the Territory of the former Yugoslavia since 1991, A/67/214, S/2012/592 (2012) 16–18.

45 United Nations Security Council, Resolution 1329, S/RES/1329 (2000) para 1.

46 Id. At the same time, the UNSC authorized an increase in the number of already established judicial category members for the ICTR. *See id.* at para 2.

47 Id. at para 3.

48 Id. at Annex I, art. 12.

49 *See* Annual Report of the International Tribunal for the Prosecution of Persons Responsible for Serious Violations of International Humanitarian Law Committed in the Territory of the former Yugoslavia since 1991, A/49/342, S/1994/1007 (1994).

50 *See id.*; Eighth Annual Report of the International Tribunal for the Prosecution of Persons Responsible for Serious Violations of International Humanitarian Law Committed in the Territory of the former Yugoslavia since 1991, A/56/352, S/2001/865 (2001) 5; Eleventh Annual Report of the International Tribunal for the Prosecution of Persons Responsible for Serious Violations of International Humanitarian Law Committed in the Territory of the former Yugoslavia since 1991, A/59/215, S/2004/627 (2004) 5–6.

51 Second Annual Report of the International Tribunal for the Prosecution of Persons Responsible for Serious Violations of International Humanitarian Law Committed in the Territory of the former Yugoslavia since 1991, A/50/365, S/1995/728 (1995) 6; Fifth Annual Report of the International Tribunal for the Prosecution of Persons Responsible for Serious Violations of International Humanitarian Law Committed in the Territory of the former Yugoslavia since 1991, A/53/216, S/1998/737 (1998) 45–50.

52 Second Annual Report of the International Tribunal for the Prosecution of Persons Responsible for Serious Violations of International Humanitarian Law Committed in the Territory of the former Yugoslavia since 1991, A/50/365, S/1995/728, *supra* note 51 at 41–42; Fifth Annual Report of the International Tribunal for the Prosecution of Persons Responsible for Serious Violations of International Humanitarian Law Committed in the Territory of the former Yugoslavia since 1991, A/53/216, S/1998/737, *supra* note 51 at 45–50; Sixth Annual Report of the International Tribunal for the Prosecution of Persons Responsible for Serious Violations of International Humanitarian Law Committed in the Territory of the former Yugoslavia since 1991, A/54/187, S/1999/846 (1999) 25–29; Tenth Annual Report of the International Tribunal for the Prosecution of Persons Responsible for

Serious Violations of International Humanitarian Law Committed in the Territory of the former Yugoslavia since 1991, A/58/297, S/2003/829 (2003) 71.

53 Third Annual Report of the International Tribunal for the Prosecution of Persons Responsible for Serious Violations of International Humanitarian Law Committed in the Territory of the former Yugoslavia since 1991, A/51/292, S/1996/665 (1996) 40–41; Fifth Annual Report of the International Tribunal for the Prosecution of Persons Responsible for Serious Violations of International Humanitarian Law Committed in the Territory of the former Yugoslavia since 1991, A/53/216, S/1998/737, supra note 51 at 45–50.

54 Fourth Annual Report of the International Tribunal for the Prosecution of Persons Responsible for Serious Violations of International Humanitarian Law Committed in the Territory of the former Yugoslavia since 1991, A/53/375, S/1997/729 (1997) 34–35; Fifth Annual Report of the International Tribunal for the Prosecution of Persons Responsible for Serious Violations of International Humanitarian Law Committed in the Territory of the former Yugoslavia since 1991, A/53/216, S/1998/737, supra note 51 at 45–50; Sixth Annual Report of the International Tribunal for the Prosecution of Persons Responsible for Serious Violations of International Humanitarian Law Committed in the Territory of the former Yugoslavia since 1991, A/54/187, S/1999/846, supra note 52 at 25–29.

55 See Seventh Annual Report of the International Tribunal for the Prosecution of Persons Responsible for Serious Violations of International Humanitarian Law Committed in the Territory of the former Yugoslavia since 1991, A/55/273, S/2000/777 (2000) 46–47.

56 Twenty-third Annual Report of the International Tribunal for the Prosecution of Persons Responsible for Serious Violations of International Humanitarian Law Committed in the Territory of the former Yugoslavia since 1991, A/71/263, S/2016/670 (2016); Assessment and Report of Judge Carmel Agius, President of the International Criminal Tribunal for the former Yugoslavia, provided to the Security Council pursuant to paragraph 6 of Security Council Resolution 1534 (2004) (18 November 2006 to 17 March 2017), S/2017/436 (2017).

57 See United Nations Security Council, Resolution 955, S/RES/955 (1994). The UNSC further made Statements "expressing once again its grave concern at the reports indicating that genocide and other systematic, widespread and flagrant violations of international humanitarian law have been committed in Rwanda," and that "determining that this situation continues to constitute a threat to international peace and security." Id. at preamble.

58 Id. at preamble.

59 Id. at para 1.

60 Id. at Annex I.

61 Id. at Annex I art 10.

62 Id. at Annex I arts 11, 12.

63 Id. at Annex art 12.

64 Id. at Annex I art. 13; Rules of Evidence and Procedure, International Criminal Tribunal for Rwanda, Rules 18, 19 (2000).

65 Rules of Evidence and Procedure, International Criminal Tribunal for Rwanda, supra note 64 at Rule 23.

66 See United Nations Security Council, Resolution 1165, S/RES/1165 (1998).

67 See United Nations Security Council, Resolution 1329, S/RES/1329 (2000).

68 See United Nations Security Council, Resolution 1431, S/RES/1431 (2002).

69 See United Nations Security Council, Resolution 1503, S/RES/1503 (2003); United Nations Security Council, Resolution 1534, S/RES/1534 (2004).

70 United Nations Security Council, Resolution 955, S/RES/955 (1994) Annex I art 15; Rules of Evidence and Procedure, International Criminal Tribunal for Rwanda, Rule 37 (2000).

71 United Nations Security Council, Resolution 955, S/RES/955 (1994) Annex I art 15(3).

72 Id. at Annex I art 16.

73 See Report of the International Criminal Tribunal for the Prosecution of Persons Responsible for Genocide and Other Serious Violations of International Humanitarian Law Committed in the Territory of Rwanda and Rwandan Citizens Responsible for Genocide and Other Such Violations Committed in the Territory of Neighbouring Countries between 1 January 1994 and 31 December 1994, A/51/399, S/1996/778 (1996); see also Second Annual Report of the International Criminal Tribunal for the Prosecution of Persons Responsible for Genocide and Other Serious Violations of International Humanitarian Law Committed in the Territory of Rwanda and Rwandan Citizens Responsible for Genocide and Other Such Violations Committed in the Territory of Neighbouring Countries between 1 January 1994 and 31 December 1994, A/52/582, S/1997/868 (1997).

74 Report of the International Criminal Tribunal for the Prosecution of Persons Responsible for Genocide and Other Serious Violations of International Humanitarian Law Committed in the Territory of Rwanda and Rwandan Citizens Responsible for Genocide and Other Such Violations Committed in the Territory of Neighbouring Countries between 1 January 1994 and 31 December 1994, supra note 73; Second Annual Report of the International Criminal Tribunal for the Prosecution of Persons Responsible for Genocide and Other Serious Violations of International Humanitarian Law Committed in the Territory of Rwanda and Rwandan Citizens Responsible for Genocide and Other Such Violations Committed in the Territory of Neighbouring Countries between 1 January 1994 and 31 December 1994, supra note 73; Third Annual Report of the International Criminal Tribunal for the Prosecution of Persons Responsible for Genocide and Other Serious Violations of International Humanitarian Law Committed in the Territory of Rwanda and Rwandan Citizens Responsible for Genocide and Other Such Violations Committed in the Territory of Neighbouring Countries between 1 January 1994 and 31 December 1994, supra note 73 at 3–4; Ninth Annual Report of the International Criminal Tribunal for the Prosecution of

Persons Responsible for Genocide and Other Serious Violations of International Humanitarian Law Committed in the Territory of Rwanda and Rwandan Citizens Responsible for Genocide and Other Such Violations Committed in the Territory of Neighbouring Countries between 1 January 1994 and 31 December 1994, A/59/183, S/2004/601 (2004) p. 19; Tenth Annual Report of the International Criminal Tribunal for the Prosecution of Persons Responsible for Genocide and Other Serious Violations of International Humanitarian Law Committed in the Territory of Rwanda and Rwandan Citizens Responsible for Genocide and Other Such Violations Committed in the Territory of Neighbouring Countries between 1 January 1994 and 31 December 1994, A/60/229, S/2005/534 (2005) p. 3.

75 See Second Annual Report of the International Criminal Tribunal for the Prosecution of Persons Responsible for Genocide and Other Serious Violations of International Humanitarian Law Committed in the Territory of Rwanda and Rwandan Citizens Responsible for Genocide and Other Such Violations Committed in the Territory of Neighbouring Countries between 1 January 1994 and 31 December 1994, supra note 73.

76 See id.

77 See Second Annual Report of the International Criminal Tribunal for the Prosecution of Persons Responsible for Genocide and Other Serious Violations of International Humanitarian Law Committed in the Territory of Rwanda and Rwandan Citizens Responsible for Genocide and Other Such Violations Committed in the Territory of Neighbouring Countries between 1 January 1994 and 31 December 1994, supra note 73 (explaining that two witnesses had been killed during the reporting period, resulting in new coordination efforts with the Rwandan Government).

78 See Third Annual Report of the International Criminal Tribunal for the Prosecution of Persons Responsible for Genocide and Other Serious Violations of International Humanitarian Law Committed in the Territory of Rwanda and Rwandan Citizens Responsible for Genocide and Other Such Violations Committed in the Territory of Neighbouring Countries between 1 January 1994 and 31 December 1994, supra note 73 at 17–19; Ninth Annual Report of the International Criminal Tribunal for the Prosecution of Persons Responsible for Genocide and Other Serious Violations of International Humanitarian Law Committed in the Territory of Rwanda and Rwandan Citizens Responsible for Genocide and Other Such Violations Committed in the Territory of Neighbouring Countries between 1 January 1994 and 31 December 1994, supra note 74 at 19; Report on the completion strategy of the International Criminal Tribunal for Rwanda, S/2008/322 (2008) 13; Report on the completion strategy of the International Criminal Tribunal for Rwanda, S/2011/731 (2011) 15–17; Report on the completion strategy of the International Criminal Tribunal for Rwanda, S/2012/836 (2012) 14–15.

79 See Report on the completion of the mandate of the International Criminal Tribunal for Rwanda as at 15 November 2015, S/2015/884 (2015) 16–19.

80 See United Nations Security Council, Resolution 1503, supra note 69; United Nations Security Council, Resolution 1534, supra note 69.

81 See id.

82 See United Nations Security Council, Resolution 1878, S/RES/1878 (2009).

83 See id.

84 See United Nations Security Council, Resolution 1901, S/RES/1901 (2009).

85 See Completion Strategy for of the International Criminal Tribunal for Rwanda, S/2004/921 (2004); Completion Strategy for of the International Criminal Tribunal for Rwanda, S/2005/336 (2005) 10–11; Report on the completion strategy of the International Criminal Tribunal for Rwanda, S/2008/322 (2008) 12–13.

86 See Completion Strategy for of the International Criminal Tribunal for Rwanda, S/2004/921 (2004) 10; Completion Strategy for of the International Criminal Tribunal for Rwanda, S/2005/336 (2005) 10–11.

87 See Completion Strategy for the International Criminal Tribunal for Rwanda (2004), supra note 86 at 10.

88 See Completion Strategy for the International Criminal Tribunal for Rwanda, S/2007/323 (2007) 9–10, Annex 5; Thirteenth Annual Report of the International Criminal Tribunal for the Prosecution of Persons Responsible for Genocide and Other Serious Violations of International Humanitarian Law Committed in the Territory of Rwanda and Rwandan Citizens Responsible for Genocide and Other Such Violations Committed in the Territory of Neighbouring Countries between 1 January 1994 and 31 December 1994, A/63/209, S/2008/514 (2008) 16–17; Report on the completion strategy for the International Criminal Tribunal for Rwanda, S/2010/259 (2009) 16–17; Report on the completion strategy of the International Criminal Tribunal for Rwanda, S/2011/731 (2011) 15–17; Report on the completion strategy of the International Criminal Tribunal for Rwanda, S/2012/836 (2012) 14–15.

89 See Agreement between the Government of the Republic of Benin and the United Nations on Enforcement of Sentences of the International Criminal Tribunal for Rwanda (1999); Agreement between the Government of the Republic of Mali and the United Nations on Enforcement of Sentences of the International Criminal Tribunal for Rwanda (1999); Agreement between the Government of the Republic of Rwanda and the United Nations on Enforcement of Sentences of the International Criminal Tribunal for Rwanda (1999); Agreement between the Government of the Republic of Senegal and the United Nations on Enforcement of Sentences of the International Criminal Tribunal for Rwanda (2010); Agreement between the Kingdom of Swaziland and the United Nations on Enforcement of Sentences of the International Criminal Tribunal for Rwanda (2000).

90 See Agreement between the United Nations and the Italian Republic on the Enforcement of Sentences of the International Criminal Court for Rwanda (2002); Accord Entre le Gouvernement de la République Française et L'Organisation des Nations Unis Concernant L'Exécution des Peines Prononcées par le Tribunal Pénal International

pour le Rwanda (1999); Agreement between the United Nations and the Government of Sweden on Enforcement of Sentences of the International Criminal Tribunal for Rwanda (2004).

91 *See* Letter dated 17 June 2002 from the Secretary-General addressed to the President of the Security Council, S/2002/678 (2002) (transmitting a report from the ICTY in which it States that there are "certain measures that it believes that it must take if it is to be in a position to achieve the objective of completing all trial activities at first instance by 2008").

92 *See* United Nations Security Council, Resolution 1503, *supra* note 69.

93 *See id.*

94 *See id.*

95 United Nations Security Council, Resolution 1966, S/RES/1966 (2010) preamble.

96 *Id.* at para 1. The MICT Statute establishes that "The Mechanism shall continue the material, territorial, temporal and personal jurisdiction of the ICTY and the ICTR . . . as well as the rights and obligations of the ICTY and the ICTR." Statute of the International Residual Mechanism for Criminal Tribunals (2010) art 1(1).

97 *Id.* at art 1(2), 1(3).

98 *Id.* at art 1(4).

99 *Id.* at art 1(5).

100 United Nations Security Council, Resolution 1966, *supra* note 95 at para 1. For the sake of continuity, each branch was located in the same city as the ICTY and the ICTR, respectively. See Statute of the International Residual Mechanism for Criminal Tribunals, *supra* note 97 at art 3.

101 United Nations Security Council, Resolution 1966, *supra* note 95 at para 9.

102 *Id.* at para 17.

103 Statute of the International Residual Mechanism for Criminal Tribunals, *supra* note 97 at art 4.

104 *Id.* at art 10.

105 *Id.* at art 10.

106 *Id.* at art 11.

107 *Id.* at arts 14, 15.

108 *Id.* at art 16(1).

109 *Id.* at art 29.

110 Rules of Procedure and Evidence, Mechanism for International Criminal Tribunals, MICT/1/Rev.1 (26 September 2016) Rule 10.

111 *Id.* at Rule 75.

112 *See* http://www.unmict.org/en/basic-documents/member-States-agreements, last accessed 5 January 2018 .

113 *See* Agreement between the Mechanism and the Government of the Federal Republic of Germany assuming the enforcement of Mr. Vujadin Popovic's prison sentence (2015); Agreement between the Mechanism and the Government of the Federal Republic of Germany assuming the enforcement of Mr. Ljubisa Beara's prison sentence (2015).

114 Agreement between the United Nations and the Government of the Republic of Benin on Enforcement of Sentences Pronounced by the International Criminal Tribunal for Rwanda or the International Residual Mechanism for Criminal Tribunals (2017).

115 Agreement between the United Nations and the Government of the Republic of Mali on the Enforcement of Sentences Pronounced by the International Criminal Tribunal for Rwanda or the International Residual Mechanism for Criminal Tribunals (2016).

116 *See* Agreement between the United Nations and the Republic of Tanzania concerning the Headquarters of the International Residual Mechanism for Criminal Tribunals (2013); Agreement between the United Nations and the Kingdom of the Netherlands concerning the Headquarters of the International Residual Mechanism for Criminal Tribunals (2015).

117 Progress report of the President of the International Residual Mechanism for Criminal Tribunals, Judge Theodor Meron (for the period from 1 July to 12 November 2012), S/2012/849 (2012) at 4, 6.

118 *Id.* at 5.

119 *Id.* at 8.

120 *See* Progress report of the President of the International Residual Mechanism for Criminal Tribunals, Judge Theodor Meron (for the period from 1 July to 12 November 2012), *supra* note 117; Assessment and progress report of the International Residual Mechanism for Criminal Tribunals, Judge Theodor Meron, for the period from 16 November 2015 to 15 May 2016, S/2016/453 (2016) 9; Assessment and progress report of the International Residual Mechanism for Criminal Tribunals, Judge Theodor Meron, for the period from 16 November 2016 to 15 May 2017, S/2017/434 (2017) p. 12; Fourth annual report of the International Residual Mechanism for Criminal Tribunal, A/71/262, S/2016/669 (2016) 12–13.

121 Assessment and progress report of the International Residual Mechanism for Criminal Tribunals, Judge Theodor Meron, for the period from 23 May 2013 to 15 November 2013, S/2013/679 (2013) 2.

122 *See generally id.*; Assessment and progress report of the International Residual Mechanism for Criminal Tribunals, Judge Theodor Meron, for the period from 16 November 2016 to 15 May 2017, *supra* note 120 at 10.

123 Assessment and progress report of the International Residual Mechanism for Criminal Tribunals, Judge Theodor Meron, for the period from 16 May 2016 to 15 November 2016, S/2016/975 (2016) at 2.

124 Id.

125 *See* ECCC, http://unictr.unmict.org/, last accessed 5 January 2018.

126 *See* Report of the Group of Experts for Cambodia established pursuant to General Assembly resolution 52/135 (18 February 1999) 6–7; United Nations General Assembly, Report of the Secretary-General on Khmer Rouge Trials, A/57/769 (2003) 3–4.

127 *See* Report of the Group of Experts for Cambodia established pursuant to General Assembly resolution 52/135 (18 February 1999), *supra* note 126 at 6–7.

128 *See id.*

129 *See id.* at 7–8; United Nations General Assembly, Report of the Secretary-General on Khmer Rouge Trials (2003), *supra* note 126 3–4.

130 *See* Report of the Group of Experts for Cambodia established pursuant to General Assembly resolution 52/135 (1999), *supra* note 126 at 7–8; United Nations General Assembly, Report of the Secretary-General on Khmer Rouge Trials (2003), *supra* note 126 at 3–4.

131 *See* Report of the Group of Experts for Cambodia established pursuant to General Assembly resolution 52/135 (1999), *supra* note 126 at pt V.

132 *See generally id.*

133 *See* United Nations General Assembly, Report of the Secretary-General on Khmer Rouge Trials (2003), *supra* note 126 at 1; United Nations General Assembly, Report of the Secretary-General on Khmer Rouge Trials (2003), *supra* note 126 at 4.

134 *See* United Nations General Assembly, Report of the Secretary-General on Khmer Rouge Trials (2003), *supra* note 126 at 1, 3.

135 *See* Agreement between the United Nations and the Royal Government of Cambodia Concerning the Prosecution Under Cambodian Law of Crimes Committed during the Period of Democratic Kampuchea (2003).

136 Id. at art 1 ("The purpose of the present Agreement is to regulate the cooperation between the United Nations and the Royal Government of Cambodia in bringing to trial senior leaders of Democratic Kampuchea and those who were responsible for the crimes and serious violations of Cambodian penal law, international humanitarian law and custom, and international conventions recognized by Cambodia that were committed during the period from 17 April 1975 to 6 January 1979.").

137 *See* Law on the Establishment of Extraordinary Chambers in the Courts of Cambodia for the Prosecution of Crimes Committed during the Period of Democratic Kampuchea (as amended 2004) art 3.

138 Agreement between the United Nations and the Royal Government of Cambodia Concerning the Prosecution Under Cambodian Law of Crimes Committed during the Period of Democratic Kampuchea, *supra* note 135 at art 3(2).

139 Id. at art 3(2)(a); *see also* Law on the Establishment of Extraordinary Chambers in the Courts of Cambodia for the Prosecution of Crimes Committed during the Period of Democratic Kampuchea, *supra* note 135 at art 9.

140 Agreement between the United Nations and the Royal Government of Cambodia Concerning the Prosecution Under Cambodian Law of Crimes Committed during the Period of Democratic Kampuchea, *supra* note 137 at art 3(2)(b); *see also* Law on the Establishment of Extraordinary Chambers in the Courts of Cambodia for the Prosecution of Crimes Committed during the Period of Democratic Kampuchea, *supra* note 137 at art 9.

141 *See* Law on the Establishment of Extraordinary Chambers in the Courts of Cambodia for the Prosecution of Crimes Committed during the Period of Democratic Kampuchea, *supra* note 137 at art 14.

142 Agreement between the United Nations and the Royal Government of Cambodia Concerning the Prosecution Under Cambodian Law of Crimes Committed during the Period of Democratic Kampuchea, *supra* note 135 at art 4.

143 Id. at art 5(1).

144 Agreement between the United Nations and the Royal Government of Cambodia Concerning the Prosecution Under Cambodian Law of Crimes Committed during the Period of Democratic Kampuchea, *supra* note 135 at art 6(1); *see also* Law on the Establishment of Extraordinary Chambers in the Courts of Cambodia for the Prosecution of Crimes Committed during the Period of Democratic Kampuchea, *supra* note 137 at art 16.

145 Agreement between the United Nations and the Royal Government of Cambodia Concerning the Prosecution Under Cambodian Law of Crimes Committed during the Period of Democratic Kampuchea, *supra* note 135 at art 6(4).

146 Id. at art 6(4).

147 Id. at art 7; *see also* Law on the Establishment of Extraordinary Chambers in the Courts of Cambodia for the Prosecution of Crimes Committed during the Period of Democratic Kampuchea, *supra* note 137 at art 23.

148 Agreement between the United Nations and the Royal Government of Cambodia Concerning the Prosecution Under Cambodian Law of Crimes Committed during the Period of Democratic Kampuchea, *supra* note 135 at art 8(1); *see also* Law on the Establishment of Extraordinary Chambers in the Courts of Cambodia for the Prosecution of Crimes Committed during the Period of Democratic Kampuchea, *supra* note 137 at ch IX. It should be noted that the Office of Administration did not become operational at the ECCC until 2007. See Report of the Secretary-General, Khmer Rouge trials, A/62/304 (2007) at 2.

149 Agreement between the United Nations and the Royal Government of Cambodia Concerning the Prosecution Under Cambodian Law of Crimes Committed during the Period of Democratic Kampuchea, *supra* note 135 at arts 8(2), 8(3).

150 Agreement between the United Nations and the Royal Government of Cambodia Concerning the Prosecution Under Cambodian Law of Crimes Committed during the Period of Democratic Kampuchea, *supra* note 35 at art 14. The contemplated agreement on services and infrastructure was entered into in 2006. *See* Supplemental Agreement between the United Nations and the Royal Government of Cambodia Auxiliary to the Agreement between the United Nations and the Royal Government of Cambodia Concerning the Prosecution Under Cambodian Law of Crimes Committed during the Period of Democratic Kampuchea, Regarding Utilities, Facilities and Services (2006).

151 Agreement between the United Nations and the Royal Government of Cambodia Concerning the Prosecution Under Cambodian Law of Crimes Committed during the Period of Democratic Kampuchea, *supra* note 135 at arts 15–17.

152 *Id.* at art 20.

153 *Id.* at art 19.

154 *Id.* at art 22.

155 *Id.* at art 23.

156 *See* Supplemental Agreement between the United Nations and the Royal Government of Cambodia, Auxiliary to the Agreement between the United Nations and the Royal Government of Cambodia Concerning the Prosecution Under Cambodian Law of Crimes Committed during the Period of Democratic Kampuchea, Regarding Safety and Security Arrangements, *supra* note 150.

157 *See* Report of the Secretary-General, Khmer Rouge trials, A/67/380 (2012) 2.

158 *See* Report of the Secretary-General, Khmer Rouge trials, A/59/432 (2004) 2–3.

159 *See* Report of the Secretary-General, Khmer Rouge trials, *supra* note 157 at 2; Report of the Secretary-General, Request for a subvention to the Extraordinary Chambers in the Courts of Cambodia, A/68/532 (2013); Report of the Secretary-General, Request for a subvention to the Extraordinary Chambers in the Courts of Cambodia, A/69/536 (2014); Report of the Secretary-General, Request for a subvention to the Extraordinary Chambers in the Courts of Cambodia, A/70/403 (2015). In 2016, the UN Secretary General requested a subvention of over $12 million in order to provide the funding requisite for the ECCC to function in the way envisioned. See Report of the Secretary-General, Khmer Rouge trials, A/71/338 (2016) 2–3.

160 Report of the Secretary-General, Khmer Rouge trials, *supra* note 157 at 9–10.

161 *Id.* at 9–10.

162 *Id.*

163 *Id.* at 10.

164 *Id.* at 11.

165 *See* Peace Agreement between the Government of Sierra Leone and the Revolutionary United Front of Sierra Leone (1999).

166 *See id.*

167 *See* Fifth report of the Secretary-General on the United Nations Mission in Sierra Leone, S/2000/751 (2000) 5–6.

168 *See* Fifth report of the Secretary-General on the United Nations Mission in Sierra Leone, S/2000/751 (2000) 2; United Nations Security Council, Resolution 1315 (2000) p. 2 (providing that the Security Council "[r]equests the Secretary-General to negotiate an agreement with the Government of Sierra Leone to create an independent special court . . . and expresses its readiness to take further steps expeditiously upon receiving and reviewing the report of the Secretary-General . . . [r]ecommends that the subject matter jurisdiction of the special court should include notably crimes against humanity, war crimes and other serious violations of international humanitarian law, as well as crimes under relevant Sierra Leonean law committed within the territory of Sierra Leone . . . the special court should have personal jurisdiction over persons who bear the greatest responsibility for the commission of the[se] crimes").

169 *See* United Nations Security Council, Resolution 1315, *supra* note 168.

170 *See* Fifth report of the Secretary-General on the United Nations Mission in Sierra Leone, *supra* note 168 at 2 (noting that, in the UN mission's interactions with a number of constituencies involved in the justice system, there was "a clear preference . . . for a national court with a strong international component in its organs (judges, prosecutors, defence-counsel and support staff) and for international assistance in funding, equipment and legal expertise"). It should be noted, however, that in the interests of security and other such factors, it was possible to relocate the Special Court either to different sites within Sierra Leone or outside Sierra Leone when necessary. See Agreement between the United Nations and the Government of Sierra Leone on the Establishment of a Special Court for Sierra Leone (2002) art 10.

171 *See* Agreement between the United Nations and the Government of Sierra Leone on the Establishment of a Special Court for Sierra Leone, *supra* note 170.

172 *Id.* at art 1; Statute of the Special Court for Sierra Leone (2002) art 1.

173 *See* Sierra Leone, Special Court Agreement (Ratification) Act (2002) art 11(2).

174 Statute of the Special Court for Sierra Leone, *supra* note 172 at art 11.

175 Agreement between the United Nations and the Government of Sierra Leone on the Establishment of a Special Court for Sierra Leone, *supra* note 171 at art 2(1).

176 *Id.* at art 12.

177 Agreement between the United Nations and the Government of Sierra Leone on the Establishment of a Special Court for Sierra Leone, *supra* note 171 at art 2(2)(c); Statute of the Special Court for Sierra Leone, *supra* note 172 at art 12.

178 Special Court for Sierra Leone, Rules of Procedure and Evidence (2008) Rule 18.

179 Id. at Rule 19.

180 Id. at Rule 23.

181 Agreement between the United Nations and the Government of Sierra Leone on the Establishment of a Special Court for Sierra Leone, supra note 171 at art 3; Statute of the Special Court for Sierra Leone, supra note 172 at art 15; Special Court for Sierra Leone, Rules of Procedure and Evidence, supra note 178 at Rules 30, 39.

182 Agreement between the United Nations and the Government of Sierra Leone on the Establishment of a Special Court for Sierra Leone, supra note 171 at art 3; Statute of the Special Court for Sierra Leone, supra note 172 at art 15.

183 Agreement between the United Nations and the Government of Sierra Leone on the Establishment of a Special Court for Sierra Leone, supra note 171 at art 3.

184 See Statute of the Special Court for Sierra Leone, supra note 172 at art 15(4).

185 Agreement between the United Nations and the Government of Sierra Leone on the Establishment of a Special Court for Sierra Leone, supra note 171 at art 4.

186 Statute of the Special Court for Sierra Leone, supra note 178 at art 16; Sierra Leone, Special Court Agreement (Ratification) Act, supra note 172 at art 3; Special Court for Sierra Leone, Rules of Procedure and Evidence (2008) Rule 33.

187 Statute of the Special Court for Sierra Leone (2002) art 16(4); Special Court for Sierra Leone, Rules of Procedure and Evidence, supra note 178 at Rule 34.

188 Agreement between the United Nations and the Government of Sierra Leone on the Establishment of a Special Court for Sierra Leone, supra note 171 at arts 5, 6; Sierra Leone, Special Court Agreement (Ratification) Act, supra note 172 art 9.

189 Agreement between the United Nations and the Government of Sierra Leone on the Establishment of a Special Court for Sierra Leone, supra note 171 at art 7.

190 Statute of the Special Court for Sierra Leone, supra note 172 at art 22(1).

191 Id. at art 22(1).

192 Id.

193 See Agreement between the Special Court for Sierra Leone and the Government of Finland on the Enforcement of the Sentences of the Special Court for Sierra Leone (2009).

194 See Amended Agreement between the Special Court for Sierra Leone and the Government of the Republic of Rwanda on the Enforcement of the Sentences of the Special Court for Sierra Leone (2009).

195 See Agreement between the Special Court for Sierra Leone and the Government of Sweden on the Enforcement of the Sentences of the Special Court for Sierra Leone (2004).

196 See Agreement between the Special Court for Sierra Leone and the Government of the Kingdom of Great Britain and Northern Ireland on the Enforcement of Sentences of the Special Court of Sierra Leone (2007).

197 Agreement between the Special Court for Sierra Leone and the Government of the Kingdom of Great Britain and Northern Ireland on the Enforcement of Sentences of the Special Court of Sierra Leone, supra note 196 at art 11; Agreement between the Special Court for Sierra Leone and the Government of Sweden on the Enforcement of the Sentences of the Special Court for Sierra Leone, supra note 195 at art 11; Agreement between the Special Court for Sierra Leone and the Government of Finland on the Enforcement of the Sentences of the Special Court for Sierra Leone, supra note 193 at art 12. However, under the agreement with Rwanda, the Special Court will pay additional amounts of the housing and enforcement costs once the prisoner is in Rwanda. Amended Agreement between the Special Court for Sierra Leone and the Government of the Republic of Rwanda on the Enforcement of the Sentences of the Special Court for Sierra Leone, supra note 194 at art 11.

198 See Statute of the Residual Special Court for Sierra Leone (2013) art 1 (providing that the functions of the Residual Special Court are to "maintain, preserve and manage [the] archives . . . provide for witness and victim protection and support; respond to requests for access to evidence by national prosecution authorities; supervise enforcement of sentences; review convictions and acquittals; conduct contempt of court proceedings; provide defense counsel and legal aid for the conduct of proceedings before the Residual Special Court; respond to requests from national authorities with respect to claims for compensation; and prevent double jeopardy.").

199 Id. at art 7.

200 See Constitution of the International Military Tribunal (1945); Judgment of the International Military Tribunal (1945); Joseph E. Persico, Nuremberg: Infamy on Trial (Penguin Random House, 1995).

201 See International Military Tribunal for the Far East (1946); Timothy P. Maga, Judgment at Tokyo: The Japanese War Crimes Trials (University Press of Kentucky, 2001); Yuma Totani, The Tokyo War Crimes Trials: The Pursuit of Justice in the Wake of World War II (Harvard University Press, 2008).

202 About the Court, International Criminal Court, https://www.icc-cpi.int/about, last accessed 5 January 2018.

203 See generally Rome Statute (1998).

204 See generally id.

205 See Crime of Aggression, International Criminal Court, https://www.icc-cpi.int/, last accessed 5 January 2018.

206 See generally Rome Statute, supra note 203.

207 Id. at art 12.

208 Id.

209 Id. at art 13.

210 Id. at art 14.

211 *Id.* at arts 13, 15.

212 *Id.* at arts 13, 16.

213 *Id.* at art 16.

214 *Id.* at art 43; *see also* Comprehensive Report on the Reorganization of the Registry of the International Criminal Court (2016).

215 Rome Statute, *supra* note 203 at art 27.

216 *Id.* at art 28.

217 *Id.* at art 26.

218 *Id.* at art 36; *see also* Report of the International Criminal Court for 2004, A/60/177 pt IV; Report of the International Criminal Court for 2006, A/61/217 pt V.

219 Rome Statute, *supra* note 203 at art 36.

220 *Id.*

221 *Id.*

222 *Id.*

223 *Id.*

224 *Id.* at art 42; *see also* Report of the International Criminal Court for 2004, A/60/177 pt V.

225 *See* Report of the International Criminal Court for 2004, A/60/177 pt V.

226 Rome Statute, *supra* note 203 at art 77.

227 *Id.*

228 *Id.*

229 *Id.* at art 79.

230 *Id.*

231 *See* The Trust Fund for Victims, Annual Report 2016 (2016) p 8.

232 *See Prosecutor v Thomas Lubanga Dyilo*, ICC – 01/04–01/06 (2012); *Prosecutor v Ahmad Al Faqi Al Mahdi*, ICC – 01/12–01/15 (2017).

233 *See Prosecutor v Ahmad Al Faqi Al Mahdi*, *supra* note 232.

234 *See* International Criminal Court, Report on cooperation challenges faced by the Court with respect to financial investigations (2015); *see also* International Criminal Court, Financial Regulations and Rules.

235 International Criminal Court, Report on cooperation challenges faced by the Court with respect to financial investigations (2015).

236 Rome Statute, *supra* note 203; *see also* Report of the International Criminal Court for 2004, A/60/177 pt. VII.

237 Regulations of the Court (2017) Ch 1 Regulation 3.

238 *Id.* at Ch 1 Regulation 4.

239 *Id.*

240 Regulations of the Court, *supra* note 237 at Regulation 41; Rules of Procedure and Evidence (2016) Rules 17, 18.

241 Regulations of the Court, *supra* note 237 at Regulation 41l Rules of Procedure and Evidence, *supra* note 240 at Rules 17, 18.

242 *See* Regulations of the Court, *supra* note 237 at Regulations 77, 81.

243 Regulations of the Prosecutor (2017) Regulations 5, 7 (explaining that the Jurisdiction, Complementarity and Cooperation Division's jurisdiction includes evaluating information, generating reports, assisting in the determination as to whether to pursue an investigation, and assisting the legal arguments throughout the litigation and appellate processes).

244 *Id.* at Regulation 8 (explaining that the Division's jurisdiction includes designing and implementing investigation systems, the protection of those involved in potential investigations, providing investigative support, and assisting with the investigative activities conducted in field offices).

245 *Id.* at Regulation 9 (explaining that the Division's jurisdiction includes assisting with legal advice during investigations, creating litigation plans, implementing litigation plans and conducting court proceedings on behalf of the Prosecution, and coordinating with the Registry).

246 *Id.* at Regulation 10 (explaining that the Service's jurisdiction includes assistance with the OTP's budget, assistance with translation services during litigation and in the field offices, and management of information).

247 *Id.* at Regulation 11 (explaining that the Service's jurisdiction includes providing all manner of legal advice and conducting legal trainings for the OTP).

248 *Id.* at Regulation 12.

249 *See* Report of the International Criminal Court to the United Nations for 2008/09, A/64/356 (17 September 2009) 15–16; Report of the International Criminal Court to the United Nations for 2011/2012 (14 August 2012) 18; *see also* Report of the International Criminal Court for 2006, A/61/217 pt VI; *see also* Report of the International Criminal Court for 2014, A/69/321 pt III; Report of the International Criminal Court for 2010, A/65/313 pt V; Report of the International Criminal Court for 2011, A/66/309 pt IV; Report of the International Criminal Court for 2008, A/63/323 pt VII; Report of the International Criminal Court for 2007, A/62/314 pt VII; Report of the International Criminal Court for 2013, A/68/314 pt IV; Report of the International Criminal Court for 2015/16, A/71/342 pt III; Report of the International Criminal Court for 2015, A/70/350 pt III. It must be noted that the ICC and the UN have executed a separate agreement which clarifies the roles and relationships assigned to each. *See* Negotiated Relationship between the International Criminal

Court and the United Nations. This includes reciprocal representation in each organization's meetings, the exchange of information, and cooperation between the ICC and the UN as organs and the Office of the Prosecutor and the UN. *See id.*

250 Report of the International Criminal Court to the United Nations for 2008/09, *supra* note 249 at 16.

251 Id. at 17; Report of the International Criminal Court for 2014, A/69/321 pt III; Report of the International Criminal Court for 2010, A/65/313 pt V; Report of the International Criminal Court for 2011, A/66/309 pt IV; Report of the International Criminal Court for 2008, A/63/323 pt. VII; Report of the International Criminal Court for 2013, A/68/314 pt IV; Report of the International Criminal Court for 2015/16, A/71/342 pt III.

252 Report of the International Criminal Court to the United Nations for 2008/09, *supra* note 249 at 17.

253 *See* The Trust Fund for Victims, Annual Report 2016, *supra* note 231 at 5.

254 *See id.* at 6.

Chapter 14

Regional organizations

Regional organizations represent a dynamic form of international organization. These entities have grown from several respected organizations to a plethora of large and small geographic groupings that are geared toward general or specific focuses. They exert significant influence well beyond their geographic regions, often have non-regional members, and frequently have overlapping memberships. Regional organizations also tend to foster concepts of future integration and the European Union has accomplished this to the point that it is more correct to refer to it as a supra-national organization. All this over the course of less than a century of international law change and adaptation which has accommodated – and indeed facilitated – the rise of regional organizations.

Organization of American States

Background

The Organization of American States (OAS) is the oldest established regional organization, having been informally founded in 1890 by States throughout the Americas who came together to establish a loose organization.[1] It was concretized as the OAS in 1948, with the purpose of addressing the issues that particularly impact the region, notably poverty and conflict.[2] As decolonization proceeded in the aftermath of World War II, the number of OAS members increased to include the majority of States in the region.[3]

Membership and voting

At present, there are 35 Member States of the OAS, which includes States from North, Central and South America.[4] In addition, there are a number of permanent observer States from around the world, although, as is common practice, these States do not have voting rights in the OAS.[5]

According to the OAS Charter, a Member State can be suspended from its full membership in the event that its democratic government is forcefully overthrown.[6] In order for this to occur, the OAS must first attempt to use its good offices to mediate the restoration of democracy and have these attempts fail.[7] After a failure of this kind, the General Assembly must vote to formally suspend the Member State, using a 2/3 majority voting requirement.[8] Similarly, when the situation in the Member State is cured, the General Assembly must obtain a 2/3 majority vote in order to reinstate it.[9]

In order to settle disputes between Member States, the OAS has established a number of mechanisms, including diplomatic channels, good offices, mediation and negotiations, conciliation, arbitration, and judicial settlement.[10]

Structure

As with the majority of organizations, there is a core set of structural organs that governs and shapes the OAS. The General Assembly, as the supreme organ of the OAS, has extensive powers, including to coordinate the OAS' activities, to ensure cooperation between the OAS and the UN, to control the OAS budget, to oversee and set requirements for the Secretariat, and to set its own rules and procedures.[11] All OAS Member States have one representative and one vote in the General Assembly.[12] In all but specially designated situations, such as votes on rules changes, the General Assembly uses an absolute majority voting system.[13]

The next highest organ in the OAS is the Permanent Council of the organization, which is composed of members from each State, who are to be credentialed as ambassadors.[14] The Permanent Council has the ability to address any measures referred to it by other OAS organs and is available to handle disputes between Member States and use its good offices to assist in their settlement.[15] Additionally, the Permanent Council serves as the oversight mechanism for the General Assembly and other OAS organs, and has the ability to set regulations requiring these organs to carry out their functions as deemed necessary.[16] All drafting of agreements between the OAS, the UN and other organizations is conducted by the Permanent Council and then sent to the General Assembly for ratification.[17]

The OAS uses a specialized organ, the Meeting of Consultation of the Ministers of Foreign Affairs, which is available for general consultation and can be convened as necessary to address specific issues.[18] The group is, as is perhaps self-evident, composed of Ministers of Foreign Affairs of each Member State or, in some instances, a deputy. Within the Meeting of Consultation, there is a specialized Advisory Defense Committee, which is to provide consultation purely on matters of military affairs.[19]

Further, there are two additional councils under the jurisdiction of the General Assembly — the Permanent Council of the Organization and the Inter-American Council for Integral Development.[20] Each of these councils contains a representative from all Member States, typically at the ministerial level.[21] Their general functions are to provide advice, reports, and other methods of consultation to the General Assembly as needed and as appropriate.[22] The councils also have the ability to create sub-organs within their own structures as deemed appropriate.[23]

In addition, the OAS has an Inter-American Juridical Committee, which provides legal consultation to the General Assembly and Member States as to compliance with OAS treaties.[24] The Inter-American Commission on Human Rights is also established in the OAS Charter — more will be said about this organ in Chapter 18.

The administrative and bureaucratic organ of the OAS is the Secretariat, headed by the OAS Secretary General.[25] Under the heading of the Secretariat fall a number of sub-organs and committees that function to administer and provide assistance to other OAS organs or to provide direct assistance to the main Charter-based organs.[26] Also within the ambit of the Secretariat is the Department of Legal Services, which is tasked with providing legal information and opinions to governmental bodies and Member States seeking advice, including those based inside the OAS.[27] A corollary to this is the Department of International Legal Affairs, which assists the OAS in reviewing potential treaties and agreements, evaluating organizational compliance with existing treaties and agreements, and assisting Member States in these evaluations.[28] Another essential aspect of the Secretariat in terms of organizational functioning is the Secretariat for Political Affairs, which includes portfolios such as the Department of Sustainable Democracy and Special Missions, Department of Electoral Cooperation and Observation, and Department of State Modernization and Good Governance.[29]

Another essential entity within the OAS is the Office of the Inspector General (OIG), which was established as an oversight entity for the General Secretariat and the bodies that it works with and supervises.[30] The purpose of the OIG is to ensure that these bodies and the Secretariat comply with the OAS' laws, rules and regulations as well as the rules and regulations generated by these bodies themselves.[31]

Functions

The purposes of the OAS include strengthening peace and security in the region,[32] promoting democracy throughout the region,[33] promoting the use of peaceful settlement of disputes arising between Member States,[34] establishing grounds for collective self-defense between Member States,[35] and promoting the development of Member States in terms of economy, cultural rights and social rights.[36] Further, there are four intersecting essential pillars of focus for the OAS: democracy, human rights, security and development.[37] With this in mind, there are separate oversight mechanisms for each of the pillars.

The Secretariat for Strengthening Democracy has oversight for the Department of Electoral Cooperation and Observation[38] (which, among other things, provides impartial observers for national elections in order to ensure that these elections follow democratic norms and the rule of law), the Department of Sustainable Democracy and Special Missions (which provides assistance with peace settlements, anti-corruption efforts, and educational assistance on political analysis),[39] and the Department of Effective Public Management (which assists with developing and implementing management plans for municipalities and States).[40]

The human rights aspects of the OAS are generally coordinated under the Inter-American Commission on Human Rights.[41] The Secretariat for Multidimensional Security has oversight of the Department to Combat Transnational Organized Crime (developing and implementing plans to address possible security threats),[42] the Secretariat of the Inter-American Committee against Terrorism (which seeks to promote coordination and cooperation between Member States to combat terrorism and potential terrorist threats to one another and in the region),[43] and the Executive Secretariat of the Inter-American Drug Abuse Control Commission.[44] Finally, the Executive Secretariat for Integral Development has oversight of the Department of Human Development and Education, the Department of Economic Development, the Department of Social Inclusion, and the Department of Sustainable Development.[45]

Several specialized organizations that have individualized standing also exist in the OAS structure, a number of which pre-date the formalized existence of the OAS in 1948. Perhaps the most prominent among these is the Pan-American Health Organization (PAHO), which exists in conjunction with the World Health Organization (WHO).[46] The Inter-American Children's Institute "helps create public policy on children in the Americas, promotes the partnership between the State and civil society, and cultivates a critical awareness of the problems affecting children and adolescents in the region."[47] Additionally, the Inter-American Commission of Women, founded in 1928, is the chief policy adviser to the OAS and its organs on broad-based issues of gender, gender-mainstreaming, and including the perspectives of gender into the organization's activities.[48] In a similar vein, the Inter-American Indian Institute was created in 1940 to advance the concerns of indigenous communities throughout the OAS region and to coordinate indigenous communities and Member States, as well as indigenous community concerns at the OAS.[49]

Connected to this is the Inter-American Institute for Cooperation on Agriculture, which promotes the use of sustainable mechanisms and the dissemination of educational practices and techniques in the agricultural sector.[50] On a somewhat more tangential level, the Pan-American Institute of Geography and History is generally focused on providing scientific and technical insights to issues that are very much at the forefront of OAS policy and concerns, such as crime, environmental disasters, and diseases.[51]

Further, the OAS system is comprised of many organs and entities that were authorized and created by the governing bodies of the OAS and function with a great degree of autonomy.[52] These include the Inter-American Committee on Natural Disaster Reduction, the Justice Studies Center of the Americas, the Administrative Tribunal of the OAS,[53] the Pan-American Development Foundation, the OAS Board of External Auditors, the Inter-American Defense Board, and the Inter-American Telecommunications Commission (CITEL).[54]

Each of these entities is structured according to a separate foundational text, setting out a structure of organs and sub-organs intended to facilitate the particular goals of the entity within the larger construct of the OAS system. For example, CITEL operates in a sphere that is, necessarily, larger than the OAS membership and region and, as a result, allows for a broad-based membership that includes UN entities and other international organizations.[55] The Inter-American Defense College, in conjunction with the Inter-American Defense Board, is organizationally focused on providing education and training techniques to those from the military, police and civilian sectors.[56]

One of the many activities undertaken by the OAS to promote the economy, cultural rights and social rights rubric is the creation of the Agreement on Cooperation and Mutual Assistance among Inter-American Port Authorities. The purpose of this agreement and the system of cooperation it enshrines is to assist in developing "port systems that are modern, flexible, economically productive, effective, rapid, and safe, and to facilitate the adoption of an Inter-American port policy attuned to Inter-American integration efforts and measures."[57] The measures provided for in this agreement include the designation of national liaisons for cooperation and dialogue,[58] the availability of experts and others to give information on direct technical assistance.[59]

An essential aspect of OAS functions involves addressing the persistent and changing methods of drug production and trafficking throughout the region. With this in mind, the OAS General Assembly members created the autonomously functioning Inter-American Drug Abuse Control Commission (CICAD).[60] This entity, which continues to function, provides a number of activities and avenues of cooperation and coordination between policy-makers and policing entities involved in issues relating to drugs and drug abuse.[61] In addition, the OAS, through the Permanent Council, approved the development of the Specific Fund for the Inter-American Program of the Action of Rio and endowed it with the ability to provide funding for CICAD's activities.[62]

Under the terms of the establishing statute, CICAD is to be comprised of 11 Member State representatives who are elected by the OAS General Assembly,[63] although Member States not elected may still attend meetings and participate as non-voting entities.[64] Additionally, it is possible for permanent observer States to attend and participate in CICAD's meetings at its discretion.[65] Each CICAD Member State has one vote and the voting requirement for measures at CICAD is a majority.[66] The specific purposes of CICAD include serving as a consultative and advisory body to the OAS, coordinating the responses and activities of entities dealing with drug-related issues, suggesting activities for the OAS to pursue, and providing guidance on future policy activities.[67] In order to provide administrative support, the OAS Secretary General is empowered to designate an officer within the OAS Secretariat to coordinate activities and needs.[68] Additionally, CICAD has the ability to liaise with other international organizations as appropriate and with permanent observer States within the OAS system.[69] Among the topic areas that have consistently been included are money laundering,[70] trafficking,[71] drug use prevention and awareness,[72] legal policy and development,[73] and cooperation with States and international organizations.[74]

In 1999, the OAS General Assembly authorized the creation of the Inter-American Committee against Terrorism (CICTE) in order to "develop cooperation to prevent, combat, and eliminate terrorist acts and activities."[75] As part of this, the Secretariat was intended to include CICTE under its rubric and provide assistance to it for administration and other necessary purposes.[76] In terms of membership, every OAS Member State is eligible to be a member of CICTE[77] and, once this step has been completed, each Member State is required to designate an official national point of contact for the purposes of liaising with CICTE and other Member States.[78]

Among the many sub-organs within the OAS is the Inter-American Council for Integral Development, under the auspices of the General Assembly, dedicated to fostering and coordinating development partnerships.[79] The platform of the Council for Integral Development centers around a number of areas relating to development, such as cooperation efforts, generating policy and discussions, and addressing issues that overlap with development such as health, poverty, and labor rights.[80] Included in the Council for Integral Development structure are a number of subcommittees that assist in the goals of the entity.[81]

African Union

Background

The African Union (AU) is the reincarnation of the Organization of American Unity (OAU), which was founded in 1963.[82] Although the OAU no longer exists as such, it formed the framework upon which the AU has been constructed and provided lessons which have informed the structure and forms of implementation used by the AU. It is for this reason that mention of the OAU as an organization is briefly made below.

The OAU was formed during the precarious political and legal transition of many African States from colonies to independent States in the midst of the Cold War and all the attendant geopolitical impacts.[83] Behind the idea of the OAU was the coordination and harmonization of Member State policies in a number of critical areas to the States and to the region as a whole, particularly politics and diplomacy, economic issues, infrastructural issues – especially those relating to communications and transportation – education and culture, health, science and technology development, and regional security and defense coordination.[84] Under the organizational system created in 1963, the OAU was comprised of four principal organs – the Assembly of Heads of State and Government, Council of Ministers, General Secretariat, and Commission of Mediation, Conciliation and Arbitration.[85]

The Assembly functioned as the supreme organ and each Member State had a seat and a vote on it. The functions of the Assembly were focused on creating policy harmonization, assisting in the functioning of the OAU and its policies, and coordinating the policies and activities of the OAU per se.[86] While technically the Assembly was to be comprised of heads of States or governments, there was the possibility for another individual with the appropriate credentials to represent them at Assembly meetings.[87] Voting for any measure other than a procedural issue required a 2/3 majority in order to be approved.[88]

As a general matter, the Council of Ministers was comprised of Foreign Ministers from each OAU Member State, although a Member State could designate another minister where appropriate – for example, where an issue under review related to a ministerial specific portfolio.[89] Each representative at the Council of Ministers had one vote and all measures required a simple majority to pass.[90] The OAU was administratively governed by the Secretariat, the head of which was the Secretary General, who was appointed by the Assembly.[91] As suggested by the title, the Commission of Mediation, Conciliation and Arbitration functioned as the dispute settlement body for Member States in the OAU system.[92]

In 1999, in the face of a changing world and political system that was no longer bi-polar, the Member States of the OAU decided to recreate an organization that would protect and promote the African continent in a new world.[93] This was done with a full recognition that the OAU had served many of its purposes, notably those relating to ending colonization and assisting in the decolonization process.[94] Similarly, the OAU noted that there were new or changing issues within the region itself, such as escalating civil conflicts that also spilled over into other Member States, the unregulated exploitation of natural resources exploitation of labor resources, and trafficking.[95] The merger of the OAU into the AU took 2 years and, ultimately, in 2001 the transition finally occurred. Currently, there are 55 AU Member States, comprising the majority of States in Africa.[96]

Membership and voting

Each Member State has one vote in the Assembly, and generally votes require a consensus.[97] In the event that the government of a Member State is created or superseded as a result of an undemocratic process, such as a coup or rigged election, the Member State is to be suspended from full AU membership.[98]

Structure

There are a number of organs established in the Constituent Act of the AU, some of which are obvious continuations, in some form, of the prior organs of the OAU. The highest organ in the AU is the Assembly of the Union, which is comprised of one member from each State – who is to be either the head of State or an appointed representative.[99] The Assembly's powers include making decisions as needed, receiving and addressing reports and information from other AU organs, creating new organs as appropriate, admitting new members, monitoring compliance of Member States with AU policies, and addressing emergency and conflict situations, particularly those occurring within the region.[100]

The AU's Executive Council is comprised of the Ministers of Foreign Affairs of each Member State.[101] The Executive Council is tasked with developing policies on a number of topic areas, particularly "foreign trade; energy, industry and mineral resources; food, agricultural and animal resources, livestock production and forestry; water resources and irrigation; environmental protection, humanitarian action and disaster response and relief; transport and communications; insurance; education, culture, health and human resources development; science and technology; nationality, residency and immigration matters; social security, including the formulation of mother and child care policies, as well as policies relating to the disabled and the handicapped."[102]

Within the Executive Council's ambit there are currently three established committees: the Ministerial Committee on Candidature; the Ministerial Committee on the Challenges of Ratification/Accession and Implementation of the OAU/AU Treaties; and the Ad-hoc Ministerial Committee on the Review of Scale of Assessment.[103] The Committee on Candidature seeks to assist AU Member States in engagement with international law and the international community through promotion of their involvement in governance mechanisms for international organizations.[104] The Committee on Ratification/Accession is in the process of complete implementation and seeks to assist Member States in full involvement in and achievement of the goals of AU instruments.[105] Finally, the Committee on Scale of Assessment evaluates the monetary assessments made to AU Member States in order to determine their appropriateness and feasibility.[106]

The Secretariat function of the AU is carried out by the AU Commission, which also has the ability to speak for and represent the AU on the international level.[107] It is headed by a Chair, who is elected by the Executive Council and assisted by staff members working in specialized portfolios.[108] Further, the Permanent Representative Committee works with the Executive Council and the Assembly to provide oversight of the quotidian needs of the organs, particularly in terms of budgeting and financial matters for the AU.[109] Each Member State has a representative on the Permanent Representative Committee as well as an internal Bureau which functions as the secretariat entity for the Committee.[110]

Additionally, the AU uses a number of specialized committees having unique portfolios, namely the Committee on Rural Economy and Agricultural Matters, the Committee on Monetary and Financial Affairs, the Committee on Trade, Customs and Immigration Matters, the Committee on Industry, Science and Technology, Energy, Natural Resources and Environment, the Committee on Transport, Communications and Tourism, the Committee on Health, Labor and Social Affairs, and the Committee on Education, Culture and Human Resources.[111] The membership of these committees is comprised of ministers with portfolios/specializations in the applicable topics.[112] The committees are tasked with providing information and consultation to the Executive Council and other organs of the AU.[113]

At the time of the transition between the OAU and the AU, the utility of a number of organs that had existed within the OAU system was evaluated. Typically, these forms of evaluation focused on the past utility of the organs as well as the potential for future use on the same or similar issues as part of the AU structure and goals.[114] In the majority of cases, these determinations were left to the future Secretary General of the AU, although they contained strong recommendations.[115]

The Constitutive Act of the AU establishes a Pan-African Parliament, a Court of Justice and a set of financial institutions, namely the African Central Bank, the African Monetary Fund and the African Investment Bank, although each of these is meant to be defined in detail in subsequent protocols.[116] The Pan-African Parliament currently serves as a largely advisory and consultative entity for the AU and associated organs rather than a fully functioning Parliament in the sense of that used by the European Union.[117] In the future, it is anticipated that the Parliament will be a vehicle toward integration of Member States' laws and rules and that it will continue to provide policy advice to the AU as an organization.[118] Under the rules of the Parliament, each Member State is allotted five representatives.[119]

The Peace and Security Council exists to address – and attempt to prevent – conflicts and threats to peace and security in the region.[120] The extent of these abilities ranges from a variety of forms of dispute settlement measures and methods, as well as the ability to use diplomacy to resolve issues and to craft peacekeeping and similar peace enforcement mechanisms.[121] Decisions regarding the use of sanctions in any form, post-conflict measures such as disarmament, and the use of humanitarian activities are within the jurisdiction of this Council.[122]

There are only 15 members on the Peace and Security Council, who are selected by the Executive Council and officially confirmed by the Assembly.[123] In the interests of preserving a power balance within the region overall, the seats on the Peace and Security Council are apportioned by sub-regions, meaning that there are separate allotments for East Africa, West Africa, North Africa, South Africa, and Central Africa in the amount of three seats per area.[124] In order to facilitate the work of the Peace and Security Council there exists a dedicated Secretariat for its operations.[125] Included in the system of the Peace and Security Council is an extensive network of committees and sub-committees that reflect the highly specialized nature of the work assigned to it.[126]

Additionally, there is an Economic, Social and Cultural Committee (ECOSOCC), which is under the jurisdiction of the Assembly.[127] ECOSOCC serves as an advisory and consultative entity only and does not have the ability to create binding AU laws or regulations.[128] This is reflected in the fact that there are no Member States who serve as members of ECOSOCC and instead it is composed of representatives from civil society throughout the AU region and from the African diaspora.[129] Included in the functions of ECOSOCC is the requirement to foster an environment in which law is generally respected and concepts of human rights and good governance can take root, both at the organizational level and at the level of Member States.[130] To facilitate the work of ECOSOCC and its utility to the AU as a whole, it is divided into a number of committees and sub-committees, each with specific expertise.[131]

Functions

The stated objectives of the AU are to foster unity and peace between Member States and on the African continent,[132] to facilitate integration of economies and political systems within the continent,[133] to present a united form of protection for the African continent against outside threats,[134] to "promote peace, security, and stability on the continent,"[135] to encourage democracy, good governance and the ability of the public to participate in the political process within Member States,[136] to promote human rights,[137] to promote sustainable development throughout the continent and within the Member States,[138] and to ensure cooperation in order to protect against and fight diseases.[139]

Recently, and in the wake of the transition from the global focus on the MDGs to the SDGs, the AU crafted "Agenda 2063: The Africa We Want," intended as a short and long-term roadmap for the future of the AU and its individual Member States.[140] Agenda 2063 includes eight topics that can be used for the continent to meet its future goals. These topics are: 1) Peace and Stability (including good governance, democracy, human rights, and security); 2) Food Security (including agricultural development, market access for African goods, food self-sufficiency, climate chance and natural resources); 3) Economic Integration (including development of infrastructure within Member States and the continent and effective use of natural resources located throughout the continent); 4) Africa's Human Capacity (including education, health resources, water access, and protection of vulnerable groups); 5) Women's and Youth Empowerment (including development of education and status for both groups); 6) Resource Mobilization (including the creation of effective resource management techniques and financing for development); 7) Effective Communication (including institutional and governmental communications as well as the development of communications infrastructure); and 8) Institutional Capacity (including the creation of mechanism for AU development of relationships with other organizations).[141]

Association of Southeast Asian Nations

Background

The Association of Southeast Asian Nations (ASEAN) has always worked as a regional organization, although the region that it works in has expanded significantly since its founding in 1967. At the time it was founded, ASEAN was comprised of Indonesia, Malaysia, the Philippines, Singapore and Thailand.[142] Over the years, as the governmental, social and legal structures of some States in the region have changed, Brunei, Vietnam, Laos and Burma have also been admitted as members.[143]

While ASEAN was created in 1967, it was not until 2008 that an official Charter for ASEAN was implemented – in the meantime ASEAN was governed by a series of agreements and accords between the Member States. Although ASEAN as such was without a formalized foundational text, from 1976 onward there was an established ASEAN Secretariat and Secretary General.[144] This organ was founded in recognition of the growing requirements of the ASEAN system as such at the time and the need for a coordinating body that could represent ASEAN within the larger world community.[145] The Secretariat was given a home in Indonesia,[146] where it enjoyed a very basic functional immunity,[147] and the Secretary General's post rotated every two years between the Member States in alphabetical order.[148] Underneath the post of Secretary General was a system of deputies and other staff members, each assigned to different portfolio groups.[149]

Membership and voting

The key to understanding ASEAN is to understand that it works through the consensus of the members both in terms of formal voting and overall policy creation. This should be remembered as the policy areas in which ASEAN works are examined and also can help explain why the ASEAN free trade area that has been touted for many years has yet to fully emerge.

Structure

ASEAN works through an established set of organs and a series of committees and groups. The key policy-making body for ASEAN is the ASEAN Summit, which is comprised of the heads of State of each Member State or their designated representatives.[150] The ASEAN Summit can either decide issues on its own or decide issues that are referred to it by the other sub-organs and entities within ASEAN.[151] It further has the ability to send issues to the appropriate sub-organs for deliberation or the provision of further information and is empowered to take action when there is an urgent need[152] – for example during a military crisis or following a natural disaster. Additionally, the ASEAN Summit alone has the ability to appoint the head of the Secretariat and to dissolve sub-organs.[153]

The ASEAN Coordinating Council consists of the foreign ministers of each State – or their equivalents – and meets at least twice a year.[154] The Coordinating Council works to coordinate ASEAN Summit meetings and also to ensure that the policy decisions made by the ASEAN Summit are in fact carried out properly by the Member States.[155] It also has the same coordination task for the actions and decisions of other ASEAN committees and councils.[156] Further, while the selection of the Secretary General is left to the ASEAN Summit, the selection of the deputy Secretaries General and other key Secretariat officials falls to the Coordinating Council.[157]

There are three designated ASEAN Community Councils within the Charter: the ASEAN Political-Security Community Council; the ASEAN Economic Community Council; and the ASEAN

Socio-Cultural Community Council.[158] The work of each of the Community Councils is reinforced by the creation of National Councils with the same portfolios.[159] This means that the Community Councils have the dual role of creating policies at the overall regional level and then overseeing the National Councils to ensure that these policies are actually being enforced at the Member State level.[160] There is no particular governmental portfolio attached to membership in a Community Council – instead, representatives are simply designated by the Member States.[161]

Further, there are ASEAN Sectorial Ministerial Bodies, which may be established as needed to provide more information on any relevant topics to the ASEAN governing organs.[162] Also at the national level are the ASEAN National Secretariats, which are responsible for coordinating regional and domestic policies and practices and serving as the voice of ASEAN at the domestic level and vice versa.[163]

In addition, there is the Committee of Permanent Representatives to ASEAN, which assists in the coordination of the multiple ASEAN organs and is able to provide guidance to the ASEAN Secretariat as needed.[164] While there is no specific ASEAN human rights court, there is the ASEAN Human Rights Body, the exact contours and legal parameters of which have yet to be fully created.[165] This means that there is uncertainty at present as to whether a human rights court will be created for ASEAN members in the future. And finally, the Charter creates the ASEAN Foundation, which is meant to work at a general level to promote ASEAN, its works and its goals throughout the region and internationally.[166]

Functions

The 2008 Charter sets out the policy goals and functions of the organization as well as the various organs that comprise its governing structure. It defines the purposes of the organization as: 1) the maintenance of regional peace and security, with particular focus on dialogue-based resolution of conflicts; 2) the promotion of regional cooperation in economic areas, security, politics, and socio-cultural areas; 3) the continued status of the region as being free of nuclear weapons; 4) the promotion of democratic values; 5) the creation of a single market similar to that created by the EU; 6) the elimination of poverty domestically and in the region; 7) the promotion of good governance, human rights and freedoms within the region and Member States; 8) the ability to respond to collective threats to the region, including organized crime and terrorism; 9) the promotion of sustainable development and environmental preservation; 10) the promotion of education; 11) the promotion of access to justice particularly for those groups that have traditionally been denied access to justice, such as women and indigenous groups; 12) the elimination of illicit drugs within the ASEAN region; 13) the encouragement of citizen participation in government and society; 14) the promotion of cultural knowledge and understanding throughout the region; and 15) the promotion of transparency through ASEAN and its organs.[167]

In order to achieve these purposes, the Charter sets out a number of principles for ASEAN and its members, including: 1) respect for sovereignty, especially State territorial sovereignty, and non-interference with internal State matters; 2) collective responsibility for maintaining peace and security in the region; 3) renunciation of the use of force if it is in violation of international law; 4) peaceful settlement of disputes; 5) the use of the rule of law and good governance mechanisms rather than force or corruption; 6) actively deciding not to use policy or other decisions in a way that would harm other members of ASEAN – this can include issues such as environmental harm through transboundary haze, as well as purely military actions; 7) respect for human rights, other cultures, languages and imprimaturs of culture; and 8) use of trade policies that better the entire region, both within the region and with external trading partners.[168]

Moving on to the workings of ASEAN, the organization's policy areas are clustered along the same topics as the Community Councils: 1) Political-Security; 2) Economics; and 3) Socio-Cultural. The Political-Security Community encompasses many broad policy areas, namely law and legal development (both within the region and domestically), defense and military cooperation and support, and the prevention of transnational crime such as the illicit drug trade and corruption.[169]

The proliferation of nuclear weapons has been a concern for ASEAN Member States over the course of decades. This manifested itself in the 1995 Treaty on the Southeast Asia Nuclear Weapons Free Zone, which reiterated the policy beliefs of Member States and also created a formalized mechanism for the implementation of its terms. Under the terms of this Treaty, the Commission for the Southeast Asia Nuclear-Weapon-Free Zone was established as the oversight body.[170] Each signatory to the treaty was apportioned one representative on the Commission and the Commission was encouraged to meet in conjunction with ASEAN meetings, although no set schedule of meeting requirements was provided.[171] This flexibility can be seen as important given the unpredictable nature of the topic regulated.

Within the Commission is the Executive Committee, which functions as a technical body, providing expertise on issues related to nuclear weapons and associated technologies and providing opinions as necessary.[172] Each Commission Member State also has a representative with one vote on the Executive Committee.[173] In the event of a significant occurrence involving nuclear energy of some sort, the affected Member State is required to submit a report to the Executive Committee[174] and, should there be a request by a Member State for a fact-finding mission, it must be approved by the Executive Committee as well.[175]

In 2007, an important aspect of the Political-Security element of ASEAN's functions was enacted in the form of the ASEAN Convention on Counter Terrorism.[176] While much of the focus of this Convention is necessarily political, significant elements of it reflect the need for law enforcement and security agencies in the region to collaborate in fighting terrorism issues while also preserving Member State sovereignty.[177] At the same time, the Convention seeks to ensure that Member State protections of and respect for human rights are maintained.[178]

The Economic Community encompasses a number of often diverse policy areas. Perhaps obviously, this is the Community under which the free trade area negotiations have been conducted and are still in the process of being conducted.[179] Additionally, however, the Community includes energy policy coordination and implementation (very important, particularly for developing States), food, agriculture and forestry policies, finance and investment, minerals[180] and natural resources (particularly gemstones, many of which are located in Member States), science and technology, tourism, telecommunications,[181] and transportation.[182] While many of these may superficially seem frivolous, they are in fact quite important to creating and maintaining viable societies and infrastructures that allow for short- and long-term growth in developing States.

ASEAN has established several entities to promote the growth and dissemination of important aspects of economic development throughout the region. For example, in 1999 the ASEAN Centre for Energy came into existence as an independent legal entity with the purpose of "initiating, coordinating and facilitating national as well as joint and collective strategies on energy."[183] The governance of the Centre was intended to be separate from the organs of ASEAN itself and instead under the supervision of a Governing Council comprised of senior energy-related leaders from the Member States.[184] On a quotidian basis, operations of the Centre were placed under the aegis of an Executive Director and associated staff.[185]

Finally, the Socio-Cultural Community encompasses the following policy areas: arts and culture (including historical preservation and indigenous culture), disaster management coordination (including for natural disasters such as tsumanis), education, the environment and sustainable development,[186] transboundary haze,[187] health care and health systems, labor standards and rights, information and communications, rural development, the development of science and technology, protection and promotion of the standing of women, and also of children.[188]

Under the terms of the ASEAN Agreement on Disaster Management and Emergency Response, Member States are to coordinate their strategies and policies regarding all aspects of disasters and disaster management, including early warning systems, loss reduction in disasters, information exchanges, standing arrangements for emergency responses, enacting disaster and emergency-related laws and regulations, and the provision of information on disasters and emergencies to neighboring Member States.[189] In order to provide governance, the Agreement establishes a Conference of the Parties assisted by the ASEAN Secretariat.[190] Additionally, the Agreement provides for the ASEAN Co-ordinating Centre for Humanitarian Assistance, which is intended to provide assistance to Member States in disaster situation.[191]

In addition, ASEAN has negotiated free trade agreements with other States and regional entities, expanding its relationships and reach as an organization.[192] However, what must be remembered is that each of these free trade agreements has to be ratified by each ASEAN Member State and is not automatically binding upon signature.

Further, in 1994 ASEAN Member States agreed to the formation of the ASEAN Fund.[193] The Fund was intended to be financed by initial and ongoing contributions from the Member States, with the purpose of assisting the funding of existing projects as well as seed funding for new endeavors within the Member States and the ASEAN area.[194]

Finally in 2000 the ASEAN Member States established the ASEAN Foundation to promote the external knowledge of ASEAN as an entity and to promote cooperation and interaction between members.[195] These internal measures are to be geared toward the promotion of development and mutual assistance, primarily through education, culture and social related activities.[196] Governance of the Foundation is to be conducted through a Board of Trustees that contains a representative from each ASEAN Member State and representatives from the internal ASEAN organizational leadership.[197]

European Union – the regional exception

Background

As with many organizations, the membership of the European Union has grown since it was created. Additionally, as with other regional organizations, the goals have shifted over time, in this case from market integration to political integration. However, unlike most regional organizations, it has progressed to become supranational in legal character and function. Under the terms of the Treaty on European Union, it is stipulated that there are areas in which the EU has exclusive competence and jurisdiction, while it is possible for there to be shared competence between the EU and the Member States for other areas.[198] Topics of particular importance in which the EU holds exclusive jurisdiction include foreign policy (notably foreign trade and investment agreements), aspects of security policy, and the creation of a common defense policy.[199]

The EU also has the ability to provide support to Member States on a number of other topics where appropriate and requested.[200]

Membership and voting

Seeking membership in the EU is an all-encompassing process through which the applicant is required to bring its laws, regulations and policies into standardization with the laws, regulations and policies of the EU itself.[201] Even if this is completed, the EU Member States must still vote to admit a State as a new member and this is no guarantee of success.[202] Currently there are 28 EU Member States, with five in the process of adapting their laws and systems with the intent of joining the EU and several others considered as potential candidates for the future.[203] Even among States not in the process of seeking membership, there are existing relationships with the EU as an organization that have established stronger ties, greater unity and increased functional liaisons across a number of fields. Some forms of these relationships include established customs unions,[204] allowing the use of the euro as a primary form of currency,[205] taxation agreements,[206] and well-established diplomatic methods and mechanisms of cooperation.[207]

Structure and Functions

The EU is comprised of many governmental structures and organs. What must be remembered is that the EU is a supranational entity, meaning that, once law is made at the Parliamentary level, with very few exceptions it becomes binding on all Member States without those States ratifying it at the domestic level. This is because, in order to join the EU, Member States agree to cede part of their sovereignty to the EU governing structure as a whole. This is quite different from regional organizations, where the treaties created require the separate approval of each Member State in order to become binding on the Member State.

At perhaps the most theory-based of governing levels within the EU is the European Council. Although all Member States are represented on the European Council, and there is a set system for such things as meeting times and the sharing of the Presidency, when the European Council makes policy decisions it does so in the form of non-binding decisions.[208] Thus, while Statements from the European Council carry a great deal of weight they do not actually apply directly to any regional or domestic legal system.[209]

Binding decisions within the EU are made by several institutions depending upon the topic and the level of degree to which the decisions are to be implemented. The main body with such authority is the European Parliament. Members of the European Parliament are directly elected by their State in proportion to the number of Parliamentary seats allotted to each Member State.[210] This allotment is based on the overall population of each Member State; however, there is a minimum number of representatives for each Member State and a maximum number of representatives for each Member State.[211] As is the case in national parliamentary bodies, when the European Parliament convenes, the Members of Parliament sit along party lines rather than by Member State represented.[212] The European Parliament is literally the parliamentary body for Europe and, as such, its resolutions and decisions are binding on all Member States.[213] Perhaps one of the most important legislative functions of the European Parliament is its responsibility to pass a budget for the European Union.[214]

The European Parliament functions using a large committee structure, in which legislation and proposed legislation receive evaluation and – potentially – approval before receiving a full Parliamentary vote. At present, the committees are: 1) Foreign Affairs; 2) Human Rights; 3) Security and Defence; 4) Development; 5) International Trade; 6) Budgets; 7) Budgetary Control; 8) Economic and Monetary Affairs; 9) Employment and Social Affairs; 10) Environment, Public Health and Food Safety; 11) Industry, Research and Energy; 12) Internal Market and Consumer Protection; 13) Transport and Tourism; 14) Regional Development; 15) Agriculture and Rural Development; 16) Fisheries; 17) Culture and Education; 18) Legal Affairs; 19) Civil Liberties, Justice and Home Affairs; 20) Constitutional Affairs; 21) Women's Rights and Gender Equality; and 22) Petitions.[215] The European Parliament and the European Council share different levels of co-legislation abilities depending on the issues involved.[216] In some instances, they share a requirement to approve a measure before it can become law, while in others Parliament has a consultative role.[217]

The second decision-making body within the EU is the Council of the European Union. The Council of the European Union is not directly elected by the Member States and instead is composed of the current ministers for each Member State.[218] A minister is selected to be sent to a Council session according to the particular topic under discussion, so, for example, the finance ministers will attend when there is a financial issue at hand. The Council of the European Union works with the Parliament to ensure that certain measures which have been recommended by other EU bodies are fully implemented.[219] It has specific responsibilities in terms of entering into international agreements on behalf of the EU and also in terms of formulating economic policy for the EU.[220]

Although foreign affairs and military policy are areas which each EU Member State controls as it sees fit, the Council of the European Union will still provide guidance and direction for these policies within the EU as a whole; however, this is non-binding on the Member States.[221]

Finally, the European Commission also has some decision-making authority and is tasked with generating recommendations and directives as to implementation of policies that have been enacted by the Parliament.[222] Each Member State designates a Commissioner, who will sit on the European Commission for a five-year term regardless of the topic at hand.[223] In addition to enforcement, the European Commission is also tasked with oversight and creating recommendations for ways to change or update enacted EU policies.[224] Further, the designated President of the European Commission is the EU's representative at international organizations of which the EU is either a member or an observer.[225]

Additionally, in order to provide for openness and transparency throughout the European system of governance and bureaucracy, the EU has established the institution of the European Ombudsman.[226] This officer, selected by the European Parliament and assisted by a dedicated staff, has the authority to receive complaints from individuals, corporations or other entities in Europe regarding any aspect of EU activity.[227] In order to ensure the impartiality of the Ombudsman as an institution, it is created as an independent entity within the EU system.[228] Ultimately, when the Ombudsman finds an occurrence of maladministration and the implicated entity has been given time to respond, he is required to forward his findings to the European Parliament for review and potential action.[229]

The Treaty on European Union establishes two advisory entities for the EU governing bodies — the Economic and Social Committee, comprised of representatives from "organizations of employers, of the employed, and of other parties representatives of civil society, notably socio-economic civil, professional and cultural areas", and the Committee of the Regions, comprised of "representatives of regional and local bodies who either hold a regional or local authority electoral mandate or are politically accountable to an elected assembly."[230] Further, a number of European agencies exist under the rubric of the EU system, ranging from those in the fields of aviation, banking and finance, food and agriculture, disease control and prevention, environmental protection, energy, and intellectual property.[231]

There are two major European Courts — the Court of Human Rights (to be discussed further in Chapter 18) and the European Court of Justice (ECJ). The ECJ is the judicial entity to which a Member State or, more rarely, an individual, will go when there is an allegation that the EU or a Member State is not enforcing its required laws and rules.[232] Each Member State of the EU has a judge on this body and there is also a quasi-prosecutor in the form of an advocate general.[233]

As an institution, the ECJ has become immensely popular and well-used, resulting in a problematic backlog of cases and issue in case completion time that has been documented on numerous occasions.[234] Although the foundational text of the ECJ allows for the creation of a number of chambers, and the ECJ is permanently in session, demand has still risen beyond the expected capacity of the ECJ's structure.[235] This issue has reached the point where it necessitates intervention by the EU system and, accordingly, several measures have been enacted.[236] Beginning in 2016, judges from specialized tribunals within the EU system, such as the European Union Civil Service Tribunal, became transferable to the General Court of the ECJ to ease the burden on currently sitting judges.[237]

The ECJ has been home to a curious and important instance of the ability of an organization to submit itself to another organization's jurisdiction. In this instance, the issue involved was the EU's accession to the European Convention for the Protection of Human Rights and Fundamental Freedoms and the subsequent question whether this would subject the EU as an organizational entity to the jurisdiction of the ECJ.[238] Ultimately, this question was answered in the affirmative and, over time, this has been concretized as an accepted fact.[239]

Additional, more specialized courts, such as the Court of Auditors, serve particularized functions within the EU system.[240] In the context of the Court of Auditors, each Member State has a representative, and together these representatives are tasked with conducting the annual audit of the EU.[241] While the auditors have the ability to audit all aspects of the EU system's account and activities, it is also possible for there to be specialized sub-chambers within the Court to handle particular technical issues.[242]

Further, there are a number of financial entities in the EU structure, as well as committees that oversee the environment and human rights issues. It is essential to remember that being a member of the EU does not automatically mean that a State is part of the eurozone. While all members of Eurozone are also members of the EU, membership in the EU does not guarantee approval for membership in the Eurozone, as this must be approved by the eurozone governing body.

As part of the EU financial structure there exists the Eurogroup, an informal entity comprised of ministers from eurozone Member States, that was created to allow for open dialogue in a less structured environment that promotes confidentiality.[243] Although the Eurogroup functions in an open manner, it was endowed with several areas in which it was required to work, notably the economic situation and economic outlook for the eurozone, the creation of budgetary policy, and the potential for and application of structural reforms in monetary policy and the eurozone.[244]

In terms of structure, the Eurogroup is headed by a President, chosen from among the ministers, who serves a two-year term during which he is meant to oversee the administration of the Eurogroup and answer questions relating to economic and financial matters from the members.[245] A good deal of background policy and research within the Eurogroup structure is conducted by the Eurogroup Working Group, which is comprised of financial and other members of the national governments of eurozone Member States.[246] Administration of the Eurogroup is a joint endeavor of several existing European Union entities.[247]

In addition to these entities within the EU system, there exists the European Atomic Energy Community (EURATOM), which is a highly specialized organ tasked with implementing and overseeing the requirements created by the EU to address the responsible generation of energy through nuclear power.[248] The terms of the Treaty required that EURATOM conduct research, policy oversight, assist in generating investment in responsible nuclear power and associated industries, establishing safety and health regulations for nuclear industries and those working in them, ensuring the safety and security of nuclear materials needed for the associated industries, and liaising with other States and international organizations on nuclear issues.[249] Included in the provisions governing EURATOM are extensive disciplinary and sanctions systems which are intended to ensure proper oversight capabilities for the organization.[250] Within EURATOM, there is a designated Agency to engage in monitoring and oversight activities, and also an advisory Scientific and Technical Committee.[251]

Brexit

It has become common for us to add new words to the English language by combining several words together to form catch phrases, just as we have become used to adding emoticons to texts. Usually these phrases are meant to be somewhat light-hearted and have very little meaning beyond the obvious. However, the recently coined term "Brexit" has a deeper and more important meaning than the simple combination of "Britain" and "exit" and threatens to undermine or, at the very least, significantly alter the EU as well as the UK and the international community.

Britain was among the first members of the EU and had a deep-seated association with the previous iterations of European organizations.[252] Recently, however, the push to become free from the EU has focused on far more than retaining the pound. There were many reasons for this, from the economic (i.e. concerns over losing jobs to those from the EU who are permitted work in the UK) to political (i.e. concerns over losing control of the law-making process as it reflects the will of the British people) to the judicial (i.e. concerns over being required to follow aspects of EU law that might have been unpopular in the UK) to the regulatory (i.e. concerns over the ability to implement environmental and other regulations without harming industries, etc).[253]

Ultimately, a referendum on whether the UK should remain in the EU was held on 23 June 2016.[254] By a vote of approximately 52 per cent to 48 per cent, voters supported leaving the EU, resulting in the then-Prime Minister and anti-Brexit campaigner, David Cameron, resigning and calling for elections of a new Parliament.[255] These elections yielded a coalition group that reflected a pro-Brexit agenda and a new Prime Minister, Theresa May.[256] The next few months saw court challenges regarding which organ was the appropriate one to officially approve withdrawal from the EU.[257] The final determination was that this decision belonged to Parliament rather than the Prime Minister and her government alone, and Parliament held a highly anticipated vote in which it approved leaving the EU.[258] As a result, on 29 March 2017, Prime Minister May formally declared that Article 50 would be triggered and the UK would begin negotiations for it to leave the EU within two years.[259] This was followed by the UK's chief representative to the EU presenting the notice of withdrawal under Article 50 to Donald Tusk, the current President of the European Council, as required under Article 50.[260]

The course of the Brexit negotiations is an unfolding one, and likely will continue to be for some time. However, according to the policy guidelines issued by the European Union, the bedrock principle for the negotiation process is that it must result in an entire agreement that covers all necessary issues rather than piecemeal attempts at cobbling one together.[261] Further, the EU has made it clear that other Member States are not to negotiate separate agreements with Britain while the EU negotiations for Brexit are ongoing.[262] The caveat to this is that the negotiation process itself is intended to progress through several phases, each addressing different issues and legal agreements.[263]

Membership in the EU requires its members to cede more sovereignty than States cede to other international or even regional organizations. Practically, this means that there are two main sources of law in each Member State – laws created by the national parliament and laws created at the European Parliament level, transferring automatically to each Member State except in certain limited instances (notably national security, public safety and public health).[264]

In addition, there are two courts for European laws, the ECJ and, as discussed in upcoming chapters regarding human rights, the European Court of Human Rights.[265] These courts determine matters between Member States themselves and between Member States and individuals located within them or affected by their activities.[266] Unlike international courts, which have limited enforcement abilities due to sovereignty issues, decisions made by both of these courts have more concrete applications because Member States have agreed to give up part of their sovereignty for the applicability of European laws.

Importantly, the Treaty of Lisbon – the newest iteration of the EU foundational texts – contains a provision under which Member States retain the ability to leave the EU provided they follow a set of procedural requirements both domestically and at the EU level.[267] Under the now infamous Article 50[268]:

1. Any Member State may decide to withdraw from the Union in accordance with its own constitutional requirements.

2. A Member State which decides to withdraw shall notify the European Council of its intention. In the light of the guidelines provided by the European Council, the Union shall negotiate and conclude an agreement with that State, setting out the arrangements for its withdrawal, taking account of the framework for its future relationship with the Union. That agreement shall be negotiated in accordance with Article 218(3) of the Treaty on the Functioning of the European Union. It shall be concluded on behalf of the Union by the Council, acting by a qualified majority, after obtaining the consent of the European Parliament.

3. The Treaties shall cease to apply to the State in question from the date of entry into force of the withdrawal agreement or, failing that, two years after the notification referred to in paragraph 2, unless the European Council, in agreement with the Member State concerned, unanimously decides to extend this period.

4. For the purposes of paragraphs 2 and 3, the member of the European Council or of the Council representing the withdrawing Member State shall not participate in the discussions of the European Council or Council or in decisions concerning it. A qualified majority shall be defined in accordance with Article 238(3)(b) of the Treaty on the Functioning of the European Union.

5. If a State which has withdrawn from the Union asks to rejoin, its request shall be subject to the procedure referred to in Article 49.

Article 50 is clear that the EU treaties will cease to be binding on the UK after the date on which withdrawal is officially completed.[269] However, prior to this there will be many issues involved in the negotiations for Brexit, a number of which are currently under negotiation as of the time of writing. Issues that must be addressed are myriad, and below is a description of only the peripheral layers involved.

Since the European project started out as an economic and industrial union, arguably the most complex and numerous issues to be determined relate to these issues. Although the United Kingdom has not joined the eurozone and does not use the euro, it is still heavily involved in the banking and financial services sector as a provider and consumer at the public and private levels. As such, determinations regarding the status of banking, foreign banks in each entity and foreign bank account holders will be extremely difficult and yet essential to the tenor of Brexit.[270] Issues also exist in the sphere of free trade agreements and treaties because the EU has acted as the chief architect and signatory of such instruments for all States, including the UK, and the UK must extricate itself and enter into new instruments at the same time that the EU and other States involved must determine how to proceed with the existing obligations.[271] Trade and customs-related issues are similarly implicated and must be determined at a relatively early stage in order to ensure that there is a continuum of these relationships.[272]

Additionally, there is the issue of amounts potentially owed by the United Kingdom to the EU as part of winding down its obligations to the organization. The requirement to pay any such amount, and the amount itself, is highly controversial and has yet to be decided; however, it could easily serve as a lynchpin to undo agreements that would allow the completion of Brexit.[273] Investments from European Union sources in the UK and the ability of UK entities to continue benefiting from funds allocated by entities such as the European banks for certain projects are also unclear at this point.[274] At the same time, taxation issues are highly important and contentious, potentially having an effect on everything from finances to tourism.[275]

Legal commitments and the applicability of everything from acts of the European Parliament to decisions of the ECJ to decisions of the European Court of Human Rights in the UK and the ability of cases pending before these bodies to proceed with any binding authority are additional matters which need clarification as part of Brexit negotiations.[276] Security plays a similarly important role in these issues, as the intertwining of the UK and EU through organizations such as EUROPOL and the EU's peacekeeping and peace enforcement activities present essential determination and policy considerations.[277]

Climate change, including participation of public and private entities in the EU carbon trading schemes, methods of climate finance, and the involvement of the UK in calculating Paris Agreement emissions standards and their implementation are serious concerns. This is particularly the case since new calculations and implementation plans would be required for multiple States and organizations.[278]

While all of these issues – and many more – are still in flux, it is clear that there will also be a need to redefine the terms of the EU as an entity in the wake of Brexit. When each new Member State joined the EU after its creation, revisions to the foundational text and other texts that relate to voting were necessary in order to maintain the balance of the voting structure. In all likelihood, the opposite will happen when the EU loses a Member State, meaning that an additional revision will be necessary for the EU structure.

Conclusions

Regional organizations abound, with a number of cooperative or competitive goals and functions, yet it is notable that these entities include States with myriad traditions and practices. One of the key lessons of this chapter is the utility of regional organizations that cut across different systems of politics, law and geography. In this way, regional organizations harness and illustrate the power of smaller organizations to generate commonality and cross-cutting goals even in situations where Member States share divergent norms.

There is a deep-seated need for these forms of organization within the current international community characterized by the tensions of globalization's potential and its conflicts and discord. In such a climate, regional organizations are able to fill voids in the interlocking yet often unconnected areas of law and policy that affect various States and regions.

Further, increased power in regional organizations has highlighted – and continues to highlight – the legitimacy of regional actors as receptacles of legal and political force and presence within the international community. This reiterates the flexibility of international organizations in their dealings with regional organizations and regional organizations in their ability to adapt to the needs of their constituencies and articulate them in a meaningful way using the law of international organizations.

A seeming threat to the role of regional organizations as a matter of international law and participation in the international community comes from the example of Brexit in the European Union. There is no doubt that Brexit has created, and will continue to create, areas of uncertainty and potential weakness within the EU. However, the lessons of this chapter suggest that there is a strong need for regional organizations to adopt and incorporate adaptability into their structures in order to ensure durability and longevity even in the wake of membership withdrawal. This is not, of course, a new possibility in the international organizations setting, as is evident by the current debate regarding the potential withdrawal of Member States from the ICC.

Notes

1 Our History, OAS, http://www.oas.org/en/about/our_history.asp, last accessed 7 January 2018.
2 Id.
3 Id.
4 Who We Are, OAS, http://www.oas.org/en/about/who_we_are.asp, last accessed 7 January 2018. It should be highlighted that, at present, Cuba is still a member although it has largely been suspended from participation since its revolution and there are some restrictions on the ability of Venezuela to participate due to its human rights and political climate.
5 Id.
6 Charter of the Organization of American States (1948) art 9.
7 Id. at art 9(a).
8 Id. at art 9(b).
9 Id. at art 9(f).
10 Id. at arts 24, 25.
11 Id. at art 54.
12 Id. at art 56.
13 Id. at art 59.

14 *Id.* at art 80; Rules of Procedure of the Permanent Council (2016) art I.

15 OAS Charter, *supra* note 6 at arts 82, 84, 85; Rules of Procedure of the Permanent Council art IV.

16 OAS Charter, *supra* note 6 at art 91(b); Rules of Procedure of the Permanent Council, *supra* note 15 at art V.

17 OAS Charter, *supra* note 6 at art 91(d).

18 *Id.* at art 61.

19 *Id.* at arts 66–69.

20 *Id.* at art 70.

21 *Id.* at art 71.

22 *Id.* at art 73.

23 *Id.* at art 77.

24 *Id.* at art 99.

25 Annual Report of the Secretary General, January–December 2007 (2007) 16; Annual Report of the Secretary General, January–December 2012 (2012); Annual Report of the Secretary General, January–December 2013 (2013); Annual Report of the Secretary General, January–December 2014 (2014); Annual Report of the Secretary General, January–December 2015 (2015).

26 Annual Report of the Secretary General, January–December 2007, *supra* note 25 at 16; Annual Report of the Secretary General, January–December 22, *supra* note 25; Annual Report of the Secretary General, January–December 2013, *supra* note 25; Annual Report of the Secretary General, January–December 2014, *supra* note 25; Annual Report of the Secretary General, January–December 2015, *supra* note 25.

27 Annual Report of the Secretary General, January–December 2007, *supra* note 15 at 18; Annual Report of the Secretary General, January–December 2009 (2009) 15–21; Annual Report of the Secretary General, January–December 2012, *supra* note 26; Annual Report of the Secretary General, January–December 2013, *supra* note 25; Annual Report of the Secretary General, January–December 2014, *supra* note 25; Annual Report of the Secretary General, January–December 2015, *supra* note 25.

28 Annual Report of the Secretary General, January–December 2007, *supra* note 25 at 90; Annual Report of the Secretary General, January–December 2012, *supra* note 25; Annual Report of the Secretary General, January–December 2013, *supra* note 25; Annual Report of the Secretary General, January–December 2014, *supra* note 25; Annual Report of the Secretary General, January–December 2015, *supra* note 25.

29 Annual Report of the Secretary General, January–December 2007, *supra* note 25 at 34–42; Annual Report of the Secretary General, January–December 2009, *supra* note 27 at 33–40; Annual Report of the Secretary General, January–December 2012, *supra* note 25; Annual Report of the Secretary General, January–December 2013, *supra* note 25; Annual Report of the Secretary General, January–December 2014, *supra* note 25; Annual Report of the Secretary General, January–December 2015, *supra* note 25.

30 Annual Report of the Office of the Inspector General for the Period January 1 to December 1 2006 (2006) 1; Annual Report of the Office of the Inspector General for the Period January 1 to December 31, 2007 (2007); Annual Report of the Office of the Inspector General for the Period January 1 to December 31, 2008, OEA/Ser.G, CP/doc.4440/09 (2009) 1–5; Annual Report of the Office of the Inspector General for the Period January 1 to December 31, 2009 (2009) 1–4; Annual Report of the Office of the Inspector General for the Period January 1 to December 31, 2010 (2010) 1–3; Annual Report of the Office of the Inspector General for the Period January 1 to December 31, 2011 (2011) 1–3; Annual Report of the Office of the Inspector General for the Period January 1 to December 31, 2012 (2012) 1–3; Annual Report of the Office of the Inspector General for the Period January 1 to December 31, 2014 (2014) 1–5; Annual Report of the Office of the Inspector General for the Period January 1 to December 31, 2015 (2015) 1–5.

31 *See* Annual Report of the Office of the Inspector General for the Period from January 1 to December 31, 2005 (2005) 1. Specifically, the OIG is empowered to "provide [] an ongoing program for appraising performance, maintaining financial integrity and measuring compliance with operational regulations, policies and procedures, safeguarding of assets, economy and efficiency in the use of resources, as well as effectiveness of program and project management for achieving desired objectives." *Id. See also* Annual Report of the Office of the Inspector General for the Period from January 1 to December 31, 2016 (2016) 3–4.

32 OAS Charter, *supra* note 6 at art 2(a).

33 *Id.* at art 2(b).

34 *Id.* at art 2(c).

35 *Id.* at art 2(d).

36 *Id.* at art 2(f), (g).

37 What We Do, OAS, http://www.oas.org/en/about/what_we_do.asp, last accessed 8 January 2018.

38 Secretariat for Strengthening Democracy, OAS, http://www.oas.org/en/spa/deco/, last accessed 8 January 2018.

39 Department of Sustainable Democracy and Special Missions, OAS, http://www.oas.org/en/spa/dsdsm/, last accessed 8 January 2018.

40 Department for Effective Public Management, OAS, http://www.oas.org/en/spa/depm/, last accessed 8 January 2018.

41 Inter-American Commission on Human Rights, OAS, http://www.oas.org/en/iachr/, last accessed 8 January 2018.

42 Department of Public Security, OAS, http://www.oas.org/dsp/english/cpo_sobre.asp last accessed 8 January 2018.

43 Inter-American Committee Against Terrorism, OAS, http://www.oas.org/en/sms/cicte/, last accessed 8 January 2018.

44 Inter-American Drug Abuse Control Commission, OAS, http://cicad.oas.org/Main/default_ENG.asp, last accessed 8 January 2018.

45 Executive Secretariat for Integral Development, http://www.oas.org/en/about/sedi.asp, last accessed 8 January 2018.

46 See Annual Report of the Secretary General, January–December 2007, supra note 25 at 96; Annual Report of the Secretary General, January–December 2010 (2010); Annual Report of the Secretary General, January–December 2012, supra note 25; Annual Report of the Secretary General, January–December 2013, supra note 25; Annual Report of the Secretary General, January–December 2014, supra note; Annual Report of the Secretary General, January–December 2015, supra note 25. PAHO began life as the Pan-American Sanitary Bureau in 1924, changing names and forms several times before it became affiliated with the WHO in 1949. See Pan-American Sanitary Code (1924); Constitution of the Pan-American Health Organization (1949).

47 See Annual Report of the Secretary General, January–December 2007, supra note 25 at 99; see also Annual Report of the Secretary General, January–December 2009, supra note 27 at 92–94; Annual Report of the Secretary General, January–December 2010, supra note 46; Annual Report of the Secretary General, January–December 2012, supra note 25; Annual Report of the Secretary General, January–December 2013, supra note 25; Annual Report of the Secretary General, January–December 2014, supra note 25; Annual Report of the Secretary General, January–December 2015, supra note 25.

48 See Annual Report of the Secretary General, January–December 2007, supra note 25 at 103; see also Annual Report of the Secretary General, January–December 2009, supra note 27 at 95–96; Annual Report of the Secretary General, January–December 2010, supra note 46; Annual Report of the Secretary General, January–December 2012, supra note 25; Annual Report of the Secretary General, January–December 2013, supra note 25; Annual Report of the Secretary General, January–December 2014, supra note 25; Annual Report of the Secretary General, January–December 2015, supra note 25. See also Agreement between the Organization of American States and the Inter-American Commission of Women (1933).

49 See Annual Report of the Secretary General, January–December 2007, supra note 25 at 110; Annual Report of the Secretary General, January–December 2009, supra note 27; Annual Report of the Secretary General, January–December 2010, supra note 46; Annual Report of the Secretary General, January–December 2012, supra note 25; Annual Report of the Secretary General, January–December 2013, supra note 25; Annual Report of the Secretary General, January–December 2014, supra note 25; Annual Report of the Secretary General, January–December 2015, supra note 25.

50 See Annual Report of the Secretary General, January–December 2007, supra note 25 at 112; Annual Report of the Secretary General, January–December 2009, supra note 27; Annual Report of the Secretary General, January–December 2010, supra note 46; Annual Report of the Secretary General, January–December 2012, supra note 25; Annual Report of the Secretary General, January–December 2013, supra note 25; Annual Report of the Secretary General, January–December 2014, supra note 25; Annual Report of the Secretary General, January–December 2015, supra note 25.

51 See Annual Report of the Secretary General, January–December 2007, supra note 25 at 106–109; Annual Report of the Secretary General, January–December 2009, supra note 27; Annual Report of the Secretary General, January–December 2010, supra note 46; Annual Report of the Secretary General, January–December 2012, supra note 25; Annual Report of the Secretary General, January–December 2013, supra note 25; Annual Report of the Secretary General, January–December 2014, supra note 25; Annual Report of the Secretary General, January–December 2015, supra note 25.

52 See Annual Report of the Secretary General, January–December 2007, supra note 25 at pt V; Annual Report of the Secretary General, January–December 2009, supra note 27 at 90–91; Annual Report of the Secretary General, January–December 2010, supra note 46; Annual Report of the Secretary General, January–December 2012, supra note 25; Annual Report of the Secretary General, January–December 2013, supra note 25; Annual Report of the Secretary General, January–December 2014, supra note 25; Annual Report of the Secretary General, January–December 2015, supra note 25.

53 See Annual Report of the Secretary General, January–December 2007, supra note 25 at pt V; Annual Report of the Secretary General, January–December 2009, supra note 27; Annual Report of the Secretary General, January–December 2010, supra note 46; Annual Report of the Secretary General, January–December 2012, supra note 25; Annual Report of the Secretary General, January–December 2013, supra note 25; Annual Report of the Secretary General, January–December 2014, supra note 25; Annual Report of the Secretary General, January–December 2015, supra note 25.

54 See Annual Report of the Secretary General, January–December 2007, supra note 25at pt V; Annual Report of the Secretary General, January–December 2009, supra note 27; Annual Report of the Secretary General, January–December 2010, supra note 46; Annual Report of the Secretary General, January–December 2012, supra note 25; Annual Report of the Secretary General, January–December 2013, supra note 25; Annual Report of the Secretary General, January–December 2014, supra note 25; Annual Report of the Secretary General, January December 2015, supra note 25.

55 *See* 2013 Annual Report, Inter-American Telecommunication Committee (2013) 3–4; 2011 Annual Report, Inter-American Telecommunication Committee (2011) 4; 2005 Annual Report, Inter-American Telecommunication Committee (2005) 3; 2008 Annual Report, Inter-American Telecommunication Committee (2008) 5; 2007 Annual Report, Inter-American Telecommunication Committee (2007) 3.

56 *See* Regulation of the Inter-American Defense College (2015).

57 *See* Agreement on Cooperation and Mutual Assistance among Inter-American Port Authorities (1995) art 2.

58 Id. at ch III.

59 Id. at ch V.

60 *See* Establishment of the Inter-American Drug Abuse Control Commission (CICAD) and Approval of Its Statute, AG/RES.813 (XVI-0/86) (1986).

61 *See id.*

62 *See* CP/RES.482 (709–87) (1987).

63 Establishment of the Inter-American Drug Abuse Control Commission (CICAD) and Approval of Its Statute, *supra* note 60 at art 3.

64 Id. at art 5.

65 Id. at art 7.

66 Id. at art 11.

67 Id. at art 20.

68 Id. at arts 23, 24.

69 Annual Report of the Inter-American Drug Abuse Control Commission (CICAD) to the General Assembly of the Organization of American States at its Thirteenth Annual Session, OEA/Ser.L/XIV.2.26, CICAD/doc.1023/99 rev.3 (2000) 27–28.

70 Id.; Annual Report of the Inter-American Drug Abuse Control Commission (CICAD) to the General Assembly of the Organization of American States at its Thirty-sixth Annual Session, OEA/Ser.1.L/XV.2.38, CICAD/doc.1474/05 rev.2 (2006) 3; Annual Report of the Inter-American Drug Abuse Control Commission (CICAD) to the General Assembly of the Organization of American States at its Thirty-ninth Regular Session, OEA/Ser.L/XV.2.45, CICAD/doc.1725/09 rev.2 corr.1 (2009) 13–14; Annual Report of the Inter-American Drug Abuse Control Commission (CICAD) to the General Assembly of the Organization of American States at its Fortieth Regular Session, OEA/Ser.L/XV.2.47, CICAD/doc.1784/10 rev.4 (2010) 12–13.

71 Annual Report of the Inter-American Drug Abuse Control Commission (CICAD) to the General Assembly of the Organization of American States at its Thirteenth Annual Session, *supra* note 69 at 3; Annual Report of the Inter-American Drug Abuse Control Commission (CICAD) to the General Assembly of the Organization of American States at its Thirty-sixth Annual Session, *supra* note 70 at 14–15.

72 Annual Report of the Inter-American Drug Abuse Control Commission (CICAD) to the General Assembly of the Organization of American States at its Thirteenth Annual Session, *supra* note 69 at 7–21; Annual Report of the Inter-American Drug Abuse Control Commission (CICAD) to the General Assembly of the Organization of American States at its Thirty-sixth Annual Session, *supra* note 70 at 7–13; Annual Report of the Inter-American Drug Abuse Control Commission (CICAD) to the General Assembly of the Organization of American States at its Thirty-ninth Regular Session, *supra* note 70 at 6–12; Annual Report of the Inter-American Drug Abuse Control Commission (CICAD) to the General Assembly of the Organization of American States at its Fortieth Regular Session, *supra* note 70 at 7–9.

73 Annual Report of the Inter-American Drug Abuse Control Commission (CICAD) to the General Assembly of the Organization of American States at its Thirty-sixth Annual Session, *supra* note 70 at 13–14.

74 2010 Annual Report of the Inter-American Drug Abuse Control Commission to the Forty First Regular Session of the General Assembly of the Organization of American States, OEA/Ser.L/XV.2.49, CICAD/doc.1861/11 rev.1 (2011) 7.

75 OAS General Assembly, Hemispheric Cooperation to Prevent, Combat and Eliminate Terrorism, AG/RES. 1650 (XXIX-O/99) (1999) para 3.

76 Id. at para 4.

77 Amendments to the Statute of the Inter-American Committee Against Terrorism, AG/RES 2010 (XXXIV-O/04) (2010) art 4.

78 Id. at art 6; *see also* Rules of Procedure of the Inter-American Committee Against Terrorism (CICTE), OEA/Ser.L/X.2.5, CICTE/doc.4/05 rev.1 (2005).

79 Annual Report of the Secretary General, January–December 2007, *supra* note 25 at 12; Annual Report of the Secretary General, January–December 2010, *supra* note 46; Annual Report of the Secretary General, January–December 2012, *supra* note 25; Annual Report of the Secretary General, January–December 2013, *supra* note 25; Annual Report of the Secretary General, January–December 2014, *supra* note 25; Annual Report of the Secretary General, January–December 2015, *supra* note 25.

80 Annual Report of the Secretary General, January–December 2007, *supra* note 25 at 13; Annual Report of the Secretary General, January–December 2010, *supra* note 46; Annual Report of the Secretary General, January–December 2012, *supra* note 25; Annual Report of the Secretary General, January–December 2013, *supra* note 25; Annual Report of the Secretary General, January–December 2014, *supra* note 25; Annual Report of the Secretary General, January–December 2015, *supra* note 25.

81 Annual Report of the Secretary General, January–December 2007, *supra* note 25 at 13; Annual Report of the Secretary General, January–December 2010, *supra* note 46; Annual Report of the Secretary General, January–December 2012, *supra* note 25; Annual Report of the Secretary General, January–December 2013, *supra* note 25; Annual Report of the Secretary General, January–December 2014, *supra* note 25; Annual Report of the Secretary General, January–December 2015, *supra* note 25.

82 African Union, https://www.au.int/, last accessed 8 January 2018.

83 *See generally* Organization of African Unity Charter (1963).

84 *See id.* at art II(2).

85 *Id.* at art VII.

86 *Id.* at art VIII.

87 *Id.* at art IX.

88 *Id.* at art X.

89 *Id.* at art XII.

90 *Id.* at art XIV.

91 *Id.* at art XVI.

92 *Id.* at art XIX.

93 *Id.*

94 *See* Algiers Declaration, Organization of African Union, AHG/Decl.1 (XXXV) (1999).

95 *See id.*

96 Member States, AU, https://www.au.int/web/en/memberStates, last accessed 8 January 2018.

97 Constituent Act of the African Union (2000) art 7.

98 *Id.* at art 30.

99 *Id.* at art 6.

100 *Id.* at art 9.

101 *Id.* at art 10.

102 *Id.* at art 13.

103 The Executive Council, African Union, https://au.int/organs/council, last accessed 8 January 2018.

104 *Id.*

105 *Id.*

106 *Id.*

107 African Union Commission, African Union, https://au.int/organs/commission, last accessed 8 January 2018.

108 *Id.*

109 Permanent Representative Committee, African Union, https://au.int/organs/prc, last accessed 8 January 2018.

110 *Id.*

111 Constituent Act of the African Union, *supra* note 97 at art 14.

112 *Id.* at art 14.

113 *Id.* at art 15.

114 *See* Decision on the Place of the African Population Commission (APC) in the African Union, AHG/Dec. 176 (XXXVIII) (2002); Decision on the Place of the OAU Labour and Social Affairs Commission in the African Union, AHG/Dec. 177 (XXXVIII) (2002); Decision on the World Solidarity and Poverty Reduction Fund, AHG/Dec. 178 (XXXVIII) (2002); Decision on the Control of Arterial Hypertension in Africa, AHG/Dec. 179 (XXXVIII) (2002).

115 *See* Decision on the Place of the African Population Commission (APC) in the African Union, *supra* note 114; Decision on the Place of the OAU Labour and Social Affairs Commission in the African Union, *supra* note 114; Decision on the World Solidarity and Poverty Reduction Fund, *supra* note 114; Decision on the Control of Arterial Hypertension in Africa, *supra* note 114.

116 Constituent Act of the African Union, *supra* note 97 at arts 17–19.

117 Pan-African Parliament, African Union, https://au.int/organs/pap, last accessed 8 January 2018.

118 *Id.*

119 *Id.*

120 *See* Peace and Security Council, African Union, https://au.int/organs/psc, last accessed 8 January 2018.

121 *See id.*

122 *See id.*

123 *See id.*

124 *See id.*

125 *See id.*

126 *See id.*

127 Constituent Act of the African Union, *supra* note 97 at arts 21, 22.

128 Economic, Social and Cultural Council, African Union, https://au.int/organs/ecosocc, last accessed 8 January 2018.

129 *Id.*

130 *Id.*

131 *Id.*

132 Constituent Act of the African Union, *supra* note 97 at art 3(a).

133 *Id.* at art 3(b).

134 *Id.* at art 3(d).

135 *Id.* at art 3(f).

136 *Id.* at art 3(g).

137 *Id.* at art 3(h).

138 *Id.* at art 3(j).

139 *Id.* at art 3(n).

140 Agenda 2063, African Union (2015).

141 *Id.* These areas build off the African Union's articulated aspirations for the future, which are "1) A prosperous Africa based on inclusive growth and sustainable development; 2) an integrated continent, politically united based on the ideals of Pan Africanism and the vision of Africa's Renaissance; 3) an Africa of good governance, democracy, respect for human rights, justice and the rule of law, 4) a peaceful and secure Africa; 5) an Africa with a strong cultural identity, common heritage, values and ethics; 6) an Africa, whose development is people-driven, relying on the potential of African people, especially its women and youth, and caring for children; 7) Africa as a strong, united, resilient and influential global player and partner." *See id.* at 2.

142 About ASEAN, http://asean.org/asean/about-asean/overview/, last accessed 10 January 2018.

143 *Id.*

144 *See* Agreement on the Establishment of the ASEAN Secretariat (1976).

145 *See id.* at preamble.

146 *See id.* at art I (2).

147 *See id.* at art XI ("The Host Country shall grant to the Secretariat, the Secretary General and the Staff such privileges and immunities as may be necessary for the performance of their duties and functions.").

148 *See id.* at art III (1).

149 *See id.* at art IV. The description of staff functions was subsequently amended to provide greater detail. *See* Protocol Amending the Agreement on the Establishment of the ASEAN Secretariat (1989); Protocol Amending the Agreement on the Establishment of the ASEAN Secretariat (1992); Protocol Amending the Agreement on the Establishment of the ASEAN Secretariat (1997).

150 Agreement on the Establishment of the ASEAN Secretariat (1976) art 7.

151 *See id.*

152 *See id.*

153 *See id.*

154 *See id.* at art 8.

155 *See id.*

156 *See id.*

157 *See id.*

158 *See id.* at art 9.

159 *See id.*

160 *See id.*

161 *See id.*

162 *See id.* at art 10.

163 *See id.* at art 13.

164 *See id.* at art 12.

165 *See id.* at art 14.

166 *See id.* at art 15.

167 ASEAN Charter (2008) art. I.

168 *See id.* at art II.

169 ASEAN Political-Security Community, ASEAN, http://asean.org/asean-political-security-community/, last accessed 10 January 2018.

170 Treaty on the Southeast Asia Nuclear Weapons Free Zone (1995) art 8.

171 *Id.*

172 *Id.* at art 9.

173 *Id.*

174 *Id.* at art 11.

175 *Id.*

176 ASEAN Convention on Counter Terrorism (2007).

177 *See id.*

178 *See id.*

179 ASEAN Economic Community, ASEAN, http://asean.org/asean-economic-community/, last accessed 10 January 2018.

180 Efforts at cooperation in this area bolster already-existing precedents for such policy coordination in the field of minerals. For example, in 2005 the ASEAN Ministerial Meeting on Minerals was created as a discussion and policy-generating entity comprised of appropriate ministers from each ASEAN Member State. *See* Ministerial Understanding on ASEAN Cooperation in Minerals (2005). In conjunction with this, the ASEAN Senior

Officials Meeting on Minerals (ASOMM) was established as an additional entity that would serve as the operational – rather than dialogue-based – portion of the Ministerial Meeting on Minerals. Id. at art 3. This included the ability to liaise with other ASEAN-based entities and to authorize new working groups within ASEAN the minerals governance system. See id.

181 Similar to the Ministerial Understanding on ASEAN Cooperation in Minerals, in 2001 the ASEAN ministers created a loose sub-organ relating to the regulation and development of telecommunications technologies. See Ministerial Understanding on ASEAN Cooperation in Telecommunications and Information Technology (2001). While there was a general agreement on periodic leadership meetings among ASEAN members, the ASEAN Telecommunications Senior Officials Meeting was created as the operational element of the Telecommunications Ministers Meeting, including generating information and policy suggestions and liaising with both the public and private sectors involved in the telecommunications industry. Id. at art 3. These entities received assistance from the ASEAN Secretariat to carry out their functions. Id. at art 4.

182 For the transportation sector, in the aftermath of the GATT agreement revisions in 1994 and the creation of a larger World Trade Organization system, the ASEAN Member States crafted a separate agreement providing for regulation of transportation sectors and goods in transit. See ASEAN Framework Agreement on the Facilitation of Goods in Transit (1995). With this in mind, the Member States were required to designate a National Transit Transportation Coordinating Council at the domestic level and these Councils were to coordinate at the organizational level through the Transit Transport Coordinating Board. Id. at art 29.

183 Agreement on the Establishment of the ASEAN Centre for Energy (1998) arts 1, 2.

184 Id. at art 3.

185 Id. at art 4.

186 For example, in 2005, ASEAN created the Agreement on the Establishment of the ASEAN Centre for Biodiversity, to "facilitate cooperation and coordination among the members of ASEAN, and with relevant national governments, regional and international organizations, on the conservation and sustainable use of biological diversity and the fair and equitable sharing of benefits arising from the use of such biodiversity in the ASEAN region." Agreement on the Establishment of the ASEAN Centre for Biodiversity (2005) art 2. The governance mechanism for the Centre is the Governing Board, comprised of representatives with the appropriate portfolios from each Member State. Agreement on the Establishment of the ASEAN Centre for Biodiversity (2005) arts 4, 5. Administration of the Centre is placed under the auspices of an Executive Director and appropriate staff members. Id. at art 6.

187 Transboundary haze was the subject of a 2002 Agreement that continues to operate and provide for a governance and coordination system within the organization. Under the terms of the ASEAN Agreement on Transboundary Haze Pollution, the ASEAN Co-ordinating Centre for Transboundary Haze Pollution Control came into existence in order to ensure cooperation between Member States with an emphasis on national responsibility and responsiveness to the issue of pollution. ASEAN Agreement on Transboundary Haze Pollution (2002) arts 5, 6. At the same time, the system created through the Centre provides for joint and/or regional responses to pollution when this is necessary or when the impacted Member State cannot thoroughly respond to the problems. Id. at arts 12, 13. Further, a Conference of the Parties for the Agreement was established in order to facilitate dialogue and cooperation between the Member States. Id. at art 18. The ASEAN Secretariat was designated as the administrative body for the Conference of the Parties. Id. at art 19.

188 ASEAN Socio-Cultural Community, ASEAN, http://asean.org/asean-socio-cultural/, last accessed 10 January 2018.

189 ASEAN Agreement on Disaster Management and Emergency Response (2005) art 4.

190 Id. at arts 21, 23.

191 Id. at art 20.

192 ASEAN External Relations, ASEAN, http://asean.org/asean/external-relations/, last accessed 10 January 2018. Examples of States with which ASEAN has established free trade agreements include China, India, Japan, New Zealand, and the Republic of Korea.

193 Agreement for the Establishment of a Fund for ASEAN (1994).

194 Id. In order to receive funding, a project has to have benefits within the ASEAN area and not be funded through one of the ASEAN Dialogue Partners. Guidelines for Utilization of the ASEAN Fund (1994) art 2.

195 See Revised Memorandum of Understanding on the Establishment of the ASEAN Foundation (2000).

196 Id. at arts IV–VI.

197 Id. at art IX.

198 Treaty on European Union (2012) arts 2(1), 2(2). The articulated areas of shared competence with Member States are: "a) internal market, b) social policy, c) economic, social and territorial cohesion, d) agriculture and fisheries, excluding the conservation of marine biological resources, e) environment, f) consumer protection, g) transport, h) trans-European networks, i) energy, j) area of freedom, security and justice, k) common safety concerns in public health matters." Id. at art 4.

199 Id. at art 2(4). Other areas of exclusive competence for the EU are: the customs union, the creation and implementation of an internal market, Eurozone monetary policy, "conservation of marine biological resources under the common fisheries policy," and commercial policy for the EU. See id. at art 3.

200 Id. at art 6. These topics are "a) protection and improvement of human health, b) industry, c) culture, d) tourism, e) education, vocational training, youth and sport, f) civil protection, g) administrative cooperation." Id. at art 6.

201 European Neighbourhood Policy and Enlargement Negotiations, Chapters of the Acquis, https://ec.europa.eu/neighbourhood-enlargement/policy/conditions-membership/chapters-of-the-acquis_en, last accessed 8 January 2018.

202 Id.

203 Countries, European Union, http://europa.eu/about-eu/countries/index_en.htm, last accessed 8 January 2018.

204 See Agreement in the form of an Exchange of Letters between the European Economic Community and the Principality of Andorra (1991); Partnership and Cooperation Agreement between the European Communities and their Member States, of the one part, and the Republic of Armenia, of the other part (1999); Partnership and Cooperation Agreement between the European Communities and their Member States, of the one part, and the Republic of Azerbaijan, of the other part (2014); Association Agreement between the European Union and the European Atomic Energy Community and their Member States, of the one part, and Georgia, of the other part (2016); Association Agreement between the European Union and the European Atomic Energy Community and their Member States, of the one part, and the Republic of Moldova, of the other part (2014).

205 See Communication from the Commission to the Council Report on the functioning of the Monetary Agreements with Monaco, San Marino and Vatican (2009); Monetary Agreement between the Italian Republic, on behalf of the European Community, and the Vatican City State, on its behalf, the Holy See (2001).

206 See Agreement between the European Community and the Principality of Andorra providing for measures equivalent to those laid down in Council Directive 2003/48/EC on taxation of savings income in the form of interest payments (2005); Partnership and Cooperation Agreement between the European Communities and their Member States and the Republic of Armenia, supra note 204; Partnership and Cooperation Agreement between the European Communities and their Member States and the Republic of Azerbaijan, supra note 204; Association Agreement between the European Union and the European Atomic Energy Community and their Member States and Georgia, supra note 204; Association Agreement between the European Union and the European Atomic Energy Community and their Member States and the Republic of Moldova, supra note 204.

207 See Andorra and the EU, https://eeas.europa.eu/headquarters/headquarters-homepage/2050/andorra-and-eu_en, last accessed 9 January 2018; Partnership and Cooperation Agreement between the European Communities and their Member States and the Republic of Armenia, supra note 204; Partnership and Cooperation Agreement between the European Communities and their Member States and the Republic of Azerbaijan, supra note 204; Association Agreement between the European Union and the European Atomic Energy Community and their Member States and Georgia, supra note 204; Association Agreement between the European Union and the European Atomic Energy Community and their Member States and the Republic of Moldova, supra note 204.

208 EU institutions and other bodies, European Union, http://europa.eu/about-eu/institutions-bodies/index_en.htm, last accessed 8 January 2018.

209 Id.

210 Id.

211 Id.

212 Id.

213 European Parliament, European Union, http://europa.eu/about-eu/institutions-bodies/european-parliament/index_en.htm, last accessed 8 January 2018.

214 Id.

215 See List of Committees, European Parliament Committees, http://www.europarl.europa.eu/committees/en/parliamentary-committees.html, last accessed 8 January 2018.

216 See Rules of Procedure of the European Parliament (2017).

217 See id.

218 Council of the European Union, European Union, http://europa.eu/about-eu/institutions-bodies/council-eu/index_en.htm, last accessed 8 January 2018.

219 Id.

220 Id.

221 Id.

222 European Commission, European Union, http://europa.eu/about-eu/institutions-bodies/european-commission/index_en.htm, last accessed 8 January 2018.

223 Id.

224 Council of the European Union, supra note 218.

225 http://europa.eu/about-eu/institutions-bodies/council-eu/index_en.htm.

226 Treaty on European Union, supra note 198 at art 228(1).

227 Id.

228 Id. at art 228(2).

229 Id. at art 228(1).

230 Id. at art 300; see also Members' Statute of the European Economic and Social Committee (2012).

231 Decentralised Agencies, European Union, https://europa.eu/european-union/about-eu/agencies/decentralised-agencies_en, last accessed 8 January 2018.

232 Court of Justice of the European Union, European Union, http://europa.eu/about-eu/institutions-bodies/court-justice/index_en.htm, last accessed 8 January 2018.

233 Id.

234 See Regulation 2015/2422 of the Parliament and the Council (16 December 2015).

235 Statute of the European Court of Justice (2016) arts 15, 17.

236 Regulation 2015/2422 of the Parliament and the Council, supra note 234.

237 Id. at art 9.

238 See Discussion document of the Court of Justice of the European Union on certain aspects of the accession of the European Union to the European Convention for the Protection of Human Rights and Fundamental Freedoms (2010).

239 See id.

240 Treaty on European Union, supra note 198 at art 286.

241 Id. at art 285.

242 Id. at art 287.

243 Working Methods of the Eurogroup, ECFIN/CEFCPE(2008)REP/50842 rev 1 (2008) 1 (providing that the Eurogroup would "discuss matters of key importance to fiscal, monetary and structural policies in the euro area, and focus on themes of particular importance for the single currency, with a forward looking bias.").

244 Id. at 1–2.

245 Id. at 2.

246 Id. at 5.

247 Id.

248 See Consolidated Version of the Treaty Establishing the European Atomic Energy Community (2009).

249 Id. at art 2.

250 Id.

251 See id. at art 134.

252 The History of the European Union, European Union, https://europa.eu/european-union/about-eu/history_en, last accessed 8 January 2018.

253 See Brexit: All you need to know about the UK leaving the EU, BBC.com, http://www.bbc.com/news/uk-politics-32810887, last accessed 8 January 2018.

254 Id.

255 Id.

256 Id.

257 Id.

258 Id.

259 Id.

260 Id.

261 Guidelines Following the United Kingdom's Notification Under Article 50 TEU, General Secretariat of the Council, EUCO XT 20004/17 (2017) 3; see also Directives for the negotiation of an agreement with the United Kingdom and Northern Ireland setting out the arrangements for its withdrawal from the European Union, General Secretariat of the Council, XT 2017/17 add 1 rev 2 (2017).

262 Guidelines Following the United Kingdom's Notification Under Article 50 TEU, supra note 261 at 3; see also Directives for the negotiation of an agreement with the United Kingdom and Northern Ireland setting out the arrangements for its withdrawal from the European Union, supra note 261.

263 Guidelines Following the United Kingdom's Notification Under Article 50 TEU, supra note 261 at 4; see also Directives for the negotiation of an agreement with the United Kingdom and Northern Ireland setting out the arrangements for its withdrawal from the European Union, supra note 261.

264 See id.

265 See id.

266 See id.

267 Treaty of Lisbon amending the Treaty of the European Union and the Treaty Establishing the European Community, 2007/C 306/01.

268 Id. at art 50.

269 Id.

270 See General Secretariat of the European Council, Guidelines Following the United Kingdom's Notification Under Article 50 TEU, EUCO XT 20004/17 (29 April 2017).

271 See id.

272 See European Commission Task Force for the Preparation and Conduct of the Negotiations with the United Kingdom under Article 50 TEU, Position paper on Customs related matters needed for an orderly withdrawal of the UK from the Union, TF50 (2017) 13/2 (20 September 2017).

273 See General Secretariat of the European Council, supra note 270.

274 See id.

275 See id.

276 *See* European Commission Task Force for the Preparation and Conduct of the Negotiations with the United Kingdom under Article 50 TEU, Position paper on Judicial Cooperation in Civil and Commercial matters, TF50 (2017) 9/2 (12 July 2017); European Commission Task Force for the Preparation and Conduct of the Negotiations with the United Kingdom under Article 50 TEU, Position paper on Ongoing Union Judicial and Administrative Procedures, TF50 (2017) 5 (12 July 2017).

277 *See* European Commission Task Force for the Preparation and Conduct of the Negotiations with the United Kingdom under Article 50 TEU, Position paper on Ongoing Police and Judicial Cooperation in Criminal matters, *supra* note 276.

278 *See generally id.*

Chapter 15

Trade, finance and banking organizations

One topic area in which there is extensive overlap and, often, coordination between international organizations clusters around trade, finance and banking. Indeed, over the course of recent decades these organizations have expanded significantly in scope, membership and areas of concentration that are outside the parameters of classical financial concerns. All this in an effort to create organizations that can better and more holistically represent and assist Member States and their constituencies in capitalizing on financial benefits and increasing the role and place of markets.

Contrast between free trade agreements, bilateral investment agreements and dedicated international organizations

In recent years, the number of free trade agreements has steadily increased between States at all different points of development. These agreements range in scope and complexity from the extremely limited[1] – which tend to contain only provisions for basic trading preferences – to the extremely broad – which fashion entirely new regimes in international law and relations, such as the North American Free Trade Agreement (NAFTA)[2] – and a vast number of forms in between.[3]

In some instances, trading arrangements have been used as the basis upon which international organizations are generated. Perhaps the most prominent example of this is the European Union, which has evolved dramatically from a post-war attempt to bring about peace through economic affiliations to become the most notable and powerful supranational entity on the world stage. At the other end of the spectrum are the instances in which international organizations have been used as devices through which free-trade agreements are negotiated and implemented between Member States and/or between Member States and non-Member States. For example, as discussed in Chapter 14, the Association of Southeast Asian Nations (ASEAN) has been a vehicle for the negotiation of an attempted free-trade agreement for the southeast Asia region. This has been in negotiations for years and has yet to be legally concretized or made operational. At the same time, ASEAN has been used as a vehicle through which Member States and non-Member States, such as Australia and New Zealand, have negotiated and implemented free-trade agreements among themselves.[4]

As such, free trade agreements are an example of the potential methods used by international organizations and conducted under their auspices, but typically do not create additional organizational structures *per se*. There are, of course, exceptions in which new organizational entities are produced through a free-trade agreement, particularly in the field of dispute resolution for the terms of the agreement. This is the case in the NAFTA regime, which is home to a dedicated Secretariat empowered to handle matters relating to disputes over the application of agreement terms by one or more of the States Parties.[5] Included in these provisions are authorizations to form panels of States and their evaluators in order to review the allegations made regarding violations of NAFTA-based obligations.[6]

Other free-trade agreements contain specific measures for the settlement of disputes and issues between the States Parties without giving rise to a set of institutions such as a secretariat. For example, the ASEAN-Australia-New Zealand Free Trade Agreement provides for an extensive arbitration and dispute settlement system between the parties but does not require the formalization of an institutional setting.[7] Over the course of the growth and development of free trade agreements as rich sources of regulations, this method of transitory entity use for dispute settlement matters alone has become standard.[8] In some instances, the establishment of a limited jurisdiction joint committee structure has been undertaken, although this in no way creates what would constitute an international organization.[9]

Similar provisions are applicable in the context of bilateral investment treaties, which are typically less extensive than free trade agreements. Recently, there has been an effort in some quarters to make bilateral investment treaties more comprehensive or to include the bulk of investment provisions in free trade agreements.[10] Either way, the institutional elements revolve around a committee structure at best, simply using *ad hoc* dispute settlement measures when the need arises.

Regardless the form of such economic agreements, they generate international relationships and could often be mistaken for forming norms similar to those used in international organizations. While this may be true, in part, they are included in this chapter to highlight the differences in form from international organizations and the reasons why it is essential to study economic organizations with care.

World Trade Organization

Background

The World Trade Organization (WTO) began its existence as a more loosely existing group of States that adhered to and implemented the General Agreement on Trade and Tariffs (GATT).[11] As a treaty-based regime, the GATT functioned to bridge the political differences existing at the global level throughout the Cold War era. However, when the Cold War ended the international community was no longer polarized to the same level and the functions of the GATT could be extended to other States and to a larger swathe of international economic and trade law.

Membership and voting

As of the time of writing, there are 164 WTO Member States and, contrary to what might be expected, most of these Member States are considered developing State members.[12] One of the newest WTO Member States is the Russian Federation, which was admitted after a long and controversial evaluation process for its laws and its economic policies.[13]

Additionally, there are 21 States that are currently classified as WTO observer States.[14] In the realm of the WTO, this means that these States are in the process of becoming Member States and there is a specific requirement that they become full-fledged WTO Member States within 10 years of starting the process.[15] The only exception to this is the Holy See, which is allowed perpetual observer status within the WTO owing to the inappropriateness of its being required to change and/or enact laws that conform with WTO laws.[16] In addition, almost all UN-affiliated international organizations are accredited as organizational observers to the WTO.[17] Unlike some other international organizations, the WTO limits the role of organizational observers to providing consultations in policy areas that are of relevance to the particular organizational observer.[18] This allows the organizational observers to give targeted, meaningful insights and advice.

Each Member State has one vote on the Ministerial Council; however, the European Communities member bloc is considered to have a number of votes that equals the number of European Communities' members which are also WTO Member States.[19] While majority rules voting occurs throughout the WTO system, there are certain instances, such as proposals for amendments to WTO documents, in which unanimity is required.[20]

Structure

In terms of organizational structure, the WTO uses a series of key legislative organs, a Secretariat and a variety of specialized councils and committees. The highest organ of the WTO is the Ministerial Council, which is comprised of representatives from each Member State.[21] The Ministerial Council has oversight powers for the Committee on Trade and Development, Committee on Balance-of-Payments Restrictions, and the Committee on Budgets, Finance and Administration.[22] One key function of the Ministerial Council is its ability to authorize a waiver from the obligations of either a Member State or group of Member States under one or more of the WTO-based treaties.[23] Perhaps the best example of the importance of this ability is in the grant – and subsequent reauthorization – of a waiver for WTO Member States wishing to become part of the Kimberley Certification Process, which seeks to combat the flow of conflict and other illicit diamonds onto the mainstream market.[24]

Below the Ministerial Council is the General Council of the WTO. The General Council is also comprised of representatives from each WTO Member State; however, it does not have the same broad-based powers.[25] The General Council is the oversight and implementation body for the WTO Dispute Settlement Body (DSB) and also for the WTO's Trade Policy Review Mechanism, a process that all Member States must undergo periodically in order to gauge their compliance with and issues in implementing the terms of various WTO-based treaties.[26] Further, the General Council has oversight powers for a variety of specialized councils, particularly the Council for Trade in Goods, Council for Trade in Services, and Council for Trade in Trade-Related Aspects of Intellectual Property Rights.[27] Each of these Councils is tasked with ensuring the implementation of specific WTO-based treaties.[28] The General Council is also the organ tasked with interacting with other international organizations and with non-governmental organizations where appropriate.[29]

As with most international organizations, the daily operations of the WTO are handled by a Secretariat. The head of the Secretariat is the Director-General, who is selected by the Ministerial Council. In addition to these standard institutionalized structures, the WTO uses a series of multi-year negotiating rounds to facilitate discussions on key issues in trade and, hopefully, to generate new treaties and agreements that address these issues.[30] Currently, the Doha round of negotiations – which began in 2001 – is still on-going, with the primary policy aim being to assist in promoting development within Member States.[31] It has led to policy agreements and declarations and is focused on the following key policy areas: agriculture, market access, services, intellectual property, trade and development, trade and the environment, facilitating trade between Member States, and the DSB system generally.[32]

In keeping with this, it should be noted that in recent years the WTO has become focused on issues that move beyond simply providing rules for the trading market and instead seeks to assist Member States and their constituencies in participating in the market.[33] This is notable in such activities as the WTO's Aid for Trade program, in which developed States provide aid to developing State members of the WTO in order to build up and enable the capacity of those States to engage in trade that complies with WTO laws and rules.[34] Through the Aid for Trade program the WTO has been able to provide assistance to Member States, particularly those in need of support for emerging issues such as environmental measures.[35] In addition to individual Member State development, Aid for Trade has come to assist in the development of regional entities and regional trade, such as that functioning in the intra-African WTO Member States.[36]

Functions

During 1994–1995, the GATT was consolidated into a more comprehensive international organization, the World Trade Organization (WTO).[37] Included in the goals of the WTO's creation was assisting in increasing global development as well as the growth of trade and services sectors.[38] Within this context, the Agreement Establishing the World Trade Organization specifies that the new organization would "provide the common institutional framework for the conduct of trade relations among its Members in matters related to the agreements and associated legal instruments" promulgated by its Member States.[39] In this context, the WTO functions as a means of administration and implementation as well as a forum for negotiation of additional treaties and the creation of new norms in international law.[40] This necessarily means that the WTO creates a forum for new trade-related treaties to be negotiated.[41]

In the context of a number of the WTO's treaties and agreements there is a series of specialized committees created within the WTO organizational structure. These committees vary in powers and expectations depending on the treaty regimes and topics they are regulating. Over time, they have produced countless measures at the WTO and have also provided important information for the entirety of the international community.[42]

For example, in the Agreement on Agriculture, a Committee on Agriculture was created to oversee and monitor the progress of the Agreement's implementation in the context of current and future rounds of policy negotiation as well as in general.[43] The mandate of the Committee on Sanitary and Phytosanitary Measures contains broader powers, such as acting as a liaison with international organizations that serve in areas directly related to relevant topics, such as the Food and Agriculture Organization (FAO).[44] Additionally, given that a key goal of the Agreement on the Application of Sanitary and Phytosanitary Measures is the harmonization of related laws and rules based on international standards, an essential function of the Committee is to review Member States' national laws in order to ensure that they are compliant.[45] Other committees exist with broad mandates that allow them latitude provided they do not act in conflict with other, more specifically tailored committees.[46] Further, where extremely technical issues form the subject of the treaty, more than one committee can be created, for example the Committee on Rules of Origin and the Technical Committee on Rules of Origin, both of which function as part of the Agreement on Rules of Origin.[47] A similar situation exists in the Committee on Subsidies and Countervailing Measures, for which subsidiary entities are authorized, such as the Permanent Group of Experts, which functions as an advisory body to the Committee.[48]

Given the extensive reach of the WTO into the realms of global policy and law, it is perhaps not surprising that it maintains a strong network of cooperation with other international organizations. The WTO's ability to do this is enshrined in several key legal texts, beginning within two years of its origin and continuing through the Doha rounds.[49] Due to the importance of some organizations' activities in the sphere of setting accepted standards in scientific or technical realms, the WTO also incorporates these standards into the rule-making and reviewing mandates of some committees where appropriate. For example, the Committee on Sanitary and Phytosanitary Measures is tasked with ensuring that the terms of the Codex Alimentarius, adopted through the FAO, are implemented by Member States as guides for food-based measures.[50] Perhaps not surprisingly, the WTO and the International Monetary Fund have signed a Cooperation Agreement that allows the organizations to work together and share information on global economic policy.[51] Similar arrangements exist between the WTO and the entities comprising the World Bank.[52] The staff of the WTO and the International Telecommunication Union share the ability to offer comments and suggestions on proposed policies in either entity and to offer suggestions for developing policy areas, including ways in which the organizations can work together and the ability to propose regulations where appropriate.[53] Further, the WTO's Aid for Trade program works in cooperation with the input and capacities of the Organization for Economic Cooperation and Development.[54] In terms of the WTO's interaction with the UN as a whole, official arrangements exist for a relationship based on reciprocity and coordination between staff members, allowing each organization input and the ability to share specific expertise and concerns where appropriate.[55] This is a blanket agreement with the UN system; however, the WTO has also entered into specific arrangements for cooperation and mutual assistance with UN agencies that are of particular importance to WTO functions and programs, such as the UN Conference on Trade and Development.[56]

International Monetary Fund

Background

The International Monetary Fund (IMF) was created as part of a newly forged attempt by the Allied powers to modernize the global financial systems in the wake of World War II.[57] This system, more commonly known as the Bretton Woods system, has served to reshape the ways in which international monetary policy and lending are conducted, and stands behind many of the evolving concepts of encouragement of development through financial assistance at the level of international organizations.[58]

Membership and voting

The vast majority of recognized States in the international community are members of the IMF[59] and membership in the IMF is necessary for a State to be eligible for membership in the World Bank Group. In order to become a member, a State must file an official application, which is reviewed first by the Executive Board and, if the Executive Board approves, is forwarded to the Board of Governors for final approval.[60] Should approval be granted, the quota and subscription requirements for the new Member State is suggested to the Board of Governors by the Executive Board, although the Board of Governors has the final ability to decide these amounts and requirements.[61] These quotas can periodically be reviewed and changed if deemed appropriate, although any such changes require approval from the States impacted before they become operational.[62]

Voting within the IMF system is determined through a calculation based on the subscription of shares that each Member State has rather than on a one State–one vote basis.[63] At the time of membership, each State is assigned a set subscription for shares and, consequentially, must pay the assigned subscription fee.[64] In terms of votes in the Board of Governors, a majority is typically sufficient for passage unless there are specific terms to the contrary.[65]

In the event a Member State wishes to withdraw from the IMF it is permitted to do so although it is required to settle its accounts with the organization as a part of its withdrawal efforts.[66] Withdrawal of a Member State is considered effective when it is properly received by the IMF.[67] Member States which fail to make the required payments to the fund or to fulfill other requisite commitments may be suspended by the IMF and, should these issues continue unabated, may fall into the category of compulsory withdrawal.[68] Determinations on whether to pursue the compulsory withdrawal under the particular circumstances at issue fall to the Executive Board first and, if the Executive Board approves, moves on to the Board of Governors.[69] Prior to making a final determination, the Board of Governors is required to provide the Member State with time to respond.[70]

Structure

The primary IMF organ in which all Member States have a voice and a vote is the Board of Governors, mimicking in many ways a corporate structure rather than the structure traditionally used by international organizations.[71] In this regime, States that joined the IMF system in 1944, when it was first created, are classified as original members of the organization, while States which subsequently seek to join and are admitted through the approval of the Board of Governors are classified as "other members."[72]

In the IMF system, the Board of Governors is the plenary body in which each Member State is permitted representation. Powers within the IMF are apportioned between the various governing entities. The Board of Governors has the broadest legislative power and is vested with the ability to handle all issues that are not otherwise apportioned to the Executive Board.[73] However, the Board of Governors maintains the ability to delegate functions to the Executive Board as a matter of discretion.[74] As a matter of structure, the Board of Governors elects a Chairman from among its membership as well as two Vice-Chairmen.[75]

The Board of Governors establishes the essential practices of the organization and can create ministerial committees.[76] To date, the Board of Governors has used this ability twice in order to form the International Monetary and Financial Committee and the Development Committee.[77] The former serves to provide advice and guidance on issues of international finance and monetary policy,[78] while the latter advises on financial aspects of development.[79]

The Executive Board of the IMF is tasked with actually performing the business of the IMF, meaning that it is the public face of the organization and interacts more openly with Member States.[80] The Executive Board is comprised of 20 total share amounts, the remaining 15 of whom are elected by the other Member States.[81] Perhaps the most important function of the Executive Board is its ability to elect a Managing Director of the IMF, who functions in a manner similar to a corporate chief executive officer.[82] The Managing Director does not come from the Executive Board and is not a member of it − instead, the office is a separate entity that holds the function of a Secretary General in other organizational systems, including the oversight of IMF staff.[83] The Managing Director and her staff create a budget proposal, which in turn must be approved by the Executive Board and, subsequently, by the Board of Governors.[84]

In order to performing oversight of the IMF's budgeting and operations, the Managing Director and Executive Board are required to appoint three outside individuals to function as a separate external audit committee.[85] This is complemented by the use of an outside auditing firm which is tasked with generating an annual audit of the IMF as a whole.[86] Accountability within the IMF context was further strengthened in 2001 when it created the Independent Evaluation Office and charged it with the task of increasing organizational credibility, governance, and oversight structure.[87]

Functions

Unlike many lending institutions, the IMF has functions besides simply lending money, a function that it will perform only when certain lending criteria have been met.[88] Among the IMF's other core functions are providing economic policy advice to Member State governments, regions, and the world economy at large, as well as working to establish currency stability and working with underdeveloped and developing States to tackle their debt issues.[89] Many of these activities have been controversial because they are seen as − or become − political acts. Overall, the purposes of the IMF focus on generating international monetary policy and cohesion,[90] assisting in the maintenance and expansion of international trade,[91] and generally ensuring stability within the international financial realm.[92]

A key aspect of the IMF's functions involves the surveillance of the international financial and monetary sectors, as well as those at the regional and national levels. In order to do this, the IMF reviews the performance of Member States on a yearly basis, and also conducts an in-depth Triennial Surveillance Review for the international system.[93]

Lending at the IMF takes many forms and can occur for a multitude of reasons. One of the most consistently used lending arrangements is the Stand-By Arrangement, which allows any Member State to receive financing when faced with problems surrounding balance of payments.[94] The loans are intended to last up to three years and are dependent on the context of the Member State and the financial issues involved.[95] Stand-By Arrangement lending is now available in advance and forms a precautionary fund that States can draw on if they need to, even where there is no immediate need.[96] Such loans require that the receiving State be subject to periodic review and monitoring by the IMF in order to determine progress in correcting the economic issues involved.[97]

Additionally, the IMF has begun offering different forms of lending and assistance that translate to the development status of the Member State seeking financing. For example, the Standby Credit Facility functions as a smaller amount, short-term lender for developing States that have made significant economic progress yet still need financing guarantees for periodic market disruptions.[98] One of the most comprehensive elements of the IMF's lending options is the Poverty Reduction and Growth Trust, which provides a number of different finance options for low-income States depending on the situations they face and their abilities.[99] Further, the IMF grants access to several forms of lines of credit options for States that have made significant economic progress.[100]

Over time, the operational function of the IMF has evolved to include capacity development assistance for Member States, particularly developing and low-income States. The bulk of these activities involves the provision of advice and technical assistance in fields such as legislative support, public finance, and general monetary system strengthening and oversight.[101] In addition, the IMF has created the Catastrophe Containment and Relief Trust to assist States facing some form of crisis in reducing debt obligations and providing necessary services to their communities, particularly in the context of public health threats.[102] Post-2015, the IMF's capacity development functions are now heavily intertwined with the implementation and achievement of the Sustainable Development Goals.[103]

World Bank Group
Background on the system

The World Bank's name is deceptive because in fact there is no one World Bank! Instead, the "World Bank Group" is a conglomerate of the International Bank for Reconstruction (IBRD), the International Development Association (IDA), the International Finance Corporation (IFC), the Multilateral Investment Guarantee Association (MIGA), and the International Centre for Settlement of Investment Disputes (ICSID).[104] Each of these entities is controlled by a separate foundational text and each has a separate governing body.[105] Within the World Bank Group is essential leadership and coordination, notably an elected President and a series of Vice-Presidents for various portfolios.

Governance of each of these bodies – except for the ICSID – is established in a more corporate-form structure that is akin to that used by the IMF. Additionally, these organizations use a slightly different voting structure for an international organization in that the voting share allotted to each Member State depends upon the subscription of shares they have taken out in the organization. This structure is quite similar to the IMF and – as will be discussed later in this chapter – to regional banking entities as well.

With the exception of the ICSID, all of the World Bank Group entities engage in lending and financing, although some, like the IBRD, lend only to State actors while others, like MIGA, are able to lend to private entities as well as State actors.[106] This means that the World Bank Group, as a whole, can provide funding and assistance to nearly all aspects of the financial and development sectors within a State.[107] In many ways this is positive, since it ensures that there is a more holistic source of funding for Member States to turn to and also in that it allows Member States to better tailor their funding requests to their actual needs. While all of this is true, it is important to note that there is constant criticism of the World Bank Group on the grounds that the group as a whole exerts too much control over developing State economies and therefore has the ability to dictate what these States will adopt in terms of domestic political and social policies.

Overall, the World Bank as an entity has embraced the potential role it can exercise in development measures, first through endorsing and working toward the accomplishment of the Millennium Development Goals and, later, through endorsing and working toward the accomplishment of the Sustainable Development Goals.[108] This is evident in the World Bank's focus on poverty reduction strategies in developing Member States and through the Heavily Indebted Countries Initiative (HIPC).[109] Additionally, through the Post-Conflict Fund, the World Bank as an entity works to provide assistance and advice to areas that are in the midst of recovering from the societal, infrastructural and economic damage caused by various forms of conflict.[110] Outside of the post-conflict realm, the World Bank as a whole prizes the role of infrastructural development funding and assistance, as evidenced by its Infrastructure Action Plan.[111]

At the global level of the World Bank, the concept of ensuring integrity in the lending and contracting process has become of paramount importance. With this in mind, and to ensure that everyone involved in these operational spheres has a clear understanding of accept practices, the World Bank has implemented a set of rules known as the Integrity Compliance Guidelines.[112]

Further, the organizations comprising the World Bank Group have, collectively, approved the implementation of a joint Sanctions Board with jurisdiction over certain forms of allegations that could lead to sanctions against contractors or projects.[113] This Board is comprised of seven members, the majority of which are selected by the IBRD, and can vary in composition depending on the organization involved in seeking sanctions.[114] For these matters, the Sanctions Board is the highest level of review possible[115] and the Sanctions Board implements the Sanctions Procedures, which are geared toward ensuring that the World Bank Group as a whole fulfills its duties regarding the proper use of its funds.[116]

The actions and decisions of the IFC and MIGA in regard to environmental and social issues are subject to oversight by the Office of the Compliance Advisor Ombudsman (CAO), which operates as an entity distinct from the World Bank itself.[117] The CAO is empowered to examine environmental and social practices on its own accord and to receive and review complaints from those impacted by activities funded or otherwise supported by IFC and MIGA.[118] As an independent entity, the CAO serves the functions of dispute resolution, evaluating compliance with the standards and rules required by the two entities, and providing advice to the two entities, the World Bank's overall leadership, and other entities as needed.[119] Guidance for the CAO and other World Bank operations generally is established through policies such as the Environmental, Health and Safety General Guidelines.[120]

Additionally, several other entities exist within the World Bank Group to ensure proper oversight and functioning of activities occurring under its rubric. One key example of this is the establishment of a dedicated Integrity Vice Presidency, which is the designated watchdog entity for fraud and corruption in all World Bank Group lending activities.[121] This entity is empowered to conduct investigations into allegations of fraud and corruption and, when there are positive findings, is authorized to issue sanctions against the offending parties.[122] Projects based on funding from either the IBRD or the IDA are subject to oversight by the World Bank Inspection Panel, which is an independent entity in the overall organizational structure that is empowered to receive complaints from outside sources – such as individuals or communities – that claim to be negatively and inappropriately affected by the project.[123] The three members of the Inspection Panel are chosen from a combination of different managerial entities within the IBRD and the IDA, and serve for an initial five-year term, which is renewable in one-year intervals.[124] At the end of an investigation, the Inspection Panel issues a report on the issues raised, which is transmitted to the appropriate Boards within the governance structure of the organization for final approval.[125] For complaints regarding projects with imminent potentials for damage, there exists the Grievance Redress Service, which is equipped to hear allegations and make determinations quickly.[126]

International Bank for Reconstruction and Development

Background

The International Bank for Reconstruction and Development (IBRD) is primarily focused on supporting efforts geared toward reconstruction in areas devastated by conflict or some other harm. Historically, the IBRD was intended to provide assistance to States in post-World War II Europe; however, this mission has grown to include the larger global sphere of conflicts and efforts to move past them through development.[127] These efforts include not only the provision of organizational financing in the short and long term[128] but also assistance in attracting private sources of funding and funding through other governmental or international organizations sources.[129] In addition to direct funding, in certain limited instances the IBRD is capable of acting as a guarantee entity[130] and now provides non-monetary assistance to promote development.[131] Further, the IBRD is empowered to act as a lender and guarantee entity for the International Finance Corporation.[132]

Membership and voting

Membership in the IBRD is connected with IMF membership status, as original IMF members who joined the IBRD at its founding are also considered original members and additional States are permitted to join the IBRD provided they are members of the IMF and meet terms required by the IBRD itself.[133] An integral part of membership is the subscription of shares in the IBRD. The requisite minimum for each member's share subscription is determined by the IBRD, although the Member State can at its discretion subscribe to more shares.[134] To meet the needs of the IBRD, it is possible for the required share subscription to be increased through appropriate organizational procedures.[135] Shares are also essential to the calculation of votes allotted per Member State.[136]

All IBRD Member States retain the right to withdraw as members. Once this decision is made, the State must transmit it to the IBRD's main office and, upon receipt of the decision at that office, the State's withdrawal is considered accepted and final.[137] The IBRD retains the right to suspend a Member State from active participation in the organization in the event that it fails to fulfill any aspect of its membership obligations.[138] Suspension from the IBRD may be cured by fulfilling the requirement at issue; however, if the suspension is not lifted within a year the Member State will be terminated from membership unless the Board of Governors determines otherwise.[139] Since initial membership in the IBRD requires membership in the IMF, it is perhaps unsurprising that, should a Member State cease to be a member of the IMF for any reason, it will cease to be a member of the IBRD unless the Board of Governors votes to the contrary.[140] Regardless the reason, should a State cease to be a member of the IBRD it must settle its accounts with the organization.[141] Similarly, should the IBRD temporarily or permanently cease to function, it must ensure that accounts with Member States and other entities are properly settled.[142]

Structure and functions

The organizational structure of the IBRD consists of three essential entities – the Board of Governors, Executive Directors and the IBRD President and associated staff members.[143] The Board of Governors consists of one representative from each Member State and, rather unusually, each representative is limited to a five-year, renewable term of office.[144] As the plenary entity of the IBRD, the Board of Governors has extensive powers; however, it can delegate all but the most critical to the Executive Directors.[145]

The task of overseeing the quotidian aspects of IBRD conduct – or any other matters delegated to it – falls within the ambit of the Executive Directors.[146] The Executive Directors' membership is limited to 12 and further defined by a mixed process of share volume and overall votes. In this system, five of the Directors are appointed based on the identities of the five Member States possessing the largest number of shares, while the remaining seven are elected by the Board of Governors.[147] In conjunction with the Executive Directors, the President and his staff are tasked with the operation of the IBRD on a practical level.[148]

Additionally, there are two standing policy entities within the IBRD system – the Advisory Council and the Loans Committees. The Advisory Council consists of seven representations from a broad number of industries involved in the international economy and international finance who are appointed by the Board of Governors.[149] Based on this wide-ranging expertise, the Advisory Council provides guidance to the IBRD as requested.[150] The Loan Committees function to oversee the implementation of loans made by the IBRD and are to include members from the regions in which the IBRD operates as well as some representation from the staff of the IBRD itself.[151]

International Development Association

Background

Unlike other organizations within the World Bank, the International Development Association (IDA) is designed to work only with the very poorest States in the international community in order to provide for some of the most basic aspects of their needs and the needs of their populations and assist in future development.

Membership and voting

States across the spectrum of development statuses are permitted to become members of the IDA and, as in other banking organizations, are required to purchase initial shares as part of their membership requirement.[152] Similarly, any Member State may withdraw from the IDA by providing the organization with notice of intent to do so. Unlike some international organizations, the IDA allows withdrawal by a Member State to become effective immediately upon receipt of notice, however a process of settling accounts with the Member State must take place.[153] Member States may be suspended by the IDA in instances where they fail to meet the requirements of membership, such as purchasing new share amounts. In these situations, the Member State must cure the issue within a year or risk having its membership in the IDA terminated entirely.[154]

Structure

The IDA's governance structure follows the standard pattern within the World Bank Group and is centered on a Board of Governors, Executive Directors, and Secretariat that is spearheaded by an organ elected President.[155] The Board of Governors, on which each Member State sits, is an entity with essential functions and governance capabilities for the IDA, including decisions on membership, the determination of share allotments per State, questions of interpretation and organizational capacity from the Executive Directors, relationships with international organizations, and any potential distributions of monies from the organization to the Member States. Any other abilities and activities are derogable to the Executive Directors.[156] Each Member State has votes commensurate with a formula based on the number of shares it subscribes to in the IDA.[157]

The IDA's Executive Directors are elected through a combination system of electoral structures.[158] As an entity, the Executive Directors have the ability to generate rules and regulations for the IDA and can serve additional functions as derogated to them by the Board of Governors.[159] The President, as chief of the Secretariat and the public representative of the IDA, has a wide range of practical responsibilities, including reporting to the Executive Directors following his election by them.[160] Staffing and other decisions are within the purview of the President in order to ensure the functioning of the organization on a daily basis.[161]

It is possible for the IDA to suspend or terminate its functions and activities when the majority of the Board of Governors votes for approval of these measures. When this happens, the organization and its Member States are still responsible for wrapping up the activities and obligations of the IDA, including the payment of outstanding debts and the apportionment of any remaining assets.[162]

Functions

To carry out this mission, the IDA's purposes include providing funding and technical support to the poorest States within the international community.[163] As a means of accomplishing this, the IDA is empowered to assist in funding measures that will raise living standards in these States, with the intent of spurring economic growth and, ultimately, self-sufficiency.[164] To assist in this, the IDA's loan and funding terms are intended to be less onerous than other international lending institutions and to promote flexibility in terms and their application.[165] It may also work in conjunction with other international organizations or interested entities in order to ensure that funds provided are coordinated to serve in the most impactful manner for the recipient State and its citizens.[166]

A prominent example of this is the IDA's involvement in the crafting and implementation of the Multilateral Debt Relief Initiative, which provides for significant debt forgiveness and repackaging for certain qualifying States in order to ensure that they are able to develop and move forward without being overwhelmed by past and current debts.[167] Further, the IDA Member States that are financially capable of doing so are required to replenish the organization's funds every three years – this in turn provides a critical funding source for the IDA's activities and demonstrates the dedication of the international community to its actions and attempts at poverty reduction in the long and short term.[168]

In compliance with international law requirements regarding respect for State sovereignty, the IDA will not provide funds to a project if the State in which it is located objects to the funding proposal.[169] As an indicator of the IDA's goal structure as it is translated into lending practice, the foundational text is specific that loans are not to be made for States or projects which could qualify for private or other funds elsewhere.[170] In this way, it is possible to view the IDA as the lender of last resort for extremely poor States.

International Finance Corporation

Background

The goals of the International Finance Corporation (IFC) center around the promotion of private investment and funding for developing States and for important projects in them.[171] As part of the same system, the IFC is intended to work together with other World Bank organizations, notably the IBRD, in order to best assist Member States.[172] Unlike other international lending organizations, the IFC does not require that there be State involvement in a project in order for it to receive support, although of course any financing from the IFC would require permission from the IFC based on sovereignty considerations.[173]

Membership and voting

As with many international organizations, there is a double classification system of members between those who were original members of the World Bank Group at its founding and States which seek to become members later.[174] Regardless the classification, all Member States are required to take out subscriptions in shares in the IFC, although the amount of the requisite shares to be subscribed varies between members.[175] The number of shares subscribed serves as the basis for determining the number of votes a Member State will exercise in the IFC system.[176]

Withdrawal from the IFC is relatively easy for a Member State to accomplish, in that it must send a formal notice to the IFC's head office and, upon receipt by the organization of that formal notice, withdrawal is effective.[177] As in other organizations within the World Bank Group, the IFC has the ability to suspend a Member State that does not comply with the terms of its membership and the issue causing suspension must be cured within a year in order to avoid termination of membership unless the Board of Governors votes otherwise.[178]

Upon termination of a State's membership in the World Bank Group, the Member State's IFC membership is also considered terminated.[179] In all situations resulting in termination of membership, the State seeking to leave must settle accounts with the IFC within established timeframes.[180] Additionally, it is possible for the IFC Board of Governors to cause the temporary or permanent termination of organizational operations through a majority vote.[181] In this situation, the IFC would be obligated to settle all accounts with Member States and other entities as part of its termination proceedings.[182]

Structure and functions

Structurally, the IFC uses the same format as most financial organizations, namely a Board of Governors, Board of Directors and President.[183] The Board of Governors is the repository of powers within the IFC system and is comprised of one Governor per Member State.[184] It is within the purview of the IFC to delegate the majority of its functions to the Board of Directors; however, there are some which it alone can exercise.[185]

The Board of Directors for the IFC serves the function of overseeing the conduct of the IFC as a whole and exercising the powers afforded to it by the Board of Governors.[186] However, the actual operation of the IFC is handled by the President and associated staff.[187] All of these actors, and others associated with the IFC, enjoy functional immunity in the course of their activities and the IFC itself enjoys standard organizational immunities and guarantees of protection where appropriate.[188]

Multilateral Investment Guarantee Association

Background

Within the World Bank Group structure, the Multilateral Investment Guarantee Association (MIGA) represents a unique blend of support for financing projects through public and private actors and funding sources. While MIGA has the capacity to operate in any Member State, it is particularly focused on States in all stages of development and serves as a guarantor of their activities and projects.[189] MIGA is intended to serve as a gap-filler for organizations within the World Bank Group and does not duplicate their activities since it has a different role to play in the financing chain than purely as a financier.[190]

Membership and voting

Every World Bank Group Member State is eligible to become a MIGA member; exceptions have been made, for example to allow Switzerland to join although it is not a part of the Group.[191] Membership in MIGA also requires subscription to a specifically determined number of shares, which are used as the basis for a Member State's voting allotment in the organization as well.[192] Once part of MIGA, a Member State retains the ability to withdraw from the organization by providing appropriate notice to the organization.[193] However, the actual withdrawal will not be complete and effective under three months following the date of notification.[194] Member States may be suspended for failure to comply with the terms and requirements of membership and the Convention.[195] Failure to cure the issue bringing about the suspension within a one-year period will result in eligibility for automatic termination of membership unless the Council of Governors decides to the contrary.[196] Regardless the cause, a State ceasing to be a MIGA member must settle accounts with the organization, including debts and any assets owed to it.[197]

It is within the power of the Board of Directors to decide that MIGA should temporarily suspend its operations in full or in part. At the discretion of the Directors, it is possible for the suspension to be lifted.[198] Decisions regarding the actual termination of activities and existence of MIGA, including the liquidation of any assets and the fulfillment of any liabilities, requires authorization from and oversight by the Council of Governors.[199]

Structure

MIGA is governed by a three-part system of a Council of Governors, Board of Directors and Secretariat that is overseen by an organizationally selected President. The Council of Governors is vested with the broadest organizational powers and has the ability to derogate some, but not all, of them to the Board of Directors if it elects to do so.[200] The non-derogable powers are those that have become standard among international organizations, such as membership decisions, questions of changing share allotments, issues on Convention construction and potential amendments, and the potential termination of MIGA.[201] All MIGA Member States have a seat on the Council of Governors, and their voting allotments are determined through the number of shares each member holds.[202]

The MIGA Board of Governors is elected by the Council of Governors and is generally charged with the regulation and oversight of the organization as a whole, and can exercise any powers that the Council derogates to it.[203] The Board of Governors is also charged with the selection and oversight of the MIGA President.[204]

Functions

To ensure compliance and to preserve the integrity of the communities and projects receiving support, MIGA has adopted the Performance Standards on Social and Environmental Sustainability as well as the requirement that all MIGA-financed projects be compliant with applicable laws and rules at the national and local levels.[205] Given the nature of financing provided by MIGA and the many communities that MIGA-financed endeavors impact, such standards are essential to the preservation of operational integrity and good faith in institutional and community-based systems. They are complemented by policies such as the Policy on Environmental and Social Sustainability.[206]

Within MIGA there exists a system of sanctions that can be applied in relation to projects that are ongoing or have been approved. The actual sanction process is a series of administrative procedures and hearings that are geared toward ensuring fairness and accuracy while at the same time protecting MIGA's operations and those affected by them.[207] Sanctions in the MIGA context can range in severity from temporary suspension of a contractor or those affiliated with a project to absolute debarment from future MIGA activities.[208] Additionally, cross-institution debarment is possible for organizations within the World Bank Group.[209]

International Centre for Settlement of Investment Disputes
Background

In 1965, the International Centre for Settlement of Investment Disputes (ICSID) was formed as a result of the ratification of the Convention on the Settlement of Disputes between States and Nationals of Other States.[210] ICSID is an independent organization that assists with and oversees the settlement of disputes between Member States and (usually) foreign investors over payments due to the investors, instances where payments are not made to investors, and similar claims.[211] At first this might not seem that important, since one might assume that these cases could be heard in a local court. However, such cases are usually not justiciable in a local court for reasons of standing or due to concerns over impartiality. Thus, the establishment of ICSID was important not only as a practical matter in order to ensure a forum for these disputes but also to provide potential investors with some sense of security in that they know that there is indeed a forum to which to take potential complaints.[212]

Structure and jurisdiction

Like other international organizations there is a legislative body – the Administrative Council – and a Secretariat for the ICSID.[213] The Administrative Council is comprised of representatives from each Member State and adopts the major rules, regulations and standards for the ICSID, as well as the budget.[214] However, the Administrative Council does not hear or comment on the disputes that are brought before the ICSID itself.[215] Rather, the Administrative Council and the Secretariat create the facilities that allow for the creation of arbitral panels and provide a general set of rules within which those who are seeking dispute settlement can operate.[216] Within the Administrative Council, each Member State has one seat and one vote,[217] which is typically cast in a system that allows measures to pass by a majority vote.[218] It is the obligation of the Administrative Council to promulgate and evaluate rules, regulations and procedures regarding the ICSID and its functions as well as to serve as the budgetary entity for the ICSID.[219]

The Secretariat comprises a dedicated staff under the aegis of a Secretary General who is elected through a 2/3 majority vote of the Administrative Council.[220] Additionally, there exist within the ICSID system designated Panels of Conciliators and Panels of Arbitrators who are tasked with evaluating claims brought before the ICSID. These individuals are selected based on their knowledge and expertise and must be chosen by the Chairman of the Administrative Council.[221] Each Panel is to consist of 10 members, and it must be highlighted that, somewhat unusually, a person with the appropriate expertise levels has the ability to serve on both Panels.[222]

Functions

In addition to arbitral proceedings, the ICSID is authorized to engage in conciliation efforts for willing parties to a dispute. Those parties wishing to avail themselves of the conciliation option are able to do so by notifying the Secretary General, who has ultimate control over whether this request is approved and placed on the appropriate Panel calendar.[223] Where arbitration is the selected method of dispute resolution, the ICSID Panel award is to be considered binding on the parties and is generally not subject to further appeal or review following issuance.[224]

Regional banking organizations
Inter-American Development Bank
Background

The Inter-American Development Bank (IADB) assists States in Latin America and the Caribbean region with projects geared toward poverty reduction and addressing issues of inequality in society.[225] In addition to regular lending practices, the IADB provides grants to Member States and projects that are in line with its goals.[226] The IADB works with Member States and private project funders and developers to forward these goals.[227] According to its most recent policy statement, the IADB's sector priorities are: "social policy for equity and productivity; infrastructure for competitiveness and social welfare; institutions for growth and social welfare; competitive regional and global international integration; and protection of the environment, response to climate change, promotion of renewable energy and ensuring food security."[228] Further, the IADB has become involved in debt relief efforts that seek to free debtor States from some of their loan obligations in order to promote their growth and development.[229]

Membership and voting

Original membership classification in the IADB is tied to founding membership in the Organization of American States (OAS) and additional regional members are able to join should they possess the requisite qualifications and be approved through the appropriate vote.[230] As in the structure of the OAS, non-regional members are possible within the IADB structure, provided they are also members of the IMF and fulfill regulatory requirements established by the IADB, including subscribing to a designated quantity of shares in the banking sector of the organization.[231]

Regardless the form of membership or their geographic locations, IADB members are required to purchase shares in amounts assessed to them at the time of membership.[232] The voting shares for each Member State in each of the IADB organs are determined by the overall shares that the Member State holds.[233]

Members of the IADB retain the right to withdraw from the organization by sending formal notification to the IADB's offices, including an effective date for the desired withdrawal.[234] However, the time to withdraw must be at the very least six months after delivery of the notice, effectively ruling out immediate withdrawal from the potential abilities of a Member State.[235] As part of withdrawing, the Member State is required to settle accounts with the IADB and there is an obligation to work with the organization to arrange for repurchase of the former Member State's capital shares in the IADB.[236]

As part of the IADB system it is possible for a Member State to be suspended for failure to pay dues or otherwise comply with the requirements of membership.[237] The voting requirements necessary to approve a suspension are, however, quite onerous, namely 3/4 of the overall votes on the Board of Governors and 2/3 of the actual Governors themselves.[238] This serves as a unique measure to ensure that these decisions are made holistically and reflect the will of the entire community rather than of one or two States with high numbers of shares and votes. A suspended member has a year to ensure that the suspension is cured – if it is not, the member can be expelled unless the Board of Governors votes otherwise.[239]

Structure

The IADB's organizational structure is similar to that used by other regional banking organizations. The primary representational organ of the IADB is the Board of Governors – containing representatives from each Member State – which is tasked with essential governance and oversight functions for the organization.[240] As the primary legislative organ for the IADB, the Board of Governors has wide-ranging authorities and powers, and can delegate the majority of them to the Board of Executive Directors subject to certain limitations.[241]

The executive functions within the IADB as a strictly banking entity are vested in the Board of Executive Directors, which is comprised of 14 members who are selected by the Board of Governors.[242] Members of the Board of Executive Directors are chosen based on a formula using share ownership or geography.[243] The Board of Executive Directors decides on specific loans and lending policies, oversees the administrative and regulatory practices of the IADB, sets interest rates on loans and other financial interactions, and takes actions that are essential for the daily lending and financing practices of the organization.[244] Additionally, the Board of Executive Directors oversees a variety of specialized committees and similar bodies.[245]

The bureaucratic arm of the IADB falls under the leadership of the President of the IADB, who serves a similar function to the Secretary General in most international organizations.[246] The President of the IADB is elected by the Board of Governors to serve a renewable, five-year term of office and is chosen from a list of those nominated by Governors.[247]

In addition to Secretariat staff, the IADB utilizes the services of employees from major private firms in the region and internationally who are seconded or otherwise attached to IADB operations and funding endeavors based on their areas of expertise.[248] This furthers the status of the IADB as a highly impactful development partner in the Latin America and Caribbean region, allowing it to benefit from a level of trust that ensures good governance in projects and with national and local governments.[249]

Suspension in the IADB context can also impact on the organization itself, particularly in situations where it is impracticable for the organization to carry out its designated functions.[250] This is envisioned as a rare occurrence and is generally thought of as an emergency measure that is intended to be temporary. On the other hand, it is also possible for the IADB to terminate as an organization following the same voting requirement necessary to suspend a Member State.[251] Should the termination be approved, the IADB is required to complete a full accounting of assets and liabilities, which will then be settled prior to official closure of the organization.[252]

Functions

In recent years, the IADB has concentrated on a number of issues under the umbrella of its priorities, such as poverty reduction, sustainability, efforts to combat climate change, infrastructural development, educational development, and efforts at regional integration.[253] Following the adoption of the Sustainable Development Goals (SDGs), the IADB and affiliated entities within the Inter-American system embraced the challenges highlighted in them and began to work them into operational policies and practices.[254] Further to this, and in the aftermath of the Paris Agreement on climate action, the IADB's work has expanded to include new and often trend-setting forms of climate finance to address the needs of individual Member States and the region as a whole.[255] The IADB also provides innovative financing programs to allow students from the region to attend the best programs in their fields of intended specialization as well as bolstering the educational systems within Member States.[256]

In order to address the potential for employment-related claims by IADB staff, the organization has created the Administrative Tribunal of the Inter-American Development Bank. The Administrative Tribunal has jurisdiction over the operations of both the IADB itself and the IIC since they are organizationally classified as one entity.[257] It is comprised of seven members, who must be from IADB Member States and must have appropriate and relevant experiences and qualifications to sit on the Administrative Tribunal.[258] In terms of governance, the Administrative Tribunal uses a President, elected from the Tribunal members, and an Executive Secretary, selected by the Board of Executive Directors.[259] Rules and regulations for cases that are brought before the Administrative Tribunal are to be generated by the Tribunal itself and explicitly are not to come from the national laws of any IADB Member States.[260] The Administrative Tribunal is the only entity within the employment dispute system at the IADB and there is no appellate entity for its decisions.[261]

To assist in overseeing the proper operations of the IADB, especially in terms of anti-corruption efforts, the IADB has created the Office of Institutional Integrity and empowered it with the ability to receive complaints, engage in investigations and issue sanctions and other findings.[262] Additionally, the Office of Institutional Integrity is tasked with undertaking educational efforts regarding corruption and anti-corruption for the public and private sectors.[263] In order to ensure impartiality within its operations, the Office of Institutional Integrity exists within the IADB system as an independent entity.[264] This Office was expanded to include an Ethics Officer to handle specialized issues within the context of integrity[265] and has grown to include assistance to IADB Member States seeking to strengthen their abilities in terms of capacity for integrity programs.[266]

European banking systems

European Central Bank and European System of Central Banks

Background and membership

The European Central Bank (ECB) controls the monetary policies and practices that are connected to the euro.[267] As part of Eurozone membership requirements, States agree that the ECB will be a supranational entity akin to the European Union and that the decisions of the ECB regarding monetary policy will be automatically adopted as part of the Member State's policies.[268] In addition, the ECB is tasked with providing advisory information to Eurozone Member States and the EU where there is a potential action or policy decision that falls within the scope of its activities.[269]

While the ECB is the overarching central bank for the purposes of the euro, the European System of Central Banks (ESCB) is the overarching banking entity for all members of the European Union, even those States that have not joined the Eurozone.[270] The ESCB is comprised of the ECB and the National Central Banks of all Member States of the European Union.[271] The ESCB is tasked with creating policies that support the common market and that attempt to ensure that there is price stability within the Member States.[272] In addition, the ESCB is required to set the monetary policy of the entire EU and to assist in the functioning of payment systems for the EU and its Member States.[273]

Generally, the ESCB is required to function independently of other EU or national institutions when making its decisions and policies.[274] However, this independence does not apply to the ECB and indeed the ECB has oversight capabilities for the ESCB.[275] It is important to stress that the dual organizations of the ECB and the ESCB are not intended to be permanent since the ESCB was created on the understanding that it would cease to exist when/if all EU Member States effectively join the Eurozone. Whether this will happen in reality is another matter.

Structure and functions

In terms of organizational structure, the ECB is comprised of the Governing Council and the Executive Board, and additionally works with the National Central Banks of Member States for purposes of coordination and implementation.[276] The Governing Council is responsible for creating and implementing guidelines to ensure that the ECB and the European System of Central Banks function according to their foundational texts.[277] Formulation of monetary policy is also accomplished at the Governing Council level,[278] as is the issuance of euro monetary instruments.[279] This includes the physical design of euro notes as well as decisions regarding whether and when to issue new notes and the quantity to issue.[280]

The membership of the Governing Council is comprised of those who sit on the Executive Board and the governors from the National Central Banks of Eurozone States.[281] All members of the Governing Council typically have one vote and votes will pass using a simple majority provided that at least 2/3 of the Governing Council's members are present.[282] There are, however, some circumstances under which the voting system is altered such that no member of the Executive Board votes and the votes of the remaining members of the Governing Council are weighted by their overall subscription shares.[283] Somewhat unusually, the foundational text for the ECB requires that there be confidentiality for all Governing Council meetings.[284]

The Executive Board takes the guidelines issued by the Governing Council and ensures their implementation on a practical level, including consultation with National Central Banks.[285] In addition, the Governing Council is allowed to delegate other functions to the Executive Board as it deems necessary.[286] The Executive Board is comprised of six members – the President and Vice-President of the ECB and four other members who possess the requisite qualifications.[287] The European Council is the body charged with appointing all of these positions.[288] The appointees must be recommended to the European Council in consultation with the European Parliament and the ECB Governing Council.[289] All members of the Executive Board have one vote and a simple majority is used for voting purposes.[290]

European Bank for Reconstruction and Development

Background

The European Bank for Reconstruction and Development (EBRD) was created following the Cold War to assist Central and Eastern European States emerging from communist regimes and in need of economic assistance.[291] The EBRD has expanded its operations and now works in areas of Asia as well as Central and Eastern Europe.[292] It identifies itself as a "transition" bank due to its focus on assisting States transitioning from communist-based market structure to free market structure.[293]

Membership and voting

The EBRD is run and owned by members who are also shareholders, and which include, rather uniquely, States as well as the European Union and the European Investment Bank.[294] Additionally, the scope of shareholders includes States from Europe, North America,[295] Asia,[296] Australasia,[297] and the Middle East.[298] All prospective members of the EBRD must also be members of the IMF in order to meet full eligibility requirements and must purchase the requisite number of shares for admission.[299]

EBRD Member States are permitted to withdraw with at least six months' notice to the organization; however, at any time during the period between notification of intent to withdraw and the effective date of withdrawal it is possible for the State to renounce the decision and remain as a Member State.[300] Withdrawing members are required to settle their accounts with the EBRD as part of their complete exit from the organization.[301] Errant members, such as those who fail to pay their membership dues, are subject to suspension of their membership rights until the issue is cured.[302] Failure to cure the issue within a year of suspension will result in the automatic termination of a State's membership in the EBRD unless the Board of Governors votes to stop this.[303]

Structure

The primary organ within the ERBD is the Board of Governors, on which representatives from all shareholders sit.[304] The EBRD Board of Governors has delegated most of its essential decision-making functions to the Board of Directors, which is the executive representational body within the EBRD system.[305] There are, however, some policy decisions that the Board of Governors cannot delegate, such as membership decisions, handling policy appeals, entering into relationships with other international organizations, the election of Directors and other executives, and deciding to terminate the organization.[306] At both the Board of Governors and Board of Directors level voting is weighted according to the shares held by each Member State.[307]

The Board of Directors is the executive representational body of the EBRD, with 23 members that are decided by geography and State identity.[308] Specifically, 11 of the 23 Directors are required to be from Belgium, Denmark, France, Germany, Greece, Ireland, Italy, Luxembourg, the Netherlands, Portugal, Spain, the United Kingdom, the European Union and the European Investment Bank.[309] Of the remaining 12 Directors' seats, four are to be held by States from Central and Eastern Europe, four by European States not otherwise represented, and four from non-European Member States.[310] The Board of Directors makes the essential decisions on the part of EBRD regarding lending and loan terms as well as general organizational operations and budgeting.[311]

The EBRD's legal representative is the President, who is elected by the Board of Governors.[312] While in office, the President liaises with the Board of Governors and the Board of Directors as well as the general staff of the organization[313] and the elected Vice-Presidents.[314] The EBRD structure includes the Office of Chief Compliance Officer to regulate the activities of the organization and the projects it funds for corruption and other potential violations of personal and/or EBRD-based integrity.[315] These include efforts to prevent money laundering, inadvertent funding of terrorist activities through project financing, and non-compliance with EBRD codes of conduct and project guidelines.[316] In order to assist in its mandate, the EBRD allows for complaints from citizens and others working on organization funded projects.[317] These offices and activities are supported by the EBRD foundational text, which sets out strict guidelines for the use of funds from the organization.[318]

Just as a Member State may terminate its membership, so too can the EBRD suspend or terminate its operations with a vote of the Board of Governors.[319] In the instance of termination, the EBRD is required to settle accounts itself, including with Member States as well as all States that have received funding.[320] The EBRD, its employees and those involved in its governance are provided standard privileges and immunities for international banks.[321]

Functions

The EBRD lends primarily to the private sector and supports projects that promote democracy and capacity-building in newly democratic States.[322] The EBRD is not a full-funding lender and caps its funding at a maximum of 35 per cent of total project funding needs.[323] Additionally, the EBRD assists projects that might otherwise not receive funding or that would receive funding but at a more burdensome rate of return.[324] Key among the operating principles for the EBRD is the respect of State sovereignty in operations and projects, the use of sound banking principles throughout the EBRD and its projects, and the legitimate ability of the recipient State to implement the project and repay the loan.[325]

Recent projects funded by the EBRD have included a number of State-specific activities that are intended to provide a benefit to the larger region and beyond, for example efforts to ensure food security in Eastern and Central Europe.[326] In an effort to provide environmental and public health safety assurances to the region and allow for safe development, the EBRD has devoted particular attention to cleanup and remediation of the Chernobyl disaster site.[327] Additionally, the EBRD has been at the forefront of regional banks seeking to incorporate essential sustainable development tenets such as the precautionary principle into its practices and, as a result, has made a concerted

effort to fund projects that support this.[328] In recent years, assistance to Member States for resettlement projects for refugees and internally displaced persons have also been encouraged and funded
by the EBRD.[329]

European Investment Bank

Background

While the European Central Bank decides monetary policy for the European Union, it does not
actually engage in banking functions. Instead, banking functions in the European Union are carried out by the European Investment Bank (EIB), which is linked to the foundational texts of the
European Union.[330] With this in mind, the EIB is explicitly required to act in ways that are in
the interests of the EU, regardless whether the lending activities it undertakes are in EU Member
States.[331] The EIB finances and lends to projects based primarily within EU Member States, although
approximately 10 per cent of its overall lending activities involve non-EU Member States.[332] These
non-EU lending activities tend to focus on projects that promote growth within developing States
and States in Eastern and Central Europe.[333] As part of its activities, the EIB may provide lending
and other services to private entities as well as to public entities provided there is State support.[334]

Membership and voting

The EIB's work is financed by the shares that all EU Member States subscribe to along with its
investment of some of its funds on the open market.[335]

Structure

The primary representative body for shareholder States in the EIB is the Board of Governors, on
which every shareholder State has a seat.[336] Typically, Finance Ministers from each Member State
hold these seats. The Board of Governors is tasked with creating credit policy guidelines for the
organization's lending practices, approving annual balance sheets, and making decisions regarding
lending policies for projects in non-EU Member States.[337]

Although the Board of Governors has many powers, essential issues on lending policies, particularly those within EU Member States, are decided by the Board of Directors.[338] The Board of
Directors is also tasked with ensuring that the EIB functions properly and in accordance with the
terms of its foundational texts.[339] In total, there are 29 members of the Board of Directors who are
selected by the Board of Governors from a list of nominees provided by the Member States.[340] Each
selected member of the Board of Directors serves for a five-year term that is renewable upon the
decision of the Board of Governors.[341] Every member of the EU is given a Director seat with voting power, and it is also possible for the EIB to bring in several outside experts to consult with the
Board of Directors, although these experts will not have voting capabilities.[342]

The EIB equivalent of a Secretariat is the Management Committee, composed of nine members
who are appointed by the Board of Governors and overseen by the Board of Directors.[343] In addition, there is an Audit Committee, which oversees the work of the EIB and ensures that all of the
EIB's policies and requirements have been complied with.[344] The Audit Committee is composed
of six members selected by and answerable to the Board of Governors.[345]Although it is under the
rubric of the EU's foundational text, the EIB retains the ability to enter into its own arrangements
with international organizations for cooperation, coordination, or other appropriate measures.[346]

Decisions regarding the EIB either suspending its operations or completely terminating its
operations are within the realm of the Board of Governors, which is also charged with overseeing
the settling of accounts and disbursing of assets when appropriate.[347]

Unlike some other international banks, the EIB explicitly avails itself of national courts or the
ECJ for disputes with public and private individuals.[348] For matters involving issues of integrity,
corruption or related allegations, the EIB has established the Ethics and Compliance Committee.[349]

This entity has jurisdiction over the activities of the EIB as well the other committees, such as the Management Committee.[350] Further, there are established procedures for handling allegations from whistleblowers and protecting them from retaliation within a number of committees and other offices within the EIB.[351]

Functions

In addition, in 2007 the EIB established the EU-Africa Infrastructure Trust Fund with the goal of facilitating the availability of long- and short-term funding to African States for the purpose of constructing or supplementing their infrastructural capacities.[352] Over time, the Fund grew to encompass a Steering Committee, comprised of European and African members, to guide its policies and priorities for project approval and funding implementation.[353] The work of the Fund itself is carried out through a dedicated Secretariat that works with the Steering Committee, other technical committees and States that are involved as funders or those that receive funds.[354]

Within the EU, the EIB's lending practices focus on encouraging environmental sustainability and related projects, promoting Member State growth, promoting regional growth, and supporting projects that will lead to job creation and the bolstering of small and medium-sized enterprises.[355] The EIB's commitment to promoting environmental and social sustainability is reflected in its requirement that proposed projects undergo stringent review for financial viability as well as environmental and social impact and potential sustainability.[356]

Asian Development Bank

Background

While there are several prominent Asian regional organizations, such as ASEAN, none is directly connected to a lending institution. Rather, the main regional financing organization is the Asian Development Bank (ADB), which works with projects that promote cooperation and growth in Asia and the Pacific Rim.[357] The ADB provides sovereign lending, financing and technical support for projects and also non-sovereign, private sector-based, lending, financing and technical support for projects.[358]

Membership and voting

The ADB has regional and non-regional Member States.[359] Regardless of a State's location, membership in a UN or UN-affiliated organization is a prerequisite for membership in the ADB.[360] Regional Member States include developed States such as Japan, Australia and New Zealand, as well as developing States throughout Asia and the Pacific Rim.[361] These developing States run the gamut of size and development needs, ranging from small island developing States such as the Maldives and Tuvalu to States that are emerging from a communist government system into the free market system such as Vietnam and Laos.[362] Interestingly, the ADB's Member States include both the People's Republic of China and Taiwan.[363] Non-regional Member States include North American and European States.[364] All Member States are required to subscribe to an assessed quantity of shares in the ADB.[365] This quantity is also used as the basis for determining a Member State's voting share within the ADB.[366]

In addition to States, the ADB is permitted to enter into relationships and work with other international organizations when this furthers the Bank's purpose.[367] While they cannot serve as members in the ADB, non-governmental organizations have a special relationship to the organization and are able to use this to foster cooperation and collaboration in a number of policy areas.[368]

All Member States in the ADB have the ability to withdraw from the organization through the provision of formal notice, which cannot become effective for at least six months after deposit.[369] Withdrawing Member States are required to settle accounts with the ADB as part of the official withdrawal process.[370] An ADB Member State may be suspended for failing to comply with organizational rules and requirements, and its membership may be terminated after a one-year suspension unless there is a vote of the Board of Governors to the contrary.[371]

Structure

In terms of organizational structure, the ADB uses the standard combination of a Board of Governors, Board of Directors and President accompanied by a staff for implementation purposes.[372] All ADB Member States have a seat on the Board of Governors.[373] However, there are only 10 seats on the Board of Directors, seven of which must be elected by the regional Member States and three of which must be elected by non-regional Member States.[374]

The Board of Governors has broad powers and also has the ability to devolve all but the most core organizational functions to the Board of Directors.[375] Additionally, Governors are authorized to revisit issues of how a particular Member State is classified on the developing to developed spectrum, which can be altered by a vote and has tremendous impacts on issues such as lending and project support to a State.[376] As the entity charged with overseeing the ADB's general operations, the Board of Directors has wide-ranging abilities that include auditing and project implementation.[377]

The President of the ADB is elected by the Board of Governors and serves multiple roles, including non-voting Chair of the Board of Directors and overall legal representative of the ADB.[378] In order to assist the President in his powers and functions, a staff is authorized and has grown to become similar to the staffs used in other regional banks and organizations.[379]

It is possible for the ADB to temporarily suspend operations with the approval of the Board of Directors and to terminate its operations completely with approval from the Board of Governors.[380] Should there be a decision to terminate operations, the ADB is required to engage in wind-up activities to settle liabilities and ensure the appropriate distribution of assets.[381]

Functions

The primary goal of ADB lending and financing operations is to support projects that will reduce poverty within individual States and the region as a whole. In order to achieve this goal, the ADB's funding operations have focused on projects addressing and mitigating the impacts of climate change, increasing access to and the quality of health care for all peoples within the region, promoting sustainable development (particularly in terms of the use of natural resources) and the development of infrastructure within States and the region.[382] The ADB is also well known for its work to combat corruption in the lending, financing and contracting sectors. In an effort to assist in these goals, the ADB created the Asian Development Bank Institute to aid in educating representatives of developing States and other organizations working in developing States on methods for successfully implementing development strategies.[383]

In terms of oversight, there are several vehicles within the ADB system. An essential aspect of this system is the Independent Evaluation Department, which examines a number of activities to ensure their compliance with ADB policies and requirements.[384] Another element of the ADB's oversight is the Accountability Mechanism, which seeks to evaluate potential issues in the application of ADB policies and projects and, subsequently, to provide suggestions on methods of addressing them.[385]

Issues involving complaints by ADB staff regarding actions of the Bank are subject to the jurisdiction of the Administrative Tribunal of the Asian Development Bank.[386] The Administrative Tribunal's membership is comprised of five individuals, who are nationals of ADB Member States, and who are versed in the legal issues involved in employment-related claims.[387] Administrative Tribunal members are appointed by the Board of Directors for three-year terms and select their own President and Vice-President.[388] It has the ability to order a variety of compensation forms, including specific performance and financial compensation.[389]

African Development Bank

Background

The African Development Bank (AfDB) provides lending and financing for both public sector and private sector projects.[390] It was founded in 1963 to promote economic growth and solidarity within Africa as a whole while also serving as a means through which to coordinate economic policies and growth plans on a regional level.[391] At the same time, one of the key understandings of the AfDB's founders was the importance of coordinating regional and non-regional economic support for African economic growth and development.[392] Throughout the AfDB's foundational texts and operational strategies there is an attempt to balance the needs and interests of the region *per se* with the needs and interests of each Member State's economic development.[393]

Membership and voting

Membership in the AfDB is open to all independent African States without any requirement of UN or other organizational membership.[394] Membership is open to non-regional States provided they are members in the African Development Fund or, at the very least, contributors to the African Development Fund.[395] The majority of African States are members of the AfDB,[396] and there are also a number of non-regional AfDB Member States, spanning North America, Europe, the Middle East and Asia.[397] Any class of membership requires subscription to AfDB shares in an amount assessed at the time of initial entry into the organization.[398] In addition to regional and non-regional Member States and partners, the AfDB has also formed partnerships with several UN-affiliated international organizations as well as private foundations and groups that can assist in financing and technical support.[399]

AfDB Member States have the ability to withdraw from the organization by providing at least six months' notice in writing.[400] A Member State may be suspended from full membership in the event it fails to comply with the terms and requirements of membership, however a 70 per cent approval vote of the Board of Governors is needed for this to occur.[401] The same percentage of votes is needed for a suspended State to be instated to full membership in the AfDB. Should this not occur within one year from the date of suspension, the State's membership in the AfDB is considered terminated.[402] When a Member State elects to withdraw from the AfDB or has its membership terminated it is required to make a settlement of liabilities to the organization.[403]

Structure

The AfDB uses the Board of Governors, Board of Directors and Presidential structure.[404] All AfDB Member States have seats on the Board of Governors, however there are only 20 seats on the Board of Directors.[405] Of these 20 seats, 13 must be elected by regional Member States and seven must be elected by the non-regional Member States.[406] As is the standard practice in banking organizations, voting power for each State is determined by the number of shares that the Member State subscribes.[407]

The Board of Governors is the highest level organ within the AfDB structure and is afforded power over the existence of the organization itself.[408] Governors can delegate many functions and decisions to the Board of Directors, however fundamental issues relating to the organization must be retained.[409] The Board of Directors has jurisdiction for the operational functions of the AfDB, while the President and his staff carry out the daily operations and decisions of the organization.[410] The President of the AfDB is elected by the Board of Governors with a requirement that the majority of African Governors vote in favor of any candidate in order for him to be approved.[411] Terms of the President are for five years and may be renewed once at the discretion of the Governors.[412]

During times of emergency, the Board of Directors has the ability to temporarily suspend the AfDB's activities and future decisions on lending.[413] Only the Board of Governors has the authority to decide that the AfDB would permanently terminate its operations, which then requires the organization to settle outstanding debts and appropriately distribute any remaining assets.[414] As an organization, the AfDB enjoys the standard privileges and immunities afforded to international organizations and those affiliated with the AfDB are afforded functional immunity.[415]

Functions

The AfDB funds projects in a variety of sectors, such as agricultural development, climate change adaptation and mitigation, the development of State infrastructure and governance capabilities, educational advancement, environment and sustainable development – including issues related to energy supply – gender equality, health care and services, the development of sustainable transportation practices, and water-based issues.[416] Further, the AfDB seeks to encourage regional integration and interdependence through its projects.[417] The AfDB receives assistance and technical support for many of these endeavors through the African Development Fund (ADF), which was founded as an organization meant to assist the AfDB in its operations.[418]

In order to provide those who are impacted by projects funded by the AfDB a venue to bring complaints regarding these projects and their implementation, the Independent Review Mechanism has been established within the AfDB organizational structure.[419] For complaints regarding fraud and other misconduct from inside the AfDB, an extensive policy to protect whistleblowers and allow for investigations into complaints has been established.[420] Complaints from staff members regarding administrative decisions relating to their employment and its terms may seek redress only from the Administrative Tribunal of the African Development Bank, which functions as an independent entity within the organization.[421] The Administrative Tribunal is composed of six judges who are appointed by the Board of Directors to three-year terms of office.[422] All judgments issued by the Tribunal are binding and there is no further appellate process available.[423]

Caribbean Development Bank

Background

From the outset, it must be noted that some Caribbean States are also members of the Inter-American Development Bank and the Organization for American States. However, the vast majority of Caribbean States are not part of either institution yet still wished to participate in a banking system that would promote the unique needs of States in the region. With that in mind, the Caribbean Development Bank (CDB) was first created in 1970.[424]

Membership and voting

While the intent of the CDB's founders was to create an entity that would provide assistance for the region, they were careful to include non-regional States in this plan as sources of funding and as a special category of members.[425] All States in the region are eligible for membership in the CDB, as are non-regional UN Member States and, unusually, international institutions.[426] Once an entity is approved for membership in the CDB it is required to take out a subscription to the number of shares assessed for it by the organization.[427] In the CDB's governance system, votes held by each Member State are decided by the number of shares held by the State.[428]

CDB Member States may withdraw from the organization by giving at least six months' notice and retain the ability to renounce the withdrawal notice at any time before it becomes effective.[429] Member States may be suspended by the Board of Directors for failing to meet an organizational requirement, for example failing to pay assessed dues, and have a year to cure the failure.[430] If the issue is not cured after a year from suspension, the State will be terminated as a member unless the Board of Governors votes to the contrary.[431] In either situation, a Member State that leaves the CDB must settle accounts with the organization.[432]

Structure

Structurally, the CDB is comprised of the Board of Governors, Board of Directors, and President of the CDB and associated staff members.[433] Every Member State appoints a representative to serve on the Board of Governors and, collectively, the Governors hold the CDB's powers.[434] In its discretion, the Board of Governors may delegate all but the most fundamental organizational powers to the Board of Directors.[435]

In contrast, the Board of Directors is comprised of 20 members, 14 of whom must be selected by Governors from the Caribbean region and six of whom must be selected by Governors from non-regional Member States.[436] Together, the Board of Directors functions as the operational arm of the CDB, exercising general powers and functions as well as those which the Board of Governors opts to delegate.[437] The quotidian operation of the CDB are administered by the President of the CDB, who is elected by the Board of Governors and serves as the official and legal representative of the organization.[438]

It is possible for the CDB to temporarily suspend its activities in response to an emergency of some sort provided the Board of Directors approves this measure.[439] It is equally possible for the Board of Governors to vote to terminate the CDB entirely, although in this situation the organization – or former organization – would still be required to settle outstanding accounts and liabilities and divide assets.[440]

Functions

Certainly the CDB is a source of financing and project support for a number of undertakings that promote economic and social development in the Caribbean, yet to conceive of it in this limited form would be incorrect.[441] The CDB also engages in technical assistance for its Member States, works to stimulate market growth and development, and assists Member States with the overall planning and implementation of their development systems so as to increase effectiveness.[442] In order to reach the fullest possible complement of development activities, the CDB has the ability to lend to both public and private entities that meet its guidelines.[443]

Given the needs of the Caribbean region, the CDB's work has a large focus on poverty reduction, infrastructural development, and climate change related issues. Poverty has been a persistent theme within the CDB's work, as has the development of Member State governmental capacities to address the needs of their communities.[444] Importantly for climate-related and emergency situations, in 2007 the CDB established the Caribbean Catastrophe Risk Insurance Facility to assist governments in certain disaster situations.[445] Recently, the CDB has embraced the terms of the Sustainable Development Goals and begun applying their tenets to its funding and support strategies and operations.[446]

Integrity is heavily regulated within the CDB context and throughout its history the organization has undertaken a number of policies and structural practices to ensure that its projects and funding mechanisms include integrity as a benchmark. From a structural standpoint, the CDB has established the Office of Integrity, Compliance and Accountability to support the application of the Strategy Framework for Integrity, Compliance and Accountability.[447] For complaints regarding the environmental and social impacts of decisions to fund projects and projects funded by the CDB there exists a Projects Complaints Mechanism as a separate entity within the Office of Integrity, Compliance and Accountability.[448] The Projects Complaints Mechanism reviews complaints from appropriate persons and entities and issues findings regarding the project's impacts and the CDB's appropriate – or inappropriate – funding of it.[449] For the regulation and oversight of CDB activities internally and with outside parties, it has promulgated a Compliance Policy to be used across organizational activities.[450] Further to this, the CDB has implemented guidelines which recipients of organizational funds must use in the selection and retention of contractors for projects financed by it.[451]

Nordic Investment Bank

Background

Comprised of eight States in the region, the Nordic Investment Bank (NIB) became operational in 1976, although throughout the course of its history the foundational text has been overhauled on several occasions.[452] Despite this, the NIB has functioned as a consistent source for financing and investment strategy for its Member States and those entities benefiting from its activities.[453]

Membership and voting

All Member States are required to subscribe to shares and hold capital stock in the NIB, and the Board of Governors has the ability to require changes to the capital stock in the NIB generally and held by each Member State in particular.[454] NIB Member States have the ability to withdraw by providing notification to the Government of Norway, effective after at least a year between the date of notification and the effective date and are required to settle accounts with the organization.[455]

Structure

The NIB is governed by a Board of Governors, Board of Directors and President, along with accompanying staff members.[456] The Board of Governors has one representative from each Member State (at present eight States in total) and together the Governors elect a Chair of the Board on a rotating basis.[457] Within the Board of Governors there is a unanimity requirement for all votes, regardless the topic or issue involved.[458] The specific powers allocated to the Board of Governors are as follows: amendment of the NIB's governing Statutes, decisions involving capital stocks in the organization, interpretation of the foundational texts, approval of reports and auditing activities, appointments to committees, and decisions regarding membership and organizational existence.[459]

The Board of Directors retains all other powers needed to operate the NIB and is the operational body for the organization.[460] As with the Board of Governors, each Member State appoints a representative to the Board of Directors and the Directors also have the ability to select a Chair on a rotating basis.[461] Within the NIB structure, the Board of Directors has the ability to hear and decide disputes between the Member States or between a Member State and the NIB.[462] Finally, the President of the NIB is selected by the Board of Directors and, in turn, has the ability to appoint staff members to carry out the official functions of the office, which involve the functional aspects of the organization.[463] One other essential organ within the NIB structure is the Control Committee, which serves as a separate entity to audit and oversee the operations and actions of the NIB itself and its constituent organs.[464] The Control Committee is comprised of 10 representatives, two from the Board of Governors and the remainder from the Nordic Council and Parliaments in Estonia, Latvia and Lithuania.[465]

The Board of Governors is afforded the power to decide if and when the NIB should terminate its activities and is, accordingly, responsible for ensuring the winding-up of operations and the handling of liabilities and assets of the organizations.[466]

Functions

The investment financing provided by the NIB falls into a number of categories, including general funding and environmental investments.[467]

As part of the NIB's oversight systems, it has created an Ombudsman role and vested it with powers over supervision of and assistance to the organizational workforce.[468] Specifically, the Ombudsman is intended to serve as a mediator in situations involving employment issues and as a source of good offices to investigate allegations of harassment or inappropriate workplace conduct.[469] In the event of employment-based disputes involving the NIB, a set of arbitration rules and procedures has been established.[470] Under these rules, an Arbitral Tribunal is established to hear complaints that cannot be settled through mediation or other dispute settlement processes.[471] The Arbitral Tribunal panel in each claim is comprised of separately selected members and is not a separate, dedicated set of fact-finders as in other international organizations settings.[472]

Essential to the NIB's activities and policies is the Compliance, Integrity and Anti-Corruption Policy that is used to guide the allowable funding decisions and project activities for the organization.[473] Issues relating to oversight for integrity, fraud, corruption and related activities are under the jurisdiction of the Office of the Chief Compliance Officer and include institutional compliance, operational compliance and conduct compliance.[474] The OCCO liaises with external actors such as project partners and also investigates allegations of wrongdoing within NIB structure.[475] Over the course of the OCCO's history it has become a larger entity comprising additional committees to allow for specialized investigations and findings based on types of allegations made.[476]

Conclusions

The trade, finance and banking sectors have expanded dramatically as private entities and in the form of international organizations that work with and in the sectors. A key lesson of this chapter is the way in which these forms of international organizations have been designed to be flexible in terms of membership, activities and purposes so as to adjust to current economic and political climates. Without the ability to do this, international organizations such as the WTO would have been unable to adapt to changes in the constitution of the international community and the ways in which this has impacted the needs of States as they attempt to build, diversify or supplement their trading systems.

Perhaps some of the most innovative and important lessons of this chapter come from the regional financial organizations, which operate to provide a dedicated area with alternative sources of funding that are integrated into the needs of the region as a whole. This reflects an awareness on the part of the organization and its Member States that has been informed by a culture of legal flexibility combined with an intimate knowledge of the needs of the region and the States that comprise it. At the same time, these organizations are highly sensitive to the cultural heritage and cultures within the region. This allows them to assess the viability and value of proposed projects in the cultural contexts and to make meaningful decisions regarding their potential funding.

Overall, the structures used by regional organizations in particular provide flexibility for the region and for both regional and non-regional members to support growth. When these attempts at support and sustainability fail, the procedures used to evaluate complaints against funding decisions and practices demonstrate the ability to flexibly address questions of legitimacy in order to act in ways that benefit the organization and the communities it is intended to serve and assist.

Notes

1 *See* Australia-New Zealand Free Trade Agreement (1983); Armenia-Kazakhstan Free Trade Agreement (2001); People's Republic of China-Singapore Free Trade Agreement (2009); Egypt-Turkey Free Trade Agreement (2007); India-Sri Lanka Free Trade Agreement (2001); Kyrgyzstan-Ukraine Free Trade Agreement (1998); Ukraine-Belarus Free Trade Agreement (2006).

2 North American Free Trade Agreement (1994).

3 *See* Australia-Chile Free Trade Agreement (2008); Japan-Brunei Free Trade Agreement (2008); New Zealand-People's Republic of China Free Trade Agreement (2008); Costa Rica-Singapore Free Trade Agreement (2013); Iceland-People's Republic of China Free Trade Agreement (2014); India-Afghanistan Free Trade Agreement (2003); Japan-India Free Trade Agreement (2011); Japan-Australia Free Trade Agreement (2015); Japan-Malaysia Free Trade Agreement (2006); Japan-Mexico Free Trade Agreement (2005); Japan-Singapore Free Trade Agreement (2002); Japan-Thailand Free Trade Agreement (2007); Laos People's Democratic Republic-Thailand Free Trade Agreement (1991); New Zealand-Malaysia Free Trade Agreement (2010); United States-Australia Free Trade Agreement (2005); United States-Colombia Free Trade Agreement (2012); Canada-Panama Free Trade Agreement (2013); Canada-Colombia Free Trade Agreement (2011).

4 *See* Agreement Establishing the ASEAN-Australia-New Zealand Free Trade Area (2009). It should be remembered that, while ASEAN as an organization has the ability to endorse such agreements, they must still be appropriately ratified by each individual Member State.

5 NAFTA, *supra* note 2 at ch 20.

6 Id.

7 *See* ASEAN-Australia-New Zealand Free Trade Agreement, *supra* note 4 at ch 17.

8 *See., e.g.,* Australia-Chile Free Trade Agreement, *supra* note 3; Japan-Brunei Free Trade Agreement, *supra* note 3; Canada-Chile Free Trade Agreement (1997); New Zealand-China Free Trade Agreement (2008); China-Singapore (2009); Costa Rica-Singapore Free Trade Agreement, *supra* note 3; Egypt-Turkey Free Trade Agreement, *supra* note 1; Taiwan-El Salvador-Honduras Free Trade Agreement (2008); Taiwan-Guatemala Free Trade Agreement (2006); Hong Kong-Chile Free Trade Agreement (2014); Hong Kong-New Zealand (2011); Iceland-China Free Trade Agreement, *supra* note 3: Japan-India Free Trade Agreement, *supra* note 3; India-Republic of Korea Free Trade Agreement (2009); India-Sri Lanka Free Trade Agreement (2001); Korea-Singapore Free Trade Agreement (2006); Kyrgyzstan-Armenia Free Trade Agreement (1995); Kyrgyzstan-Kazakhstan Free Trade Agreement (1995); Kyrgyzstan-Moldova Free Trade Agreement (1996); Kyrgyzstan-Russian Federation Free Trade Agreement (1993); Kyrgyzstan-Ukraine Free Trade Agreement (1998); Kyrgyzstan-Uzbekistan Free Trade Agreement (1998); Singapore-Panama Free Trade Agreement (2005); Switzerland-China Free Trade Agreement (2014); Thailand-New Zealand Free Trade Agreement (2005); Turkey-former Yugoslav Republic of Macedonia Free Trade Agreement (2000); Turkey-Syria Free Trade Agreement (2007); United States-Morocco Free Trade Agreement (2006); United States-Panama Free Trade Agreement (2012); Canada-Panama Free Trade Agreement, *supra* note 3; Canada-Peru Free Trade Agreement (2009); Australia-Singapore Free Trade Agreement (2003).

9 *See, e.g.,* Iceland-Faroe Islands Free Trade Agreement (2006); Iceland-Afghanistan Free Trade Agreement (2003); Japan-Australia Free Trade Agreement, *supra* note 3; Japan-Malaysia Free Trade Agreement (2006); Japan-Mexico Free Trade Agreement, *supra* note 3; Japan-Philippines Free Trade Agreement (2008); Japan-Singapore Free Trade Agreement (2002); Japan-Switzerland Free Trade Agreement (2009); Japan-Thailand Free Trade Agreement (2007); Japan-Vietnam Free Trade Agreement (2009); Jordan-Singapore Free Trade Agreement (2005); Australia-China Free Trade Agreement (2015); Korea-Chile Free Trade Agreement (2004); New Zealand-Malaysia Free Trade Agreement, *supra* note 3; China-Nicaragua Free Trade Agreement (2008); Pakistan-Malaysia Free Trade Agreement (2008); Panama-Taiwan Free Trade Agreement (2004); Pakistan-Sri Lank Free Trade Agreement (2005); China-Peru Free Trade Agreement (2010); Australia-Thailand Free Trade Agreement (2005); Turkey-Albania Free Trade Agreement (2008); Turkey-Chile Free Trade Agreement (2011); Turkey-Georgia Free Trade Agreement (2008); Turkey-Mauritius Free Trade Agreement (2013); Turkey-Montenegro Free Trade Agreement (2010); Turkey-Morocco Free Trade Agreement (2006); Turkey-Serbia Free Trade Agreement (2010); Turkey-Tunisia Free Trade Agreement (2005); Ukraine-Macedonia Free Trade Agreement (2001); Ukraine-Moldova Free Trade Agreement (2005); Montenegro-Ukraine Free Trade Agreement (2013): United States-Australia Free Trade Agreement, *supra* note 3; United States-Singapore Free Trade Agreement (2004); United States-Jordan Free Trade Agreement (2001); Korea-Australia Free Trade Agreement (2014); United States-Bahrain Free Trade Agreement (2006); CAFTA-DR (2009); United States-Chile Free Trade Agreement (2004); United States-Colombia Free Trade Agreement, *supra* note 3; United States-Korea Free Trade Agreement (2012); United States-Oman Free Trade Agreement (2009); United States-Peru Free Trade Agreement (2009); Canada-Korea Free Trade Agreement (2015); Canada-Honduras Free Trade Agreement (2014); Canada-Jordan Free Trade Agreement (2012); Canada-Colombia Free Trade Agreement, *supra* note 3; Canada-European Union Free Trade Agreement (2009); Canada-Costa Rica Free Trade Agreement (2002).

10 *See* Australia-Chile Free Trade Agreement, *supra* note 8; Japan-Brunei, Free Trade Agreement, *supra* note 8; New Zealand-China Free Trade Agreement, *supra* note 8; Costa Rica-Singapore Free Trade Agreement, *supra* note 8; India-Korea Free Trade Agreement (2009); Japan-Mexico Free Trade Agreement (2005); Japan-Singapore Free Trade Agreement (2002); Australia-China Free Trade Agreement (2015); Korea-Chile Free Trade Agreement (2004); New Zealand-Malaysia Free Trade Agreement, *supra* note 9; Singapore-Panama Free Trade Agreement (2006); Australia-Thailand Free Trade Agreement (2005); United States-Australia Free Trade Agreement (2005); United States-Singapore Free Trade Agreement (2004); Korea-Australia Free Trade Agreement (2014); United States-Chile Free Trade Agreement (2004); United States-Korea Free Trade Agreement (2012); United States-Peru Free Trade Agreement, *supra* note 9 (2009); Canada-Korea Free Trade Agreement, *supra* note 9; Canada-Honduras Free Trade Agreement, *supra* note 9; Canada-Panama Free Trade Agreement, *supra* note 8.

11 *See* General Agreement on Trade and Tariffs (1947).

12 Members and Observers, WTO, https://www.wto.org/english/thewto_e/whatis_e/tif_e/org6_e.htm, last accessed 8 January 2018. When considering Member States it should be remembered that, as discussed in Chapter 14, the European Union/European Community is a member of the WTO and is represented at the WTO by the President of the European Commission or his assigned representative.

13 *See* id.

14 Id.

15 Id.

16 Id.

17 International intergovernmental organizations granted observer status to WTO bodies, http://wto.org/english/thewto_e/igo_obs_e.htm, last accessed 8 January 2018.

18 Members and Observers, *supra* note 12.

19 GATT (1994) art IX(1).

20 *Id.* at art X(2).

21 *See* Ministerial Conferences, WTO, http://wto.org/english/thewto_e/minist_e/minist_e.htm, last accessed 8 January 2018.

22 GATT, *supra* note 19 at art IV(7).

23 *Id.* at art IX.

24 *Id.* at art IX(3).

25 *Id.* at art IV(2). This does not mean that the General Council is removed from key decisions in the WTO system, as it is tasked with approving the organization's budget. *See id.* at art VII.

26 *Id.* at art IV(3), (4).

27 *Id.* at art IV(5).

28 *Id.* at art IV.

29 *Id.* at art V.

30 *See* The Doha Round, WTO, http://wto.org/english/tratop_e/dda_e/dda_e.htm, last accessed 8 January 2018.

31 *See id.*

32 *See id.*

33 *See* Building trade capacity, WTO, http://wto.org/english/tratop_e/devel_e/build_tr_capa_e.htm, last accessed 8 January 2018. For example, the Agreement on Agriculture preamble provides that "under the reform programme should be made in an equitable way among all Members, having regard to non-trade concerns, including food security and the need to protect the environment; having regard to the agreement that special and differential treatment for developing countries is an integral element of the negotiations, and taking into account the possible negative effects of the implementation of the reform programme on least-developed and net food-importing developing countries." *See* Agreement on Agriculture (1995) preamble. The Agreement on the Application of Sanitary and Phytosanitary Measures similarly noted the role that relevant laws and rules play in the development process for many States and the concomitant need to provide protections. *See* Agreement on the Application of Sanitary and Phytosanitary Measures (1995) preamble ("Recognizing that developing country Members may encounter special difficulties in complying with the sanitary or phytosanitary measures of importing Members, and as a consequence in access to markets, and also in the formulation and application of sanitary or phytosanitary measures in their own territories, and desiring to assist them in their endeavours in this regard"). *See also* Agreement on Technical Barriers to Trade (1995) preamble.

34 *See* WTO, Aid for Trade at a Glance 2007, 1st Global Review (2007).

35 *See id.*; WTO, Aid for Trade at a Glance, Maintaining Momentum (2009); WTO, Aid for Trade at a Glance 2011, Showing Results (2011); WTO, Aid for Trade at a Glance 2015, Reducing Trade Costs for Inclusive, Sustainable Growth (2015).

36 *See* WTO, Promoting connectivity in Africa: The role of Aid for Trade in boosting intra-African Trade (2007); Asian Development Bank, Aid for Trade in Asia and the Pacific: Promoting Connectivity for Inclusive Development (2017); WTO Aid for Trade at a Glance, Maintaining Momentum (2009); WTO, Aid for Trade at a Glance 2011, *supra* note 35; WTO, Aid for Trade at a Glance 2015, *supra* note 35.

37 About the WTO, http://wto.org/english/thewto_e/whatis_e/wto_dg_stat_e.htm, last accessed 8 January 2018.

38 Agreement Establishing the World Trade Organization (1995) preamble. In the preamble, the Member States recognized "that their relations in the field of trade and economic endeavour should be conducted with a view to raising standards of living, ensuring full employment and a large and steadily growing volume of real income and effective demand, and expanding the production of and trade in goods and services, while allowing for the optimal use of the world's resources in accordance with the objective of sustainable development, seeking both to protect and preserve the environment and to enhance the means for doing so in a manner consistent with their respective needs and concerns at different levels of economic development." *Id.*

39 *Id.* at art II(1).

40 *Id.* at arts III(1) ("The WTO shall facilitate the implementation, administration and operation, and further the objectives, of this Agreement and of the Multilateral Trade Agreements, and shall also provide the framework for the implementation, administration and operation of the Plurilateral Trade Agreements."), III(2) ("The WTO shall provide the forum for negotiations among its Members concerning their multilateral trade relations in matters dealt with under the agreements in the Annexes to this Agreement. The WTO may also provide a forum for further negotiations among its Members concerning their multilateral trade relations, and a framework for the implementation of the results of such negotiations, as may be decided by the Ministerial Conference.").

41 *See id.*

42 *See* WTO Annual Report 2000 (2000); WTO Annual Report 2002 (2002); WTO Annual Report 2003 (2003); WTO Annual Report 2004 (2004); WTO Annual Report 2005 (2005); WTO Annual Report 2006 (2006); WTO Annual Report 2007 (2007); WTO Annual Report 2008 (2008); WTO Annual Report 2009 (2009); WTO Annual Report 2010 (2010); WTO Annual Report 2011 (2011); WTO Annual Report 2012 (2012); WTO Annual Report 2013 (2013); WTO Annual Report 2014 (2014); WTO Annual Report 2015 (2015); WTO Annual Report 2016 (2016).

43 Agreement on Agriculture, *supra* note 33 at arts 17, 18.

44 Agreement on the Application of Sanitary and Phytosanitary Measures (1995) art 12(3).

45 *Id.* at art 12(4). *See also* Agreement on Trade-Related Investment Measures (1995) art 7; Agreement on Implementation of Article VII of the General Agreement on Tariffs and Trade 1994 (1995) art 18.

46 Agreement on Technical Barriers to Trade (1995) art 13; Agreement on Import Licensing Procedures (1995) art 4.

47 Agreement on Rules of Origin (1995) art 4.

48 *See* Agreement on Subsidies and Countervailing Measures (1995) art 24.

49 *See* The WTO and other organizations, https://www.wto.org/english/thewto_e/coher_e/coher_e.htm, last accessed 8 January 2018.

50 *See* Agreement on the Application of Sanitary and Phytosanitary Measures, *supra* note 44 at art 12.3.

51 *See* WTO News, WTO and IMF sign cooperation agreement (9 December 1996) https://www.wto.org/english/news_e/pres96_e/pr062_e.htm, last accessed 8 January 2018.

52 *See* WTO News, WTO and World Bank sign cooperation agreement (28 April 1997), https://www.wto.org/english/news_e/pres97_e/pr72_e.htm, last accessed 8 January 2018.

53 *See* Agreement between the International Telecommunication Union and the World Trade Organization (2000).

54 WTO, The WTO and the Organization for Economic Cooperation and Development (OECD), https://www.wto.org/english/thewto_e/coher_e/wto_oecd_e.htm, last accessed 8 January 2018.

55 *See* Arrangements for Effective Cooperation with other Intergovernmental Organizations: Relations between the WTO and the UN, WT/GC/W/10 (1995).

56 *See* Memorandum of Understanding between the World Trade Organization and the United Nations Conference on Trade and Development (2003).

57 *See* IMF Articles of Agreement (1944).

58 *See id.* The name Bretton Woods is derived from a remote holiday destination in the American State of New Hampshire, where the political and economic leaders of the Allies and their associated met in 1944 to decide the details of the post-war economic world. Benn Steil, *The Battle of Bretton Woods* (Princeton University Press 2013).

59 Currently, there are 189 IMF Member States. *See* IMF Members' Quotas and Voting Power, and IMF Board of Governors, http://www.imf.org/external/np/sec/memdir/members.aspx, last accessed 9 January 2018.

60 By-Laws, Rules and Regulations of the International Monetary Fund (2016) art I (21).

61 *Id.* at art I (21)(b).

62 *See* IMF Annual Report 2016 (2016) 8 (noting that the attempted reform of quotas for the United States failed to pass the US Congress as required and, as such, as not operational).

63 *See id.*

64 *See* IMF Articles of Agreement, *supra* note 57 at art III(i).

65 IMF By-Laws, *supra* note 60 at art I(11).

66 *See* IMF Articles of Agreement, *supra* note 57 at arts XXVI, XXIV.

67 *Id.* at art XXVI(1).

68 *See id.* at art XXIV(2).

69 IMF By-Laws, *supra* note 60 at art I(22).

70 *Id.*

71 IMF Articles of Agreement, *supra* note 57 at art XII sect 2.

72 *Id.* at art II(2).

73 *Id.* at art XII(2)(a).

74 *Id.* at art XII(2)(b).

75 *See id.* at art I(7).

76 *See* IMF By-Laws, *supra* note 60 at art I(7).

77 *See* IMF, Governance Structure, http://www.imf.org/external/about/govstruct.htm, last accessed 9 January 2018.

78 *See* IMF, A Guide to Committees, Groups and Clubs, https://www.imf.org/en/About/Factsheets/A-Guide-to-Committees-Groups-and-Clubs#IC, last accessed 9 January 2018. ("The IMFC advises and reports to the IMF Board of Governors on the supervision and management of the international monetary and financial system, including on responses to unfolding events that may disrupt the system.").

79 *See id.* (explains that the reason for establishing the Committee was "to advise the Board of Governors of the IMF and the World Bank on critical development issues and on the financial resources required to promote economic development in developing countries.").

80 By-Laws, Rules and Regulations of the International Monetary Fund at art XII sect 3.

81 *Id.* at art XII sect 3.

82 *Id.* at art XII sect 4.

83 *Id.* at art XII (4).

84 *See id.* at art I(20).

85 *Id.* at art I(20)(c).

86 *Id.* at art I(20)(d).

87 *See* IMF Annual Report 2015: Tackling Challenges Together (2015) 73–74.

88 *Id.*

89 *Id.*

90 *See* IMF Articles of Agreement, *supra* note 57 at art I(i) ("To promote international monetary cooperation through a permanent institution which provides the machinery for consultation and collaboration on international monetary problems.").

91 *See id.* at art I(ii) ("To facilitate the expansion and balanced growth of international trade, and to contribute thereby to the promotion and maintenance of high levels of employment and real income and to the development of the productive resources of all members as primary objectives of economic policy.").

92 *See id.* at arts I(iii) ("To promote exchange stability, to maintain orderly exchange arrangements among members, and to avoid competitive exchange depreciation."), I(iv) ("To assist in the establishment of a multilateral system of payments in respect o current transactions between members and in the elimination of foreign exchange restrictions which hamper the growth of world trade."), art I(v) ("To give confidence to members by making the general resources of the Fund temporarily available to them under adequate safeguards, thus providing them with opportunity to correct maladjustments in their balance of payments without resorting to measures destructive of national and international property.").

93 *See* IMF, IMF Surveillance, http://www.imf.org/en/About/Factsheets/IMF-Surveillance, last accessed 9 January 2018.

94 *See* IMF Stand-by Arrangement, http://www.imf.org/en/About/Factsheets/Sheets/2016/08/01/20/33/Stand-By-Arrangement, last accessed 9 January 2018.

95 *See id.*

96 *See id.*

97 *See id.*

98 *See id.*

99 *See* IMF Support for Low-Income Countries, https://www.imf.org/en/About/Factsheets/IMF-Support-for-Low-Income-Countries, last accessed 9 January 2018.

100 For example, the Flexible Credit Line option "was created as part of the process of reforming how the IMF lends money to countries that find themselves in a cash crunch, with the idea of tailoring its lending instruments to the diverse needs and circumstances of member countries." *See* The IMF's Flexible Credit Line (FCL), http://www.imf.org/en/About/Factsheets/Sheets/2016/08/01/20/40/Flexible-Credit-Line, last accessed 9 January 2018.

101 *See* IMF, Capacity Development, http://www.imf.org/external/np/ins/english/capacity_wwd.htm, last accessed 9 January 2018.

102 *See* IMF Annual Report 2015: Tackling Challenges Together (2015) 6, 12–13. The CCRT focuses on assistance to States in the immediate crisis phase and in the post-crisis phase, when rebuilding and regrouping as a society are most necessary. *Id.* at 13.

103 *See id.* at 16–18

104 About Us, World Bank Group, http://web.worldbank.org/WBSITE/EXTERNAL/EXTABOUTUS/0,,pagePK:50004410~piPK:36602~theSitePK:29708,00.html, last accessed 9 January 2018.

105 *See id.*

106 *Id.*

107 *Id.*

108 *See* The World Bank Annual Report 2004 v 1 (2004) 6; The World Bank Annual Report 2005 v 1 (2005) 12.

109 *See* The World Bank Annual Report 2004 v 1, *supra* note 108 at 6–7.

110 *See id.* at 12–13.

111 *See* The World Bank Annual Report 2005 v 1, *supra* note 108 at 15–16.

112 *See* Summary of World Bank Group Integrity Compliance Guidelines (2010).

113 *See* IBRD, IDA, IFC and MIGA, Sanctions Board Statute (2010).

114 *Id.* at art V.

115 *See id.* at art XIV.

116 World Bank Group, Sanctions Procedures art I sect. 1.01 (noting that the sanctions "regime protects Bank funds and serves as a deterrent upon those who might otherwise engage in the misuse of the proceeds of Bank financing").

117 CAO Operational Guidelines (2013) sect 1.1.

118 *Id.* The Guidelines explain that "the CAO process provides communities and individuals with access to a grievance mechanism that offers redress for negative environmental and/or social impacts associated with IFC/MIGA projects. This includes impacts related to business and human rights in the context of the IFC Policy and Performance Standards on Environmental and Social Sustainability." *Id.*

119 *Id.* at sect 1.2.

120 *See* World Bank, Environmental, Health and Safety General Guidelines (2007).

121 *See* World Bank, Integrity Vice Presidency, http://www.worldbank.org/en/about/unit/integrity-vice-presidency, last accessed 9 January 2018.

122 *See id.*

123 *See* World Bank Inspection Panel, Resolution Nos. IBRD 93–10, IDA 93–6 (1993) art 12 ("The Panel shall receive requests for inspection presented to it by an affected party in the territory of the borrower which is not a single individual (i.e., a community of persons such as an organization, association, society or other grouping

of individuals), or by the local representative of such party or by another representative in the exceptional cases where the party submitting the request contends that appropriate representation is not locally available and the Executive Directors so agree at the time they consider the request for inspection.").

124 See id. at arts 2–10.

125 See The Inspection Panel at the World Bank, Operating Procedures (2016).

126 World Bank, Grievance Redress Service, http://www.worldbank.org/en/projects-operations/products-and-services/grievance-redress-service, last accessed 9 January 2018.

127 See International Bank for Reconstruction and Development, Who We Are, http://www.worldbank.org/en/who-we-are/ibrd, last accessed 9 January 2018.

128 International Bank for Reconstruction and Development, Articles of Agreement (2012) art I(i) (including in the purposes of the IBRD "to assist in reconstruction and development of territories of members by facilitating the investment of capital for productive purposes, including the restoration of economies destroyed or disrupted by war, the reconversion of productive facilities to peacetime needs and the encouragement of the development of productive facilities and resources in less developed countries."). This is reflected in the explicit requirement that IBRD funding be made "with equitable consideration to projects for development and projects for reconstruction alike." Id. at art III(1)(a).

129 Id. at art I(ii) ("to promote private foreign investment by means of guarantees or participations in loans and other investments made by private investors; and when private capital is not available on reasonable terms, to supplement private investment by providing, on suitable conditions, finance or productive purposes").

130 See id. art III(4).

131 See International Bank for Reconstruction and Development, Who We Are, supra note 127.

132 See IBRD Articles of Agreement, supra note 128 at art III(6).

133 Id. at art II (1).

134 Id. at art II (3).

135 Id. at art II (3).

136 Id. at art V (3).

137 Id. at art VI(1).

138 Id. at art VI(2).

139 Id. Allowing an errant member to retain membership in the IBRD without curing the issue after more than a year requires a 2/3 majority vote.

140 Id. at art VI(3). In this extraordinary instance, a 3/4 majority vote is required to retain membership. Id.

141 Id. at art VI(4).

142 Id. at art VI(5).

143 Id. at art V(1).

144 Id. at art V(2)(a).

145 Id. at art V(2)(b). The non-derogable decisions allotted solely to the Board of Governors relate to the admission of new members, the creation and alterations of membership criteria, changes to the amount of retained capital stock, the suspension of Member States, questions of interpretation regarding the Articles of Agreement, the creation of agreements with other international organizations, the suspension or permanent disbanding of the IBRD, and whether and how to distribute IBRD assets. Id.

146 Id. at art V(4).

147 Id. at art V(4)(b).

148 Id. at art V(5). The President is selected by the Executive Director and appoints his staff. Id.

149 Id. at art V(6). Specifically, the requirements are that the members of the Advisory Council be "representatives of banking, commercial, industrial, labor and agricultural interests, and with as wide a national representation as possible." Id.

150 Id. at art V(6)(a).

151 Id. at art V(7).

152 International Development Association Articles of Agreement (1960) art II. As in other international financial organizations, it is possible for the requisite share amounts to be increased periodically at the discretion of the IDA. See id. at art III(1). Where there are issues in a Member State providing the necessary funds as appraised in its appropriate currency, it is possible for another Member State to cover this amount on behalf of the impacted State. Id. at art III(2).

153 Id. at art VII(1), (4).

154 Id. at art VII(2).

155 Id. at art VI(1).

156 Id. at art VI(2).

157 Id. at art VI(3).

158 Id. at art VI(4).

159 Id.

160 Id. at art VI(5).

161 Id.

162 Id.

163 Id. at art I; International Development Association: The World Bank's Fund for the Poorest (2017).

164 IDA Articles of Agreement, *supra* note 152 at art I; International Development Association: The World Bank's Fund for the Poorest, *supra* note 163.

165 IDA Articles of Agreement, *supra* note 152 at art I.

166 *See id.* at art V(4).

167 For a discussion of this, *see* International Development Association, IDA's Implementation of the Multilateral Debt Relief Initiative (2006).

168 *See* World Bank, How does the IDA work? http://ida.worldbank.org/about/how-does-ida-work, last accessed 9 January 2018. In 2016, at the 18th IDA replenishment, the total amount pledged by donors was US$ 75 billion, signifying a high-water mark for the support of the international community toward IDA activities. *See* World Bank, Global Community Makes Record $75 Billion Commitment to End Extreme Poverty, http://www.worldbank.org/en/news/press-release/2016/12/15/global-community-commitment-end-poverty-ida18, last accessed 9 January 2018; International Development Association, Contributions to the Eighteenth Replenishment (2016).

169 IDA Articles of Agreement, *supra* note 152 at art V.

170 *Id.* ("Financing provided by the Association shall be for purposes which in the opinion of the Association are of high developmental priority in the light of the needs of the area or areas concerned and, except in special circumstances, shall be for specific projects . . . The Association shall not provide financing if in its opinion such financing is available from private sources on terms which are reasonable for the recipient or could be provided by a loan of the type made by the Bank.").

171 International Finance Corporation, Articles of Agreement (2012) arts 1(i) (noting that the IFC "in association with private investors, assist[s] in financing the establishment, improvement and expansion of productive private enterprises which would contribute to the development of its member countries by making investments, without guarantee of repayment by the member government concerned, in most cases where sufficient private capital is not available on reasonable terms"), 1(ii) (noting that the IFC functions to "seek to bring together investment opportunities, domestic and foreign private capital, and experienced management."), 1(iii) (noting that the IFC functions to "seek to stimulate, and to help conditions conducive to, the flow of private capital, domestic and foreign, into productive investment in member countries").

172 *Id.* at art 1.

173 *Id.* at arts III(1), III(3)(ii).

174 *Id.* at art II (1).

175 *Id.* at art II (3).

176 *Id.* at art V (2).

177 *Id.* at art V(1).

178 *Id.* at art V. These decisions require a majority vote from the Board of Governors. *Id.*

179 *Id.* at art V(3).

180 *Id.* at art V(4).

181 *Id.* at art V(5).

182 *Id.*

183 *Id.* at art IV (1).

184 *Id.* at art IV (2).

185 *Id.* at art IV (2)(c). The issues which cannot be delegated relate to membership and admission, suspension of members, changes to the capital stock, interpretation of the Articles of Agreement, creation of relationships with international organizations, ceasing or suspending IFC operations, issuing dividends, and amending the foundational text. *Id.*

186 *Id.* at art IV (4).

187 *Id.* at art IV (5).

188 *Id.* at art VI.

189 Convention Establishing the Multilateral Investment Guarantee Agency (1985) art 2; *see also* Multilateral Investment Guarantee Agency, Operational Policies (2015).

190 Convention Establishing MIGA, *supra* note 189 at art 2; MIGA Operational Policies, *supra* note 189.

191 Convention Establishing MIGA, *supra* note 189 at art 4; MIGA Commentary on the Convention Establishing the Multilateral Investment Guarantee Agency (1985) 3.

192 Convention Establishing MIGA, *supra* note 189 at arts 5, 6.

193 *Id.* at art 51; MIGA Commentary on the Convention Establishing the Multilateral Investment Guarantee Agency, *supra* note 191 at 33.

194 Convention Establishing MIGA, *supra* note 189 at art 51.

195 *Id.* at art 52; MIGA Commentary on the Convention Establishing the Multilateral Investment Guarantee Agency, *supra* note 191 at 33–34.

196 Convention Establishing MIGA, *supra* note 189 at art 52.

197 *Id.* at art 53.

198 *Id.* at art 54.

199 *Id.* at art 55.

200 *Id.* at art 30.

201 *Id.* at art 31.

202 *Id.* at arts 31, 39, 40; MIGA Commentary on the Convention Establishing the Multilateral Investment Guarantee Agency, *supra* note 191 at 27.

203 Convention Establishing MIGA, *supra* note 189 at arts 32, 41; MIGA Commentary on the Convention Establishing the Multilateral Investment Guarantee Agency, *supra* note 191 at 27–28.

204 Convention Establishing MIGA, *supra* note 189 at art 33; MIGA Commentary on the Convention Establishing the Multilateral Investment Guarantee Agency, *supra* note 191 at. 28.

205 *See* MIGA Performance Standards on Social and Environmental Sustainability (2013). These standards relate to social and environmental assessment, labor and working conditions, pollution prevention and control, public health and safety, land acquisition and community resettlement, biodiversity and sustainable natural resources, indigenous peoples, and the protection of cultural heritage. *Id.*

206 *Id.*

207 *See* MIGA Sanctions Procedures (2013) arts II, IV, V.

208 *See id.* at art IX.

209 *See id.* at art XII.

210 *See* History of the ICSID Convention v 1 (1970) ii.

211 *See* ICSID, https://icsid.worldbank.org/en/, last accessed 12 January 2018.

212 *See* About ICSID, https://icsid.worldbank.org/en/Pages/about/default.aspx, last accessed 12 January 2018.

213 ICSID and the World Bank Group, https://icsid.worldbank.org/en/Pages/about/ICSID%20And%20The%20World%20Bank%20Group.aspx, last accessed 12 January 2018.

214 *See id.*

215 *See id.*

216 Administrative Council, ICSID, https://icsid.worldbank.org/en/Pages/about/Administrative-Council.aspx, last accessed 12 January 2018.

217 *See* ICSID Convention (1965) arts 4, 7(2).

218 *See* ICSID Administrative and Financial Regulations (2006) Regulation 7.

219 *See* ICSID Convention, *supra* note 217 at art 6(1) (1965) (providing that the Administrative Council's functions are to "adopt the administrative and financial regulations of the Centre; adopt the rules of procedure for the institution of conciliation and arbitration proceedings; adopt the rules of procedure for conciliation and arbitration proceedings . . .").

220 *See id.* at arts 9, 10. Specifically, the Secretary General's functions are to serve as "the legal representative and the principal officer of the Centre and shall be responsible for its administration, including the appointment of staff . . . [and] shall perform the function of registrar and shall have the power to authenticate arbitral awards rendered pursuant to this Convention." *Id.* at art 11; *see also* ICSID Administrative and Financial Regulations, *supra* note 218 at Regulation 10 (regarding staff appointments).

221 *See* ICSID Convention, *supra* note 217 at arts 12–15; ICSID Administrative and Financial Regulations, *supra* note 218 at (2006) Regulation 21.

222 *See* ICSID Convention, *supra* note 217 at sect 4 (1965).

223 *See id.* at art 28 (1965); *see also* ICSID Rules of Procedure for Conciliation Proceedings (2006) Rule 1.

224 *See* ICSID Convention, *supra* note 217 at art 53; ICSID Rules of Procedure for Arbitration Proceedings (2006) ch. VII.

225 About Us, IADB, http://www.iadb.org/en/about-us/about-the-inter-american-development-bank,5995.html, last accessed 9 January 2018.

226 *Id.*

227 Our Priorities and Areas of Action, IADB, http://www.iadb.org/en/about-us/our-priorities-and-areas-of-action,6007.html, last accessed 9 January 2018.

228 Mandates, IADB, http://www.iadb.org/en/about-us/mandates,6280.html, last accessed 9 January 2018.

229 *See* Debt Relief, IADB, http://www.iadb.org/en/about-us/debt-relief,6898.html, last accessed 9 January 2018.

230 IADB Agreement, *supra* note 230 at art II(1).

231 *Id.*; General Rules Governing Admission of Nonregional Countries to Membership in the Bank (1995) sect 2, 4.

232 IADB Agreement, *supra* note 230 at art II(3).

233 *Id.* at art VIII sect 4.

234 *Id.* at art IX sect 1.

235 *Id.*

236 *Id.* at art IX sects 1, 3. In instances that are over 6 months in negotiation duration without an agreement on effecting the repurchase of these shares, both parties agree that the repurchase amount will be the book value of the shares on the date that withdrawal was completed. *Id.* at sect 3(d).

237 *Id.* at art IX sect 2.

238 *Id.*

239 *Id.*

240 *Id.* at art VIII sect 2; *see also* Board of Governors, IADB, https://www.iadb.org/en/about-us/board-of-governors%2C1325.html, last accessed 9 January 2018.

241 *See* IADB Agreement, *supra* note 230 at art VIII sect 2. The specific powers that cannot be derogated are similar to those in the international banks, namely membership and admissions, changes to the capital stocks or other IADB financial holdings, election of the IADB President, decisions regarding membership suspensions, payment

decisions for directors and others, interpretation of the Articles of Agreement, creation of relationships with other international organizations, decisions regarding auditor selection and contracting, and termination of the IADB itself. *Id.*

242 *Id.* at art VIII sect 3; Inter-American Development Bank, Board of Executive Directors Regulations (2014) pt II sect 2.

243 IADB Agreement, *supra* note 230 at art VIII sect 3.

244 *Id.*

245 *Id.*; Inter-American Development Bank, Board of Executive Directors Regulations, *supra* note 242 at pt III, sects 7, 8. Within this committee structure, there are six mandated standing committees: Audit, Budget and Financial Policies, Organization, Human Resources and Board Matters, Policy and Evaluation, Programming, and Steering. Inter-American Development Ban, Standing Committees of the Board of Executive Directors: Consolidated Procedures (2016) art II.

246 IADB Agreement, *supra* note 230 at art VIII sect 5(a).

247 *Id.*; Inter-American Development Bank, Regulations for the Election of the President of the Bank (2014) sect 2.

248 Inter-American Development Bank, 2015 Partnership Report (2015) 7.

249 *Id.*

250 IADB Agreement, *supra* note 230 at art X sect 1.

251 *Id.* at art X sect 2.

252 *Id.* at art X sects 3, 4.

253 *See* Inter-American Development Bank, Sustainability Report (2007); Inter-American Development Bank, Sustainability Report (2008); Inter-American Development Bank, Annual Report 2009 (2009); Inter-American Development Bank, Sustainability Report (2010); Inter-American Development Bank, Sustainability Report (2011); Inter-American Development Bank, Annual Report 2011 (2011); Inter-American Development Bank, Annual Report 2012 (2012); Inter-American Development Bank, Annual Report 2014 (2014); Inter-American Development Bank, Sustainability Report 2015 (2015); Inter-American Development Bank, 2016 Partnership Report (2016); Inter-American Development Bank, Sustainability Report 2016 (2016).

254 Inter-American Development Bank, 2015 Partnership Report (2015) 4–5.

255 *See id.* at 12–25.

256 *See id.* at 26–29.

257 Statute of the Inter-American Development Bank (2013) art I. In terms of covered claims, the Administrative Tribunal is authorized to hear claims from "an Employee of the Bank or the Corporation [in which the employee] alleges non-observance of his or her contract of employment or terms and conditions of appointment." *Id.* at art. 2.

258 *Id.* at art III(1) (2013); Rules of Procedure of the Administrative Tribunal (2013) art 1(1).

259 *See* Statute of the Inter-American Development Bank, *supra* note 257 at art V; Rules of Procedure of the Administrative Tribunal, *supra* note 258 at art 4.

260 Statute of the Inter-American Development Bank (2013) art VII.

261 *Id.* at art VIII (2013).

262 *See* IADB, Office of Institutional Integrity 2004 (2004); IADB Office of Institutional Integrity, Annual Report 2010 (2010).

263 *See* IADB, Office of Institutional Integrity 2004, *supra* note 262; IADB Office of Institutional Integrity, Annual Report 2010, *supra* note 262.

264 IADB Office of Institutional Integrity, Annual Report 2007 (2007); IADB Office of Institutional Integrity, Annual Report 2010, *supra* note 262 3; IADB Office of Institutional Integrity, Annual Report 2015 (2015).

265 *See* IADB Office of Institutional Integrity, Annual Report 2008 (2008) 2.

266 *Id.* at 4.

267 The European Central Bank, European Central Bank, http://www.ecb.int/ecb/html/index.en.html, last accessed 9 January 2018.

268 ECB, ESCB and the Eurosystem, European Central Bank, http://www.ecb.int/ecb/orga/escb/html/index.en.html, last accessed 9 January 2018.

269 European Central Bank Agreement (2016) Protocol 4 art. 4.

270 *Id.*

271 *Id.*

272 *Id.* at art 2.

273 *Id.* at art 3.

274 *Id.* at art 7.

275 *Id.* at arts 8, 9.

276 *Id.* at arts 10–14.

277 *Id.* at art 12(1).

278 *Id.*

279 *Id.* at art 16.

280 *Id.*

281 *Id.* at art 10(1).

282 *Id.* at art 10(2).

283 *Id.* at art 10(3).

284 *Id.* at art 10(4).

285 *Id.* at art 12(1).

286 *Id.*

287 *Id.* at art 11.

288 *Id.* at art 11(1).

289 *Id.* at art 11(2).

290 *Id.* at art 11(5).

291 Agreement Establishing the European Bank for Reconstruction and Development at art 1 (1991); History of the EBRD, EBRD, http://www.ebrd.com/who-we-are/history-of-the-ebrd.html, last accessed 9 January 2018.

292 *Id.*

293 *Id.* Specifically, the designated purpose of the EBRD is to "foster the transition towards open market-oriented economies and to promote private and entrepreneurial initiative in the Central and Eastern European countries committed to and applying the principles of multiparty democracy, pluralism and market economics." *Id. See also* European Bank for Reconstruction and Development, Transition Report 2016–17 (2017).

294 EBRD Agreement, *supra* note 291 at arts 3–5 (1991). Our Shareholders, EBRD, http://www.ebrd.com/pages/about/who/shareholders.shtml, last accessed 9 January 2018.

295 These States are Canada, Mexico and the United States. *Id.*

296 Japan is the Member State referenced here. *Id.*

297 These States are Australia and New Zealand. *Id.*

298 These States are Cyprus, Egypt, Israel, Jordan, Morocco, Tunisia, and Turkey. *Id.*

299 EBRD Agreement, *supra* note 291 at art 3; By-Laws of the European Bank for Reconstruction and Development (1990) sect 14 ("When submitting an application to the Board of Governors, with a recommendation that the applicant country be admitted to membership, the Board of Directors, inter alia after a report, in consultation with the applicant country, by the President, shall recommend to the Board of Governors the number of shares of capital stock to be subscribed and such other conditions as, in the opinion of the Board of Directors, the Board of Governors may wish to prescribe.").

300 EBRD Agreement, *supra* note 291 at art 37.

301 *See id.* at art 39.

302 *Id.* at art 38; EBRD By-Laws, *supra* note 299 at sect 15.

303 EBRD Agreement, *supra* note 291 at art 38. In this instance, the State must receive a 2/3 majority vote from the Board of Governors. *Id.*

304 *Id.* at art 23 (1991); Board of Governors, ERBD, http://www.ebrd.com/shareholders-and-board-of-governors.html, last accessed 9 January 2018.

305 *See* EBRD Agreement, *supra* note 291 at art 24.

306 *Id.*

307 *Id.* at art 29.

308 *Id.* at art 26. While this number has traditionally been used by the EBRD, its foundational text does provide for an increase or decrease in the size of the Board of Directors if the Board of Governors approves. *Id.*

309 *See id.*

310 *See id.*

311 *Id.* at art 27 ("The Board of Directors shall be responsible for the direction of the general operations of the Bank and, for this purpose, shall, in addition to the powers assigned to it expressly by this Agreement, exercise all the powers delegated to it by the Board of Governors, and in particular: i) prepare the work of the Board of Governors; ii) in conformity with the general directions of the Board of Governors, establish policies and take decisions concerning loans, guarantees, investment in equity capital, borrowing by the Bank, the furnishing of technical assistance and other operations of the Bank; iii) submit the audited accounts for each financial year for approval of the Board of Governors at each annual meeting; and iv) approve the budget of the Bank.").

312 *Id.* at art 30.

313 *Id.*

314 *Id.* at art 31.

315 *See* European Bank for Reconstruction and Development, Anti-Corruption Report 2008 (2009) 3; European Bank for Reconstruction and Development, Anti-Corruption Report 2009 (2010); European Bank for Reconstruction and Development, OCCO's Integrity and Anti-Corruption Report (2015); European Bank for Reconstruction and Development, Integrity and Anti-Corruption Report (2016).

316 *See* European Bank for Reconstruction and Development, Anti-Corruption Report 2008, *supra* note 315 at 3; European Bank for Reconstruction and Development, Anti-Corruption Report 2009, *supra* note 315.

317 European Bank for Reconstruction and Development, Anti-Corruption Report 2010, *supra* note 315 at 7; European Bank for Reconstruction and Development, Project Complaint Mechanism Annual Report for 2010 (2011); European Bank for Reconstruction and Development, Project Complaint Mechanism Annual Report 2012 (2013); European Bank for Reconstruction and Development, Enforcement Policy and Procedures: The mechanism to combat fraud and corruption in EBRD projects (2015); European Bank for Reconstruction and Development, Project Complaint Mechanism Annual Report 2015 (2016).

318 *See* EBRD Agreement, *supra* note 291 at art 8 (setting out the terms and conditions for lending).

319 *Id.* at arts 40, 41 (1991).

320 *Id.* at arts 42, 43 (1991).

321 *See id.* at ch. VIII (1991); Headquarters Agreement Between the Government of the United Kingdom of Great Britain and Northern Ireland and the European Bank for Reconstruction and Development (1991).

322 *See* EBRD Agreement, *supra* note 291 at art 2.

323 *See id.* at art 2; Products and Services, EBRD, http://www.ebrd.com/what-we-do/products-and-services.html, last accessed 9 January 2018.

324 EBRD Agreement, *supra* note 291 at art 2.

325 *See id.* at art 9.

326 *See* European Bank for Reconstruction and Development, Private Sector for Food Security Initiative Annual Report (2014).

327 *See* European Bank for Reconstruction and Development, Transforming Chernobyl (2015).

328 *See* European Bank for Reconstruction and Development, Guidance Note: EBRD Performance Requirement 6 (2014); European Bank for Reconstruction and Development, Environmental and Social Policy (2014); European Bank for Reconstruction and Development, Environmental and Social Policy: Report on the Invitation to the Public to Comment (2014); European Bank for Reconstruction and Development, Green Economy Transition Approach (2015).

329 *See* European Bank for Reconstruction and Development, Resettlement Guidance and Good Practice (2014).

330 Statute of the European Investment Bank (2013) preamble, art 1; Treaty on the Functioning of the European Union (2007) art 309 ("The task of the European Investment Bank shall be to contribute, by having recourse to the capital market and utilising its own resources, to the balanced and steady development of the internal market in the interest of the Union.").

331 Statute of the EIB, *supra* note 330 at art 18(1).

332 *Id.* at art 16.

333 About, EIB, http://www.eib.org/about/index.htm, last accessed 9 January 2018; European Investment Bank, Report on results of EIB operations out the EU (2013); European Investment Bank, Report on results outside the EU (2014); European Investment Bank, Report on results outside of the EU (2015).

334 Statute of the EIB, *supra* note 330 at art 19.

335 Structure, EIB, http://www.eib.org/about/structure/index.htm, last accessed 9 January 2018.

336 Statute of the EIB, *supra* note 330 at art 7; The Board of Governors, EIB, http://www.eib.org/about/structure/governance/board_of_governors/index.htm, last accessed 9 January 2018.

337 Statute of the EIB, *supra* note 330 at art 7.

338 *Id.* at arts 7–9; Board of Directors, EIB, http://www.eib.org/about/structure/governance/board_of_directors/index.htm, last accessed 9 January 2018.

339 Statute of the EIB, *supra* note 330 at art 9.

340 *Id.* at art 9(2).

341 *Id.* at art 9.

342 *Id.* at art 10.

343 *Id.* at art 11. The Management Committee's extensive powers are defined as follows: "The Management Committee shall be responsible for the current business of the Bank, under the authority of the President and the supervision of the Board of Directors. It shall prepare the decisions of the Board of Directors, in particular decisions on the raising of loans and the granting of finance, in particular in the form of loans and guarantees; it shall ensure that these decisions are implemented." *Id. See also* European Investment Bank, 2010 Annual Statement on Corporate Governance at the European Investment Bank (2010); European Investment Bank, 2011 Annual Statement on Corporate Governance at the European Investment Bank (2012); European Investment Bank, 2012 Annual Statement on Corporate Governance at the European Investment Bank (2013).

344 Statute of the EIB, *supra* note 330 at art 12; European Investment Bank, 2010 Annual Statement on Corporate Governance, *supra* note 343; European Investment Bank, 2011 Annual Statement on Corporate Governance, *supra* note 343; European Investment Bank, 2012 Annual Statement on Corporate Governance, *supra* note 343.

345 Statute of the EIB, *supra* note 330 at art 12.

346 *Id.* at art 16. The EIB has used this ability to enter into agreements with other European banking entities regarding shared areas of operation and financing. It has also entered into arrangements with other regional organizations and international organizations for policy areas such as money-laundering and fraud. *See, e.g.,* Tripartite Agreement between the European Commission, the European Court of Auditors, and the European Investment Bank (2016).

347 Statute of the EIB, *supra* note 330 at art 25.

348 *Id.* at art 28.

349 *See* European Investment Bank, Ethics and Compliance Committee Operating Rules (2016).

350 *See* European Investment Bank, Management Committee Code of Conduct (2011) art 1.7; European Investment Bank, Code of Conduct for the Members of the Audit Committee (2011) art 4.

351 *See* EIB Management Committee Code of Conduct, *supra* note 350 at art 1.17.

352 *See* European Investment Bank, EU-Africa Infrastructure Trust Fund Annual Report (2007); European Investment Bank, EU-Africa Infrastructure Trust Fund Annual Report (2009); European Investment Bank, EU-Africa Infrastructure Trust Fund Annual Report (2010); European Investment Bank, EU-Africa Infrastructure Trust Fund

Annual Report (2011); European Investment Bank, EU-Africa Infrastructure Trust Fund Annual Report (2012); European Investment Bank, EU-Africa Infrastructure Trust Fund Annual Report (2013); European Investment Bank, EU-Africa Infrastructure Trust Fund Annual Report (2014); European Investment Bank, EU-Africa Infrastructure Trust Fund Annual Report (2015); European Investment Bank, EU-Africa Infrastructure Trust Fund Annual Report (2016).

353 *See* European Investment Bank, EU-Africa Infrastructure Trust Fund Annual Report (2008) 6–7; EU-Africa Infrastructure Trust Fund Annual Report, *supra* note 352.

354 *See id.*; EU-Africa Infrastructure Trust Fund Annual Report, *supra* note 352; EU-Africa Infrastructure Trust Fund Annual Report, *supra* note 352; EU-Africa Infrastructure Trust Fund Annual Report, *supra* note 352; EU-Africa Infrastructure Trust Fund Annual Report, *supra* note 352; EU-Africa Infrastructure Trust Fund Annual Report, *supra* note 352; EU-Africa Infrastructure Trust Fund Annual Report, *supra* note 352; EU-Africa Infrastructure Trust Fund Annual Report, *supra* note 352.

355 *Id.*

356 *See* European Investment Bank, Sustainability Report (2013); European Investment Bank, Sustainability Report (2014); European Investment Bank, Sustainability Report (2015).

357 *See* Agreement Establishing the Asian Development Bank (1965) art 1; History, ADB, https://www.adb.org/about/history, last accessed 9 January 2018.

358 ADB Agreement, *supra* note 357 at art 2; Financing Operations, ADB, http://www.adb.org/about/main, last accessed 9 January 2018.

359 Members, ADB, http://www.adb.org/about/members, last accessed 9 January 2018.

360 ADB Agreement, *supra* note 357 at art 3(1).

361 *Id.* at art 3(1).

362 *Id.*

363 *Id.*

364 *Id.*

365 *Id.* at arts 4–6.

366 *Id.* at art 33.

367 *Id.* at art 2(v). *See also* Memorandum of Understanding with regard to Cooperation between the Asian Development Bank and the European Bank for Reconstruction and Development; Memorandum of Understanding on Administrative Arrangements between the Asian Development Bank, and the International Bank for Reconstruction and Development, and the International Development Association (2001); Memorandum of Understanding between Asian Development Bank and European Investment Bank (2007); Memorandum of Understanding for Strengthening Co-operation between Asian Development Bank and Asian Infrastructure Investment Bank (2016).

368 *See* Asian Development Bank, Cooperation between Asian Development Bank and Nongovernment Organization (1998).

369 ADB Agreement, *supra* note 357 at art 41.

370 *Id.* at arts 41, 43.

371 *Id.* at art 42.

372 *Id.* at ch VI.

373 *Id.* at art 27.

374 *Id.* at art 30.

375 *See id.* at art 28. The powers that cannot be exercised by any body other than the Board of Governors include admission of members, changes is capital stock, decisions regarding the suspension of a Member State, questions of interpretation of the Articles of Agreement, arrangements with other international organizations, appointment of other organization officers, issues of operational financing, amendment of the Articles of Agreement, and decisions regarding the termination of the ADB's operations and functions. *Id.*

376 ADB Agreement, *supra* note 357 at art 28(4).

377 *Id.* at art 31.

378 *Id.* at art 34.

379 *Id.* at art 34.

380 *Id.* at arts 44, 45.

381 *Id.* at art 47.

382 Asian Development Bank, Annual Report (2005); Asian Development Bank, Annual Report (2006); Asian Development Bank, Annual Report (2009); Asian Development Bank, Annual Report (2010); Asian Development Bank, Annual Report (2011); Asian Development Bank, Annual Report (2012); Asian Development Bank, Annual Report (2013); Asian Development Bank, Annual Report (2014); Asian Development Bank, Annual Report (2015); Asian Development Bank, Annual Report (2016).

383 *See* Statute of the Asian Development Bank Institute (2004).

384 *See* Asian Development Bank, Independent Evaluation Annual Report (2012); Asian Development Bank, Independent Evaluation Annual Report (2013); Asian Development Bank, Independent Evaluation Annual Report (2014); Asian Development Bank, Independent Evaluation Annual Report (2016); Asian Development Bank, Independent Evaluation Annual Report (2017).

385 *See* Asian Development Bank, Accountability Mechanism Policy (2012) 1–3; ADB Accountability Mechanism Annual Report 2016: Improving Lives Through the Accountability Mechanism (2016).
386 Statute of the Administrative Tribunal of the Asian Development Bank (2016) art II ("The Tribunal shall hear and pass judgment upon any application by which an individual member of the staff of the Bank alleges non-observance of the contract of employment or terms of appointment of such staff member.").
387 *Id.* at art IV.
388 *Id.* at arts IV, V; Rules of the Asian Development Bank Administrative Tribunal (2016) Rule 2.
389 Statute of the Administrative Tribunal, *supra* note 217 386 at art X.
390 Home, African Development Bank, http://www.afdb.org/en/, last accessed 9 January 2018.
391 *See* Establishing the African Development Bank (2016) preamble.
392 *Id.*
393 This is true even in the Stated purpose of the AfDB "to contribute to the sustainable economic development and social progress of its regional members individually and jointly." *Id.*
394 *Id.* at art 3(1).
395 *Id.* at art 3(3).
396 Countries, AfDB, http://www.afdb.org/en/countries/, last accessed 9 January 2018.
397 Partnership, AfDB, http://www.afdb.org/en/topics-and-sectors/topics/partnerships/, last accessed 9 January 2018.
398 AfDB Agreement, *supra* note 391 at art 6.
399 *See* ADB-UNESCO Cooperative Programme Revised Agreement (1969); Agreement between the United Nations Development Programme and African Development Bank (1977); Memorandum of Understanding on Working Arrangements between the African Development Bank and the African Development Fund and the Food and Agriculture Organization of the United Nations (1991); Cooperation Agreement between the African Development Fund and the African Development Fund and the World Health Organization (1994); Cooperation Agreement between the African Development Fund and the African Development Fund and the Southern African Development Community (1998); Memorandum of Understanding between African Development Bank and African Development Fund and International Bank for Reconstruction and Development and International Development Association (2000); Memorandum of Understanding between the United Nations Development Programme and the African Development Bank and the African Development Fund (2001); Memorandum of Understanding between the Secretariat of the World Trade Organization and the African Development Bank and the African Development Fund (2002); Amendment to the Cooperative Agreement between the African Development Bank and African Development Fund and United Nations Population Fund (2003); Cooperative Agreement between the International Labor Organization and the African Development Bank and the African Development Fund (2004); Memorandum of Understanding on an Enhanced Strategic Partnership for Cooperation in the African Countries (2005); Memorandum of Understanding between the United Nations Children's Fund and the African Development Bank and the African Development Fund (2005); Memorandum of Understanding between United Nations Human Settlements Programme and the African Development Bank and the African Development Fund (2006); Memorandum of Understanding between the World Conservation Union and the African Development Bank and the African Development Fund (2008); Technical Cooperation on India-Africa Economic Cooperation between the Government of the Republic of India and the African Development Bank and the African Development Fund (2010); General Cooperation Arrangement between the Republic of Korea and the African Development Bank and the African Development Fund: Korea-Africa Economic Development Trust Fund (2013).
400 AfDB Agreement, *supra* note 391 at art 43.
401 *Id.* at art 44(1).
402 *Id.* at art 44(2).
403 *Id.* at art 45.
404 *Id.* at art 4.
405 *Id.* at arts 29, 33.
406 *Id.* at art 33.
407 *Id.* at art 35.
408 *Id.* at art 29.
409 *Id.* at art 29. The retained powers relate to membership issues, key financial decisions relating to the structure of the AfDB, decisions regarding agreements with international organizations, and election of Board of Directors members. *Id.*
410 *See id.* at arts 32, 37.
411 *Id.* at art 36.
412 *Id.*
413 *Id.* at art 46.
414 *Id.* at arts 46–49.
415 *Id.* at ch VII.
416 *See id.*; African Development Bank, Report by the Boards of Directors of the African Development Bank and the African Development Fund covering the period January 1 to December 31, 2004 (2005); African Development

Bank, Report by the Boards of Directors of the African Development Bank and the African Development Fund covering the period January 1 to December 31, 2005 (2006); African Development Bank, Report by the Boards of Directors of the African Development Bank and the African Development Fund covering the period January 1 to December 31, 2006 (2007); African Development Bank, Report by the Boards of Directors of the African Development Bank and the African Development Fund covering the period January 1 to December 31, 2007 (2008); African Development Bank, Report by the Boards of Directors of the African Development Bank and the African Development Fund covering the period January 1 to December 31, 2008 (2009); African Development Bank, Report by the Boards of Directors of the African Development Bank and the African Development Fund covering the period January 1 to December 31, 2009 (2010); African Development Bank, Report by the Boards of Directors of the African Development Bank and the African Development Fund covering the period January 1 to December 31, 2010 (2011); African Development Bank, Report by the Boards of Directors of the African Development Bank and the African Development Fund covering the period January 1 to December 31, 2011 (2012); African Development Bank, Report by the Boards of Directors of the African Development Bank and the African Development Fund covering the period January 1 to December 31, 2011 (2012); African Development Bank, Report by the Boards of Directors of the African Development Bank and the African Development Fund covering the period January 1 to December 31, 2013 (2014); African Development Bank, Report by the Boards of Directors of the African Development Bank and the African Development Fund covering the period January 1 to December 31, 2014 (2015); African Development Bank, Report by the Boards of Directors of the African Development Bank and the African Development Fund covering the period January 1 to December 31, 2015 (2016); African Development Bank, Report by the Boards of Directors of the African Development Bank and the African Development Fund covering the period January 1 to December 31, 2016 (2017); African Development Bank, AfDB Trust Funds Annual Report (2009); African Development Bank, Investing in Gender Equality for Africa's Transformation (2014).

417 See African Development Bank, Regional Integration Policy and Strategy (RIPoS) 2014–2023 (2015); Regional Integration, AfDB, http://www.afdb.org/en/topics-and-sectors/topics/regional-integration/, last accessed 9 January 2018.

418 See ADB Agreement, supra note 391 at art 2 ("The purpose of the Fund shall be to assist the Bank in making an increasingly effective contribution to the economic and social development of the Bank's members and to the promotion of cooperation (including regional and sub-regional cooperation) and increased international trade, particularly among such members. It shall provide finance on concessional terms for purposes which are of primary importance for and serve such development.").

419 See African Development Bank/African Development Fund Boards of Directors, Resolution B/BD/2010–10 – F/BD/2010–04 (2010) (amending the original statute creating the Independent Review Mechanism); African Development Bank/African Development Fund Boards of Directors, Resolution B/BD/2015/03 – F/BD/2015/02 (2015) (providing further amendments and updates to the original statute); African Development Bank Group, Independent Review Mechanism Operating Rules and Procedures (2015); see also African Development Bank, Independent Review Mechanism Annual Report (2006); African Development Bank, Independent Review Mechanism Annual Report (2007); African Development Bank, Independent Review Mechanism Annual Report (2009); African Development Bank, Independent Review Mechanism Annual Report (2010); African Development Bank, Independent Review Mechanism Annual Report (2011); African Development Bank, Independent Review Mechanism Annual Report (2012); African Development Bank, Independent Review Mechanism Annual Report (2013); African Development Bank, Independent Review Mechanism Annual Report (2014); African Development Bank, Independent Review Mechanism Annual Report (2015).

420 African Development Bank, Whistle Blowing and Complaints Handling Policy (2007); see also African Development Bank, Integrity and Anti-Corruption Department Progress Report 2009–2010 (2011); African Development Bank, Integrity and Anti-Corruption Department Progress Report 2011–2012 (2013); African Development Bank, Integrity and Anti-Corruption Department Annual Report 2013 (2014); African Development Bank, Integrity and Anti-Corruption Department Annual Report 2014 (2015).

421 See Statute of the Administrative Tribunal of the African Development Bank (2007).

422 Id. at art VI.

423 Id. at art XII.

424 See Agreement Establishing the Caribbean Development Bank (2007) preamble, art 1 ("The purpose of the Bank shall be to contribute to the harmonious economic growth and development of the member countries in the Caribbean . . . and to promote economic co-operation and integration among them, having special and urgent regard to the needs of the less developed members of the region.").

425 See id. at preamble.

426 Id. at art 3.

427 Id. at art 6.

428 Id. at art 32; By-Laws of the Caribbean Development Bank (1999) sect 21.

429 CDB Agreement, supra note 424 at art 40.

430 Id. at art 41; CDB By-Laws, supra note 428 at sect 22.

431 CDB Agreement, supra note 424 at art 41.

432 Id. at art 42.

433 Id. at art 25.

434 Id. at arts 26, 27.
435 Id. art 27. As in many international organizations, the retained powers center on issues of structural finance, membership, CDB termination, amendments to the foundational text, and agreements with international organizations and States. Id.
436 Id. at art 29.
437 Id. at art 30.
438 Id. at art 33.
439 Id. at art 43.
440 Id. at arts 44–46.
441 Id. at art 2.
442 Id.
443 See Caribbean Development Bank, Lending Policies (2016); see also Caribbean Development Bank, Private Sector Development Strategy (2004); Caribbean Development Bank, Private Sector Development Policy & Operational Guidelines (2013).
444 See, e.g., Caribbean Development Bank, Annual Report (2004); Caribbean Development Bank, Annual Report (2006); Caribbean Development Bank, Annual Report (2008); Caribbean Development Bank, Annual Report (2009); Caribbean Development Bank, Annual Report (2010); Caribbean Development Bank, Annual Report (2011); Caribbean Development Bank, Annual Report (2012); Caribbean Development Bank, Annual Report (2013); Caribbean Development Bank, Annual Report (2014); Caribbean Development Bank, Climate Resilience Strategy 2012–2017 (2012).
445 Caribbean Development Bank, Annual Report (2007) 3.
446 See Caribbean Development Bank, Strategic Plan 2015–2019 (2014); Caribbean Development Bank, Annual Report (2015); Caribbean Development Bank, Annual Report (2016).
447 Caribbean Development Bank, Strategic Framework for Integrity, Compliance and Accountability (2015); Caribbean Development Bank, Whistleblower Policy (2015).
448 See Caribbean Development Bank, Projects Complaint Mechanism (2015).
449 See id.
450 See Caribbean Development Bank, Compliance Policy (2015); see also Caribbean Development Bank, Procedures for Dealing with Fraud and Corruption in CDB-Financed Projects (2014).
451 See Caribbean Development Bank, Guidelines for the Selection and Engagement of Consultants by Recipients of CDB Financing (2011).
452 Nordic Investment Bank, Constituent Documents: Introduction (2017). The eight current NIB Member States are Denmark, Estonia, Finland, Iceland, Latvia, Lithuania, Norway and Sweden. See Agreement between Denmark, Estonia, Finland, Iceland, Latvia, Lithuania, Norway and Sweden concerning the Nordic Investment Bank (2005) preamble.
453 See id. at art 1 ("The purpose of the Nordic Investment Bank . . . is to make financing available in accordance with sound banking principles and taking into account socio-economic considerations, to carry into effect investment projects of interest to the Member countries and other countries which receive such financing."). See also Nordic Investment Bank, Annual Report (1998); Nordic Investment Bank, Annual Report (1999); Nordic Investment Bank, Annual Report (2000); Nordic Investment Bank, Annual Report (2001); Nordic Investment Bank, Annual Report (2002); Nordic Investment Bank, Annual Report (2003); Nordic Investment Bank, Annual Report (2004); Nordic Investment Bank, Annual Report (2005); Nordic Investment Bank, Annual Report (2007); Nordic Investment Bank, Annual Report (2009); Nordic Investment Bank, Annual Report (2010); Nordic Investment Bank, Annual Report (2011); Nordic Investment Bank, Annual Report (2012); Nordic Investment Bank, Annual Report (2013); Nordic Investment Bank, Integrity Report (2014); Nordic Investment Bank, Integrity Report (2015); Nordic Investment Bank, Integrity Report (2016).
454 NIB Agreement, supra note 452 at art 3.
455 Id. at art 18.
456 Statutes of the Nordic Bank (2017) sect 13.
457 Id. at sect 14.
458 Id.
459 Id.
460 Id. at sect 15.
461 Id.
462 NIB Agreement, supra note 452 at art 16.
463 NIB Statutes, supra note 456 at sect 16.
464 Id. at sect 17; Rules of Procedure for the Control Committee (2016).
465 NIB Statutes, supra note 456 at sect 17; Rules of Procedure for the Control Committee, supra note 463 at sect 2.
466 NIB Agreement, supra note 452 at sect 18.
467 See NIB Statutes, supra note 456 at sect 7; Nordic Investment Bank, Sustainability Policy and Guidelines (2012). See also Nordic Investment Bank, Annual Report (1998); Nordic Investment Bank, Annual Report (1999); Nordic Investment Bank, Annual Report (2000); Nordic Investment Bank, Annual Report (2001); Nordic Investment Bank, Annual Report (2002); Nordic Investment Bank, Annual Report (2003); Nordic Investment Bank, Annual Report (2004); Nordic Investment Bank, Annual Report (2005); Nordic Investment Bank, Annual

Report (2007); Nordic Investment Bank, Annual Report (2009); Nordic Investment Bank, Annual Report (2010); Nordic Investment Bank, Annual Report (2011); Nordic Investment Bank, Annual Report (2012); Nordic Investment Bank, Annual Report (2013); Nordic Investment Bank, Integrity Report (2014); Nordic Investment Bank, Integrity Report (2015); Nordic Investment Bank, Integrity Report (2016).

468 Nordic Investment Bank, Rules for the Ombudsman (2009) rule 4.

469 *See generally id.*

470 *See* Nordic Investment Bank, Arbitration Regulations (2005). The same rules and procedures are shared with the subsidiary Nordic Development Fund and Nordic Environment Financing Company. *Id.*

471 Nordic Investment Bank, Arbitration Regulations (2005) preamble.

472 *Id.* at sects 5, 6.

473 *See* Nordic Investment Bank, Compliance, Integrity and Anti-Corruption Policy (2016).

474 *See* Investigations and Enforcement Policy – Corruption, Misconduct and Complaints (2016); Nordic Investment Bank, Speaking-up and Whistleblowing Policy (2016); Nordic Investment Bank, Integrity Report (2010) sect 2; Nordic Investment Bank, Integrity Report (2011–2012).

475 *See* Investigations and Enforcement Policy – Corruption, Misconduct and Complaints (2016); Nordic Investment Bank, Speaking-up and Whistleblowing Policy (2016); Nordic Investment Bank, Integrity Report, supra note 274 at sect 3; Nordic Investment Bank, Integrity Report (2011–2012).

476 *See, e.g.,* Nordic Investment Bank, Integrity Report (2013); Nordic Investment Bank, Integrity Report (2014); Nordic Investment Bank, Integrity Report (2015); Nordic Investment Bank, Integrity Report (2016).

Chapter 16

Sector and industry-focused organizations

In international law, no less than in domestic law, specific sectors and industries play essential roles in defining various aspects of law and society. The international organizations selected for discussion in the following chapter demonstrate this and provide insights into topics that are essential to development and growth as well as the creation of meaningful laws and rules for their regulation.

World Health Organization

Background

The World Health Organization (WHO) operates as an independent institution within the overall UN-affiliated organization framework and is charged with coordinating the global response of the UN system to health threats and general health policy.[1] The WHO was created in 1945 and became legally effective in 1948 when the WHO Constitution went into operation.[2] The overall goal of the WHO is for all peoples to attain the "highest possible level of health" and, accordingly, each State is deemed to have the responsibility to provide healthcare and assistance to all citizens.[3] With this in mind, the WHO is authorized to carry out many functions in order to assist States in fulfilling their obligations and to act as an international source of laws, policy and coordination in these fields.[4] In order to comply with its purposes and goals, the WHO is enabled to enter into a variety of professional and scientific capacities and undertakings that go beyond the standard enunciated functions for international organizations.[5] This includes the ability to coordinate with other international organizations on issues relating to health and health policy, particularly in times of emergency.[6]

Membership and voting

Membership in the WHO is available to States that are members of the UN and generally the process of obtaining membership is very simple.[7] Currently, every recognized State within the international community is a member of the WHO and, accordingly, has the right to a seat on the WHO Health Assembly.[8] In addition, it is possible for a territory to hold Associate Member status in the WHO, for example if it is a territory that is under the control of another State but exercises significant autonomy.[9]

In addition to participation in WHO governing bodies and dues payments, WHO Member States are required to submit annual reports to the WHO.[10] These reports are meant to provide the WHO as an institution with information on the status of health as a whole within the Member State[11] and also must explain the ways in which the State has – or has not – complied with the Conventions, agreements and regulations promulgated by the WHO.[12] States are required to provide the WHO with information on their overall health-related legal regimes[13] and must provide additional information to the WHO in the event that it is requested.[14] These reports and forms of information are essential to chart the implementation of WHO policies and the ways in which Member States handle health and related issues.[15]

Should a WHO Member State fail to meet its dues payment requirement or in any other way violate the obligations of membership, it may be suspended by the Health Assembly.[16] In the event the issue triggering suspension is cured, the Health Assembly may vote to terminate the suspension and allow the State to resume its status as a full Member State.[17]

Structure

The Health Assembly is in many ways similar to the UN General Assembly in that it is the plenary entity within the WHO.[18] The Health Assembly is scheduled to meet once a year and is chaired by a President who is elected by its members.[19] The Health Assembly sets the overall policy direction of the WHO and elects members of the WHO Executive Board, which is the equivalent of the UN

Security Council in terms of organizational structure, as well as the Director-General of the WHO Secretariat.[20] Importantly in the WHO context, the Health Assembly is tasked with adopting proposed Conventions and agreements relating to organization-related issues.[21] In addition, the Health Assembly is tasked with adopting regulations that relate to the organization's functions, perhaps most importantly those relating to the imposition of quarantines and other measures that are aimed at stopping the transmission of disease.[22] These regulations become binding on all Member States once they are promulgated, due to their technical nature and essentially apolitical character.[23] Further, the WHO as an organization has the ability to create a variety of sub-organizations and entities.[24] Despite this relative independence, the Health Assembly is required to send reports on its activities to ECOSOC, reinforcing its status as a UN affiliated entity.[25]

The WHO Executive Board is the equivalent of the UN Security Council. The Executive Board is comprised of 34 members who are elected by the Health Assembly.[26] However, unlike the UN Security Council, there are no permanent members of the Executive Board and Member States of the Executive Board must be geographically balanced rather than taking into account any particular State identity.[27] The Executive Board makes the highest-level policy decisions for the WHO, provides health policy advice to the Health Assembly, has the ability to submit suggestions to the Health Assembly, and takes whatever measures are necessary to address health emergencies when the Health Assembly cannot be convened in time.[28] In the course of carrying out the latter ability the Executive Board has the ability to coordinate with and provide approvals to the WHO Director-General and Secretariat for necessary assistance for disasters and epidemics.[29] Independently or with the Health Assembly, the Executive Board is authorized to convene conferences at any level in a Member State, region, or internationally in order to address health or related issues.[30]

The WHO Secretariat is headed by the Executive Board selected Director-General, who is confirmed to the post by vote of the Health Assembly.[31] The Director-General serves a titular role as the secretary of all WHO organs and sub-organs, although he holds this position as a non-voting member.[32] As part of the Director-General's functions, he has the ability to interact with the national health systems in Member States when necessary, and can also establish relationships with non-governmental organizations and other international organizations as appropriate.[33] A critical part of the Director-General's function in the WHO structure is the creation of a budget for approval by the Health Assembly.[34] Selections of Secretariat staff members also fall within the purview of the Director-General, provided they comply with requirements established by the Health Assembly and the organization per se.[35]

Under the terms of the WHO Constitution, the Health Assembly is authorized periodically to create regional WHO-based organizations where it is deemed appropriate.[36] These committees are meant to provide coordinated assistance and guidance on issues that are of particular importance to WHO Member States within the given area.[37] They are governed by committees with representatives of the Member States in the region and have powers and obligations assigned to them by the Health Assembly.[38] The seats of WHO regional organizations are located in the respective regional offices, each overseen by a Regional Director who exercises functions similar to the head of a secretariat.[39] At present, there are established WHO regional offices for Africa, the Americas (the Pan American Health Organization), South-East Asia, Europe, Eastern Mediterranean, and Western Pacific.[40]

Functions

An essential WHO function is the creation, implementation and updating of the International Health Regulations (IHRs), which are geared toward preventing and addressing the spread of a number of diseases between States and within the international community.[41] The IHRs further allow for the designation of public health emergencies at the international level by the WHO

Director-General, which can trigger a number of results including special meetings of the WHO organs and the imposition of travel restrictions or the declaration of a pandemic.[42] In such situations, there are established procedures for the designation of national contact points to coordinate treatment efforts and to ensure that sovereignty concerns are addressed.[43] Readers may be familiar with these efforts from recent cases of pandemics such as avian influenza.

Part of the WHO's coordination with other international organizations involves an extensive collaboration with the Food and Agriculture Organization (FAO) through which the two entities work together to create and implement the Codex Alimentarius. The Codex, which regulates food safety and security, is largely crafted by the FAO with input from the WHO. The organizations work together to ensure appropriate implementation and drafting of updates through the Codex Alimentarius Commission, convened under the auspices of the Joint FAO/WHO Food Standards Programme.[44] Within this Commission there are set rules and procedures that govern the ways in which the Commission itself functions, ostensibly creating a separate sub-organ of both organizations that is responsible to each of them.[45]

In essence, the WHO works in every major area of health care and health concern, from SARS to maternal health to environmental contamination to obesity to access to water and food.[46] One final area of WHO policy that should be mentioned is that of disease outbreak and control thereof. The WHO has established the Global Alert and Response (GAR) system, which is tasked with monitoring the outbreak, or potential outbreak, of disease around the world and assisting in the coordination of relevant information-sharing and response.[47]

Food and Agriculture Organization

Background

Food is a persistent issue within the international community and international law, fueling everything from famine and humanitarian disaster to conflict to humanitarian responses and relief. In order to address these issues, the Food and Agriculture Organization (FAO) was created as a UN-affiliated international organization and tasked with addressing issues of food access as well as food quantity and quality.[48]

Membership and voting

Membership in the FAO is open to all States that are willing to conform with the requirements of the organizational constitution and able to garner the necessary number of votes from the FAO Conference.[49] Additionally, Associate Membership status is available to entities that are not completely independent yet wishing to join the FAO as separate territories.[50]

After four or more years of membership in the FAO, a Member State is eligible to withdraw from the organization by providing notice of the intention to do so to the Director-General.[51] Following this, there is a one-year mandatory waiting period before the withdrawal becomes effective in the eyes of the organization.[52] As part of the winding up process for membership, withdrawing States are required to ensure that their outstanding obligations are met.[53]

Structure

The main organizational body of the FAO is the Conference, the equivalent of the UN General Assembly, in which each Member State has a seat and a vote.[54] While the Conference has the ability to create committees and other organs as it sees fit, it is required at the very least to create and maintain a Committee on World Food Security.[55] The Conference is tasked with deciding the general policy direction of the FAO, has the power to approve the FAO's budget, and make international, regional and domestic legal and policy recommendations to members regarding issues of food and agriculture.[56] Perhaps most importantly, the Conference has the ultimate responsibility for adopting Conventions, agreements or other international instruments.[57] In furtherance of the FAO's specialized role, it has the ability to provide other international organization with guidance and information relating to issues that are within the FAO's functions.[58]

Similar to the WHO, the FAO may create regional offices, referred to as Regional Conferences, with the goal of ensuring the proper functioning of the FAO's mandate at regional and national levels.[59] As currently established, there are Regional Conferences in Africa, Asia and the Pacific, Europe, Latin America and the Caribbean, and the Near East, very closely approximating those used by the WHO.[60]

In the FAO system, the Council of the Organization is the UN Security Council equivalent.[61] There are 49 seats on the Council of the Organization,[62] and these seats are filled by the Conference without restrictions based on designated permanent members or geographical balance attempts.[63] Within the Council of the Organization there are a number of designated subsidiary entities and committees, including for financing, legal matters, and issues associated with food on the commodities markets.[64] Given the technical – and often compartmentalized – nature of food and agriculture issues, such committees are highly necessary.[65] Additionally, the Council has the ability to send Conventions or other international instruments to the Conference for a vote on whether they should be adopted by the FAO as a whole.[66]

Either of the main legislative bodies within the FAO system has the ability to create a new sub-organ for a number of topic areas.[67] These sub-organs may be made open to the entirety of the FAO's membership or the specific States and regions that are most impacted by the issues at hand, depending on the appropriateness of the membership approach.[68] In addition, when a particular issue merits it, the FAO can establish a working group or study group to determine the contours and dynamics involved in an issue or set of issues.[69]

The general secretariat function of the FAO is overseen and headed by the Director-General, who is appointed to the post by the Conference and is eligible to serve up to two terms of four years.[70] The Director-General is also tasked with representing the FAO at meetings of other international organizations and Member States, and has the ability to attend meetings of both the Conference and Council, although he is without voting rights in these forums.[71] Official work of the FAO is carried out by a staff that is selected and appointed by the Director-General with a mandate to, among other things, be of an international nature so as to reflect the makeup of the organization.[72]

Functions

The FAO has several distinct functions. It is in part a scientific organization in that it is required to examine issues involved in agriculture and food production so that food quality and quantity can be overseen.[73] This scientific function also takes into account the key issue of food security, which involves not only ensuring the quality of food and agricultural stocks but also measures taken by governments to ensure that there are adequate food reserves to protect their populations in the event of a natural disaster, conflict or simply a drastic increase in food prices which would make it difficult for the general population to access sufficient food.[74] The FAO is also a policy organization in that it is required to create international Conventions and standards and also to assist regions and States with legal and regulatory measures necessary to address issues relating to food and agriculture.[75] Finally, the FAO is an oversight entity in that it oversees the educational and environmental policies and practices at the international, regional and domestic level as they relate to food and agriculture issues.[76]

Within the system of sub-organs established in the FAO there is a range of subject areas and intended protections that mirrors the range of activities undertaken by the organization itself. In the realm of the preservation of food resources, the FAO has created sub-organs such as the

Asia-Pacific Fisheries Commission with the intent of ensuring the continued existence of fish as viable food sources for the region and for the international market.[77] Membership in the Asia-Pacific Fisheries Commission was opened to UN Member States and, once a member of the Commission, each Member State is afforded one seat and one vote.[78] The Commission was given – and has used – the ability to create committees and similar associated entities as needed to carry out its work and mission.[79]

At the same time, the FAO is home to sub-organs created in response to a disease outbreak that threatens food stocks and food security. A vivid example of this is the European Commission for the Control of Foot-and-Mouth Disease, which was established within the FAO structure and continues this role.[80] Similar responses have been made to disasters that threaten certain aspects of the food supply, such as the creation of the Commission for Controlling the Desert Locust in the Central Region.[81]

While food tends to be most associated with the work of the FAO, it must be remembered that the organization's jurisdiction extends to all forms of cultivation and agriculture, including non-food related purposes. An example of a sub-organ which supports this form of work is the International Poplar Commission, which works to ensure the protection and preservation of poplar and willow trees, including for scientific and touristic purposes.[82]

The FAO created the Global Information and Early Warning System on Food and Agriculture in order to provide information on food shortages, issues with production of food, and food security.[83] As noted, the FAO promulgates the Codex Alimentarius, which creates guidelines and rules for food content, food production, and agricultural practices.[84] These guidelines are not immediately binding as a matter of law, however they are typically accepted by FAO Member States and incorporated into domestic law at some level due to the technical nature of their content.[85] This is quite useful for ensuring that there is uniformity in the food safety practices used for food products around the world and can also provide developing States with rules that might otherwise be quite costly to test and create.[86]

The FAO has adopted the Sustainable Development Goals (SDGs) as part of its operational strategy, seeking to incorporate them into its functions and to coordinate with other international organizations to work toward their achievement.[87] Given the increasing impacts of conflict on broad swathes of the civilian population, in extreme numbers and severity, for example the recent fight against IS and the devastation caused by the group on those in its wake, the FAO has begun to operate in this field of emergencies as well.[88]

Oversight of the FAO's activities, funding and operational mandates is within the jurisdiction of the Office of the Inspector General, which exists as a separate entity within the organization's structure.[89] This mandate is fulfilled through a system that stresses the importance of auditing, investigations, and publicity of the outcomes.[90] After several years in existence, the Office of the Inspector General's jurisdiction was expanded to include employment-related complaints and allegations regarding improper conduct.[91] Further, a Compliance Review system for allegations that the FAO's operations violate established guidelines and practices relating to environmental and social standards now exists within the overall apparatus of the Office of the Inspector General.[92] However, the Compliance Review system is intended to operate as a separate entity within the Office of the Inspector General.

International Labour Organization

Background

In the post-World War II world, most organizations affiliated with the League of Nations have been discredited to some extent and replaced by independent organizations or UN-affiliated organizations. One of the few exceptions to this trend is the International Labour Organization (ILO), which was founded in the immediate aftermath of World War I and continues to function as a vibrant organization in modern international law.[93] However, the foundational text and associated agreements of the ILO have been updated to reflect the realities and needs of modern international law and the issues it involves, demonstrating its organizational tenacity.

From the outset, the ILO has existed to promote international peace through the achievement of social justice through labor standards and rights.[94] Over the course of its organizational history, the ILO has functioned in a system in which domestic laws and rules surrounding labor practices and protections have been – and still are – uneven, resulting in the ILO viewing part of its function as attempting to fill these gaps.

Membership and voting

Following World War II, it was agreed that ILO Member States prior to the war would automatically retain their membership status, and it was further agreed that all original UN Member States could join the ILO through notification of the Director-General.[95] In addition, new members were – and still are – allowed to join through the proper systemic requirements involving approval of admission by the General Conference.[96] At the other end of the spectrum, an ILO Member State has the ability to withdraw from the organization after a two-year notification period.[97] As part of withdrawal, the terminating member must settle outstanding accounts with the ILO and even after a State is withdrawn as an ILO member it is required to honor its commitments to ILO Conventions and agreements unless they are repealed through the appropriate State legislative methods.[98] Withdrawal from the ILO is not dispositive, however, in that former Member States have the ability to reapply for membership in the organization although they must do so in the same way that any first time applicant would.[99]

All ILO members have a seat on the ILO General Conference, which has the typical functions of the main governing body of any international organization.[100]

Structure

The General Conference is charged with deciding what issues are in need of an international instrument, whether a Convention, agreement or resolution is necessary, and what the terms of the instrument should be.[101] This does not obviate the need for individual States to ratify the appropriate instruments – or officially agree to them, depending on the form used – but it does shift the site of negotiation to the General Conference.[102]

There is, however, another feature of the General Conference and the ILO's secondary organ, the Governing Body, that differs drastically from other international organizations. As established in the UN Charter and often replicated by international organizations regardless whether they are affiliated with the UN, only States sit on this body. It would be inconceivable for a union representative to sit on the UN Security Council, for example. And yet, this is exactly what happens on the General Conference and Governing Body under the moniker of the Tripartite system or "tripartism" that has come to define the ILO.[103]

At the General Conference, a State must appoint two State-based delegates – such as a representative from the Department of Labor – as well as delegates representing employers/industry and employees/workers within the State.[104] This includes the right of each of the four delegates from a Member State to an individual vote.[105] At this point, one might wonder why such a system was implemented when it appears to fly in the face of the State-centered focus of international organization governance and fundamental tenets of State sovereignty that underpin international law. The idea behind this system is that it is more effective to involve all aspects of labor with the creation of policy as opposed to imposing policy on them without understanding the impacts of the policy in practice.

The ILO Governing Body is comprised of 56 members.[106] Only 28 members are direct State representatives, with the remaining seats equally apportioned between employers/industry representatives and workers' representatives.[107] At the State representative level, 10 of the 28 members must be from "States of chief industrial importance"[108] and the remaining members are to be elected by the General Conference regardless of industrial status.[109] The employers/industry members are elected to the Governing Body by the combined employers/industry delegates sitting at the General Conference, and the same practice is used for the employee-representative members.[110]

The ILO is similar to other international organizations in that it elects a Director General to lead the Secretariat – the Labour Office in this instance – and depends on the Secretariat to facilitate the daily functioning of the organization.[111] At the ILO level, the Director-General is elected by the Governing Body and has the ability to appoint the necessary staff members to assist in carrying out the organization's operations.[112] In addition to standard secretariat functions, the Labour Office is required to take an active role in the gathering and dissemination of information regarding issues within the ILO's purview to the public as well as States, industries and employee groups.[113]

In addition, the ILO Constitution makes provisions for a complaint settlement function within the ILO system.[114] Under the terms of these provisions, a Member State may complain to the Governing Body about another Member State's alleged failure to comply with an ILO instrument.[115] The Governing Body then examines the allegations and can send the issue to a Commission of Inquiry – a subsidiary body within the ILO system – for an opinion if it finds that there are sufficient grounds.[116] At the Commission of Inquiry level, all States involved have the ability to offer statements before a decision is rendered.[117] In the event there is a negative finding against the complained-of Member State, the Commission of Inquiry will make recommendations as to how to remedy the situation involved.[118] In the event that these recommendations are not complied with the Governing Body has the ability to refer the matter to the International Court of Justice.[119] It should be noted these complaints are relatively rare – indeed, only 12 have been brought during the history of the ILO.

Functions

The ILO works to promote four strategic objectives: 1) the promotion of standards and other regulations that protect those who are working and the right to work in general; 2) the creation of job opportunities that reflect gender equality and that involve the payment of a decent wage; 3) the enhancement of social protection through the ability and right to work; and 4) the creation of a consistent and meaningful dialogue between States, employers/industry and employees/workers.[120] In recognition of the holistic impact of work on one's life and, conversely, of one's life, skills and status on one's work, the ILO acts in a variety of areas that are not strictly labor-related.[121] For example, the ILO is active in the promotion of protections for vulnerable populations, such as children, indigenous groups and those with disease, in terms of labor law and law as a general matter.[122] Its efforts also target industries that have the potential to undermine the concept and application of decent working conditions, such as forced labor and unsafe working conditions.[123]

Throughout the ILO's history, one of its most important functions has consistently been the development of Conventions and agreements that reflect important issues of labor policy. If a Member State ratifies an ILO Convention or agreement it is also required to provide periodic reports to the Secretariat regarding implementation and issues with implementation.[124] In the event a Member State does not ratify an ILO Convention or agreement it still has reporting requirements, this time encompassing statements as to why the particular instrument has not been ratified and whether there are laws in effect which relate to the subject of the instrument.[125]

The vast majority of the ILO's Conventions seek to promote and require the regulation of an industrial sector or practice; however, they do so in a way that is dependent on each signatory

State's compliance with the terms of the regime, namely incorporating them into national law regimes.[126] Given the scope of the ILO's activities and the cross-cutting nature of labor issues, the ILO is authorized to create and maintain relationships with other international organizations and sub-organizations. Since its inception, the ILO has actively seized on this ability and created a number of these relationships, which are often governed through joint committees.[127]

Issues involving complaints raised in the context of employment at the ILO are to be settled by the Administrative Tribunal of the International Labour Organization rather than by resort to the local court system of a host State. Within the Tribunal setting, there are judges, including designated judges to serve as the President and Vice-President, and a Registry office to handle the functional aspects of the Tribunal's operations.[128] Complainants to the Tribunal have the ability to represent themselves in its proceedings or may involve certain, highly experienced individuals to act as their representatives.[129]

International Maritime Organization

Background

The International Maritime Organization (IMO) is a regulatory organization for the conduct of many aspects of commercial shipping, fishing and general uses of the sea.[130] It is a UN-affiliated international organization subject to its own foundational text and procedures.[131] The IMO became operational in the 1950s, at a time when maritime commerce was changing and there was a recognition that the regulation of the many aspects of the industry needed to change as well. Over time, the IMO has seen changes to its foundational text in order to reflect the needs and interests of the maritime and associated industries, as well as such public policy issues as environmental regulation and safe labor standards.

The foundation of the IMO was reflective of several primary areas of international, national, and commercial concern. These clustered around concerns over safety and uniformity in the industry,[132] using the highest practicable standards to ensure safety and efficiency in international maritime commerce,[133] encouraging freedom of maritime access and commerce and the reduction in discriminatory practices in the maritime industry,[134] and only subsequently included issues such as environment and trade preferences that would implicate WTO regimes.[135]

Membership and voting

Membership in the IMO is open to members of the UN and for States that have been granted a status in the UN, as well as to non-UN Member States, for whom the requirements for admission are more stringent.[136] Associate membership status is available for non-self-governing territories and entities.[137] It is possible for a State to lose its membership in the IMO if it loses its status within the UN, or when the UN General Assembly or Security Council orders that the IMO terminate the membership.[138] For every IMO organ, the general rule is that each Member State has one vote.[139]

At the time of writing, there are 170 IMO Member States, with several other States in the process of becoming members.[140] The majority of important seafaring States are members along with a number of other States with varying degrees of connection to the sea and maritime commerce.[141] In addition, the IMO allows international organizations to serve as observer entities provided they have expertise in a policy area that the IMO works on and can contribute to the IMO's work.[142] Non-governmental organizations that meet the same criteria are also eligible for consultative status at the IMO.[143]

On the opposite end of the spectrum, Member States may withdraw from the IMO by informing the UN Secretary-General, who then transmits the notice of withdrawal to the IMO.[144] Withdrawals are deemed to be effective after a year from the date of notification.[145]

Structure

Structurally, the IMO uses a system that is very similar to those used by other organizations, particularly those affiliated with the UN. The Assembly is the representative body for all IMO Member States.[146] It debates issues, creates the program of work for the IMO, and handles budgetary issues for the organization.[147] It also is responsible for electing members to the Council, which is a supervisory entity for the IMO.[148]

Although the job of the Assembly is to elect members to the Council, there are some parameters in which they must work, dictated by the establishment of multiple classes of Council representation.[149] Class A representatives are to be the "10 States with the largest interest in providing international shipping services."[150] Class B representatives are to be "10 other States with the largest interest in international seaborne trade."[151] Finally, Class C representatives are 20 States not falling into the first two categories but still having a significant connection to the industry and, it is hoped, representing a wide geographical range of Member States.[152]

In addition to its oversight work, the Council reviews a variety of specialized committees that have been established within the IMO.[153] Perhaps the most important of these committees is the Maritime Safety Committee, which has a wide mandate that generally covers all technical aspects of ensuring the safety of ships and their operations while at sea.[154] When the Assembly proposes any form of safety-related guideline, the Maritime Safety Committee is charged with reviewing it and providing comments if necessary.[155] In this sense, it is similar to the work of US Senatorial or Congressional committees on specialized topics.

Further, there are many highly technical committees and sub-committees and also a legal committee to assist Member States and the organization with drafting of laws and policies.[156] As the highest-level organ in the IMO, the Council has the ability to enter into agreements and relationships with other international organizations on its behalf.[157]

To complete the daily work of the IMO, there is also a Secretariat headed by the Council-selected Secretary-General.[158] The Secretary-General is the main public representative of the IMO and has the ability to appoint staff members to fulfill the Secretariat's functions.[159]

Functions

The Maritime Environment Protection Committee has grown in importance since the spate of oil spills and disasters that have occurred over the past 20 years.[160] The purpose of this Committee is to propose and review measures that seek to stop these and other forms of pollution, along with other topics that relate to environmental protection – for example, the requirements for cleaning a ship before it is launched into a different body of water.[161] This includes enforcement of existing and future agreements and relationships with other international organizations.[162]

The Legal Committee is comprised of all members and has jurisdiction to consider any legal instruments or issues that are generally within the purview of the IMO.[163] The Legal Committee works in conjunction with, and can report to, the Assembly and the Council as appropriate, ensuring that it has full breadth of scope over the entirety of the organization. Given the scope of its work, the Legal Committee has authorization to engage in dialogue and connections with other relevant international organizations and their committees and/or organs.[164] Should the Legal Committee generate draft agreements, Conventions, or other legal instruments it is obligated to send them to the Council for review and follow-up as appropriate.[165]

Over the course of time, the IMO has developed some extremely influential Conventions and agreements for the entirety of the international community and international law. For example, in recent years the International Convention on Maritime Search and Rescue has gained in value due to the prevalence of refugees seeking assistance at sea and encountering problems with vessel seaworthiness.[166] In this context, and the subsequent political fallout from it, this Convention has been applied in ways that might have been unforeseen at the time yet are an evolution of the meaning and spirit of the instrument terms. Another example is the Convention for the Suppression of Unlawful Acts Against the Safety of Maritime Navigation and its Protocol for the Suppression of Unlawful Acts Against the Safety of Fixed Platforms Located on the Continental Shelf, which together are important to the fight against maritime piracy.[167]

In the maritime environmental realm, the IMO has crafted Conventions that are far more extensively applied and meaningful than simply in the industrial context. Examples include the International Convention for the Prevention of Pollution from Ships (MARPOL),[168] which addresses pollution from oil and other substances; the International Convention Relating to Intervention on the High Seas in Cases of Oil Pollution Casualties;[169] the Convention on the Prevention of Marine Pollution by Dumping of Wastes and Other Matter;[170] and the International Convention for the Control and Management of Ships' Ballast Water and Sediments.[171] Another example is the International Convention for the Safety of Life at Sea (SOLAS), which provides seminal terms for the protection of merchant seamen and others engaged in seafaring activities.[172]

International Civil Aviation Organization

Background

Founded in 1944, the International Civil Aviation Organization (ICAO) is essentially the equivalent of the IMO for the aviation industry. As with the IMO, ICAO is an UN-affiliated international organization that currently counts all but two recognized States in the UN system as Member States.[173] ICAO was founded on the belief that the aviation industry required a system of regulation and coordination and that the aviation industry could serve as either a method of growth and international cooperation or a method of conflict if not properly subject to common laws and rules.[174]

Membership and voting

Membership is open to all UN Member States. A Member State may withdraw from ICAO by providing official notice to the Government of the United States, which is then required to forward that notice to the ICAO Secretariat.[175] Withdrawal from ICAO becomes effective one year after official notice of intent to withdraw is received.[176]

Structure

ICAO's equivalent of the UN General Assembly is the Assembly, which has a representative of every Member State, each of whom has the ability to vote.[177] The Assembly is tasked with guiding ICAO's organizational policies and with handling budgetary measures for the organization.[178] Additionally, the Assembly has the ability to delegate powers to the Council as it sees fit and, conversely, may decide to revoke any such delegation of powers and resume the exercise of powers.[179]

Within ICAO's structure the equivalent of the UN Security Council is the Council. The Council uses a membership system that is very similar to the IMO in that it is dependent on the status of States as users and facilitators of civil aviation.[180] This means that, of the 36 Member States on the Council, "States of chief importance in air transport, States which make the largest contribution to the provision of facilities for air navigation, and States whose designation will ensure that all major areas of the world are represented."[181] Each Member State sitting on the Council has a vote, and the Council has the ability to delegate issues to committees and subcommittees to take votes of approval.[182] At the Council level, those States not holding a seat on the Council have the right to attend and participate in discussions that impact them provided they do not exercise a vote.[183]

The Council's work includes both mandatory and permissive functions. Mandatory functions include the adoption of various forms of industry-related regulations and standards, as well as oversight of key technical committees.[184] They also include significant reporting requirements to the Assembly, the administration of ICAO finances and budgetary oversight, investigatory and reporting requirements for violation of ICAO rules and instruments, and the recommendation of international standards for aviation practices.[185] Permissive functions include significant research and policy suggestions on issues facing the international aviation industry and community, conducting research into issues that have an impact for ICAO at the organizational level, and conducting research into potentially problematic aviation practices at the request of a Member State.[186]

A further key component of the governance structure of ICAO is the Air Navigation Commission. The Air Navigation Commission is a smaller sub-group of ICAO that is composed of 19 members who are nominated and elected by the Council and who have significant backgrounds in relevant scientific fields.[187] It serves as an advisory body to the Council on technical matters and their relation to current and proposed policy.[188] Finally, ICAO's daily work is overseen and implemented by a Secretariat, which is under the direction of an appointed Secretary-General.[189]

Functions

An essential function of ICAO that is set out in the foundational text and has been used to define the organization ever since is the ability to create agreements, rules and regulations that are technically based and that Member States agree to support.[190] ICAO works in four policy areas: safety, security, environmental protection and sustainable development of air transport.[191] Included in these policy areas are many very technical issues and problems, emerging issues – such as the impacts of the industry on the environment in the long and short term[192] and addressing the best way to handle emerging threats to the security of the aviation industry.[193] In addition to promulgating Conventions in these areas, ICAO is quite active in establishing guidelines and regulations for the industry on a flexible basis, which is important given the changing nature of the aviation industry.

Throughout its history, ICAO has been proactive in the creation of international instruments that reflect the changing needs and capacities of the international aviation industry.[194] As part of its policy and operational strategies, ICAO has also come to incorporate new issue areas, such as security from attack and the protection of the environment.[195]

World Intellectual Property Organization

Background

Intellectual property figures heavily in the work of the WTO. However, the intellectual property needs of the international community extend far beyond this scope, and are instead regulated by the World Intellectual Property Organization (WIPO), which counts nearly all UN Member States as part of its regime.[196]

Membership and voting

Membership in WIPO is available to two different categories of States. First, States that have joined an existing treaty regime for intellectual property (referred to as a "union") are automatically eligible to become WIPO members.[197] Second, States that are not part of a union but are UN Member States or members of a UN-affiliated organization and who are specifically invited by the WIPO General Assembly are eligible for membership as well.[198] Additionally, international organizations and non-governmental organizations are eligible for membership in WIPO as observers.[199] Conversely, it is possible for any WIPO Member State to withdraw as a member by providing notification to the Director General and waiting six months for the notification to become official.[200]

Structure

The plenary organ of WIPO is the General Assembly, in which all eligible Member States have one seat and one vote.[201] General Assembly powers and functions include the ability to elect the WIPO Director General, review and comment on reports from other WIPO organs and sub-organs, budgetary approvals for the organization, approval of methods for compliance with and implementation of international instruments involving WIPO, and issuing invitations for membership to qualifying non-Member States.[202]

Rather unusually, the next layer of the WIPO system, the Conference, is also comprised of representatives from each WIPO State rather than a smaller, elected group.[203] Within the Conference, each Member State has one seat and one vote to exercise.[204] The Conference's functions are partly budgetary in terms of approval and planning and partly policy oriented in terms of discussion of methods to address new issues facing the intellectual property community and artists and inventors generally.[205]

Within the WIPO system, an additional organ is the Coordination Committee, which is comprised of a limited membership based on representatives from the different union regimes.[206] The Coordination Committee is tasked with evaluating potential policies, issues and instruments that impact on at least two of the unions and also serves as the entity that provides initial nominees for WIPO Director General.[207] Each Coordination Committee member has one vote in the Committee system.[208]

Secretariat functions for WIPO are exercised by the International Bureau, which is overseen by the Director General.[209] In addition to the oversight function, the Director General is responsible for the approval of initial staff hiring and is the official representative of WIPO in the international community, including at other international organizations.[210]

In addition to these organs, WIPO is governed through a series of committees and conferences that are authorized to focus on specific areas of law, technical practice and policy in intellectual property regimes. Some of these committees have been made permanent given the importance and recurring nature of their focuses.[211] The permanent entities are the Budget Committee,[212] the Committee on Development and Intellectual Property,[213] the Intergovernmental Committee on Intellectual Property and Genetic Resources, Traditional Knowledge and Folklore,[214] and the Advisory Committee on Enforcement.[215] The standing committees are established for certain policy issues that are of particular importance, although not necessarily of the same duration in importance as the permanent committees.[216] As of the time of writing, these committees are the Standing Committee on the Law of Patents,[217] the Standing Committee on the Law of Trademarks, Industrial Designs and Geographical Indications,[218] the Standing Committee on Copyright and Related Rights,[219] and the Committee on WIPO Standards.[220]

Functions

The overarching goal of WIPO is to create uniformity in the intellectual property realm, allowing artists and inventors easier and more thorough access to protections for their work regardless the venue in which it is created and shown.[221] To accomplish this, WIPO is empowered to craft international instruments relating to intellectual property and associated concerns, assist Member States with questions regarding the application of WIPO rules and instruments, and serve as a source of guidance for the international regulation of intellectual property per se.[222]

One of the tasks assigned to the committees is the evaluation of potential treaties and agreements on certain topics relating to intellectual property. Once a committee believes there is progress toward the potential adoption of an international instrument, it is then forwarded to an established diplomatic conference, which is responsible for the final negotiations of an instrument.[223] These conferences are convened for the purpose of a specific instrument only.

Examples of treaty regimes created by WIPO for the purposes of protecting and encouraging development of artistic and scientific works include the Beijing Treaty on Audiovisual Performances,[224] Budapest Treaty on the International Recognition of the of Deposit of Microorganisms for the Purposes of Patent Procedure,[225] Marrakech Treaty to Facilitate Access to Published Works for Persons Who Are Blind, Visually Impaired, or Otherwise Print Disabled,[226] Convention for the Protection of Producers of Phonograms Against Unauthorized Duplication of Their Phonograms,[227] Patent Law Treaty,[228] Singapore Treaty on the Law of Trademarks,[229] WIPO Copyright Treaty,[230] and WIPO Performances and Phonograms Treaty.[231]

Conclusions

Sector and industry-specific international organizations seem to offer the likelihood of creating laws and rules that are segmented and have little relevance outside that sector or industry. This chapter has demonstrated that the opposite is indeed true and that there are cross-cutting issues among these organizations which get to the heart of their purposes and functions, such as the protection of different constituencies from harm and the promotion of new technologies that are in accordance with legal and societal concerns and protections.

The lessons of this chapter illustrate the flexibility of international organizational structures necessary to accommodate industrial and/or sectoral needs and concerns rather than creating transient organizations or affiliations for issue-specific concerns. While this might have resulted in more sophisticated organizational designs, it nevertheless has led to durability of organizations that would not have otherwise existed in these fields. This level of durability and continued use, even when the organizational structures might require updating to reflect current legal, technological and political realities, demonstrates the continued legitimacy of industry and sectoral-specific organizations.

This chapter further illustrates the power of international law and the law of international organizations to accommodate the challenges faced by various industries and sectors over time and throughout various settings of economy, technology and geography. In a rapidly developing climate for business and technology, these powers of accommodation are essential to allow for growth and stability to co-exist for the benefit of the international community and domestic communities.

Notes

1 *See* World Health Organization, http://www.who.int/about/en/, last accessed 11 January 2018.
2 *See* History of WHO, World Health Organization, http://www.who.int/about/history/en/index.html, last accessed 11 January 2018.
3 World Health Organization Constitution (1948) preamble, art 1.
4 *Id.* at art 2.
5 *Id.*
6 *Id.* Since the WHO was founded, it has become the preeminent international organization for handling and coordinating responses to public health disasters and epidemics.
7 *Id.* at arts 3, 4.
8 Governance, World Health Organization, http://www.who.int/governance/en/index.html, last accessed 11 January 2018; WHO Constitution, *supra* note 3 art 10. Given the technical nature of the WHO's mandate and subject area, it is highly preferred that those sent to represent a Member State at the Health Assembly have a health background and are attached to a health portfolio in their home State's government. *Id.* at art 11.
9 WHO Constitution, *supra* note 3 at art 8; World Health Assembly, Rights and Obligations of Associate Members and Other Territories (1948).

10 WHO Constitution, *supra* note 3 at art 61.

11 Id.

12 Id. at art 62.

13 Id. at art 63.

14 Id. at art 65.

15 Id. at ch XIV.

16 Id. at art 7.

17 Id.

18 Id. at ch. IV; *see also* Rules of Procedure of the World Health Assembly (2014).

19 WHO Constitution, *supra* note 3 at arts 13, 16.

20 Id. at art 18.

21 Id. at art 19. *See* Agreement between the United Nations and the World Health Organization (1948) (providing for, among other things, reciprocal representation between the organizations, sharing of relevant information generated by each organization, of the ability of the WHO to assist the General Assembly, Trusteeship Council); Agreement between the International Labor Organization and the World Health Organization (1948) (providing for, among other things, reciprocal representation, the establishment of joint committees, and information sharing); Agreement between the Food and Agriculture Organization and the World Health Organization (1948) (providing for, among other things, reciprocal representation, the establishment of joint committees, and information sharing); Agreement between the United Nations Educational, Scientific and Cultural Organization and the World Health Organization (1948) (providing for, among other things, reciprocal representation, the establishment of joint committees, and information sharing); Agreement between the International Atomic Energy Agency and the World Health Organization (1959) (providing for, among other things, reciprocal representation, the establishment of joint committees, and information sharing); Agreement between the United Nations Industrial Development Organization and the World Health Organization (1989) (providing for, among other things, reciprocal representation, the establishment of joint committees, and information sharing); Agreement between the Commission of the African Union and the World Health Organization (2012) (affirming the relationship between the organizations and defining the scope of information sharing, coordination and other activities to be undertaken between them).

22 WHO Constitution, *supra* note 3 at art 21.

23 International Health Regulations, World Health Organization, http://www.who.int/features/qa/39/en/index.html, last accessed 11 January 2018.

24 WHO Constitution, *supra* note 3 at art 2; *see also* Regulations for Expert Advisory Panels and Committees (2002).

25 *See* WHO Constitution, *supra* note 3.

26 Id. at art 24. As with the Health Assembly, there is a requirement that those selected as representatives to the Executive Board have individual knowledge of health and related issues. Id.

27 *See id.*

28 Id. at art 28; *see also* Rules of Procedure of the Executive Board of the World Health Organization (1996).

29 WHO Constitution, *supra* note 3 at art 28(i).

30 Id. at art 41.

31 Id. at art 31.

32 Id. at art 32.

33 Id. at art 33.

34 Id. at art 34.

35 Id. at arts 35–37; Staff Regulations of the World Health Organization (2009).

36 WHO Constitution, *supra* note 3 at art 46, 50.

37 Id. at art 47.

38 Id.

39 Id. at art 52.

40 *See* World Health Organization, WHO Regional Offices, http://www.who.int/about/en/, last accessed 11 January 2018.

41 World Health Organization, International Health Regulations (2016) 1.

42 Id.

43 Id. at 1–2. However, there have been consistent problems in the application of the IHRs in times of crisis, such as in the recent Ebola outbreak. *See* Report of the Review Committee on the Role of the International Health Regulations (2005) in the Ebola Outbreak and Response, A69/21 (2016).

44 *See* Statutes of the Codex Alimentarius Commission (2016); Rules of Procedure of the Codex Alimentarius Commission (2016); Joint FAO/WHO Food Standards Programme, Codex Alimentarius Commission Procedural Manual 25th edn (2016).

45 *See* Statutes of the Codex Alimentarius Commission, *supra* note 44; Rules of Procedure of the Codex Alimentarius Commission, *supra* note 44.

46 *See* Health topics, World Health Organization, http://www.who.int/topics/en/, last accessed 11 January 2018; World Health Organization, Report of the Commission on Ending Childhood Obesity: implementation plan, A70/31 (2017).

47 Global Alert Response, World Health Organization, http://www.who.int/csr/alertresponse/en/, last accessed 11 January 2018.

48 *See* About FAO, Food and Agriculture Organization, http://www.fao.org/about/en/, last accessed 11 January 2018.

49 *See* FAO Constitution (1948) art II; Food and Agriculture Organization, Rules of the Organization (2009) Rule XIX.

50 *See id.*

51 *See* FAO Constitution, *supra* note 49 at art XIX.

52 *See id.* at art XIX.

53 *See id.*

54 Id. at art III.

55 Id.; FAO Rules of the Organization, *supra* note 49 at Rule XXXIII.

56 FAO Constitution, *supra* note 49 at art IV.

57 Id. at art XIV.

58 Id. at art IV(4).

59 Id. at art IV(6).

60 FAO Rules of the Organization, *supra* note 49 at Rule XXXV.

61 FAO Constitution, *supra* note 49 at art V.

62 Id.

63 Id.

64 Id. Under the heading of general support and advice to the Council are the Programme Committee, Finance Committee and Committee on Constitutional and Legal Matters. Id. at art V(6)(a); FAO Rules of the Organization, *supra* note 49 at Rules XXVI, XXVII, XXXIV. In order to provide policy and regulatory assistance to the Council exist the Committee on Commodity Problems, Committee on Fisheries, Committee on Forestry, and Committee on Agriculture. FAO Constitution, *supra* note 49 at art V(6)(b); FAO Rules of the Organization, *supra* note 49 at Rules XXIX, XXX, XXXI, XXXII.

65 FAO Constitution, *supra* note 49 at art V; FAO Rules of the Organization, *supra* note 49 at Rule XXIV.

66 FAO Constitution, *supra* note 49 at art XIV.

67 Id. at art. VI; FAO Rules of the Organization, *supra* note 49 at Rules XIII–XV.

68 *See* FAO Constitution, *supra* note 49 at art VI.

69 Id.

70 Id. at art VII; FAO Rules of the Organization, *supra* note 49 at Rule XXXVII.

71 FAO Constitution, *supra* note 49 at art VII; FAO Rules of the Organization, *supra* note 49 at Rule XXXVIII.

72 FAO Constitution, *supra* note 49 at art VIII; FAO Rules of the Organization, *supra* note 49 at Rule XL.

73 FAO Constitution, *supra* note 49 at art 1; FAO Rules of the Organization, *supra* note 49 at Rule XXXV.

74 FAO Constitution, *supra* note 49 at art. 1; FAO Rules of the Organization, *supra* note 49 at Rule XXXV.

75 FAO Constitution, *supra* note 49 at art. 1; FAO Rules of the Organization, *supra* note 49 at Rule XXXV.

76 FAO Constitution, *supra* note 49 at art. 1; FAO Rules of the Organization, *supra* note 49 at Rule XXXV.

77 *See* Asia-Pacific Fishery Commission (1997).

78 Id. at arts I, II.

79 Id. at art III.

80 *See* Constitution of the European Commission for the Control of Foot-and-Mouth Disease (2015).

81 *See* Agreement for the Establishment of a Commission for Controlling the Desert Locust in the Central Region (2005).

82 *See* Convention Placing the International Poplar Commission within the Framework of FAO (1977).

83 *See* Global Information and Early Warning System on Food and Agriculture, Food and Agriculture Organization, http://www.fao.org/giews/english/index.htm, last accessed 11 January 2018.

84 Codex Alimentarius, http://www.codexalimentarius.org/about-codex/en/, last accessed 11 January 2018.

85 *See id.*

86 *See id.*

87 *See* Food and agriculture: Driving action across the 2030 Agenda for Sustainable Development (2017).

88 *See* Food and Agriculture Organization, Iraq – Agriculture damage and loss needs assessment (2017).

89 *See* Charter of the Food and Agricultural Organization, Office of the Inspector General (2013).

90 Id. at art I. As is explained, the Office of the Inspector General "helps the Organization accomplish its objectives by bringing a systematic, disciplined approach to evaluate and improve the effectiveness of risk management, control and internal governance processes." Id. at art I(2).

91 *See* Food and Agriculture Organization, Office of the Inspector General Investigations Unit – Guidelines for Internal Administrative Investigations by the Office of the Inspector General (2016); Food and Agriculture Organization, Office of the Inspector General – Policy Against Fraud and Other Corrupt Practices (2015); Food and Agriculture Organization, Policy on the Prevention of Harassment, Sexual Harassment and Abuse of Authority (2015).

92 *See* Food and Agriculture Organization, Compliance Reviews Following Complaints Related to the Organization's Environmental and Social Standards Guidelines (2015).

93 *See* Gerry Rodgers et al., *The International Labour Organization and the quest for social justice, 1919–2009* (2009) ch. 1; Origins and History, International Labour Organization, http://www.ilo.org/global/about-the-ilo/history/lang—en/index.html, last accessed 11 January 2018.

94 *See* Constitution of the International Labor Organization (1944) preamble. As the preamble further explains, "conditions of labour exist involving such injustice, hardship and privation to large numbers of people as to produce unrest so great that the peace and harmony of the world are imperilled; and an improvement of those conditions is urgently required; as, for example, by the regulation of the hours of work, including the establishment of a maximum working day and week, the regulation of the labour supply, the prevention of unemployment, the provision of an adequate living wage, the protection of the worker against sickness, disease and injury arising out of his employment, the protection of children, young persons and women, provision for old age and injury, protection of the interests of workers when employed in countries other than their own, recognition of the principle of equal remuneration for work of equal value, recognition of the principle of freedom of association, the organization of vocational and technical education and other measures." *Id.*

95 *Id.* at art 1; International Labour Organization, Membership in the International Organization: Information Guide (2014) 1.

96 *Id.*

97 ILO Constitution, *supra* note 94 at art 1.

98 *Id.*

99 *Id.*

100 *Id.* at art 3.

101 *Id.* at art 19; Rodgers et al., *supra* note 93 at 19–29.

102 ILO Constitution, *supra* note 94 at art 19.

103 *Id.* at art 7; Rodgers et al., *supra* note 93 at 10–18; International Labour Organization, Membership in the International Organization: Information Guide (2014) 2.

104 ILO Constitution, *supra* note 94 at art 6.

105 *Id.* at art 4. The determination as to which States constitute "States of chief industrial importance" is to be made by a specific committee within the Governing Body's structure, although ultimately the matter can be decided by the Conference if there are issues in the methodology or other aspects of decision-making used. *Id.*

106 *Id.* at art 7.

107 *Id.*

108 *Id.*

109 *Id.*

110 *Id.*

111 *Id.* at arts 8–10.

112 *Id.* at art 9. It must be noted that the rules used for appointment of staff members by the Director-General are created and overseen by the Governing Body as well.

113 *Id.* at art 10.

114 *Id.* at art 26.

115 *Id.*

116 *Id.*

117 *Id.*

118 *Id.* at art 29.

119 *Id.* at art 30.

120 *See* Rodgers et al., *supra* note 93, at 45–90; Missions and Objectives, International Labor Organization, http://www.ilo.org/global/about-the-ilo/mission-and-objectives/lang—en/index.htm, last accessed 11 January 2018.

121 *See* Topics, International Labor Organization, http://www.ilo.org/global/topics/lang—en/index.htm, last accessed 11 January 2018.

122 *See* Worst Forms of Child Labour Convention (No. 182) (1999); Discrimination (Employment and Occupation) Convention (No. 111) (1958); Maternity Protection (No. 3) (1919); Abolition of Penal Sanctions (Indigenous Workers) Convention (No. 104) (1955); Indigenous and Tribal Populations Convention (No. 107) (1957); Indigenous and Tribal Peoples Convention (No. 169) (1989); Night Work Convention (No. 171) (1990); Maternity Protection Convention (No. 183) (2000).

123 *See* Abolition of Forced Labour Convention (No. 105) (1957); Minimum Age (Underground Work) Convention (No. 123) (1965); Benzene Convention (No. 136) (1971); Working Environment (Air Pollution, Noise and Vibration) Convention (No. 148) (1977); Chemicals Convention (No. 170) (1990).

124 *See* ILO Constitution, *supra* note 94 at art 19; Membership in the International Organization: Information Guide, *supra* note 95 at 3.

125 ILO Constitution, *supra* note 94 at art 19; Membership in the International Organization: Information Guide, *supra* note 95 at 3–4.

126 *See* Labour Inspection (Agriculture) Convention, No. 129 (1969); Employment Policy Convention, No. 122 (1964); Labour Inspection Convention, No. 81 (1947); Convention No. 111, *supra* note 122; Equal Remuneration Convention, No. 100 (1951); Convention, No. 182, *supra* note 122; Minimum Age Convention No. 138 (1973); Abolition of Forced Labour Convention, No. 105 (1957); ILO Forced Labour Convention, No. 29

(1930); Freedom of Association and Protection of the Right to Organize Convention, No. 87 (1948); Agreement between Liaison between the International Labour Organization and the European Economic Community (1958).

127 *See, e.g.,* Agreement Concerning Co-Operation between the International Labour Organization and the European Atomic Energy Community (1960); Agreement concerning Co-Operation between the International Labour Organization and the European Coal and Steel Community (1953); Agreement between the International Labour Organization and the Asian Productivity Organization (1965); Agreement between the International Labour Organization and the League of Arab States (1958); Memorandum of Understanding between the International Labour Organization and the Pan-American Health Organization to support Latin America and Caribbean countries in the extension of social protection in health to excluded populations (1999); Memorandum of Understanding between the International Labour Organization and the Organization of Eastern Caribbean States (2008); Agreement between the International Labour Organization and the Organization of Central American States (1965); Agreement between the International Labour Organization and the Organization of American States (1950); Agreement between the International Labour Organization and the Caribbean Development Bank (1998); Agreement between the International Labour Organization and the Organization of African Unity (1965); Memorandum of Understanding between the International Labour Organization and the East African Community (2001); Cooperation Agreement between the African Development Bank and the African Development Fund and the International Labour Organization (2004); Agreement between the International Labour Organization and the International Fund for Agricultural Development (1978); Commission for Technical Co-Operation in Africa South of the Sahara (1954); Memorandum of Understanding between the International Labour Organization and the United Nations Office for Project Services (2015); Memorandum of Understanding for cooperation between the United Nations International Drug Control Programme and the International Labour Organization (1994); Memorandum of Understanding concerning Co-operation between the International Labour Organization and the United Nations Centre for Human Settlements (UNHABITAT) (1984); Memorandum of Understanding between the United Nations Economic Commission for Africa and the International Labour Organization (2016); Memorandum of Understanding between the United Nations Economic and Social Commission for Asia and the Pacific and the International Labour Organization (2015).

128 *See* Rules of the Administrative Tribunal of the International Labour Organization (2014) arts 1, 2.

129 *Id.* at art 5, 6.

130 Introduction to IMO, http://www.imo.org/About/Pages/Default.aspx, last accessed 11 January 2018.

131 *Id.*

132 IMO Convention (1958) art 1(a) ("To provide machinery for co-operation among Governments in the field of governmental regulation and practices relating to technical matters of all kinds affecting shipping engaged in international trade; to encourage and facilitate the general adoption of the highest practicable standards in matters concerning the maritime safety, efficiency of navigation and prevention and control of marine pollution from ships; and to deal with administrative and legal matters related to the purposes set out in this Article.").

133 *Id.*

134 *Id.* at art 1(b) ("To encourage the removal of discriminatory action and unnecessary restrictions by Governments affecting shipping engaged in international trade so as to promote the availability of shipping services to the commerce of the world without discrimination; assistance and encouragement given by a Government for the development of its national shipping and for purposes of security does not in itself constitute discrimination, provided that such assistance and encouragement is not based on measures designed to restrict the freedom of shipping of all flags to take part in international trade.").

135 *Id.* at arts 1(d), 1(e).

136 *Id.* at arts 5–7.

137 *Id.* at art 9.

138 *Id.* at art 10.

139 *Id.* at pt XIII.

140 International Labour Organization, Country profile, http://www.ilo.org/dyn/normlex/en/f?p=NORMLEXPUB:11003:0::NO:::, last accessed 11 January 2018.

141 Membership, IMO, http://www.imo.org/About/Membership/Pages/Default.aspx, last accessed 11 January 2018.

142 *Id.*

143 *Id.*

144 IMO Convention, *supra* note 132 at art 73.

145 *Id.* at art 73.

146 *Id.* at pt III; Structure of IMO, IMO, http://www.imo.org/About/Pages/Structure.aspx, last accessed 11 January 2018.

147 IMO Convention, *supra* note 132 at pt III.

148 *Id.* at pt III.

149 *Id.* at art 17.

150 Id. Currently these States are: China, Greece, Italy, Japan, Norway, Panama, Republic of Korea, Russian Federation, United Kingdom, and the United States. Id.

151 Id. Currently these States are: Argentina, Bangladesh, Brazil, Canada, France, Germany, India, Netherlands, Spain, and Sweden. Id.

152 Id. Currently these States are: Australia, Bahamas, Belgium, Chile, Cyprus, Denmark, Egypt, Indonesia, Kenya, Liberia, Malaysia, Malta, Mexico, Morocco, Peru, Philippines, Singapore, South Africa, Thailand, and Turkey. Id.

153 Id. at art 21.

154 Id. at art 29 (explaining that the specific mandate for the Maritime Safety Committee is comprised of "proposals for safety regulations or for amendments to safety regulations which the Committee has developed; recommendations and guidelines which the Committee has developed; [and] a report on the work of the Committee since the previous session of the Council").

155 Id. at art 21.

156 Id. at pt X.

157 Id. at art 25.

158 Id. at pt XI.

159 Id. at art 22.

160 Id. at pt IX.

161 Id. at art 21.

162 Id. at art 38.

163 Id. at art 33.

164 Id.

165 Id. at art 34.

166 International Convention on Maritime Search and Rescue (1985).

167 Convention for the Suppression of Unlawful Acts Against the Safety of Maritime Navigation and its Protocol for the Suppression of Unlawful Acts Against the Safety of Fixed Platforms Located on the Continental Shelf (2010).

168 International Convention for the Prevention of Pollution from Ships (1983).

169 International Convention Relating to Intervention on the High Seas in Cases of Oil Pollution Casualties (1969).

170 Convention on the Prevention of Marine Pollution by Dumping of Wastes and Other Matter (2006).

171 International Convention for the Control and Management of Ships' Ballast Water and Sediments (2007).

172 See International Convention for the Prevention of Pollution from Ships (1980).

173 Member States, ICAO in Brief, http://www.icao.int/MemberStates/Member%20States.English.pdf, last accessed 11 January 2018.

174 Convention on International Civil Aviation (2006) preface ("[T]he future development of international civil aviation can greatly help to create and preserve friendship and understanding among the nations and peoples of the world, yet its abuse can become a threat to the general security; and . . . it is desirable to avoid friction and to promote that cooperation between nations and peoples upon which the peace of the world depends.").

175 Id. at art 95.

176 Id.

177 Id. at art 48; How it works, ICAO in Brief, https://www.icao.int/about-icao/pages/how-it-works.aspx, last accessed 11 January 2018.

178 ICAO Convention, supra note 174 at art 48.

179 Id. at art 49.

180 Id. at art 50.

181 Id.

182 Id. at art 52.

183 Id. at art 53.

184 Id.

185 Id. at art 54.

186 Id. at art 55.

187 Id. at art 56.

188 Id. at art 57.

189 Id.

190 Id. at ch VI.

191 Strategic Objectives, ICAO, https://www.icao.int/about-icao/Council/Pages/Strategic-Objectives.aspx, last accessed 11 January 2018.

192 Environmental Protection, ICAO, http://www.icao.int/environmental-protection/Pages/default.aspx, last accessed 11 January 2018.

193 Security, ICAO, http://www.icao.int/Security/Pages/default.aspx, last accessed 11 January 2018.

194 See Consolidated Text of the Convention for the Suppression of Unlawful Seizure of an Aircraft, 1970 and the Protocol Supplementary to the Convention for the Suppression of Unlawful Seizure of Aircraft, 2010 (2010); Consolidated Text of the Convention on Offences and Certain Other Acts Committed Onboard Aircraft, 1963, and the Protocol to Amend the Convention on Offences and Certain Other Acts Committed Onboard Aircraft, 2014 (2014); International Civil Aviation Organisation, Annual Report of the Council (2007); International

Civil Aviation Organisation, Annual Report of the Council (2008); International Civil Aviation Organisation, Annual Report of the Council (2009); International Civil Aviation Organisation, Annual Report of the Council (2011); International Civil Aviation Organisation, Annual Report of the Council (2012); International Civil Aviation Organisation, Annual Report of the Council (2013).

195 *See* International Civil Aviation Organisation, Global Aviation Safety Plan 2017–2019 (2016); International Civil Aviation Organization, On Board a Sustainable Future: 2016 Environmental Report (2016).

196 World Intellectual Property Organization, Inside WIPO, http://www.wipo.int/about-wipo/en/, last accessed 11 January 2018.

197 Convention Establishing the World Intellectual Property Organization (1979) art 5.

198 Id.

199 World Intellectual Property Organization, Observers, http://www.wipo.int/about-wipo/en/observers/index.html, last accessed 11 January 2018.

200 WIPO Convention, *supra* note 197 at art 18.

201 *Id.* at art 6; General Rules of Procedure of WIPO (1979) Rule 7.

202 WIPO Convention, *supra* note 197 at art 6.

203 *Id.* at art 7; WIPO General Rules of Procedure, *supra* note 201 at Rule 7

204 WIPO Convention, *supra* note 197 at art 7.

205 *Id.* at art 7.

206 *Id.* at art 8.

207 *Id.*

208 *Id.*

209 *Id.* at art 9.

210 *Id.*

211 World Intellectual Property Organization, Policy, http://www.wipo.int/policy/en/, last accessed 11 January 2018.

212 World Intellectual Property Organization, Budget Committee, http://www.wipo.int/meetings/en/topic.jsp?group_id=101, last accessed 11 January 2018.

213 World Intellectual Property Organization, Committee on Development and Intellectual Property, http://www.wipo.int/policy/en/cdip/, last accessed 11 January 2018.

214 World Intellectual Property Organization, Intergovernmental Committee on Intellectual Property and Genetic Resources, Traditional Knowledge and Folklore, http://www.wipo.int/tk/en/igc/, last accessed 11 January 2018.

215 World Intellectual Property Organization, Advisory Committee on Enforcement, http://www.wipo.int/enforcement/en/ace/, last accessed 11 January 2018.

216 World Intellectual Property Organization, Policy, http://www.wipo.int/policy/en/, *supra* note 211.

217 World Intellectual Property Organization, Standing Committee on the Law of Patents, http://www.wipo.int/policy/en/scp/, last accessed 11 January 2018.

218 World Intellectual Property Organization, Standing Committee on the Law of Trademarks, Industrial Designs and Geographical Indications, http://www.wipo.int/policy/en/sct/, last accessed 11 January 2018.

219 World Intellectual Property Organization, Standing Committee on Copyright and Related Rights, http://www.wipo.int/policy/en/sccr/, last accessed 11 January 2018.

220 World Intellectual Property Organization, Committee on WIPO Standards, http://www.wipo.int/cws/en/, last accessed 11 January 2018.

221 WIPO Convention, *supra* note 197 at preamble.

222 *Id.* at art 4.

223 World Intellectual Property Organization, Diplomatic Conferences, http://www.wipo.int/meetings/en/topic.jsp?group_id=109, last accessed 11 January 2018.

224 Beijing Treaty on Audiovisual Performances (2012).

225 Budapest Treaty on the International Recognition of the of Deposit of Microorganisms for the Purposes of Patent Procedure (1980).

226 Marrakech Treaty to Facilitate Access to Published Works for Persons Who Are Blind, Visually Impaired, or Otherwise Print Disabled (2013).

227 Convention for the Protection of Producers of Phonograms Against Unauthorized Duplication of Their Phonograms (1971).

228 Patent Law Treaty (2000).

229 Singapore Treaty on the Law of Trademarks (2006).

230 WIPO Copyright Treaty (1996).

231 WIPO Performances and Phonograms Treaty (1996).

Chapter 17

Military and policing organizations

An essential aspect of statehood and sovereignty is control over the military and policing functions within the State. While this is as true today as it was when the Montevideo factors for statehood were promulgated in 1933, international organizations focusing on military and policing operations have grown dramatically and with them has come a way to re-envision concepts such as international peacekeeping and peacebuilding. This chapter examines organizations which have been influential in bringing about these changes and furthering these activities in the international settings.

Organization for the Prohibition of Chemical Weapons

Background

The Organization for the Prohibition of Chemical Weapons (OPCW) might seem an odd choice for the opening profile in a chapter on military and policing organizations. It is, after all, an organization devoted to the restriction of warfare conduct and weaponry access and usage. However, the choice of including the OPCW here was made with a distinct understanding that seeking to limit the use of the most severe forms of weaponry is as much an attempt to protect military personnel as it is to protect civilians. Seen from this perspective, the OPCW is arguably a military-focused organization that must be studied and understood in order to frame the ways in which military organizations function.

As noted in the preamble of the Convention on the Prohibition of the Development, Production, Stockpiling, and Use of Chemical Weapons and On Their Destruction which creates the OPCW, the concept of restricting chemical weapons came into existence at the international level in the aftermath of World War I.[1] The use of chemical weapons such as mustard gas had been pioneered during the war with fatal and grotesque consequences that many in the international community sought to curtail. In this way, the Convention and the OPCW were successful outgrowths of painful lessons learned in combat.

The OPCW was created with the purpose of overseeing and ensuring the implementation of the Convention terms, ensuring that there is oversight of chemical agents and the demobilization where appropriate, and allowing for the development of future policies relating to chemical weapons and their use.[2] One of the most important functions of the OPCW is to oversee the verification process for decommissioning of chemical weapons.[3]

Membership and voting

Given the relationship between the OPCW and the goals of the Convention, membership in the organization is necessarily available to all States Parties to the Convention.[4] This relationship also alters the impacts of failure to pay membership dues. Rather than suspension from the organization or termination of membership, non-payment of dues after two years or more results in the suspension of a Member State's voting power alone and even this can be overridden if the Conference of the States Parties believes that there is reason to do so.[5] A Member State has the ability to withdraw from the Convention – and thus the OPCW – at its election, "if it decides that extraordinary events, related to the subject-matter of this Convention, have jeopardized the supreme interests of its country."[6]

Structure

Within the OPCW governance structure there are three key organs, the Conference of the States Parties, the Executive Council and the Technical Secretariat.[7] The Conference of the States Parties consists of a representative from each Member State, and each Member State has one vote in all matters.[8] As the chief policy-making organ of the OPCW, the Conference has extensive powers, including over the capacities and jurisdiction of the Executive Council and Technical Secretariat.[9] Additional functions of the Conference include budgeting for the OPCW, the election of members to the Executive Council, selection of the Technical Secretariat, creation of sub-organs in the OPCW as appropriate, and review suggested guidelines or agreements.[10]

The Executive Council is comprised of 41 Conference-appointed members, who sit on the Council on a rotating basis between the Member States. When appointing Member States, the Conference is meant to take into account factors such as geographical distribution, the State's connections to the chemical industry, the State's technical capabilities, and the balance of the international political situation at the time.[11] The role of the Council is to ensure that the Convention and associated agreements are properly implemented, enter into and maintain relationships with international organs and other States, and address issues of non-compliance with the Convention or other problems or its implementation.[12]

In the confines of the OPCW, the Technical Secretariat plays a far more specific role than do most secretariats. As a primary matter, the Technical Secretariat has the duty to oversee and implement verification proceedings under the terms of the Convention.[13] It is also responsible for the preparation of reports to the Council and Conference, budgetary arrangements and preparations, serving as a provider of technical advice to the Member States as needed, and negotiation of necessary verification treaties.[14] The Technical Secretariat is under the control of the Director General, an office that is appointed by the Conference and oversees the activities of the Secretariat's staff, along with the work of sub-committees such as the Inspectorate.[15]

Functions

Over time, the OPCW has created specialized sub-organs in order to carry out its functions and duties under the terms of the Convention. For example, in 2004 the OPCW authorized the creation of the Scientific Advisory Board in order to allow all components of the organization to function with the scientific knowledge necessary to complete their roles under the Convention.[16] To complement this, in 2015 the Conference of the States Parties created the Advisory Board on Education and Outreach to assist in public outreach on matters undertaken by the OPCW and related to the Convention.[17] In order to ensure the proper functioning of the Convention and the OPCW's tasks, particularly verification processes, the Conference created a Confidentiality Commission and also enabled it to work as a source of conflict resolution if and when necessary.[18]

The OPCW has established relationships with other international organizations, such as the UN, to foster cooperation and information sharing on matters related to the interests of all organizations.[19]

North Atlantic Treaty Organization

Background

The North Atlantic Treaty Organization (NATO) was founded shortly after the end of World War II and at the beginning of the Cold War as a collective self-defense entity for Western Europe, the US and Canada.[20] This was essential to the political, security and legal aspects of the plans of NATO Member States since an armed attack on any Member State would be deemed an armed attack on all of them and would be sufficient grounds for NATO as a collective to take action against the aggressor. In the political climate of the time this was vital. At its core, NATO is intended to be a political and military alliance, both of which are of increasing importance in the face of modern threats such as terrorism and cyber-based crimes.[21] However, while NATO is intended as an organization for the protection of the Member States through the use of force if necessary, internally the Member States have agreed that they will refrain from the use of force or the threat of the use of force against one another and in general.[22]

While the Soviet bloc equivalent to NATO – the Warsaw Pact – ceased to exist in the aftermath of end of the Cold War, NATO has continued to exist and has become an increasingly global military organization in recent years.[23] NATO has expanded its membership to include many Eastern European States that were not eligible for membership during the Cold War due to geography and politics,[24] and has established working partnerships with individual States and regional organizations across the world.[25]

Membership and voting

Membership in NATO was originally set at a small number of States and open to the possibility of an increase in the event that another European State sought membership. Early in NATO's history, four new members – Greece, Turkey, the Federal Republic of Germany and Spain – were admitted but otherwise membership remained static.[26] However, from 1991 onward, 13 new members, largely from Eastern Europe, have been admitted and added to the functionality of NATO as an organization.[27] At present, a Member State has the ability to withdraw from NATO by presenting a notice to the Government of the US.[28]

Structure

There is one primary decision-making entity within the NATO structure – the North Atlantic Council.[29] The North Atlantic Council meets on a weekly basis and its membership rotates between the Member States' foreign or defense ministers depending on the issues facing the Council at the time.[30] Each Member State has a representative and a vote.[31] Notably, all decisions taken by NATO must be by consensus – this is especially important when issues related to the use of force arise.[32] Every Member State has a permanent representative to NATO and subsidiary staff stationed at NATO's headquarters in Brussels, Belgium.[33]

In addition to the North Atlantic Council, there are a number of subsidiary committees that handle issues that are very technical or require a particular expertise.[34] For example, the Military Committee is tasked with handling issues associated with deployment of NATO forces although it is still subject to the oversight of the North Atlantic Council.[35] Additionally, the Nuclear Planning Group works to address issues of nuclear warfare and weaponry that have occupied NATO since its inception.[36] The Nuclear Planning Group continues to maintain a continuous portfolio that adapts to the current needs of the NATO community regarding nuclear issues and nuclear policy.[37]

One other NATO associated organ is the NATO Parliamentary Assembly.[38] This is an organ that is technically outside the realm of the official organs of NATO. Its function is to allow parliamentary/Congressional representatives from NATO Member States to meet and discuss issues that are facing their States, the region and NATO as a whole.[39] The NATO Parliamentary Assembly has no power over NATO but rather serves as a liaison body between NATO and its Member States with the goal of ensuring that NATO as an organization understands the views of its Member States and that the Member States learn the views of NATO as an organizational entity.[40]

In line with the structure and needs of the organization, the work of NATO is divided into civilian and military branches. The military aspects of NATO's operations are divided between an office in Norfolk, Virginia and an office in Mons, Belgium.[41] For all daily operations there is an established Secretariat[42] and for field operations there is a separated Allied Command structure.[43]

Within the civilian branch are the NATO Headquarters offices themselves along with the national Permanent Delegations to NATO and the International Staff. The International Staff encompasses a number of entities, including the Political Affairs and Security Policy Division, Operations Division, Emerging Security Challenges Division, Defence Policy and Planning Division, Defence

Investment Division, Public Diplomacy Division, Executive Management, NATO Headquarters Consultation, Command and Control Staff, the Office of Financial Controller, Office of the Controller of the Senior Resource Board, Office of the Chairman of the Civil and Military Budget Committees, International Board of Auditors for NATO, and NATO Administrative Tribunal.[44]

Within the military branch are the Military Committee, International Military Staff, Allied Command Operations, Allied Command Transformation, and other associated command and staff organizations.[45] In addition, a number of sub-organizations and agencies exist within the NATO organizational structure, including those which are extremely broad in scope and those which are extremely narrow in scope.[46]

Functions and operations

Recent NATO activities have included providing active duty troops and peacekeeping forces in conflicts around the world, such as the conflicts in Afghanistan and Libya, policing of the Mediterranean for and providing assistance with refugees utilizing an unsafe maritime route to Europe, and peacekeeping forces in the former Yugoslavia during the various conflicts that took place during its breakup.[47] NATO forces have not only served in a military and peacekeeping capacity, they have also provided training and guidance to military forces in States that need assistance, particularly post-conflict States and newly created States such as Kosovo.[48] NATO forces also work to prevent maritime piracy and to detect and prevent potential terrorist threats in areas that impact NATO Member States.[49]

Further, NATO has begun deploying its forces on humanitarian missions, such as providing assistance to those who are impacted by natural disasters.[50] In order to prevent natural ecological disasters and the underlying security threats they pose, NATO has begun working in the realm of environmental protection, including through liaisons with other international organizations and non-governmental organizations.[51] However, in recent meetings NATO has signaled an intent to refocus undertakings on the protection of territorial Europe and also the seaways that connect the various coasts of the Atlantic.[52]

Peacekeeping

United Nations Peacekeeping Operations

Background

The UN Charter provides for a standing UN military force to be at the ready in order to handle issues that threaten international peace and security. However, as noted, due to political tensions after the Cold War this idea never came to fruition. Instead, when faced with threats to peace and security early in its existence, the UN began a series of peacekeeping operations that would soon come to define the way in which the organization responds to issues that can or do represent a threat to international peace and security.[53]

Under the terms of the Charter, the UN has the ability to authorize the international community to use force against an errant State or regime – as it did with the 2003 invasion of Iraq – however, this is a separate consideration from the decision to deploy peacekeeping forces. In the situation where direct force is authorized, the UN is allowing the international community to violate the internal sovereignty of a State in order to preserve peace and security. This means that the permission of the State about to be attacked is not needed for force to be used – indeed, to require this would seem rather nonsensical.

In terms of organizational structure, UN peacekeeping is overseen by the UN Security Council and the UN General Assembly and certain aspects of its functions are overseen by various UN Commissions and Committees.[54] The entity that is most directly involved in its oversight is the UN

Department of Peacekeeping Operations (DPKO), which is tasked with finding peacekeepers and also with making arrangements for peacekeepers within the host State. It has extensive powers over the management and oversight of individual peacekeeping operations and peacekeeping within the UN context.[55] Additionally, the UN DPKO works in contexts other than military operations, for example in the Office of Rule of Law and Security Institutions.[56]

Creation and authorization

UN peacekeeping forces operate in a different legal and political realm than standard military forces and operations. The UN Security Council, which is arguably the primary UN organ tasked with authorizing the deployment of peacekeepers, cannot insist that a State accept peacekeepers – rather, it must enter into an agreement with the State to which it seeks to send peacekeepers.[57] This agreement, typically referred to as a host State agreement or status of forces agreement, will provide the conditions upon which the peacekeepers may be present in the State and any restrictions on their presence and activities, for example that the use of firearms by peacekeepers is prohibited unless fired on first.[58] The agreement will also reiterate that peacekeeping forces are not intended to undermine the sovereignty of the host State and that the host State retains its full political authority, including the ability to evict the peacekeepers from its territory.[59]

What do peacekeeping forces do? The answer is quite nuanced, as it depends on the needs of the State, which can change over time.[60] Some peacekeepers are intended to provide immediate protection to vulnerable populations while others are intended to ensure calm in potentially volatile situations, such as before, during, or after an election in a State that has been plagued with conflict.[61] Although technically peacekeeping forces are not intended for permanent deployment in host States, there are instances where UN peacekeepers have been deployed for years.[62] It is also possible for peacekeeping forces to leave a State for any number of reasons and then return to the same State due to continued instability.[63] This has happened in the Democratic Republic of the Congo and Haiti, to give two very prominent examples.[64] At present there are 16 active UN peacekeeping operations throughout the world.[65] In addition, it must be noted that there is a trend toward including peace building and capacity building as part of the UN peacekeeping system in order to create a more lasting system of governance in the host States.

Typically, UN peacekeeping operations are authorized by the UN Security Council for finite periods of time with the possibility of renewal should the UN Security Council believe it to be appropriate and necessary.[66] Thus, when the authorization expires, it is up to the UN Security Council to determine whether to renew it and what the exact parameters of the renewal should be.[67]

Staffing

Who are the peacekeepers? This too depends on the circumstances. Since there is no standing UN military, the DPKO will put out a call for peacekeepers once it receives a mandate to create a peacekeeping operation from the UN Security Council. All UN Member States are eligible to provide peacekeeping forces – comprised of members of their own national military forces – and receive payment in exchange.[68] For developed States this payment is often far below what the State would pay its military forces and so the State supplements the amount for the selected soldiers.[69] For many developing States, however, this stipend is much higher than the average wage and so selection for a peacekeeping operation is akin to a raise.[70] There is no vetting process for those selected to participate in a peacekeeping operation unless the State independently decides to implement one.[71]

Command structure

Once deployed, peacekeepers are overseen by an allied command made of military personnel from a variety of States.[72] However, while the peacekeepers operate as a UN force under a joint command they are subject solely to the laws of their home State unless the home State decides to waive them.[73] This has created many issues, not the least of which is the seemingly endemic trend of sexual abuse perpetuated by peacekeepers, most often against vulnerable populations of the host State, such as young children and those who must depend on the UN for food and security.[74]

European Union
Background

It is within the power of the European Union to create peacekeeping and similar forms of military and civilian missions under the terms of the European Common Security and Defence Policy.[75] The Policy allows for this provided that these missions are carried out with the approval of the European Council and that they are conducted for finite, renewable terms, as used in the UN peacekeeping structure.[76] Funding for these missions must be raised through the EU as an organization, and typically comes from Member States.[77]

Creation and authorization

From the outset, it must be noted that the EU's operations tend to incorporate authorizations from the UN to carry out certain military and civilian objectives, making them less like the traditional, non-combative forms of peacekeeping that may come to mind. This does not, however, mean that the peacekeeping role is minimized or taken lightly at the EU level, and indeed even when acting in a military capacity there are elements of peacekeeping in EU operations, for example, as the entity that is responsible for ensuring the military and security aspects of the Dayton Peace Accords in the areas that are part of the former Yugoslavia.[78]

Many of the EU's operations are peacekeeping in nature but have a stronger military authorization than a standard peacekeeping operation. For example, this duality is emblematic of the ways in which the EU has addressed the issue of maritime piracy. In order to respond to the growing threats from and incidents of maritime piracy in terms of economy, maritime transportation, access to food and vital supplies, and the protection of the lives of the crew members who are often taken hostage, the EU enacted its European Union Naval Force, with a particular focus on Somalia.[79]

A primary method of enforcing the maritime protections at the EU level is Operation Atalanta, which offers military protection for shipping and maritime transport at the same time as it assists the Somali military with training to fight piracy and protect its maritime boundaries, and provides safety training to local fishing populations.[80] Similar activities have been authorized for the EU in the Mediterranean region as a response to the human rights tragedies occurring as a result of perilous sea crossing attempts by desperate migrants.[81]

In other settings, the EU has engaged in a joint form of activity in which it provides traditional military support with peacekeeping activities in which the local populations are to be protected at the same time as they receive training and assistance for future capacities.[82] In many instances, such deployments have functioned in conjunction with UN peacekeeping activities, such as actions to support elections and the implementation of ceasefires.[83] Recently, as part of the Quartet, the EU agreed to establish and operate a European Union Border Assistance Mission for the Rafah Crossing Point in the Palestinian territory after the Israeli forces moved out.[84] In addition to military-focused operations, the EU has used and continues to use assistance in training and operations for police in areas needing assistance. This has led, for example, to the creation of an EU police advisory force for the former Yugoslav Republic of Macedonia.[85]

Recently, for example in the Republic of Georgia, EU civilian peacekeeping forces were requested to assist in the preservation of peace and the protection of a State from outside forces that threatened destabilization.[86] Additionally, the EU has engaged in Rule of Law building activities under the rubric of peacekeeping and peace-building operations, for example in Iraq.[87] It has also engaged in activities that are of very limited protective scope and are intended to provide support for certain aspects of a larger peace operation, such as the agreement to provide aviation security assistance in South Sudan.[88]

Status of forces agreements

Operations in a State are, of course, governed through status of forces agreements between the EU and the State.[89] Further, the EU also has established agreements with States that act as transit points for troops en route to and from the peacekeeping venues.[90] These allow the EU troops to travel for limited reasons and in limited locations without interruption and also require them to observe local laws in the process.[91] The EU has taken an expansive view on the participation of affiliated yet non-Member States in the activities of the EU forces, and frequently allows them to participate through separate agreements directly with the EU.[92]

INTERPOL

Background

Unlike States or peacekeeping operations that have policing components, INTERPOL does not have its own police force. Contrary to depictions in film, there are no INTERPOL police officers waiting to arrest those who are put on any of its well-known lists. Rather, INTERPOL is an international police organization that coordinates information on police activities and criminals between Member States and facilitates the designation of criminals as wanted based on certain types of crime that they are alleged to have committed.[93] While this might seem rather esoteric at first, it is in practice quite important, especially given the ability of criminals to use technology and easy international travel in order to hide their activities or evade capture.[94] Also, criminals – particularly organized crime groups dealing in drugs or trafficking in humans – often seek refuge in States with weakly developed policing systems and technology, meaning that INTERPOL's training of local police forces and facilitation of information sharing can be vital to stopping these forms of criminality.[95]

Membership and voting

Nearly all recognized States are INTERPOL Member States.[96] All Member States have the ability to vote and possess one vote each, although voting rights may be suspended in the event of non-payment of dues.[97] In addition, it is possible for international organizations and non-member police entities to serve as observers to INTERPOL's proceedings, although they do so without possessing the ability to vote.[98]

Structure

INTERPOL's main governing organs are the General Assembly and the Executive Committee, a Secretariat, the National Central Bureaus, the Advisers, and the Commission for the Control of Files.[99] The General Assembly is comprised of representatives from all INTERPOL Member States, each of whom has one vote, and functions similarly to the UN General Assembly in terms of the scope of its abilities.[100] These include budgetary functions, the creation and implementation of rules and regulations for the organization, approving agreements and other instruments, and the creation of specialized committees within the INTERPOL system.[101]

The General Assembly also elects the 13 members of the Executive Committee, none of which are permanent members, but four of which must be the President and three Vice Presidents of INTERPOL.[102] The Executive Committee is the oversight body for the daily functioning of the

Secretariat and INTERPOL generally and ensures that the decisions of the General Assembly are implemented.[103]

In turn, the Secretariat functions to administer the workings of INTERPOL, including the many liaison functions between various States, international organizations and INTERPOL itself.[104] It also oversees a number of offices and sub-offices that reflect the priority areas of the organization.[105]

In order to ensure that there is communication between INTERPOL and its Member State policing entities, there are also National Central Bureaus for each of the Member States.[106] The National Central Bureaus are the liaison points between INTERPOL and domestic policing entities and are typically a separate division within the domestic policing force.[107] For example, in the US there is a special National Central Bureau in Washington that is tasked with coordinating the actions of INTERPOL with all domestic policing entities – federal, State and local – and vice versa.[108] While the National Central Bureaus do not have decision-making roles *per se*, they serve a vital function in the implementation of the decisions issued by the General Assembly, Executive Committee and Secretariat.

Within the INTERPOL system of governance there is the ability to create committees or other sub-organs in order to address important issues. These committees are generated at the commencement of each General Assembly term and given the appropriate functions as needed.[109]

Functions

INTERPOL currently focuses on a variety of crimes and crime areas. Its overall goals center on the promotion of coordination and cooperation between States' policing entities in order to allow for the application of international laws and principles in a more uniform manner.[110] Additionally, INTERPOL was formed in an effort to create a strong network of police entities that can effectively combat crime in multiple and evolving forms.[111]

Corruption is an issue that plagues States at all levels of development and in particular threatens the development of poorer States because it undermines their infrastructure and the proper use of government funds to develop the State's economic, social and environmental policies.[112] Crimes against children – ranging from sex crimes to internet crimes to child soldiering – are areas in which INTERPOL actively works to prevent the victimization of children and to identify those who have victimized children.[113] Due to the evolving nature of this form of crime, INTERPOL is particularly active in facilitating the transfer of information on criminal practices between States and also in educating police officers on what to look for when investigating these crimes.[114] This dovetails with INTERPOL's work in the cybercrime area, which also includes financial crimes[115] and hacking.[116]

Perhaps unsurprisingly, INTERPOL also focuses on organized crime networks throughout the world, including those that traffic in drugs,[117] firearms and weapons,[118] counterfeit or otherwise illicit goods,[119] and human beings.[120] INTERPOL's human trafficking program focuses on trafficking for all purposes, from sex and prostitution to labor and, increasingly, to trafficking in human organs.[121] It is also perhaps unsurprising that INTERPOL works extensively in areas connected to terrorism detection and prevention[122] and also maritime piracy.[123]

In addition, there are some relatively new crime areas in which INTERPOL acts. One of these areas is pharmaceutical crime, which typically involves the selling of counterfeit medications or the diversion of legitimate medications to the black market.[124] Another area is vehicle crime, involving the theft of vehicles from one State in order to resell them in another State – for example, the theft of vehicles off the street in the US in order to sell in the Chinese market, where they can often fetch high prices.[125] For those familiar with the television show *White Collar*, it might be interesting to know that the references to INTERPOL's involvement in thefts of works of art is indeed accurate and that this is another crime area in which INTERPOL concentrates.[126] Finally, INTERPOL has become heavily involved in environmental crimes, such as illegal poaching of animals for parts or skins, and pollution activities.[127] Further, there are emerging issues and practices such as the identification of disaster victims that have fallen within INTERPOL's scope of interest.[128]

Given the importance of cooperation between INTERPOL and other entities in order for its mandate to be successful, the organization has created a number of agreements with other international and regional organizations.[129] These agreements are all important, however some are more essential to the functioning of INTERPOL's systems. For example, the arrangement between INTERPOL and the UN regarding the activities of the UN Sanctions Committee is essential for there to be enforcement of sanctions orders through the INTERPOL list system.[130] In another key example, an agreement between the International Criminal Court (ICC) and INTERPOL allows for information exchange and notice issuance where appropriate to the scope of the ICC's functions and INTERPOL's jurisdiction.[131] Overall, some of these agreements are focused on specific issues or topics of concern,[132] while others are open-ended agreements that allow for broad-based cooperation.[133]

Finally, a word about the notices issued by INTERPOL. INTERPOL will issue a color-coded notice once it has been asked by a National Central Bureau to do so, or the UN Security Council has provided INTERPOL with information regarding an arrest warrant, criminal decision or other pending criminal summons for an individual suspected of being on the run.[134] If approved by INTERPOL, the notice is then communicated to all INTERPOL offices and National Central Bureaus for dissemination to local law enforcement.[135] If an individual who is the subject of the notice is located in another State, the idea is that he will be arrested by the appropriate authorities in that State, held, and then the proper extradition process will start so that he can be sent back to the State that is charging him with a crime.[136]

INTERPOL uses a number of color codes to denote allegations and their severity. At the most serious end of a very serious list, red notices indicate that the person being sought is wanted for extradition, usually as the result of a major offense or allegation of a major offense.[137] Yellow notices indicate that the person(s) subject to the notice are missing or may have been kidnapped. In this instance, the point is to locate and assist the person who is the subject of the notice rather than to make an arrest.[138]

Blue notices request information regarding a "person's identity, location or activities in relation to a crime," while Orange notices will be used "to warn of an event, person, object or process representing a serious and imminent threat to public safety."[139] Black notices indicate that a jurisdiction has found unidentified human remains and is requesting information on or leading to their identity.

Green notices "provide warnings and intelligence about persons who have committed criminal offences and are likely to repeat these crimes in other countries."[140] Purple notices indicate a request for information on the methods and instruments that are used by criminals in the commission of their crimes.[141] INTERPOL-UN Security Council Special Notices are used for individuals who have become the subject of a UN Security Council sanction – for example, charged war criminals.[142]

EUROPOL

Background

The European Union has established its own version of INTERPOL – EUROPOL – to serve similar coordination and facilitation functions for policing between EU Member States in regard to serious crimes and/or crimes involving two or more States in the European Union.[143] Although EUROPOL is identified as being the EU's law enforcement agency, it does not have police officers or direct powers of arrest. Rather, it works with the policing entities within Member States to identify criminals, criminal networks and other threats to safety and then the national policing entity has the responsibility to carry out arrests or other activities.[144] In addition to the implementation of investigations at the EUROPOL level, it has the ability to request that Member States initiate investigations into significant crimes occurring at the State level.[145] EUROPOL also coordinates with several non-EU States, particularly the US, Canada, Norway and Australia.[146]

Membership and voting

Membership in EUROPOL is open to all EU Member States. In addition to the implementation of investigations at the EUROPOL level, it has the ability to request that Member States initiate investigations into significant crimes occurring at the State level.[147] EUROPOL also coordinates with several non-EU States, particularly the US, Canada, Norway and Australia.[148]

Structure

EUROPOL's work is overseen by the EU Council of Ministers for Justice and Home Affairs.[149] In addition, each national parliamentary body has oversight and information gathering abilities in order to ensure that its policing activities are being conducted in accordance with national standards when they involve EUROPOL.[150] At the practical level, the Director and the office of the Directorate carries on the day to day Secretariat functions for EUROPOL and are overseen by the Management Board, which serves as the equivalent of the INTERPOL Executive Committee.[151]

All EUROPOL Member States have a representative on the Management Board.[152] The Management Board is responsible for the creation of annual working programs for EUROPOL as an organization, generation of the budget for the organization, formation of an anti-fraud policy for the organization, internal organization audits, settlement of the organization in disputes between the Member States, and creating guidelines for EUROPOL's functions.[153] To assist in the internal audit requirement, an Internal Audit division has been established as part of EUROPOL.[154]

A key function of the Management Board is the oversight of the Executive Director of EUROPOL, the office responsible for the management of the organization in practice.[155] Within the EUROPOL structure there is extensive protection of data to which policing entities have access and which may be shared between policing agencies and others, in accordance with the EU's provisions for the protection of privacy.[156]

Additionally, there are EUROPOL National Units in each EU Member State of EUROPOL, which function as coordinating elements and as the main communication vehicle regarding crimes that rise to the level of serious crimes or cross-border crimes.[157] Included as part of the National Units are specifically designated liaison officers that are meant to be the conduits of information between the EUROPOL level and the State level.[158] These are intended to serve the same information coordination function as the National Central Bureaus in the INTERPOL system.[159] To ensure that there is parity and continuity within EUROPOL, the organization has established a Cooperation Board which is comprised of representatives from the National Units of each Member State.[160] In conjunction with EUROPOL, it is also possible for Member States to utilize joint teams for the investigation of cross-border crimes.[161]

Functions

In recent years, EUROPOL has become heavily involved in issues such as human trafficking and cross-border organized criminal activity.[162] Other examples of key areas of criminal investigation include narcotics, counterfeiting and other measures involving the euro and currency in general, sex crimes, and cybercrimes.[163]

EUROPOL has the authority to enter into agreements with international organizations and regional organizations, as well as other EU entities.[164] It also retains the ability to enter into agreements with individual States regarding cooperation, information-sharing and enforcement.[165]

Conclusions

As noted at the beginning of this chapter, military and policing activities are essential State functions regardless the criteria being used to determine the validity of statehood. The ability to create and make operational international organizations capable of exercising these functions is a testament to the importance and capacity of organizations within the larger international community and system.

A portion of these abilities arguably stems from international organizations being seen as fundamentally different forms of actors in the international system in military and policing situations because their identities and functions are not tied to a particular State. Rather, they act – at least in theory – at the behest of the international community, making them less of a threat to serve as proxy entities for the exercise of foreign State control than traditional military or policing assistance from a particular State. Along with this, international organizations can be used as reliable assistance in exercising core State functions and roles because of perceptions of good actor status from the legal and political perspectives.

As a result, international organizations such as those discussed in this chapter can act and be accepted in ways that individual States cannot. There is a limit to this, however, and the overdependence on organizational flexibility to condone military and policing activities where the foundational text does not contemplate them can result in legal uncertainty and potential harm for the States and individuals involved.

Notes

1 Convention on the Prohibition of the Development, Production, Stockpiling, and Use of Chemical Weapons and On Their Destruction (1996) preamble.
2 *Id.* at art VIII (1).
3 *Id.* at art VIII (5).
4 *Id.* at art VIII (2).
5 *Id.* at art VIII (8).
6 *Id.* at art XVI.
7 *Id.* at art VIII (4).
8 *Id.* at art 9.
9 *Id.* at arts 19, 20.
10 *Id.* at art 21.
11 *Id.* at art 23; OPCW, Rules of Procedure of the Executive Council (1997) Rule 1.
12 Chemical Weapons Convention, *supra* note 2 at arts 30–36.
13 *Id.* at art 37; Rules of Procedure of the Executive Council, *supra* note 11 at Rule 11.
14 Chemical Weapons Convention, *supra* note 2 at arts 38–39; Rules of Procedure of the Executive Council, *supra* note 11 at Rule 11.
15 Chemical Weapons Convention, *supra* note 2 at arts 41–43; Rules of Procedure of the Executive Council, *supra* note 11 at Rule 9.
16 *See* OPCW, Decision: Scientific Advisory Board, C-II/DEC.10/Rev.1 (2004); OPCW, Rules of Procedure for the Scientific Advisory Board and Temporary Working Groups of Scientific Experts (2011).
17 *See* OPCW, Decision: Establishment of an Advisory Board on Education and Outreach, C-20/DEC.9 (2015).
18 *See* OPCW, Operating Procedures of the Confidentiality Commission, C-II/DEC.14 Annex (1997).
19 OPCW, Decision: Relationship Agreement between the United Nations and OPCW, EC-MXI/DEC.1 (2000).
20 *See* North Atlantic Treaty (1949) preamble ("The Parties to this Treaty reaffirm their faith in the purposes and principles of the Charter of the United Nations and their desire to live in peace with all peoples and all governments. They are determined to safeguard the freedom, common heritage and civilisation of their peoples, founded on the principles of democracy, individual liberty and the rule of law. They seek to promote stability and well-being in the North Atlantic area. They are resolved to unite their efforts for collective defence and for the preservation of peace and security. They therefore agree to this North Atlantic Treaty."); What is NATO, http://www.nato.int/welcome/brochure_WhatIsNATO_en.pdf, last accessed 11 January 2018. In 2010, the NATO members – old and new – recommitted themselves to the concept of collective self-defense and assistance of Member States. *See* NATO, Strategic Concept for the Defence and Security of the Members of the North Atlantic Treaty Organization (2010) p 14 ("The greatest responsibility of the Alliance is to protect and defend our territory and our populations against attack, as set out in Article 5 of the Washington Treaty. The Alliance does not consider any country to

be its adversary. However, no one should doubt NATO's resolve if the security of any of its members were to be threatened."). Further, in 2010 NATO members restated the modern goals of the organization: "We, the political leaders of NATO, are determined to continue renewal of our Alliance so that it is fit for purpose in addressing the 21st Century security challenges. We are firmly committed to preserve its effectiveness as the globe's most successful political-military Alliance. Our Alliance thrives as a source of hope because it is based on common values of individual liberty, democracy, human rights and the rule of law, and because our common essential and enduring purpose is to safeguard the freedom and security of its members. These values and objectives are universal and perpetual, and we are determined to defend them through unity, solidarity, strength and resolve." NATO, Strategic Concept for the Defence and Security of the Members of the North Atlantic Treaty Organization (2010) 35.

21 *See* Active Engagement in Cooperative Security: A More Efficient and Flexible Partnership Policy (2010) (outlining ways in which NATO will encourage increased capacity building through relationships with its Member State and non-Member State parties); Political Military Framework for Partner Involvement in NATO-led Operations (2010); NATO, The Secretary General's Annual Report (2011); NATO, Strategic Concept for the Defence and Security of the Members, *supra* note 20.

22 *See* North Atlantic Treaty, *supra* note 20 at art 1 ("The Parties undertake, as set forth in the Charter of the United Nations, to settle any international dispute in which they may be involved by peaceful means in such a manner that international peace and security and justice are not endangered, and to refrain in their international relations from the threat or use of force in any manner inconsistent with the purposes of the United Nations.").

23 *Id.* at art 1.

24 NATO Member Countries, NATO, http://www.nato.int/cps/en/natolive/nato_countries.htm, last accessed 11 January 2018. At present, there are 29 NATO Member States. *Id.*

25 NATO, Strategic Concept for the Defence and Security of the Members, *supra* note 20 at 19–22; What is NATO, *supra* note 20.

26 *See* Protocol to the North Atlantic Treaty on the Accession of Greece and Turkey (1951); Protocol to the North Atlantic Treaty on the Accession of the Federal Republic of Germany (1954); Protocol to the North Atlantic Treaty on the Accession of Spain (1981).

27 *See* Protocol to the North Atlantic Treaty on the Accession of the Czech Republic (1997); Protocol to the North Atlantic Treaty on the Accession of the Republic of Hungary (1997); Protocol to the North Atlantic Treaty on the Accession of the Republic of Poland (1997); Protocol to the North Atlantic Treaty on the Accession of the Republic of Bulgaria (2003); Protocol to the North Atlantic Treaty on the Accession of the Republic of Estonia (2003); Protocol to the North Atlantic Treaty on the Accession of the Republic of Latvia (2003); Protocol to the North Atlantic Treaty on the Accession of the Republic of Lithuania (2003); Protocol to the North Atlantic Treaty on the Accession of Romania (2003); Protocol to the North Atlantic Treaty on the Accession of the Slovak Republic (2003); Protocol to the North Atlantic Treaty on the Accession of the Republic of Slovenia (2003); Protocol to the North Atlantic Treaty on the Accession of the Republic of Albania (2009); Protocol to the North Atlantic Treaty on the Accession of the Republic of Croatia (2009); Protocol to the North Atlantic Treaty on the Accession of Montenegro (2016).

28 North Atlantic Treaty, *supra* note 20 at art 13.

29 *Id.*

30 *Id.*

31 *Id.*

32 *Id.*

33 *Id.*

34 *Id.*

35 *Id.*

36 *See* NATO, Nuclear Planning Group https://www.nato.int/cps/en/natohq/topics_50069.htm, last accessed 11 January 2018.

37 *Id.*

38 *See id.*

39 *Id.*

40 *Id.*

41 *Id.*

42 *Id.*

43 *See* NATO, Structure, http://www.nato.int/cps/en/natolive/structure.htm#MS, last accessed 11 January 2018.

44 *Id.*

45 *Id.*

46 *Id.*

47 *See* NATO, The Secretary General's Annual Report (2011); NATO, The Secretary General's Annual Report (2012); NATO, The Secretary General's Annual Report (2013); NATO, The Secretary General's Annual Report (2014); NATO, The Secretary General's Annual Report (2015); NATO, Strategic Concept for the Defence and Security of the Members, *supra* note 20; Declaration by the North Atlantic Treaty Organisation (NATO) and the Government of the Islamic Republic of Afghanistan on an Enduring Partnership (2010).

48 NATO, Strategic Concept for the Defence and Security of the Members, *supra* note 20; Secretary General's Annual Report (2012), *supra* note 47; Secretary General's Annual Report (2013), *supra* note 47; Secretary General's Annual Report (2014), *supra* note 47; Secretary General's Annual Report (2015), *supra* note 47; NATO, NATO's role in Kosovo, https://www.nato.int/cps/en/natohq/topics_48818.htm, last accessed 11 January 2018; Warsaw Summit Communique (2016).

49 NATO, Strategic Concept for the Defence and Security of the Members, *supra* note 20; Secretary General's Annual Report (2012), *supra* note 47; Secretary General's Annual Report (2013), *supra* note 47; Secretary General's Annual Report (2014), *supra* note 47; Secretary General's Annual Report (2015), *supra* note 46; Alliance Maritime Strategy (2011); Warsaw Summit Communique, *supra* note 48.

50 NATO, Strategic Concept for the Defence and Security of the Members, *supra* note 20; Secretary General's Annual Report (2012), *supra* note 47; General's Annual Report (2013), *supra* note 47; Secretary General's Annual Report (2014), *supra* note 47; General's Annual Report (2015), *supra* note 47; Warsaw Summit Communique, *supra* note 48.

51 NATO, Environment – NATO's stake, https://www.nato.int/cps/en/natohq/topics_91048.htm?, last accessed 11 January 2018.

52 *See* North Atlantic Treaty Organization, Press Conference: NATO Secretary Jens Stoltenberg following meeting of the North Atlantic Council at the level of Defence Ministers (8 November 2017) https://www.nato.int/cps/en/natohq/opinions_148417.htm?, last accessed 11 January 2018.

53 About Us, UN Peacekeeping Operations, http://www.un.org/en/peacekeeping/about/, last accessed 11 January 2018.

54 *Id.*; *see* United Nations General Assembly, A comprehensive strategy to eliminate future sexual exploitation and abuse in United Nations peacekeeping operations, A/59/710 (2005); United Nations General Assembly, Comprehensive report on strengthening the capacity of the United Nations to manage and sustain peace operations, A/61/858 (2007); United Nations Security Council, Women and peace and security, S/RES/465 (2009); United Nations General Assembly, Implementation of the recommendations of the Special Committee on Peacekeeping Operations, A/64/753 (2009); United Nations General Assembly, Strengthening the capacity of the United Nations to manage and sustain peacekeeping operations, A/65/624 (2010); United Nations General Assembly, Report of the Special Committee on Peacekeeping Operations, A/68/19 (2014); United Nations General Assembly, The future of United Nations peace operations: implementation of the recommendations of the High Level Independent Panel on Peace Operations, A/70/357 – S/2015/682 (2015); United Nations Department of Peacekeeping Operations, A New Partnership Agenda: Charting a New Horizon for UN Peacekeeping (2009); United Nations Department of Peacekeeping Operations, The New Horizon Initiative: Progress Report No. 1 (2010); United Nations Department of Peacekeeping Operations, The New Horizon Initiative: Progress Report No. 2 (2011);

55 Examples of UNDPKO regulatory activity include: United Nations Peacekeeping Operations, Handbook on United Nations Multidimensional Peacekeeping Operations (2003); United Nations Peacekeeping Operations, Principles and Guidelines (2008); United Nations Peacekeeping Operations, Office of Rule of Law and Security Institutions, DDR in Peace Operations: A Retrospective (2010); United Nations Department of Peacekeeping Operations, Gender Equality in UN Peacekeeping Operations (2010); United Nations General Assembly, Disarmament, demobilization, and reintegration, A/65/741 (2010);

56 United Nations Peacekeeping Operations, Sustainable Peace Through Justice and Security (2009); United Nations Peacekeeping Operations, Sustainable Peace Through Justice and Security (2010); United Nations Peacekeeping Operations, Sustainable Peace Through Justice and Security (2011); United Nations Peacekeeping Operations, Sustainable Peace Through Justice and Security (2012); United Nations Peacekeeping Operations, Office of Rule of Law and Security Institutions, Justice & Corrections Update (2014); United Nations Peacekeeping Operations, Office of Rule of Law and Security Institutions, Justice & Corrections Update (2016); United Nations Peacekeeping Operations, Office of Rule of Law and Security Institutions, Justice & Corrections Update (2017); United Nations Department of Peacekeeping Operations, Handbook for Judicial Affairs Officers in United Nations Peacekeeping Operations (2013).

57 *Id.*

58 *Id.*

59 *Id.*

60 What is peacekeeping?, UN Peacekeeping Operations, http://www.un.org/en/peacekeeping/operations/peacekeeping.shtml, last accessed 11 January 2018.

61 *Id.*

62 *Id.*

63 *Id.*

64 *See* United Nations Peacekeeping, MONUSCO Fact Sheet, https://peacekeeping.un.org/en/mission/monusco, last accessed 11 January 2018; United Nations Peacekeeping, MINUJUSTH Fact Sheet, https://peacekeeping.un.org/en/mission/minujusth, last accessed 11 January 2018.

65 Current operations, UN Peacekeeping Operations, http://www.un.org/en/peacekeeping/operations/current.shtml, last accessed 11 January 2018.

66 *See, e.g.*, United Nations Security Council, Res. 1497, S/RES/1497 (2003) (establishing a UN peacekeeping mission in Liberia in order to assist in enforcing a ceasefire); United Nations Security Council, Res. 1529, S/RES/1529 (2004) (establishing another UN peacekeeping mission in Haiti); United Nations Security Council,

Res. 1590, S/RES/1590 (2005) (establishing a UN peacekeeping mission in Sudan); United Nations Security Council, Res. 1657, S/RES/1657 (2006) (allowing for the deployment of UN peacekeeping troops to the Cote D'Ivoire); United Nations Security Council, Res. 1996, S/RES/1996 (2011) (establishing the UN Mission in the Republic of South Sudan).

67 *See, e.g.*, United Nations Security Council, Res. 1288, S/RES/1288 (2000) (extending the UN Interim Force in Lebanon); United Nations Security Council, Res. 1292, S/RES/1292 (2000) (extending the UN Mission for a Referendum in the Western Sahara); United Nations Security Council, Res. 1301, S/RES/1301 (2000) (extending the UN Mission for a Referendum in the Western Sahara); United Nations Security Council, Res. 1303, S/RES/1303 (2000) (extending the UN Peacekeeping Force in Cyprus); United Nations Security Council, Res. 1309, S/RES/1309 (2000) (extending the UN Mission for a Referendum in the Western Sahara); United Nations Security Council, Res. 1310, S/RES/1310 (2000); United Nations Security Council, Res. 1324, S/RES/1324 (2000) (extending the UN Mission for a Referendum in the Western Sahara); United Nations Security Council, Res. 1331, S/RES/1331 (2000) (extending the UN Peacekeeping Force in Cyprus); United Nations Security Council, Res. 1337, S/RES/1337 (2001) (extending the UN Interim Force in Lebanon); United Nations Security Council, Res. 1359, S/RES/1359 (2001) (extending the UN Mission for a Referendum in the Western Sahara); United Nations Security Council, Res. 1394, S/RES/1394 (2002) (extending the UN Mission for a Referendum in the Western Sahara); United Nations Security Council, Res. 1416, S/RES/1416 (2000) (extending the UN Peacekeeping Force in Cyprus); United Nations Security Council, Res. 1461, S/RES/1461 (2003) (extending the UN Interim Force in Lebanon); United Nations Security Council, Res. 1463, S/RES/1463 (2003) (extending the UN Mission for a Referendum in the Western Sahara); United Nations Security Council, Res. 1523, S/RES/1523 (2004) (extending the UN Mission for a Referendum in the Western Sahara); United Nations Security Council, Res. 1525, S/RES/1525 (2004) (extending the UN Interim Force in Lebanon); United Nations Security Council, Res. 1583, S/RES/1583 (2005) (extending the UN Interim Force in Lebanon); United Nations Security Council, Res. 1626, S/RES/1626 (2005) (extending the UN Mission in Sierra Leone); United Nations Security Council, Res. 1642, S/RES/1642 (2005) (extending the UN Peacekeeping Force in Cyprus); United Nations Security Council, Res. 1655, S/RES/1655 (2006) (extending the UN Interim Force in Lebanon); United Nations Security Council, Res. 1658, S/RES/1658 (2006) (extending the UN Stabilization Mission in Haiti); United Nations Security Council, Res. 1675, S/RES/1675 (2006) (extending the UN Mission for a Referendum in the Western Sahara); United Nations Security Council, Res. 1687, S/RES/1687 (2006) (extending the UN Peacekeeping Force in Cyprus); United Nations Security Council, Res. 1743, S/RES/1743 (2007) (extending the UN Stabilization Mission in Haiti); United Nations Security Council, Res. 1750, S/RES/1750 (2007) (extending the UN Mission in Liberia); United Nations Security Council, Res. 1754, S/RES/1754 (2007) (extending the UN Mission for a Referendum in the Western Sahara); United Nations Security Council, Res. 1755, S/RES/1755 (2007) (extending the UN Mission in the Sudan); United Nations Security Council, Res. 1813, S/RES/1813 (2008) (extending the UN Mission for a Referendum in the Western Sahara); United Nations Security Council, Res. 1818, S/RES/1818 (2008) (extending the UN Peacekeeping Force in Cyprus); United Nations Security Council, Res. 1828, S/RES/1828 (2008) (extending the UN Mission in the Sudan); United Nations Security Council, Res. 1836, S/RES/1836 (2008) (extending the UN Mission in Liberia); United Nations Security Council, Res. 1871, S/RES/1871 (2009) (extending the UN Mission for a Referendum in the Western Sahara); United Nations Security Council, Res. 1873, S/RES/1873 (2009) (extending the UN Peacekeeping Force in Cyprus); United Nations Security Council, Res. 1908, S/RES/1908 (2010) (extending the UN Mission for a Referendum in the Western Sahara); United Nations Security Council, Res. 1927, S/RES/1927 (2010) (extending the UN Stabilization Mission in Haiti); United Nations Security Council, Res. 1935, S/RES/1935 (2010) (extending the UN Mission in the Sudan); United Nations Security Council, Res. 1979, S/RES/1979 (2011) (extending the UN Mission for a Referendum in the Western Sahara); United Nations Security Council, Res. 1986, S/RES/1986 (2011) (extending the UN Peacekeeping Force in Cyprus); United Nations Security Council, Res. 1990, S/RES/1990 (2011) (extending the UN Mission in the Sudan); United Nations Security Council, Res. 2044, S/RES/2044 (2012) (extending the UN Mission for a Referendum in the Western Sahara); United Nations Security Council, Res. 2058, S/RES/2058 (2012) (extending the UN Peacekeeping Force in Cyprus); United Nations Security Council, Res. 2070, S/RES/2070 (2012) (extending the UN Stabilization Mission in Haiti); United Nations Security Council, Res. 2089, S/RES/2089 (2013) (extending the UN Peacekeeping Force in Cyprus); United Nations Security Council, Res. 2099, S/RES/2099 (2013) (extending the UN Mission for a Referendum in the Western Sahara); United Nations Security Council, Res. 2104, S/RES/2104 (2013) (extending the UN Mission in the Sudan); United Nations Security Council, Res. 2116, S/RES/2116 (2013) (extending the UN Mission in Liberia); United Nations Security Council, Res. 2148, S/RES/2148 (2014) (extending the UN Mission in the Sudan); United Nations Security Council, Res. 2168, S/RES/2168 (2014) (extending the UN Peacekeeping Force in Cyprus); United Nations Security Council, Res. 2180, S/RES/2180 (2014) (extending the UN Stabilization Mission in Haiti); United Nations Security Council, Res. 2197, S/RES/2197 (2015) (extending the UN Stabilization Mission in Haiti); United Nations Security Council, Res. 2205, S/RES/2205 (2015) (extending the UN Mission in the Sudan); United Nations Security Council, Res. 2215, S/RES/2215 (2015) (extending the UN Mission in Liberia); United Nations Security Council, Res. 2234, S/RES/2234 (2015) (extending the UN Peacekeeping Force in Cyprus); United Nations Security Council, Res. 2265, S/RES/2265 (2016) (extending the UN Mission in the Sudan); United Nations Security Council, Res. 2308, S/RES/2308 (2016) (extending the UN Mission in Liberia); United Nations Security Council, Res. 2313, S/RES/2313 (2016) (extending the UN

Stabilization Mission in Haiti); United Nations Security Council, Res. 2350, S/RES/2350 (2017) (extending the UN Stabilization Mission in Haiti).

68 Forming a new operation, UN Peacekeeping Operations, http://www.un.org/en/peacekeeping/operations/newoperation.shtml, last accessed 11 January 2018.

69 Alexandra R. Harrington, *Victims of Peace: Current Abuse Allegations Against UN Peacekeepers and the Role of Law in Preventing Them in the Future*, ILSA Journal of Comparative and International Law (2005).

70 Id.

71 Id.

72 Id.

73 Id.

74 Id.

75 *See* European Union External Action, European Common Security and Defence Policy (2017).

76 *See* id.

77 *See* id.

78 *See* EUFOR, EUFOR – Mission & Mandate, Operation Althea (2016).

79 *See* European Union Naval Force Somalia Operation Atalanta, Information Booklet (2017). The EU also works to combat piracy in other areas through the use of multi-purpose forces. *See* European Union, Council Decision 2013/367/CFSP (2013) (relating to the European Union Mission on Regional Maritime Capacity Building in the Horn of Africa).

80 *See* Naval Force Somalia Operation Atalanta, *supra* note 79.

81 *See* European Union, Council Decision 2015/778 (2015) (establishing the European Union military operation in the Southern Central Mediterranean).

82 European Union, Council Decision 2014/482/CFSP (2014) (extending the parameters of the EU force in Niger); European Union, EU Military Operation in Eastern Chad and North Eastern Central African Republic (EUFOR Tchad/RCA) (2009); European Union, EU mission in support of security sector reform in the Republic of Guinea-Bissau (EU SSR GUINEA-BISSAU) (2010); European Union, Council Decision 2012/389/CFSP (2012) (relating to the creation of the European Union Capacity Building Mission in Somalia); European Union, Council Joint Action 2005/824/CFSP (2005) (extending the European Union Police Mission in Bosnia and Herzegovina); European Union, Political and Security Committee Decision EUPM/3/2007 ("concerning the appointment of the Head of Mission/Police Commissioner of the European Union Police Mission in Bosnia and Herzegovina"); European Union, Council Joint Action 2007/405/CFSP (2007) (regarding the European Union police mission undertaken in the framework of reform of the security sector (SSR) and its interface with the system of justice in the Democratic Republic of the Congo); European Union, Council Decision 2012/392/CFSP (2012) (establishing the European Union CSDP mission in Niger); European Union, Council Decision 2013/233/CFSP (2013) (establishing the European Union Integrated Border Management Assistance Mission in Libya).

83 *See, e.g.*, Council Joint Action 2006/319/CFSP (2006) (relating to the European Union operation in support of the United Nations Organisation Mission in the Democratic Republic of the Congo (MONUC) during the election process).

84 *See* Council Joint Action 2005/889/CFSP (2005) (establishing the European Union Border Assistance Mission for the Rafah Crossing Point); Political and Security Committee Decision EUPOL COPPS/1/2007 (2007) ("concerning the extension of the mandate of the Head of Mission/Police Commissioner of the European Union Police Mission for the Palestinian Territories").

85 Council of the European Union, Council establishes an EU police advisory team in the former Yugoslav Republic of Macedonia (2005).

86 *See* European Union, Council Joint Action 2008/736/CFSP (2008) (creating the European Union Monitoring Mission in Georgia). The established mandate of this mission was to: "provide civilian monitoring of Parties' actions, including full compliance with the six-point Agreement and subsequent implementing measures throughout Georgia, working in close coordination with partners, particularly the United Nations (UN) and the Organisation for Security and Cooperation in Europe (OSCE), and consistent with other EU activity, in order to contribute to stabilisation, normalization and confidence building whilst also contributing to informing European policy in support of a durable political solution for Georgia." Id.

87 *See* European Union, Political and Security Committee Decision EUJUST LEX-IRAQ/2/2011 (2011) (relating to the European Union Integrated Rule of Law Mission in Iraq); European Union Common Security and Defence Policy, EU Integrated Rule of Law Mission for Iraq (2014).

88 *See* European Union, Council Decision 2012/312/CFSP (2012) (relating to the European Union Aviation Security CSDR Mission in South Sudan); European Union Common Security and Defence Policy, European Union Aviation Security Mission in South Sudan (2014).

89 *See, e.g.*, Agreement between the European Union and the Central African Republic on the status of the European Union-led forces in the Central African Republic (2008); Agreement between the European Union and the Republic of Guinea-Bissau on the Status of the European Union Mission in Support of Security Sector Reform in the Republic of Guinea-Bissau (2008).

90 *See, e.g.*, Agreement between the European Union and the Republic of Cameroon on the status of European Union-led Forces in transit within the territory of the Republic of Cameroon (2008).

91 *See, e.g.*, id.

92 *See, e.g.*, Agreement between the European Union and the Republic of Albania on the participation of the Repub-lic of Albania in the European Union military operation in the Republic of Chad and in the Central African Republic (2008); Agreement between the European Union and the Russian Federation on the participation of the Russian Federation in the European Union military operation in the Republic of Chad and in the Central African Republic (2008); European Union, Council Decision 2008/783/CFSP (2008) (relating to the Agree-ment between the European Union and the Republic of Croatia on the participation of the Republic of Croatia in the European Union military operation in the Republic of Chad and in the Central African Republic); European Union, Council Decision 2003/157/CFSP (2003) (relating to the Agreement between the European Union and the Republic of Poland on the participation of this State to the European Union Police Mission in Bosnia and Herzegovina).

93 About INTERPOL, http://www..int/About-/Overview, last accessed 11 January 2018.

94 Id.

95 Id.

96 Member Countries, INTERPOL, http://www..int/Member-countries/World, last accessed 11 January 2018.

97 General Regulations of the International Criminal Police Organization-INTERPOL (2014) art 18; Rules of Pro-cedure of the General Assembly (2004) art 36.

98 General Regulations of INTERPOL, *supra* note 97 at art 8; Rules of Procedure of the General Assembly, *supra* note 97 at art 6.

99 *See* Constitution of the International Criminal Police Organisation-INTERPOL (1997) at art 5.

100 *See id.* at art 6.

101 *See id.* at arts 8, 11; Rules of Procedure of the General Assembly, *supra* note 97 at art 1.

102 *See* Constitution of INTERPOL, *supra* note 99 at art 15.

103 *See id.* at art 22; Rules of Procedure of the Executive Council (2013) art 4.

104 *See* Constitution of INTERPOL, *supra* note 99 at art 26.

105 *See id.*

106 *See id.* at arts 31–35.

107 *See id.*

108 *See* Member Countries, United States, INTERPOL, http://www..int/Member-countries/Americas/United-States, last accessed 11 January 2018.

109 General Regulations of INTERPOL, *supra* note 97 at art 35; Rules of Procedure of the General Assembly, *supra* note 97 at ch VIII.

110 *See* Constitution of INTERPOL, *supra* note 99 at art 1.

111 *See id.*

112 INTERPOL, Annual Report (2010); INTERPOL, Annual Report (2011); INTERPOL, Annual Report (2012); INTER-POL, Annual Report (2013); INTERPOL, Annual Report (2014); INTERPOL, Annual Report (2015); Corruption, Crime Areas, INTERPOL, http://www..int/Crime-areas/Corruption/Corruption, last accessed 11 January 2018.

113 Annual Report (2010), *supra* note 112; Annual Report (2011), *supra* note 112; Annual Report (2013), *supra* note 112; Annual Report (2014), *supra* note 112; Annual Report (2015), *supra* note 112; Crimes against children, Crime areas, INTERPOL, http://www..int/Crime-areas/Crimes-against-children/Crimes-against-children, last accessed 11 January 2018.

114 *See, e.g.*, INTERPOL, INTERPOL Handbook on DNA Data Exchange and Practice (2009).

115 Annual Report (2010), *supra* note 112; Annual Report (2011), *supra* note 112; Annual Report (2012), *supra* note 112; Annual Report (2013), *supra* note 112; Annual Report (2014), *supra* note 112; Annual Report (2015), *supra* note 112; Financial crime, Crime areas, INTERPOL, http://www..int/Crime-areas/Financial-crime/Financial-crime, last accessed 11 January 2018.

116 INTERPOL Fact Sheet, The INTERPOL Data Protection Office (2017); Cybercrimes, Crime areas, INTERPOL, http://www..int/Crime-areas/Cybercrime/Cybercrime, last accessed 11 January 2018.

117 Annual Report (2010), *supra* note 112; Annual Report (2011), *supra* note 112; Annual Report (2012), *supra* note 112; Annual Report (2013), *supra* note 112; Annual Report (2014), *supra* note 112; Annual Report (2015), *supra* note 112; Drugs, Crime areas, INTERPOL, http://www..int/Crime-areas/Drugs/Drugs, last accessed 11 January 2018.

118 Annual Report (2010), *supra* note 112; Annual Report (2011), *supra* note 112; Annual Report (2012), *supra* note 112; Annual Report (2013), *supra* note 112; Annual Report (2014), *supra* note 112; Annual Report (2015), *supra* note 112; Firearms, Crime areas, INTERPOL, http://www..int/Crime-areas/Firearms/Firearms, last accessed 11 January 2018.

119 INTERPOL Office of Legal Affairs, Countering Illicit Trade in Goods: A Guide for Policy-Makers (2014); Annual Report (2010), *supra* note 112; Annual Report (2011), *supra* note 112; Annual Report (2012), *supra* note 112; Annual Report (2013), *supra* note 112; Annual Report (2014), *supra* note 112; Annual Report (2015), *supra* note 112; Trafficking in illicit goods, Crime areas, INTERPOL, http://www..int/Crime-areas/Trafficking-in-illicit-goods/Trafficking-in-illicit-goods, last accessed 11 January 2018.

120 Annual Report (2010), *supra* note 112; Annual Report (2011), *supra* note 112; Annual Report (2012), *supra* note 112; Annual Report (2013), *supra* note 112; Annual Report (2014), *supra* note 112; Annual Report (2015), *supra* note 112; Trafficking in human beings, Crime areas, INTERPOL, http://www..int/Crime-areas/Trafficking-in-human-beings/Trafficking-in-human-beings, last accessed 11 January 2018.

121 *See id.*

122 Annual Report (2010), *supra* note 112; Annual Report (2011), *supra* note 112; Annual Report (2012), *supra* note 112; Annual Report (2013), *supra* note 112; Annual Report (2014), *supra* note 112; Annual Report (2015), *supra* note 112; Terrorism, Crime areas, INTERPOL, http://www..int/Crime-areas/Terrorism/Terrorism, last accessed 11 January 2018.

123 Annual Report (2010), *supra* note 112; Annual Report (2011), *supra* note 112; Annual Report (2012), *supra* note 112; Annual Report (2013), *supra* note 112; Annual Report (2014), *supra* note 112; Annual Report (2015), *supra* note 112; Maritime Piracy, Crime areas, INTERPOL, http://www..int/Crime-areas/Maritime-piracy/Maritime-piracy, last accessed 11 January 2018.

124 Annual Report (2010), *supra* note 112; Annual Report (2011), *supra* note 112; Annual Report (2012), *supra* note 112; Annual Report (2013), *supra* note 112; Annual Report (2014), *supra* note 112; Annual Report (2015), *supra* note 112; Pharmaceutical Crime, Crime areas, INTERPOL, http://www..int/Crime-areas/Pharmaceutical-crime/Pharmaceutical-crime, last accessed 11 January 2018.

125 Annual Report (2010), *supra* note 112; Annual Report (2011), *supra* note 112; Annual Report (2012), *supra* note 112; Annual Report (2013), *supra* note 112; Annual Report (2014), *supra* note 112; Annual Report (2015), *supra* note 112; Vehicle crime, Crime areas, INTERPOL, http://www..int/Crime-areas/Vehicle-crime/Vehicle-crime, last accessed 11 January 2018.

126 Annual Report (2010), *supra* note 112; Annual Report (2011), *supra* note 112; Annual Report (2012), *supra* note 112; Annual Report (2013), *supra* note 112; Annual Report (2014), *supra* note 112; Annual Report (2015), *supra* note 112; Works of art, Crime areas, INTERPOL, http://www..int/Crime-areas/Works-of-art/Works-of-art, last accessed 11 January 2018.

127 INTERPOL Environmental Security Sub-Directorate, Pollution Crime Forensic Investigation Manual (2014); Annual Report (2010), *supra* note 112; Annual Report (2011), *supra* note 112; Annual Report (2012), *supra* note 112; Annual Report (2013), *supra* note 112; Annual Report (2014), *supra* note 112; Annual Report (2015), *supra* note 112; International Consortium on Combating Wildlife Crime, Guidelines on Methods and Procedures for Ivory Sampling and Laboratory Analysis (2014); Environmental crime, Crime areas, INTERPOL, http://www.int/Crime-areas/Environmental-crime/Environmental-crime, last accessed 11 January 2018.

128 *See* INTERPOL Fact Sheet, Disaster victim identification (2017).

129 *See* Constitution of INTERPOL, *supra* note 99 at art 41. *See, e.g.,* Arrangement on Co-operation between the International Criminal Police Organization-INTERPOL and the United Nations in relation to the activities of Peacekeeping Operations and Special Political Missions, Supplementary to the Co-operation Agreement between the United Nations and the International Criminal Police Organisation-INTERPOL (2009); Arrangement on Cooperation between the International Criminal Police Organisation-INTERPOL and the United Nations in relation to Direct Access by United Nations Department of Safety and Security to the INTERPOL Information System, Supplementary to the Cooperation Agreement between the United Nations and the INTERPOL (2014); Cooperation Agreement between the United Nation and the International Criminal Police Organisation-INTERPOL (1997).

130 *See* Arrangement on Co-operation between the International Criminal Police Organization-INTERPOL and the United Nations in relation to the United Nations Security Council Sanctions Committees Supplementary to the Cooperation Agreement between the International Criminal Police Organization-INTERPOL and the United Nations (2009).

131 Co-operation Agreement between the Office of the Prosecutor of the International Criminal Court and the International Criminal Police Organization-INTERPOL (2004).

132 *See, e.g.,* Co-operation Agreement on Direct Access to and Use of INTERPOL's Police Information System between The International Criminal Police Organisation-INTERPOL and Central Asian Regional Information and Coordination Centre for Combatting Illicit Trafficking of Narcotic Drugs, Psychotropic Substances and their Precursors (2012); Memorandum of Understanding between the International Criminal Police Organization-INTERPOL and the Office of Audit and Investigations of the United Nations Development Programme (2011); Cooperation Agreement between the ICPO-INTERPOL General Secretariat and European Police College (2008); Memorandum of Mutual Understanding in Terms of Co-operation and Interaction in the Field of Counterterrorism Information Sharing between the International Criminal Police Organization-INTERPOL and the Anti-Terrorism Centre of the Commonwealth of Independent States (2008); Joint Initiative of the Secretary General of INTERPOL and the Director of Europol on Combatting the Counterfeiting of Currency, in Particular the Euro (2001); Co-operation Agreement between the International Criminal Police Organisation-INTERPOL and the Special Tribunal for Lebanon (2009); Arrangement on Cooperation between the International Criminal Police Organisation-INTERPOL and the United Nations in Relation to Joint Activities with the United Nations Office of Drugs and Crime Supplementary to the Cooperation Agreement between INTERPOL and the United Nations (2016); Working Agreement between the International Criminal Police Organisation-INTERPOL and the European Agency for the Management of Operational Cooperation at the External Borders of the Member States of the European Union – FRONTEX (2009); Co-operation Agreement between the International Criminal Police Organisation-INTERPOL and the Special Court for Sierra Leone (2003); Memorandum of Understanding between the International Criminal Police Organisation-INTERPOL and the United Nations Interim Administration Mission in Kosovo on Co-operation in Crime Prevention and Criminal Justice (2002).

133 See, e.g., Memorandum of Understanding on Co-operation between the International Criminal Police Organization-INTERPOL and the World Customs Organization (1998); Memorandum of Understanding between the International Criminal Police Organization-INTERPOL and the Secretariat of the Basel Convention (1999); Co-operation Agreement between the Economic Community of West African States (ECOWAS) and the International Criminal Police Organization-INTERPOL (2004); Memorandum of Understanding as Mentioned in Article 4(1) of the Agreement between INTERPOL and Europol (2008); Memorandum of Understanding between the International Criminal Police Organization-INTERPOL and the Commission of the African Union (2011); Co-operation Agreement between the Economic and Monetary Community of Central Africa and the International Criminal Police Organization-INTERPOL (2001); Acuerdo de Cooperacion entre la Organizacion Internacional de Policia Criminal (INTERPOL) y la Secretaria General de la Comunidad Andina (2003); Memorandum of Understanding between the General Secretariat of ICPO-INTERPOL and the Secretariat of the Convention on International Trade in Endangered Species of Wild Fauna and Flora (CITES) (1998); Cooperation Agreement between the International Criminal Police Organisation-INTERPOL and the East African Community (2012); Memorandum of Understanding on cooperation between EUROJUST and the International Criminal Police Organisation (2013); Cooperation Agreement between the European Central Bank and the International Criminal Police Organisation (2004); Cooperation Agreement between the International Criminal Police Organisation-INTERPOL and the International Organisation for Migration (2014); Cooperation Agreement between the International Atomic Energy Association and the International Criminal Police Organisation-INTERPOL (2006); Memorandum of Understanding on Cooperation between the International Criminal Police Organisation-INTERPOL and the International Civil Aviation Organisation (2000); Agreement of Co-operation between the International Maritime Organisation and the International Criminal Police Organisation-INTERPOL (2005); Co-operation Agreement between the International Criminal Police Organisation-INTERPOL and the Caribbean Community (CARICOM); Memorandum of Understanding between the International Criminal Police Organisation-INTERPOL and the Commonwealth of Australia (2014); General Agreement between the General Secretariat of the International Criminal Police Organisation-INTERPOL and the General Secretariat of the Organization of American States (2000); Cooperation Agreement between the Southern African Development Community and the International Criminal Police Organisation-INTERPOL (2011).

134 Id.

135 Id.

136 Id.

137 INTERPOL, Red Notices, https://www..int/-expertise/Notices/Red-Notices, last accessed 11 January 2018.

138 INTERPOL, Yellow Notices, https://www..int/-expertise/Notices/Yellow-Notices, last accessed 11 January 2018.

139 INTERPOL, Blue Notices, https://www..int/-expertise/Notices, last accessed 11 January 2018; INTERPOL, Orange Notices, https://www..int/-expertise/Notices/Orange-notices-%E2%80%93-public-versions, last accessed 11 January 2018.

140 INTERPOL, Green Notices, https://www..int/-expertise/Notices, last accessed 11 January 2018.

141 INTERPOL, Purple Notices, https://www..int/-expertise/Notices/Purple-notices-%E2%80%93-public-versions, last accessed 11 January 2018.

142 INTERPOL, INTERPOL-United Nations Security Council Special Notices, https://www..int/-expertise/Notices/Special-Notices, last accessed 11 January 2018.

143 General Provisions, Objectives and Tasks of Europol (1999) art 3 ("Europol shall support and strengthen action by the competent authorities of the Member States and their mutual cooperation in preventing and combating serious crime affecting two or more Member States, terrorism and forms of crime which affect a common interest covered by a Union policy . . . Europol's objectives shall also cover related criminal offences. The following shall be considered to be related criminal offences: (a) criminal offences committed in order to procure the means of perpetrating acts in respect of which Europol is competent; (b) criminal offences committed in order to facilitate or perpetrate acts in respect of which Europol is competent; (c) criminal offences committed in order to ensure the impunity of those committing acts in respect of which Europol is competent.").

144 Id. at art 5.

145 Id. at art 6.

146 Id.

147 Id.

148 Id.

149 Id. at art 52.

150 Id. at art 51.

151 Id. at art 53.

152 Id. at art 10.

153 Id. at art 11.

154 See Charter of EUROPOL's Internal Audit Function (2009); European Commission, Strategic Plan 2016–2020 Internal Audit Service (2016); European Commission, Management Plan Internal Audit Service (2017).

155 General Provisions, Objectives and Tasks of Europol, supra note 143 at art 16.

156 Id. at arts 17–19.

157 Id. at art 7.

158 Id. at art 8.
159 See id.
160 Id. at art 45.
161 See European Union, Council Decision 2002/465/JHA (2002); European Union, Council Decision 2017/C 18/01 (2017); European Union General Secretariat of the Council, Joint Investigation Teams Practical Guide, 6128/1/17 (2017).
162 See EUROPOL, Migrant smuggling on board international trains (2015); EUROPOL, EUROPOL Work Programme 2010 (2009); EUROPOL, EUROPOL Preliminary Work Programme 2011 (2010); EUROPOL, EUROPOL Work Programme 2012 (2011); EUROPOL, EUROPOL Work Programme 2013 (2012); EUROPOL, EUROPOL Work Programme 2014 (2013); EUROPOL, EUROPOL Work Programme 2015 (2014).
163 See EUROPOL, EUROPOL Programming Document 2017–2019 (2017); EUROPOL, EUROPOL Work Document (2016); EUROPOL, EUROPOL Review: General Report on EUROPOL Activities (2009); EUROPOL, EUROPOL Review: General Report on EUROPOL Activities (2010); EUROPOL, EUROPOL Review: General Report on EUROPOL Activities (2011); EUROPOL, EUROPOL Review: General Report on EUROPOL Activities (2012); EUROPOL, EUROPOL Review: General Report on EUROPOL Activities (2013); EUROPOL, EUROPOL Review: General Report on EUROPOL Activities; EUROPOL, EUROPOL Review: General Report on EUROPOL Activities (2015); EUROPOL Work Programme 2010, supra note 162; EUROPOL Preliminary Work Programme 2011, supra note 162; EUROPOL Work Programme 2012, supra note 162; EUROPOL Work Programme 2013, supra note 162; EUROPOL Work Programme 2014, supra note 162; EUROPOL Work Programme 2015, supra note 162.
164 Administrative Agreement on Co-operation between the European Commission and the European Police Office (2003); Administrative Arrangement between the European Police Office and the European Anti-Fraud Office (2004); Agreement between Eurojust and Europol (2004); Agreement between the European Police Office and the European Central Bank (2014); Agreement on Operational Cooperation between the European Police Office and the European Agency for the Management of Operational Cooperation at the External Borders of the Member States of the European Union (FRONTEX) (2008); Agreement on Strategic Co-operation between the European Union Agency for Network and Information Security and the European Police Office (2014); Agreement on Strategic Co-operation between the Office for Harmonisation in the Internal Market and the European Police Office (2013); Agreement on Strategic Cooperation between the European Centre for Disease Prevention and Control and the European Police Office (2011); Cooperation Agreement between EUROPOL and the European Monitoring Centre for Drugs and Drug Addiction (2001); Cooperation Agreement between the United Nations Office on Drugs and Crime and the European Police Office (2004).
165 Agreement between the European Police Office and Ukraine on Strategic Co-operation (2009); Agreement on co-operation between the European Police Office and the Russian Federation (2003); Agreement on Cooperation between the European Police Office and the Republic of Turkey (2004); Agreement on Strategic Co-operation between the European Police Office and the Ministry of Public Security of the People's Republic of China (2017).

Chapter 18

Human rights organizations and bodies

Chapter contents

Human rights concerns have become prevalent in the years since the end of World War II and this has led to the development of international law and international organizations surrounding human rights law. Although there has been a rise in the discussion of human rights during this time, there has also been a consistent stream of human rights violations, in wartime and peacetime, on a grand scale and an individual scale.

Treaty-based bodies

Human Rights Committee

The Human Rights Committee was established as a result of the International Covenant on Civil and Political Rights (ICCPR), which was adopted by the international community in 1966 and entered into force in 1976.[1] The ICCPR and the International Covenant on Economic, Social and Cultural Rights (ICESCR) were adopted at the same time and originally were meant to be one combined treaty. However, during the Cold War years there was a split between the Western states, which emphasized the importance of civil and political rights, and the Communist states, which emphasized the importance of economic, social and cultural rights and were not as supportive of the concept of civil and political rights. In addition to the larger legal and societal implications, this split meant that violations of each treaty were to be reported to separate international bodies.

In terms of the rights protected and guaranteed under the ICCPR, the treaty begins by providing that "all peoples have the right to self-determination,"[2] and goes on to provide that "all peoples may . . . freely dispose of their natural wealth and resources."[3] These, and many of the early provisions of the ICESCR, are the same. Non-discrimination and gender discrimination are essential to the ICCPR, and Member States are to ensure that their laws reflect these provisions.[4]

The ICCPR goes on to provide for the right to life,[5] protection from "torture or cruel, inhuman or degrading treatment or punishment,"[6] freedom from slavery,[7] freedom from arbitrary arrest or detention,[8] and the right of those who are arrested or accused of a crime to have basic trial rights.[9] In addition, the ICCPR contains the freedom of movement within the Member State, provided that a person is legally in the Member State,[10] some protections for non-citizens in terms of presence and removal from the Member State,[11] the right to privacy,[12] the right to "freedom of thought, conscience and religion,"[13] the right to opinions,[14] the right to freedom of expression,[15] and the right to freedom of assembly.[16]

Outside of this, the ICCPR provides for other protections, such as family rights and the right to freely enter into marriage,[17] the rights of children to legal protection, an identity and a nationality,[18] voting rights for eligible citizens and the right of citizens of a Member State to seek and hold office,[19] and the general rights of ethnic and cultural minority communities to preserve their identity.[20] Some provisions of the ICCPR may be derogated from in the event that there is a legitimate emergency declared in the Member State. However, even then there are some rights, such as the right to life, to a free trial, and anti-slavery protections, which cannot be derogated from even in an emergency.[21]

All of these rights sound laudable. However, the question then becomes their enforceability within the international community. The ICCPR's answer to this was to create the Human Rights Committee and vest it with powers.[22] Some of these powers are more administrative, such as overseeing the process in which all Member States submit reports chronicling their implementation of the ICCPR, commenting on them and issuing statements which clarify the scope of ICCPR terms, while others are essentially judicial.[23] The judicial component includes the ability of the Human Rights Committee to hear complaints from Member States regarding the alleged non-compliance of other Member States with the terms of the ICCPR[24] and complaints from individuals regarding the alleged non-compliance of a Member State with the terms of the ICCPR.[25] The individual complaint mechanism was created through a separate protocol to the ICCPR that was implemented at the same time as the ICCPR itself.[26]

Within the framework of the Protocol to the ICCPR creating the Human Rights Committee, a Secretariat is established to handle the implementation of the Covenant terms, including working with a designated Special Rapporteur for the intake and general administration of complaints brought to the Human Rights Committee.[27] Since the time it was founded, the Human Rights Committee has received nearly 3000 complaints regarding the conduct of 92 States in the international community, over half of which proceeded to the admissibility phase of determination at the very least.[28] Over time, the range of entities able to interact with the Human Rights Committee has expanded and now includes non-governmental organizations as well as State-based entities, international organizations, individuals and experts.[29] Additionally, the Human Rights Committee works closely with State-based, official human rights bodies and also works to foster the creation of these entities where they do not exist within a Member State's governance regime.[30]

In terms of membership, there are 18 members of the Human Rights Committee, who are elected by the conference of ICCPR Member States.[31] As with many such positions, two persons from the same Member State cannot sit on the Human Rights Committee at the same time and the selection of the members is meant to take geographical representation into account.[32] Each State sitting on the Hunan Rights Committee has one vote to exercise in determinations regarding complaints and any other matters that come before it.[33]

In order to bring an individual complaint there are certain justiciability thresholds which must be cleared first. Perhaps the most obvious threshold is that the ICCPR Member State must also have signed on to the protocol as well.[34] In addition, the complaining individual must have sought and exhausted all applicable judicial remedies at the domestic level,[35] the complaining individual must use his/her name and not bring an anonymous complaint,[36] the complaint cannot be an abuse of the complaint system function,[37] and the complainant cannot also be seeking or have sought review of the same issue by another international tribunal or institution.[38] If these requirements are met, the Human Rights Committee will inform the Member State of the complaint and seek a response from the Member State within six months.[39] Following this, the complaining individual has the opportunity to respond to the Member State's submission and then the Human Rights Committee issues a report which states its findings as to whether there has been a violation of the ICCPR.[40]

If there is a violation, the Human Rights Committee can issue a set of requirements and recommend that there be some type of monetary compensation given by the Member State, although none of these are binding on the State Party at the domestic level.[41] Despite this, the Human Rights Committee is a very popular venue for individual complaints, particularly because bringing this type of complaint will frequently generate information on what happened in a particular case – for example, where a person went after he was "disappeared" – and provides some recognition of what happened to the person involved and her family. This pattern will remain the same throughout all of the human rights bodies discussed in this chapter, with the exception of the European Court of Human Rights.

Committee on Economic, Social and Cultural Rights

The Committee on Economic, Social and Cultural Rights was created under the auspices of the ICE-SCR,[42] although it only recently became empowered to hear individual complaints against Member States.[43] This is due to the slow progress of Member States in agreeing to be subject to the jurisdiction of the Committee on these matters. The essential issue is the ability of the rights contained in the ICESCR to be decided on, since many of them are highly subjective – for example, the meaning of the "highest attainable" standard for healthcare, discussed below.[44]

As with all human rights bodies that seek to assure the implementation of treaty terms, it is important to understand the instrument's terms themselves. Many of the initial rights, such as self-determination and non-discrimination, are exactly the same as those contained in the ICCPR.[45] However, after these initial terms there is a distinct divergence between the two treaties.

The ICESCR moves on to provide for the right of people to work, and specifically for the right of people to "just and favorable" working conditions, for example fair wages, healthy working conditions, and the right to rest and leisure time.[46] In connection with working rights, the ICESCR provides for the right to form and participate in trade unions,[47] and the right to social security.[48] The ICESCR protects the rights and integrity of the family, including for new mothers who are working,[49] and the rights of all peoples to an adequate standard of living that allows them to provide the basics needed for survival, particularly as enshrined in the right to freedom from hunger.[50] Under the terms of the ICESCR, there is a right to "the enjoyment of the highest attainable standard of physical and mental health,"[51] the right to an education (although this encompasses a guarantee of primary-level education and then a tapered right afterward),[52] the right "to take part in cultural life,"[53] and the right to benefit from one's intellectual property.[54]

The Committee has the same administrative functions as the Human Rights Committee and, as noted, now has the ability to receive individual complaints. The Committee is selected in a similar way to the Human Rights Committee. There are, however, several differences in the justiciability requirements for individual complaints brought to the Committee. As with the Human Rights Committee, there is a requirement that the individual have exhausted all relevant domestic remedies, that the complaint falls within the scope of the ICESCR, that the complaint not be pending before or have been decided by another international tribunal, that the applicable Member State be bound to the protocol, and that the complaint not be anonymous.[55] For the purposes of the Committee's jurisdiction, however, there is a requirement that the complaint not be based loosely on facts that are not personally known – such as facts gleaned through the internet[56] – and that the disadvantage caused by the alleged harm be reasonably significant.[57]

The procedure followed by the Committee as it decides a complaint and the ability of the Committee to issue decisions, as well as their binding nature at the domestic level, are the same as used by the Human Rights Committee.[58] However, it is important to highlight that the Committee has the express ability to request that the complained-of Member State take actions to protect those who have complained from harm, including harm from State actors.[59] In this context, it should be noted that non-governmental organizations have been given a significant place as a source of information and policy guidance for the Committee.[60]

Committee on the Rights of the Child

The Convention on the Rights of the Child (CRC) came into force in 1990 and has since become one of the most ratified international instruments in international law. It seeks to reinforce the essential human rights guaranteed under previous international instruments for children and to ensure that their particular needs are accounted for in law and policy. At the same time, it promotes the role of children in society and their unique insights into matters that will impact them now and in the future.

As an essential matter, the CRC defines the very terms of childhood, setting it as those in the age range from birth to 18 years.[61] The basic rights guaranteed to children under the CRC include non-discrimination based on their status, beliefs, ethnicity, or other characteristics, as well as based on the status of their parents,[62] and the right to life.[63] The child is vested with the right to a name[64] – and to have that name registered by the appropriate State – and the right to a nationality.[65] An underlying theme of the CRC is the preservation of family and family connections for children unless doing so would be detrimental to their health or safety.[66] Within parameters that are safe, children are guaranteed the right to freedom of expression,[67] freedom of thought, conscience and religion,[68] and freedom of association.[69] As a general matter, the State and society as a whole is to protect children from violence and other danger that would cause harm or interfere with their status as children.[70] Children such as refugee children – either on their own or with their parents – are also to be afforded the rights contained in the CRC.[71] Those children with mental or physical disabilities are also given special protections under the CRC and are provided with recognition of rights in law. [72] Health as a general matter is protected for children, using the standard of enjoying the "highest attainable standard of health and facilities for treatment of illness and rehabilitation of health."[73] Additionally, the CRC enshrines the "right of every child to a standard of living adequate for the child's physical, mental, spiritual, moral and social development."[74] Further, the CRC vests children with the right to education at tapered stages ranging from primary school through university level.[75] This is complemented by a recognized right to leisure and play as essential parts of childhood.[76]

One of the most important aspects of the CRC is the creation and implementation of the "best interests of the child" standard, which is meant for use as a primary consideration by all entities making decisions involving the interests or general welfare of a child.[77] This is an enduring aspect of the CRC that has become extremely important in the meaningful application of the CRC by States Parties. The best interests of the child standard functions in tandem with another vital element of the CRC, the evolving capacities standard, which recognizes that a child's abilities and capacities change and grow over time, and that practices regarding the input of a child should change accordingly.[78]

Included in the terms of the CRC are provisions to establish the Committee on the Rights of the Child as the primary oversight body for the CRC's adoption by States Parties.[79] The Committee on the Rights of the Child is comprised of 18 members, each of whom is elected by a plenary of the CRC States Parties as a whole and serve for four-year terms.[80] The daily requirements of administration for the Committee on the Rights of the Child are attended to by staff members provided through the UN Secretariat who function in a secretariat-like capacity, and funding for the Committee is also provided by the UN.[81]

The Committee on the Rights of the Child receives and reviews reports on compliance and areas of concern from CRC States Parties and provides guidance to States Parties on the meanings of various aspects of the CRC.[82] States are required to provide reports and information to the UN at periodic intervals and have the ability to answer requests for information from various international organizations, largely those affiliated with the UN.[83] While an Optional Protocol creating a procedure for children or their representatives to communicate complaints regarding State Party behavior to the Committee on the Rights of the Child was adopted by the UN General Assembly in 2011, the majority of States have not ratified it and it has yet to begin issuing opinions.[84]

Committee Against Torture

The Committee Against Torture (CAT) oversees the implementation of the Convention Against Torture, under which Member States agree that they will take necessary measures to prevent the commission of acts of torture in their jurisdiction.[85] While the ICCPR contains a provision allowing for limited derogation from some of its provisions in times of national emergency, the CAT is equally explicit in stating that its conditions are non-derogable.[86]

Additional provisions of the CAT include non-refoulement,[87] criminalization requirements for acts of torture under the Member State's penal law,[88] that those allegedly responsible for them be promptly be apprehended and charged,[89] and that there be a system for assistance to those who are tortured.[90]

The CAT serves the standard administrative functions that most treaty-based human rights committees serve, such as reporting requirements from States Parties and commenting functions on important questions involving the Convention's terms and its application.[91] The CAT's functions are assisted through the availability of a staff provided by the UN Secretary General, which acts in the capacity of a secretariat, including essential roles such as collecting complaints (discussed below), collecting and disseminating reports and arranging meetings.[92] Additionally, the Committee has jurisdiction to hear qualifying individual complaints.[93]

Unlike the other committees, the CAT is somewhat smaller in membership, having only 10 members at any given time, each of which has one vote.[94] Given the gravity of the subject matter of torture, the Committee also has the ability to initiate its own investigation when it receives credible information that a Member State is engaging in such acts.[95]

In terms of complaints initiated by individuals, the Committee generally uses the same justiciability standards as do other committees, except that the Committee is authorized to hear complaints brought on behalf of the alleged victim of torture rather than solely by those who are the direct victims.[96] This may not seem overly important; however, when one considers that many victims of torture continue to be held in state custody, and thus are not in a position to complain themselves, the importance of this provision is clear.

Similarly, where it is proved that pursuing a case throughout the fullest extent of the domestic judiciary would be pointless, or even constitute a threat to the safety of the victim, the exhaustion requirement can be waived by the Committee.[97] Again, the point is to reflect the unique position that victims of torture often find themselves in. Once jurisdiction has been established, the implicated State Party has the opportunity to respond to the allegations as is the standard procedure in complaints proceedings, and the CAT may request further information from each party to the complaint before issuing a finding.[98]

In practical terms, more claims involving torture have been brought to the Human Rights Committee – which does have jurisdiction over them due to the essential terms of the ICCPR – than to the CAT. However, a good number of complaints have also been brought to the CAT and have yielded positive findings for the aggrieved individual.

Committee on the Elimination of All Forms of Discrimination Against Women

The Committee on the Elimination of All Forms of Discrimination Against Women oversees the implementation of the Convention on the Elimination of All Forms of Discrimination Against Women (CEDAW) and also hears individual complaints regarding Member State violations of CEDAW.

CEDAW sets out essential rights and guarantees for women around the world. As an overarching matter – and indeed as the treaty name suggests – CEDAW seeks to target discrimination against women in their personal and public lives.[99] Under CEDAW, Member States are to ensure that all aspects of their law and jurisprudence enshrine the concept of equality between men and women and also that these laws and pieces of jurisprudence target discrimination against women.[100] Included in these requirements is the need for Member States to attempt to change the social and cultural patterns within society that condone or perpetuate discrimination against women.[101]

In terms of specific rights, CEDAW guarantees the rights of women to vote,[102] to seek and hold public office,[103] to participate in public debate,[104] the right to hold a nationality regardless of the nationality of their husband,[105] the right to determine the nationality of their children,[106] the right to access education that is equal to that provided to men,[107] the right to access information on family planning and other health issues,[108] the right to equal employment access,[109] the right to equal pay,[110] the right to social security,[111] the right to safe working conditions,[112] freedom from discrimination based on marital status or maternity status,[113] the right to health care,[114] the right to financial independence, such as the ability to conduct banking without male approval,[115] the provision of equal rights and opportunities to women in rural conditions,[116] the right to the same legal status as men in all legal proceedings,[117] and the freedom to marry (or not) and equal rights as regards family decisions when married.[118]

As the issues facing women continue to evolve and emerge, so too do the methods of applying the terms of CEDAW to meeting these needs and providing assistance to women and society and a whole. For example, issues relating to the rights and treatment of migrant women have become increasingly important and, accordingly, studied by the CEDAW Committee in order to provide recommendations and guidance for the future.[119] Another key issue has been and continues to be the ways in which international law and individual States address gender-based violence in conflict and non-conflict settings. This has been the subject of much discussion and constant reappraisal by the CEDAW Committee in order to ensure that the best possible protections are afforded to women the world over.[120] These discussions function in tandem with discussions by the CEDAW Committee regarding the general post-conflict status of women.[121]

In the event there is an individual complaint regarding these rights, it may go to the CEDAW Committee provided that it meets the justiciability requirements.[122] In the context of the CEDAW Committee, the standard system of soliciting information and issuing a finding on behalf of the Committee applies and there is no appeal from its decision.[123]

Committee on the Elimination of Racial Discrimination

The Committee on the Elimination of Racial Discrimination is the oversight body for the International Convention on the Elimination of Racial Discrimination (CERD). CERD is one of the oldest human rights Conventions in the modern international human rights system, having been enacted in 1965 and entering into force in 1969.[124]

CERD at its core contains a wide-ranging statement on the part of Member States, condemning racial discrimination and undertaking to prevent all forms of racial discrimination in their jurisdiction.[125] In order to implement this, Member States agree to make the propagation of racist ideology punishable as a matter of law.[126] The statement sets out a list of rights which Member States agree should be enjoyed by all and not be impacted upon by racial discrimination.[127]

The Committee on the Elimination of Racial Discrimination is comprised of 18 members[128] and is tasked with administrative and judicial functions.[129] As with the Committee Against Torture, the Committee on the Elimination of Racial Discrimination is able to hear complaints from individuals or those speaking on their behalf.[130] In addition, given that racial discrimination often impacts an entire group or community rather than just one individual, the Committee on the Elimination of Racial Discrimination is authorized to hear complaints from groups as a whole.[131] For the purposes of evaluating complaints and for other activities such as evaluating reports from States Parties, the Committee on the Elimination of Racial Discrimination allows input from nongovernmental organizations, national human rights entities and similar sources of information to be received and considered.[132]

Committee on Migrant Workers

One of the newer international human rights treaties is the International Convention on the Protection of the Rights of All Migrant Workers and Members of Their Families (Migrant Workers Convention).[133] Although it has met the required number of States Parties to become effective, the Migrant Workers Convention has not been ratified by the majority of States in the international community, including the US and the majority of States in the EU.

The Migrant Workers Convention seeks to protect legal and illegal migrant workers and their families and recognizes that these groups are often vulnerable as a result of gaps in the law that allow them to be exploited.[134] The Migrant Workers Convention represents an attempt to balance the human rights considerations applicable to these workers and their families with the immigration policies of Member States and their sovereign rights to enact such policies.[135]

To operationalize the requirements of the Migrant Workers Convention there exists the Committee on the Protection of the Rights of All Migrant Workers and Members of Their Families (Committee on Migrant Workers), which functions in the same manner as the other human rights instrument-based committees.[136] Initially, provisions are made for 10 members of the Committee on Migrant Workers, with that number scheduled to increase to 14 after certain targets for ratifications of the Convention on Migrant Workers are achieved.[137] Given the subject matter under the jurisdiction of the Committee on Migrant Workers, it is intended that those who serve on the Committee represent a balance of geography and States that send and receive migrant workers.[138] Functional needs for the Committee on Migrant Workers are to be provided by the UN Secretary General in order to ensure that a quasi-secretariat body exists for the benefit of the Committee.[139]

The Committee on Migrant Workers is intended to review reports and communications from States Parties regarding compliance with the terms of the Convention on Migrant Worker and has the ability to establish necessary procedure for the reporting aspects of its functions.[140] Reflecting the subject matter of the Convention on Migrant Workers, it is intended that the International Labor Organization review the reports issued by the States Parties and the Committee on Migrant Workers and generally work with the Committee as appropriate to provide insights into topics of importance to migrant workers, their families, and the States from which and to which they travel.[141] The Committee on Migrant Workers has the ability to liaise with additional international organizations and other entities as appropriate for the completion of its mandate under the Convention on Migrant Workers.[142]

Additionally, the Convention on Migrant Workers creates a complaint system under the auspices of the Committee on Migrant Workers, provided as always that a State Party agrees to be under its jurisdiction.[143] This complaint system functions in the same manner as the other human rights complaints proceedings and results in non-appealable findings from the Committee.[144]

Committee on the Rights of Persons with Disabilities

Among the newest international human rights treaties is the Convention on the Rights of Persons with Disabilities (CRPD). The CRPD requires that Member States recognize the legal equality of those with disabilities and that they work to ensure that this equality is reflected in all facets of the Member State's laws and rules.[145] Special protections are established for women with disabilities and children with disabilities as they are regarded to be more likely to be vulnerable at law and within society.[146] The rights guaranteed in the CRPD include the right to life,[147] special protections for the people with disabilities during disasters and humanitarian emergencies,[148] equality before the law,[149] access to justice,[150] standard rights to personal integrity and freedom from cruel or inhuman punishment,[151] freedom from exploitation and violence,[152] freedom of movement,[153] the right to live independently and to be part of the community,[154] freedom of thought and expression,[155] the protection of privacy and the personal living space of people with disabilities,[156] the right to education and equality of education,[157] the right to health and rehabilitation,[158] the right to employment,[159] the right to an adequate standard of living,[160] the right to public participation,[161] and the right to participation in sports, culture and leisure.[162]

The CRPD also establishes the Committee on the Rights of Persons with Disabilities, the powers of which are supplemented through an Optional Protocol. General functions of a secretariat for the Committee on the Rights of Persons with Disabilities are carried out by a staff provided by the UN Secretary General.[163] Through the Optional Protocol, the Committee is granted the ability to hear individual complaints as well as receive and issue reports and engage in other activities on a par with the other human rights instrument bodies.[164]

The Committee on the Rights of Persons with Disabilities, which is composed of an initial 12 members and rises to 18 after certain membership benchmarks have been met, functions in the same way as the other human rights committees and has the ability to receive individual complaints or complaints from groups.[165] The procedure used by the Committee to evaluate the initial justiciability of the complaint and, if appropriate, the overall merits of the complaint, are the same as used by the other human rights committees.[166] In assessing complaints, reports or other aspects of its functions, the Committee on the Rights of Persons with Disabilities is empowered to liaise with international organizations or other appropriate entity to gain insights and expertise.[167]

UN High Commissioner for Refugees

In the years immediately following the end of World War II, the UN General Assembly created the UN High Commissioner for Refugees as an affiliated organization with the goal of assisting those who were displaced by the conflict.[168] At the time, those displaced were largely victims of the bombings, forced deportations and utter devastation caused by the war. Over time, however, those classified as refugees have expanded in scope as diverse and increasingly dire situations for human rights and basic survival of individuals and communities emerged throughout the world.[169] Concerns over refugees and displaced persons have resulted in several Conventions and international instruments that guarantee rights for refugees and those who are rendered stateless.[170] These are among the core laws that the UNHCR is charged with upholding and overseeing.

The UNHCR's name is in fact quite deceptive, as the organization works with many other vulnerable populations. For example, the UNHCR helps internally displaced persons – those who were forced to flee from one portion of a State to another rather than outside the State, as refugees are forced to do – as well as those who are seeking asylum in another State, those who were refugees but are now in the position where they are able to return home, and those who are, for whatever reason, rendered stateless, meaning that they are unable to claim any legal connection to a State.[171]

Regardless the conflict involved, the UNHCR is intended to provide necessary protections for those impacted as well as to work with States to ensure that their activities are commensurate with international law requirements and principles.[172] Perhaps most importantly, the UNHCR is instrumental in the determination of whether, as a matter of international law tenets that the majority of States have embraced, an individual should be classified as a refugee for the purpose of receiving protections.[173]

Under the terms of the UNHCR Statute, the organization is charged with generating international instruments that protect refugees and displaced persons, supporting efforts at national and international levels to provide protections to refugees and displaced persons, assisting in the repatriation or assimilation of affected persons, monitoring the activities and policies of state governments that impact on refugees and displaced persons, and coordinating work with other international organizations and non-governmental organizations, States and private entities.[174]

The High Commissioner is elected by the UN General Assembly and is responsible for appointing staff members and establishing the works of his office.[175] Funding and resources for the UNHCR are allocated by the UN, rendering it subject to the audit functions of the UN.[176] Although there is a designated High Commissioner, governance and oversight of the UNHCR as an entity is decided by an Executive Committee that is appointed by ECOSOC.[177] Additionally, there exists an Inspector General's Office to oversee the conduct of all aspects of the UNHCR's activities and the activities of those organizations and contractors working with the UNHCR.[178]

Beyond this high-level structure, the UNHCR works across all boundaries, from international to regional to national, to assist refugees in terms of laws and policies and also in terms of the functioning of refugee camps and other areas where refugees are located.[179]

The UNHCR works in both emergency and long-term situations.[180] It is an unfortunate reality that conflicts often drag on for years and, even when they are over, it can be years until a durable solution can be achieved. In the meantime, refugees must find a place to live and methods of survival for themselves and their families. Throughout these situations, the UNHCR works with refugees and those affected by conflict in order to ensure that they are afforded at least the basic protections of international law.[181]

Regional human rights systems

Inter-American Human Rights System

The Inter-American Human Rights system, which falls under the rubric of Organization of American States (OAS), is the oldest established regional human rights system in use today. Its origins can be traced to the 1948 American Declaration on Human Rights, a non-binding statement in which the members of the OAS agreed to the core principles of human rights law.[182] The Declaration was, however, simply a statement of beliefs and aspirations and there was no institutionalized system for the implementation of human rights protections until the 1969 American Convention on Human Rights.[183] Over time, the Inter-American Human Rights system has come to include not only the American Convention on Human Rights but also specialized Inter-American treaties on human rights issues.[184]

The American Convention contains protections for civil and political rights as well as economic, social and cultural rights.[185] In terms of civil and political rights, the American Convention guarantees the right to legal recognition for individuals,[186] the right to life,[187] the right to humane treatment, especially in the context of the criminal justice system,[188] freedom from slavery and conditions akin to slavery,[189] the right to personal liberty, including freedom from arbitrary arrest,[190] the protection of trial rights,[191] the right to personal privacy,[192] the freedom of religion,[193] thought and expression,[194] the right of assembly,[195] family and child rights,[196] the right of everyone to a name and a nationality,[197] the freedom of movement,[198] and the right to participate in government, including through voting and standing for office.[199] Further, the Inter-American Commission on Human Rights and the Inter-American Court of Human Rights have jurisdiction over the specialized human rights instruments that have been implemented in addition to the American Convention.

In terms of economic, social and cultural rights, the American Convention guarantees that the provisions of the OAS Charter will be respected, namely that "each State has the right to develop its cultural, political and economic life freely and naturally . . . [i]n this free development, the State shall respect the rights of the individual and the principles of universal morality."[200] While the American Convention does allow for derogations in times of national emergency, there are limitations on derogations for core human rights.[201]

The American Convention establishes a two-layer system for the protection and enforcement of these rights.[202] The first layer within this system is the Inter-American Commission on Human Rights, which is comprised of seven members elected by the OAS General Assembly.[203] The executive officers of the Inter-American Commission, namely the President, Vice-President and Second Vice-President, are elected by the overall membership of the Commission and are the public face of the Commission as well as the internal source of problem solving.[204] In order to implement the activities of the Inter-American Commission, the OAS Secretary General has the ability to appoint an Executive Secretary to preside over the Executive Secretariat and its staff.[205]

The Commission has several specific responsibilities under the American Convention: developing awareness of human rights within the region[206]; issuing legislative and constitutional recommendations to Member States to ensure that their legal systems offer the appropriate protections of human rights as set out in the American Convention;[207] preparing studies and reports on important human rights issues in the region or within a specific Member State;[208] receiving and requesting information on how the Member States are complying (or not) with their obligations under the American Convention;[209] providing information and advice to the OAS General Assembly on human rights issues when this is requested;[210] receiving, hearing and taking action on petitions regarding allegations of specific human rights violations by Member States;[211] and submitting annual human rights reports to the OAS General Assembly.[212] In addition, it has the ability to create specialized rapporteurships and working groups for specific topics as necessary.[213]

To carry out these functions and to provide advice and training to Member States, State courts and other judicial and prosecutorial entities within Member States, the Inter-American Commission – through the OAS Secretary General – has the ability to enter into direct agreements with these States.[214] Additionally, the OAS Secretary General has the ability to conclude agreements with other States, international organizations and entities on behalf of the Inter-American Human Rights Commission.[215]

Many of these functions are essentially administrative and have evolved into an extensive system of human rights-based information-gathering on the part of the Inter-American Commission. The Inter-American Commission has a quasi-judicial function in its ability to receive, hear and issue preliminary requirements for petitions from individuals or groups regarding alleged human rights violations.[216] Provided a petition is deemed judiciable, using the same general requirements as used by the international human rights committees, the implicated Member State will have the ability to respond, the petitioning individual will have the ability to add further information, and then the Inter-American Commission will issue its findings.[217] If it finds that there has been an action implicating the human rights protections guaranteed under the Inter-American system, the Inter-American Commission will issue recommendations for remedying the situation and ask that the petition be revisited within a set period of time (three months to a year, depending on the severity of the violations) to determine the level of Member State compliance.[218]

In the event of continued non-compliance by a Member State or where the issues involved in the petition are particularly grave or novel, the Inter-American Commission has the power to refer a petition to the Inter-American Court of Human Rights.[219]

The Inter-American Court is comprised of seven judges who are elected by the OAS General Assembly.[220] It is a separate entity within the Inter-American Human Rights system and is not required to act on the requests of the Inter-American Commission. As in other courts discussed throughout this book, judges on the Inter-American Court elect a President and Vice President from amongst themselves and these officers, in turn, oversee the functioning of the judiciary and answer questions of order that arise.[221] Where appropriate, a permanent commission of judges within the Inter-American Court can provide guidance of specific issues as well.[222] The functions exercised by a Registry in other court systems are exercised by a Secretary, Deputy Secretary and office of Secretariat in the Inter-American Court system.[223]

Once the Inter-American Court receives a petition from the Inter-American Commission and agrees to hear the case, it then opens a full judicial hearing into the matter, receiving arguments and evidence from all involved parties. It is important to note that the Inter-American Commission is a necessary party in each case at the Inter-American Court level; however, alleged victims of human rights abuses have the ability to bring in their own counsel or allow the Inter-American Commission to act on their behalf.[224] Where appropriate, the Inter-American Court is authorized to issue interim protective or other measures to prevent harms from occurring during the pendency of a trial.[225]

If there is a finding of culpability on the part of the Member State, the Inter-American Court can impose fines and require information to be provided (i.e. on the whereabouts of a disappeared person) or laws to be changed to prevent the wrong from happening in the future.[226] It can, and often does, also require non-pecuniary reparations be taken to commemorate the victim, such as erecting memorials to victims of disappearance, and can require the State to provide medical and other assistance to family members of the victim who were directly impacted by the violations (i.e. psychological counseling to those who survived a massacre).[227]

Since its inception, the Inter-American Court has heard over 330 cases involving some of the most egregious human rights violations. These violations have included massacres of villages, particularly those belonging to indigenous communities, torture, rape, extra-judicial killing, forced disappearances, forced deportations, the stealing of children from political dissidents, and the deprivation of poor children of nearly every human right provided for under the American Convention and subsequent Inter-American instruments of human rights protection. Although the Inter-American Court's decisions are not binding at the domestic level, they have shed a great deal of light on these practices and have empowered groups and new governments to address these issues.

European Court of Human Rights

The European Court of Human Rights is a product of the European Convention on Human Rights, which binds European Union Member States. The initial iteration of the European Convention was adopted in 1950 and the rights that fall under it have been expanded several times through the years via the use of protocols.[228]

The 1950 European Convention, which predated the European Union as an organization, set out the basic rights and freedoms guaranteed by the Member States, including the right to life,[229] the protection of individuals from torture,[230] the protection of individuals from slavery,[231] the right to personal liberty and personal security,[232] standard trial rights,[233] protection of privacy and family life,[234] freedom of thought, religion and conscience,[235] freedom of expression and assembly,[236] the right to marry or not as one sees fit,[237] and the right to a remedy from the State in the event that one's rights are violated.[238] The European Convention also allows for the derogation of certain rights in times of national emergency, although the core rights, such as the right to life, cannot be derogated even in these situations.[239]

The 1952 Protocol created protections of private property rights,[240] the right to an education,[241] and the right to free elections.[242] Protocol 4, enacted in 1953, provided for the freedom of movement,[243] the prohibition of imprisonment for debt,[244] the prohibition of Member States expelling their own nationals,[245] and the prohibition of collective expulsion of aliens by Member States.[246] Protocol 6, enacted in 1983, specifically relates to the prohibition of the death penalty in the territories of the Member States.[247] Protocol 7 combines several topics, providing additional safeguards to aliens who are in the process of being expelled from a Member State,[248] the right to criminal case appeals,[249] protection from double jeopardy,[250] and spousal equality as a matter of law.[251] The overall protection of individuals from discrimination was added to the European Convention through Protocol 12 in 2000.[252]

The 1950 European Convention also establishes the European Court of Human Rights.[253] Unlike other human rights committees and courts that set a certain number of members, the European Convention requires that the number of members be equal to the number of Member States.[254] The Parliamentary Assembly for the Convention ultimately elects the judges, who must possess moral character and be eligible for service on the highest of their home State courts.[255] The European Court judges are responsible for the election of the President and Vice President of the Court from among their ranks.[256]

The functions of the European Court at the operational level are carried out by the Registry, which is headed by a designated Registrar and consists of a number of staff members who facilitate the different stages of claims that exist in the Court's jurisdiction.[257]

Claims may be brought to the European Court either by Member States or by individuals who fulfill the justiciability requirements.[258] In certain instances where there is a tangible threat involved, it is possible for the European Court to issue interim measures and protections.[259] The European Court also has the ability to issue advisory opinions where it is requested to do so by a Member State.[260] A new tool available to the European Court is the Pilot-Judgment Procedure, through which the Court renders a single decision for a single case that is emblematic of a number of similar cases stemming from the same underlying problem and attempts to use that decision as a tool to craft a solution to the problem as a whole.[261] This is still considered to be in the embryonic stage but offers the ability to clear Court backlog and speed up the access to justice time necessary.

From the outset, the European Court of Human Rights was intended to function as an entity that provided oversight to States. However, this was before the formation of the European Union as an organization that could, arguably, act in ways that violate the human rights of those under its jurisdiction. After many years of discussion and debate, the European Union has acceded to European Convention on Human Rights and, consequently, to the jurisdiction of the European Court of Human Rights, allowing its activities to be judged based on human rights standards.[262] This is rather unusual in the realm of international organizations, although it is more logical in the realm of the EU given the relationship between the EU, its Member States and their citizens.

In the discussion on international criminal courts it was noted that there are often different chambers within such courts and that these chambers hear various aspects of the proceedings pending before the court as a whole. The same structure is utilized in the European Court, where there is the lower ranking Plenary Chamber – typically consisting of one judge – and the Grand Chamber, where the very serious cases are heard and decided.[263] It is possible to analogize this structure to the two-layer structure used by the Inter-American Human Rights system in that there is a first layer that serves as a vetting layer for the second layer. Due to the supranational structure of the EU and its affiliated organs, decisions issued by the European Court are binding at the domestic level for Member States, marking a key difference between the European Court and the rest of the human rights bodies discussed in this chapter.[264]

At the time it was created, the European Court's crafters could not have envisioned the role it would have in the organizational behemoth that is the European Union. The issue areas it was intended to address were certainly numerous, however the population and territory to which they would be applied were circumscribed and the willingness of the covered population to resort to the European Court could not have been imagined at its current levels. As time and history have shown, the European Court has become a preeminent international juridical body, let alone human rights body, and is now facing a pressing overload of cases. Even with expansions to chambers and judges' ranks, the European Court still faces the unfortunate reality that it cannot meet the number of cases brought before it in a timely manner that promotes justice and efficiency.

This is not a new issue, and indeed has been plaguing the European Court for over a decade.[265] A number of suggestions for handling this situation have been offered, ranging from additional chambers to alternate dispute resolution to tightening jurisdictional requirements.[266] To address these suggestions, the European Court established the "Interlaken Process," named after the Interlaken Declaration through which it began, to evaluate proposals and determine how to implement them while balancing the rights of individuals and the duties of Member States.[267] In the past several years, there have been efforts to impose more stringent jurisdictional requirements for cases in order to reduce the workload and these have had some impacts in reducing the quantity of new cases at the European Court, although this has not been a sustained effect.[268]

African Court of Human and Peoples' Rights

The African Court of Human and Peoples' Rights is the newest regional human rights court and has jurisdiction over alleged violations of the African Charter on Human and Peoples' Rights. It should be highlighted here that the designation of "peoples'" rights as well as human rights indicates that the protections contained in the Charter – and under the jurisdiction of the Court – are intended to apply to indigenous and tribal groups as well as individuals *per se*.

The African Charter requires Member States to take all measures necessary to implement its terms within the scope of their domestic laws.[269] The specific rights and protections in the African Convention include freedom from discrimination,[270] the right to life,[271] the right to legal equality,[272] the right to personal dignity,[273] freedom from slavery,[274] the right to personal liberty and personal security,[275] standard trial rights,[276] freedom of religion and conscience,[277] the right to information,[278] freedom of expression,[279] freedom of assembly,[280] freedom of movement and protection from mass expulsion from a Member State,[281] the right to participate in government,[282] the right to property,[283] the right to work and safe working conditions,[284] the right to the highest attainable standard of health,[285] the right to education,[286] family rights and protections,[287] and the right to self-determination and existence for peoples.[288] In addition, the African Charter sets out duties of those who are covered by its protections, namely to respect and protect the family, to serve and protect their community, to work and pay taxes, to be tolerant and supportive of a variety of cultures, and to support African unity.[289]

The African Charter establishes the African Commission on Human and Peoples' Rights, an 11-member organization that is tasked with overseeing the implementation of the Convention.[290] The African Commission has several responsibilities, key among them: undertaking studies and writing reports on key issues facing the Member States and African continent;[291] education and outreach on these issues to all levels of constituencies, communities and groups;[292] creating model legislation for Member States to use in implementing human rights responsibilities;[293] working with other AU and international organizations;[294] and interpreting the meaning of the Convention where necessary.[295]

The African Commission also has the ability to evaluate complaints from Member States against each other and may also receive complaints from other entities, such as individuals and groups, regarding Member State conduct.[296] In these instances, the African Commission has the ability to use a similar fact-finding procedure and to issue findings regarding the conduct of Member States.[297]

The African Court was established through a subsequent protocol to the African Charter.[298] The Court is composed of 11 judges and can hear all forms of issues that relate to the Charter, including those that have been brought before the Commission.[299] Unlike the Inter-American Court, there are many other venues to African Court jurisdiction that do not require clearance by the African Commission.[300]

The African Court conducts public hearings on the claims before it[301] and issues opinions reflecting whether there has been a violation of the Charter and, if so, what the appropriate penalties might be.[302] In addition, the African Court has jurisdiction to issue advisory opinions upon specific request, provide good offices and dispute settlement mechanisms in order to settle disputes amicably, and to re-interpret its judgments in the event this is deemed appropriate.[303]

Within the African Court structure the sitting judges elect a President and Vice-President for the Court from among themselves.[304] As in other systems, the President and Vice-President of the African Court act as the chief decision-makers for the Court's operations, including questions of procedure.[305] The African Court uses the Registry for its administration entity, with the Registrar elected by the Court and the officers and staff members of the Registry appointed to provide essential services and expertise.[306]

Conclusions

At its most fundamental level, human rights laws and practices represent some of the most intimate forms of relationship between the individual and the State. Through the emergence and functions of human rights-focused international organizations, this relationship has now made space for organizations to share in this privileged space between State and individual.

In this position, international organizations are able to function as sources of oversight of State practices regarding their human rights obligations and to generate meaningful dialogue as well as case law or factual findings. This is furthered through the flexibility that is demonstrated in allowing international organizations to hear complaints regarding human rights system violations by States while at the same time being sites of discussion regarding future steps for the development of human rights norms at the international and domestic levels. In addition, international organizations have the ability to act as intermediaries in cases and issues where neither side wants to lose face by being seen as giving in.

Notes

1 International Covenant on Civil and Political Rights (1966); International Covenant on Economic, Social and Cultural Rights (1966).

2 International Covenant on Civil and Political Rights, *supra* note 1 at art. 1(1).

3 *Id.* at art 1(2).

4 *Id.* at arts 2, 3.

5 *Id.* at art 6. It should be noted, however, that this protection specifically does not require Member States to abolish the death penalty in order to be in compliance, although it does require that Member States using the death penalty do so only for the most egregious crimes and that the imposition of the death penalty not be done arbitrarily. *See id.* However, a protocol to the ICCPR does seek to implement a ban on the death penalty outright. *See* United Nations General Assembly, Second Optional Protocol to the International Covenant on Civil and Political Rights, aiming at the abolition of the death penalty, GA Res. 44/128 (1989). Further, in this context it is important to understand that the right to life does not have an anti-abortion connotation as in American jurisprudence. Instead, the right to life means the right of an individual to be free from state killing. *Id.*

6 International Covenant on Civil and Political Rights, *supra* note 1 at art 7.

7 *Id.* at art 8.

8 *Id.* at art 9(1).

9 *Id.* at arts 9–11, 14, 15.

10 *Id.* at art 12.

11 *Id.* at art 13.

12 *Id.* at art 17.

13 *Id.* at art 18.

14 *Id.* at art 19(1).

15 *Id.* at art 19(2).

16 *Id.* at art 21.

17 *Id.* at art 23.

18 *Id.* at art 24.

19 *Id.* at art 25.

20 *Id.* at art 27.

21 *Id.* at art 4.

22 *Id.* at pt IV.

23 *See generally id.* at pt IV.

24 *Id.* at art 41. It should be noted that no Member State has ever brought a complaint against another Member State under any of the human rights bodies discussed in the international human rights bodies section of this chapter.

25 *See* Optional Protocol to the International Covenant on Civil and Political Rights (1966).

26 *See id.*

27 *See* Human Rights Committee, The mandate of the Special Rapporteur on New Communications and Interim Measures, CCPR/C/110/3 (2014); Rules of Procedure of the Human Rights Committee, CCPR/C/3/Rev.8 (2005) art V; Rules of Procedure of the Human Rights Committee, CCPR/C/Rev.9 (2011) art V; Rules of Procedure of the Human Rights Committee, CCPR/C/Rev.10 (2012) art V.

28 *See* Human Rights Committee, Consideration by the Human Rights Committee at its 114th, 115th, and 116th sessions of communications received under the Optional Protocol to the International Covenant on Civil and Political Rights, CCPR/C/116/3 (2016) 3.

29 *See* Human Rights Committee, The relationship of the Human Rights Committee with non-governmental organizations, CCPR/C/104/3 (2012).

30 *See* Human Rights Committee, Paper on the relationship between of the Human Rights Committee with national human rights institutions, CCPR/C/106/3 (2012).

31 *Id.* at arts 28–29.

32 *Id.* at art 31.

33 Rules of Procedure of the Human Rights Committee (2005), *supra* note 27 at art 50; Rules of Procedure of the Human Rights Committee (2011), *supra* note 27 at ch X; Rules of Procedure of the Human Rights Committee (2012), *supra* note 27 at ch X.

34 Optional Protocol to the International Covenant on Civil and Political Rights, *supra* note 25 at art 1.

35 *Id.* at art 2.

36 *Id.* at art 3.

37 *Id.*

38 *Id.* at art 5.

39 *Id.* at art 4.
40 *Id.* at art 5.
41 *Id.*
42 *See* International Covenant on Economic, Social and Cultural Rights, *supra* note 1.
43 *See* Committee on Economic, Social and Cultural Rights, Provisional rules of procedure under the Optional Protocol to the International Covenant on Economic, Social and Cultural Rights, E/C.12/49/3 (2012).
44 *See* Committee on Economic, Social and Cultural Rights, An Evaluation of the Obligation to Take Steps to the "Maximum of Available Resources" Under an Optional Protocol to the Covenant, E/C.12/2007/1 (2007); Committee on Economic, Social and Cultural Rights, Statement on the obligations of States parties regarding the corporate sector and economic, social and cultural rights, E/C.12/2011/1 (2011); Committee on Economic, Social and Cultural Rights, Statement on the importance and relevance of the right to development, E/C.12/2011/2 (2011); Committee on Economic, Social and Cultural Rights, Statement in the context of the Rio +20 Conference on "the green economy in the context of sustainable development and poverty eradication," E/C.12/2012/1 (2012); Committee on Economic, Social and Cultural Rights, Social protection floors: an essential element of the right to social security and of the sustainable development goals, E/C.12/2015/1 (2015); Committee on Economic, Social and Cultural Rights, Duties of States towards refugees and migrants under the International Covenant on Economic, Social and Cultural Rights, E/C.12/2017/1 (2017).
45 *See* International Covenant on Economic, Social and Cultural Rights, *supra* note 1 at arts 1–5.
46 *Id.* at arts 6–7.
47 *Id.* at art 8.
48 *Id.* at art 9.
49 *Id.* at art 10.
50 *Id.* at art 11.
51 *Id.* at art 12.
52 *Id.* at art 13.
53 *Id.* at art 14(1)(a).
54 *Id.* at art 14(1)(c).
55 Optional Protocol to the International Convention on Economic, Social and Cultural Rights (2008) art 3.
56 *Id.* at art 3(e).
57 *Id.* at art 4.
58 *See generally id.*
59 *Id.* at art. 13.
60 *See* Committee on Economic, Social and Cultural Rights, Substantive issues arising in the implementation of the International Covenant on Economic, Social and Cultural Rights, E/C.12/2000/6 (2000).
61 Convention on the Rights of the Child (1989) art 1. Note that, in some circumstances, it is possible for a State's laws to deviate from this standard. *Id.*
62 *Id.* at art 2.
63 *Id.* at art 6.
64 *Id.* at art 7.
65 *Id.* at art 8.
66 *Id.* at arts 9, 10.
67 *Id.* at art 13.
68 *Id.* at art 14.
69 *Id.* at art 15.
70 *Id.* at art 19.
71 *Id.* at art 22.
72 *Id.* at art 23.
73 *Id.* at art 24.
74 *Id.* at art 27.
75 *Id.* at arts 28, 29.
76 *Id.* at art 31.
77 *Id.* at arts 3(1), 21.
78 *Id.* at art 5.
79 *Id.* at art 43.
80 *Id.*; Committee on the Rights of the Child, Rules of Procedure, CRC/C/Rev.4 (2015) Rules 11, 12.
81 Convention on the Rights of the Child, *supra* note 61 at arts 43(11), 43(12); Committee on the Rights of the Child, Rules of Procedure, *supra* note 80 at Rule 29.
82 Convention on the Rights of the Child, *supra* note 61 at art 44. Importantly, the reporting process is now able to include input from children in order to more accurately reflect their perspectives. *See* Committee on the Rights of the Child, Working methods for the participation of children in the reporting process of the Committee on the Rights of the Child, CRC/C/66/2 (2014).
83 Convention on the Rights of the Child, *supra* note 61 at arts 44, 45.
84 *See* United Nations General Assembly, Optional Protocol to the Convention on the Rights of the Child on a communications procedure, A/RES/66/138 (2012); Committee on the Rights of the Child, Rules of procedure

under the Optional Protocol to the Convention on the Rights of the Child on a communications procedure, CRC/C/62/3 (2013).

85 *See* Convention Against Torture (1985) art 2.

86 Id. art 2(2).

87 Id. at art 3.

88 Id. at art 4.

89 Id. at arts 5–8.

90 Id. at art 14.

91 Committee Against Torture, Overview of Working Methods (2015) arts II, III.

92 Committee Against Torture, Rules of Procedure, CAT/C/3/Rev.4 (2002) ch V; Committee Against Torture, Rules of Procedure, CAT/C/3/Rev.5 (2011) ch V.

93 *See* Committee Against Torture, Rules of Procedure (2011), *supra* note 92 at pt II.

94 Committee Against Torture, *supra* note 85 at art 17; Committee Against Torture, Rules of Procedure (2002), *supra* note 92 at art 49; Committee Against Torture, Rules of Procedure (2011), *supra* note 92 at Rule 11.

95 Committee Against Torture, *supra* note 85 at art 20.

96 Id. at art 22.

97 Id.

98 Committee Against Torture, Rules of Procedure (2002), *supra* note 92 at ch XVII.

99 *See generally* Convention on the Elimination of All Forms of Discrimination Against Women (1979).

100 Id. at arts 2–6.

101 Id. at art 5.

102 Id. at art 7.

103 Id.

104 Id.

105 Id. at art 8.

106 Id.

107 Id. at art 10.

108 Id.

109 Id. at art 11.

110 Id.

111 Id.

112 Id.

113 Id.

114 Id. at art 12.

115 Id. at art 13.

116 Id. at art 14.

117 Id. at art 15.

118 Id. at art 16.

119 *See* Committee on the Elimination of All Forms of Discrimination Against Women, General recommendation No. 26 on women migrant rights, CEDAW/C/2009/WP.1/R (2009).

120 *See* Committee on the Elimination of All Forms of Discrimination Against Women, General recommendation No. 35 on gender-based violence against women, updating general recommendation No. 19, CEDAW/C/2009/GC/35 (2017).

121 *See* Committee on the Elimination of All Forms of Discrimination Against Women, General recommendation No. 30 on women in conflict prevention, conflict and post-conflict situations, CEDAW/C/2009/GC/30 (2013).

122 Optional Protocol to the Convention on the Elimination of All Forms of Discrimination Against Women (1999) (establishing the CEDAW complaints system).

123 Id.

124 Convention on the Elimination of Racial Discrimination (1969).

125 Id. at arts 2–3.

126 Id. at art 4.

127 Id. at art 5.

128 Id. at art 8.

129 *See generally* id. at pt. II.

130 Id. at art 14.

131 Id.

132 *See* Committee on the Elimination of Racial Discrimination, Working Methods (2015).

133 International Convention on the Protection of the Rights of All Migrant Workers and Members of Their Families (2016).

134 *See* id.; Office of the United Nations High Commissioner for Human Rights, The International Convention on Migrant Workers and its Committee, Fact Sheet No. 24 Rev. 1 (2005).

135 International Convention on the Protection of the Rights of All Migrant Workers and Members of Their Families (2016); International Convention on Migrant Workers and its Committee, Fact Sheet No. 24 Rev. 1, *supra* note 134.

136 International Convention on the Protection of the Rights of All Migrant Workers and Members of Their Families, *supra* note 133 at art 72.

137 *Id.* at art 72(1)(b).

138 *Id.* at art 72(2)(a).

139 *Id.* at art 72(7).

140 *Id.* at art 74.

141 *Id.* at art 74(2).

142 *Id.* at art 74; Committee on the Protection of the Rights of All Migrant Workers and Members of Their Families, Statement by the Committee on the Protection of the Rights of All Migrant Workers and Members of Their Families on its relationship with civil society organizations, CMW/C/21/2 (2014).

143 International Convention on the Protection of the Rights of All Migrant Workers and Members of Their Families, *supra* note 133 at arts 76, 77.

144 *Id.*

145 Convention on the Rights of Persons with Disabilities (2006) arts 4–5, 9.

146 *Id.* at arts 6–7.

147 *Id.* at art 10.

148 *Id.* at art 11.

149 *Id.* at art 12.

150 *Id.* at art 13.

151 *Id.* at arts 14–15.

152 *Id.* at art 16.

153 *Id.* at art 18.

154 *Id.* at art 19.

155 *Id.* at art 21.

156 *Id.* at arts 22–23.

157 *Id.* at art 24.

158 *Id.* at arts 25–26.

159 *Id.* at art 27.

160 *Id.* at art 28.

161 *Id.* at art 29.

162 *Id.* at art 30.

163 *Id.* at art 34; Committee on the Rights of Persons with Disabilities, Working methods of the Committee on the Rights of Persons with Disabilities, CRPD/C/5/4 (2011) pt I; Committee on the Rights of Persons with Disabilities, Rules of Procedure, CRPD/C/1/Rev.1 (2016) Rule 23.

164 Convention on the Rights of Persons with Disabilities, *supra* note 145 at art 35; Optional Protocol to the Convention on the Rights of Persons with Disabilities (2008); Working methods of the Committee on the Rights of Persons with Disabilities (2011), *supra* note 163 at pts I, IV.

165 Convention on the Rights of Persons with Disabilities, *supra* note 145 at arts 14, 34; Optional Protocol to the Convention on the Rights of Persons with Disabilities, *supra* note 164; Working methods of the Committee on the Rights of Persons with Disabilities (2011), *supra* note 163 at pt IV.

166 *See* Convention on the Rights of Persons with Disabilities, *supra* note 145; Optional Protocol to the Convention on the Rights of Persons with Disabilities, *supra* note 164; Working methods of the Committee on the Rights of Persons with Disabilities (2011), *supra* note 163 at pt IV.

167 Convention on the Rights of Persons with Disabilities, *supra* note 145 at art 38; Optional Protocol to the Convention on the Rights of Persons with Disabilities, *supra* note 164; Working methods of the Committee on the Rights of Persons with Disabilities (2011), *supra* note 163 at pts II, IV; Committee on the Rights of Persons with Disabilities, Rules of Procedure (2016), *supra* note 163 at Rules 30, 49–53.

168 *See* Statute of the Office of the United Nations High Commissioner for Refugees (1950) Introductory Note; About Us, UNHCR, http://www.unhcr.org/pages/49c3646c2.html, last accessed 14 January 2018.

169 *See* Statute of the Office of the United Nations High Commissioner for Refugees, *supra* note 168 at Introductory Note; UNHCR, http://www.unhcr.org/cgi-bin/texis/vtx/home, last accessed 14 January 2018.

170 *See* Convention Relating to the Status of Refugees (1951); Protocol Relating to the Status of Refugees (1967); Convention relating to the Status of Stateless Persons (1954); Convention on the Reduction of Statelessness (1961).

171 *See* Who We Help, UNHCR, http://www.unhcr.org/pages/49c3646c11c.html, last accessed 14 January 2018.

172 Statute of the Office of the United Nations High Commissioner for Refugees, *supra* note 168 at art 1 ("The United Nations High Commissioner for Refugees, acting under the authority of the General Assembly, shall assume the function of providing international protection, under the auspices of the United Nations, to refugees who fall within the scope of the present Statute and of seeking permanent solutions for the problem of refugees by assisting Governments and, subject to the approval of the Governments concerned, private organizations to facilitate the voluntary repatriation of such refugees, or their assimilation within new national communities.").

173 *See* UNHCR, Handbook and Guidelines on Procedures and Criteria for Determining Refugee Status under the 1951 Convention and the 1967 Protocol Relating to the Status of Refugees (2011); Executive Committee of the High Commissioner's Programme, Refugee Status Determination, EC/67/SC/CRP.12 (2016).

174 Statute of the Office of the United Nations High Commissioner for Refugees, *supra* note 168 at art 8.

175 Id. at art 13.

176 Id. at arts 20, 22.

177 Id.; United Nations Economic and Social Council, Establishment of the Executive Committee of the Programme of the United Nations High Commissioner for Refugees, E/RES/642 (XXV) (1958).

178 See UNHCR, Inspector General's Office, http://www.unhcr.org/inspector-generals-office.html, last accessed 14 January 2018.

179 *See* Governance and Organization, UNHCR, http://www.unhcr.org/en-us/governance.html, last accessed 14 January 2018.

180 *See* What We Do, UNHCR, http://www.unhcr.org/pages/49c3646cbf.html, last accessed 14 January 2018.

181 Id.

182 *See* American Declaration on Human Rights (1948).

183 Id.; Conferencia Especializada Interamericana sobre Derechos Humanos, Actas y Documentos (1969).

184 *See* Inter-American Convention to Prevent and Punish Torture (1987); Protocol to the American Convention on Human Rights to Abolish the Death Penalty (1991); Inter-American Convention on the Prevention, Punishment and Eradication of Violence Against Women (1995); Inter-American Convention on Forced Disappearances of Persons (1996); Inter-American Convention on the Elimination of All Forms of Discrimination against Persons with Disabilities (2001); Inter-American Democratic Charter (2001).

185 *See generally* Inter-American Convention to Prevent and Punish Torture, *supra* note 184; Protocol to the American Convention on Human Rights to Abolish the Death Penalty, *supra* note 184; Inter-American Convention on the Prevention, Punishment and Eradication of Violence Against Women, *supra* note 184; Inter-American Convention on Forced Disappearances of Persons, *supra* note 184; Inter-American Convention on the Elimination of All Forms of Discrimination against Persons with Disabilities, *supra* note 184; Inter-American Democratic Charter, *supra* note 184.

186 American Declaration on Human Rights, *supra* note 182 at art 3.

187 Id. at art 4.

188 Id. at art 5.

189 Id. at art 6.

190 Id. at art 7.

191 Id. at art 8.

192 Id. at art 11.

193 Id. at art 12.

194 Id. at art 13.

195 Id. at art 15.

196 Id. at arts 17, 19.

197 Id. at arts 18, 20.

198 Id. at art 22.

199 Id. at art 23.

200 Charter of the Organization of American States (1948) art 17.

201 Id. at ch. IV.

202 American Convention on Human Rights (1969) chs VII, VIII.

203 Id. at arts 34–36; Rules of Procedure of the Inter-American Commission on Human Rights (2013) art 1.

204 Rules of Procedure of the Inter-American Commission on Human Rights, *supra* note 203 at arts 6, 10.

205 Id. at art 11.

206 American Convention on Human Rights, *supra* note 202 at art 41.

207 Id. at art 41.

208 Id.; *see, e.g.*, Inter-American Commission on Human Rights, Access to Information, Violence against Women, and the Administration of Justice in the Americas (2015); Inter-American Commission on Human Rights, Criminalization of Human Rights Defenders (2015); Inter-American Commission on Human Rights, Situation of Human Rights in the Dominican Republic (2015); Inter-American Commission on Human Rights, Indigenous Peoples Communities of African Descent Extractive Industries (2015); Inter-American Commission on Human Rights, Situation of Human Rights in Guatemala (2016); Inter-American Commission on Human Right, Human Mobility: Inter-American Standards (2015); Inter-American Commission on Human Rights, Missing and Murdered Indigenous Women and Girls in British Colombia, Canada (2014).

209 American Convention on Human Rights, *supra* note 202 at art 41; *see, e.g.*, Inter-American Commission on Human Rights, Annual Report 2014 (2015) ch IV (discussing the specific human rights practices in Venezuela and Cuba); Inter-American Commission on Human Rights, Annual Report 2015 (2016) ch IV (discussing the specific human rights practices in Venezuela and Cuba); Inter-American Commission on Human Rights, Annual Report 2016 (2017) ch V (discussing the specific human rights practices in Cuba, Honduras and Guatemala).

210 American Convention on Human Rights, *supra* note 202 at art 41; *see, e.g.*, Inter-American Commission on Human Rights, Annual Report 2014, *supra* note 209 at v II (containing the Annual Report of the Office of the Special Rapporteur for Freedom of Expression); Inter-American Commission on Human Rights, Annual Report 2015, *supra* note 209 at v II (containing the Annual Report of the Office of the Special Rapporteur for Freedom of Expression); Inter-American Commission on Human Rights, Annual Report 2016, *supra* note 209 at v II (containing the Annual Report of the Office of the Special Rapporteur for Freedom of Expression).

211 American Convention on Human Rights, *supra* note 202 at art 41.

212 *Id.* at art 41; *see, e.g.*, Inter-American Commission on Human Rights, Annual Report 2014, *supra* note 209.

213 Rules of Procedure of the Inter-American Commission on Human Rights (2013) art 15.

214 *See, e.g.*, Acuerdo de Cooperacion entre la Corte Suprema de Justicia de la Republica del Paraguay y la Secretaria General de la Organizacion de los Estados Americanos por medio de la Secretaria Ejecutiva de la Comision Interamericana de Derechos Humanos (2013); Acuerdo de Cooperacion General entre la Secretaria General de la Organizacion de los Estados Americanos y la Comision de Derechos Humanos del Distrito Federal de los Estados Unidos Mexicanos (2012).

215 *See* Memorandum of Understanding between the General Secretariat of the Organization of American States through the Inter-American Commission on Human Rights and the Danish Institute for Human Rights (2015).

216 *See* Inter-American Commission on Human Rights, Petition and Case System (2010); Inter-American Commission on Human Rights, Strategic Plan 2011–2015: 50 years Defending Human Rights: Results and Challenges (2015).

217 American Convention on Human Rights, *supra* note 202 at art 50.

218 *Id.* at art 50.

219 *Id.* at art 51; Statute of the Inter-American Court of Human Rights (1979).

220 American Convention on Human Rights, *supra* note 202 at arts 52–54; Statute of the Inter-American Court of Human Rights (1979) art 4

221 Rules of Procedure of the Inter-American Court of Human Rights (2009) arts 4, 5; Statute of the Inter-American Court of Human Rights, *supra* note 21 at arts 12, 13.

222 Rules of Procedure of the Inter-American Court of Human Rights, *supra* note 221 at art 6.

223 *Id.* at ch II; Statute of the Inter-American Court of Human Rights, *supra* note 219 at art 14.

224 Rules of Procedure of the Inter-American Court of Human Rights, *supra* note 221.

225 *Id.* at art 27.

226 American Convention on Human Rights, *supra* note 202 at art 63.

227 *Id.* at art 63.

228 Convention for the Protection of Human Rights and Fundamental Freedoms and Protocol (1950); *See* The Right Honourable the Lord Woolf, Review of the Working Methods of the European Court of Human Rights (2005) Introduction. As has been highlighted, the European Court of Human Rights was conceived of in order to prevent the recurrence of such grave human rights violations as were perpetrated during World War II and not for a formally unified European structure. *Id. See also* European Court of Human Rights, Annual Report 2001 (2002) 8; European Court of Human Rights, Annual Report 2005 (2005) 8.

229 European Convention, *supra* note 228 at art 2.

230 *Id.* at art 3.

231 *Id.* at art 4.

232 *Id.* at art 5.

233 *Id.* at arts 6–7.

234 *Id.* at art 8.

235 *Id.* at art 9.

236 *Id.* at arts 10–11.

237 *Id.* at art 12.

238 *Id.* at art 13.

239 *Id.* at art 15.

240 1953 Protocol to the Convention for the Protection of Human Rights and Fundamental Freedoms art 1.

241 *Id.* at art 2.

242 *Id.* at art 3.

243 *Id.* Protocol 4 to the Convention for the Protection of Human Rights and Fundamental Freedoms (1953) art 2.

244 *Id.* at art 1.

245 *Id.* at art 3.

246 *Id.* at art 4.

247 *See* generally Protocol 6 to the Convention for the Protection of Human Rights and Fundamental Freedoms (1983).

248 Protocol 7 to the Convention for the Protection of Human Rights and Fundamental Freedoms (1983) art 1.

249 *Id.* at art 2.

250 *Id.* at art 4.

251 Protocol 7 to the Convention for the Protection of Human Rights and Fundamental Freedoms, *supra* note 248 at art 5.

252 *See* generally Protocol 12 to the Convention for the Protection of Human Rights and Fundamental Freedoms (2000).

253 *See* European Convention, *supra* note 228 at sect II.

254 Id. at art 20.

255 Id. at arts 21–22.

256 Id. at art 25; European Court of Human Rights, Rules of the Court (2016) ch II.

257 *See* European Convention, *supra* note 228 at art 24; European Court of Human Rights, Rules of the Court, *supra* note 256 at ch III.

258 European Convention, *supra* note 228 at arts 33–36.

259 European Court of Human Rights, Rules of the Court: Practice Directions – Request for interim measures (2016).

260 *See* Protocol No. 16 to the Convention on the Protection of Human Rights and Fundamental Freedoms (2013); European Court of Human Rights, Explanatory Report: Protocol No. 16 to the Convention on the Protection of Human Rights and Fundamental Freedoms (2013); European Court of Human Rights, Rules of the Court (2016) ch IX.

261 European Court of Human Rights, The Pilot-Judgment Procedure (2009).

262 *See* European Court of Human Rights, Accession by the European Union to the European Convention on Human Rights (2010).

263 *See* European Court of Human Rights, Accession by the European Union to the European Convention on Human Rights at sect. II.; European Court of Human Rights, Rules of the Court (2016) ch V.

264 *See* European Court of Human Rights, Accession by the European Union to the European Convention on Human Rights, *supra* note 263 at art 46. In limited circumstances there is a possibility of having the case re-examined by the Council of Ministers, although this is a rare occurrence. Id.

265 *See* The Right Honourable the Lord Woolf, Review of the Working Methods of the European Court of Human Rights (2005). At the time Lord Woolf wrote his findings in 2005 he noted that over 44,000 new complaints had been brought to the European Court in 2004 and that the total number of cases pending before the Court was over 82,000. Id. at 4.

266 *See* id.; European Court of Human Rights, Opinion of the Court on the Wise Persons' Report (2007); High Level Conference on the Future of the European Court of Human Rights, Interlaken Declaration (2010); European Court of Human Rights, Interlaken Follow-up: Principle of Subsidiarity (2010); High Level Conference on the Future of the European Court of Human Rights, Brighton Declaration (2012).

267 *See* European Court of Human Rights, The Interlaken Process and the Court (2012).

268 *See* European Court of Human Rights, The Interlaken Process and the Court: 2015 Report (2015) 3; *cf* European Court of Human Rights, The Interlaken Process and the Court: 2016 Report (2016) 3.

269 African Convention on Human and Peoples' Rights (1987) art 1.

270 Id. at art 2.

271 Id. at art 4.

272 Id. at art 3.

273 Id. at art 5.

274 Id.

275 Id. at art 6.

276 Id. at art 7.

277 Id. at art 8.

278 Id. at art 9.

279 Id.

280 Id. at art 11.

281 Id. at art 12.

282 Id. at art 13.

283 Id. at art 14.

284 Id. at art 15.

285 Id. at art 16.

286 Id. at art 17.

287 Id. at art 18.

288 Id. at arts 20–24.

289 Id. at art 29.

290 *See* id. at pt II.

291 Id. at art 45.

292 Id.

293 Id.

294 Id.

295 Id.

296 *See* id. at pt III.

297 Id.

298 *See* Protocol to the African Charter on Human and Peoples' Rights on the Establishment of an African Court on Human and Peoples' Rights (2003).
299 *Id.* at art 3.
300 *Id.* at art 5.
301 *Id.* at art 10.
302 *Id.* at art 27.
303 African Court of Human and Peoples' Rights, Rules of the Court (2009) Rule 26, pt V.
304 *Id.* at Rules 9, 10.
305 *Id.* at Rule 11.
306 *Id.* at pt II.

Chapter 19

Environmental organizations

Chapter contents

The final chapter in this section discusses environmental organizations in the international system. The inclusion of these organizations – and the treaty regimes giving rise to them – in the last chapter should by no means be seen as indicating that they are in any way least. Indeed, issues of environment and regulation at the international organization levels are of ever-increasing import and presence in international and domestic dialogue. And, as set out in the Conclusion chapter, such issues form the crux of many aspects of current and future issues in the international community and in international law *per se*. As such, it is essential to first set out the essential organizations to discussions and actions involving environmental law and policy.

United Nations Framework Convention on Climate Change and implementing entities

Background

The UN Framework Convention on Climate Change (UNFCCC) was adopted in 1992 with the goal of addressing greenhouse gas emissions and other contributing factors to climate change at the international level.[1] Underlying its foundations were core beliefs of the international community relating to the need for a concerted, international response to climate change that sought to balance principles of equity, fairness and sustainability with those of sovereignty and fundamental tenets of international law.[2] Some of the terms of the UNFCCC were ultimately left to subsequently adopted legal instruments, particularly the Kyoto Protocol and the 2016 Paris Agreement, to implement.[3]

Membership and structure

In order to assess the implementation of the UNFCCC, as well as to provide UNFCCC Member States with a permanent structure in which to hold discussions on future protocols and other developments, a Conference of the Parties was created within the terms of the UNFCCC itself.[4] Every Member State has a representative and vote at the Conference.[5] The Conference as a whole was deemed the "supreme body" of the UNFCCC, having the ability to: examine whether and how the terms and principles of the UNFCCC are being enforced by the Member States;[6] enable Member States to exchange knowledge and information regarding climate change, especially newly emerging scientific and technical information (aka technology transfer);[7] assist Member States in holding discussions regarding common climate change-related issues;[8] examine whether and how the terms of the UNFCCC are impacting climate change and associated issues, especially on the emission of identified greenhouse gases;[9] create reports and other publications regarding the UNFCCC and aspects of its implementation;[10] suggest changes to the UNFCCC which might be adopted by the Member States;[11] create sub-committees or other organs that are deemed necessary;[12] create rules and procedures for committees and also for conducting meetings;[13] and seek the input of other international organizations as well as non-governmental organizations (NGOs) and others with knowledge on the subject areas covered in the UNFCCC.[14]

Under the terms set out in the UNFCCC, the Conference meets every year,[15] although it can meet in between these times if necessary.[16] Each year the site of the Conference rotates and the chief of the delegation of the host State is deemed to be the nominal convener of the Conference. Full membership in the Conference is granted to UNFCCC Member States, however representatives from other UN-associated international organizations, as well as international organizations generally and accredited NGOs, are able to hold observer status.[17]

In order to implement the terms of the UNFCCC and oversee the Conference there is a UNFCCC Secretariat.[18] The Secretariat is charged with facilitating the Conference's yearly meetings, representing the Conference at meetings of other international organizations, and performing the general administrative work needed to ensure that the terms of the UNFCCC are properly carried out.[19] The UNFCCC specifically created several "subsidiary bodies" deemed necessary to ensure the proper implementation of its terms, such as the Subsidiary Body for Scientific and Technical Advice,[20] the Subsidiary Body for Implementation,[21] and the Financial Mechanism.[22]

The Subsidiary Body for Scientific and Technical Advice is open to all UNFCCC Member States and is intended to convene representatives from different disciplines that are necessary to providing the background required for technical advice on climate change.[23] It is intended to provide information on the current and potential future states of knowledge regarding climate change and climate change-related impacts, as well as serving the function of providing answers to and information on specific questions posed to it by the UNFCCC Member States and organization.[24]

The Subsidiary Body on Implementation is similarly open to all UNFCCC Member States, however representatives are to be from the government sector and possessing knowledge relating to climate change.[25] It is tasked with providing information on the current state of practice regarding climate change legislation and regulations, and with providing information on the potential climate change implications of proposed legislation and regulations.[26]

In a different vein from the subsidiary bodies, the Financial Mechanism is intended to assist in the implementation of financial policy-based funding between States or entities, as well as concepts and practices such as technology transfers.[27] Membership in the Financial Mechanism must be conducted equitably between the Member States, and it is required that the system for organizational governance and oversight utilize and promote transparency and good business practices.[28]

In terms of withdrawal, a Member State has the ability to leave the UNFCCC system – and associated protocols – by giving written notice, which is effective after a one-year period from the date of official notification.[29]

Functions

The UNFCCC enshrines many principles of international environmental law and requires that the measures taken by States to react to and attempt to mitigate climate change be related to each State's development status and presumed abilities stemming from this status, better known as "common but differentiated responsibilities."[30] In order to achieve this, the UNFCCC establishes two sets of States, those regarded as developed[31] and those regarded as developing and thus at a disadvantage in implementing meaningful climate change policies owing to the likely financial and other burdens.[32]

Kyoto-Protocol and associated entities

Kyoto Protocol

In recent years, the UNFCCC Conferences of the Parties have been heavily broadcast in the media and have been notable for their failures to reach permanent agreements for handling the new environmental issues that are facing the international community. However, this was not always the case, as the Conference was able to adopt the Kyoto Protocol in 1997 in order to guide law, policy and scientific activities in the environmental context.[33]

The key element of the Kyoto Protocol was the creation of more nuanced categories of States – Annex I for developed States and Annex II for developing States – in terms of requirements that they reduce their greenhouse gas emissions, particularly their carbon emissions.[34] These requirements placed a heavier burden on developed States than developing States, which was one of the reasons that the US failed to ratify the Kyoto Protocol. The Kyoto Protocol involved far more than a focus on carbon or other greenhouse gases in and of themselves, and indeed much of it centered on creating new and distinctive innovations in industry, agriculture, and other economic practices in order to promote sustainable development, environmental growth, economic growth and reductions in greenhouse gas emissions.[35] Also included in these terms was a focus on information-sharing and knowledge exchanges so as to promote parity in the domestic and international realms of environmental law and practice.[36]

Further, the Kyoto Protocol outlined a system that may be used to create a carbon trading market at the option of the States Parties.[37] Although no truly international carbon market has been created in the aftermath of the Kyoto Protocol, the European Union used this outline to form the EU Emissions Trading System, which functions as perhaps the most successful and visible form of carbon trading scheme devised to date.[38] In addition to carbon trading systems, the Kyoto Protocol created two other organizational entities that relate to carbon trading systems: the Clean Development Mechanism and Joint Implementation.

Subsequent to the creation of these entities through the Kyoto Protocol, the Adaptation Fund was created with a specific mandate of providing assistance to those particularly vulnerable States that are in the position of needing to adapt quickly and expansively.[39] The Adaptation Fund receives resources from the revenues generated by the Clean Development Mechanism's operations.[40] It is governed by an Adaptation Fund Board and managed by a specialized Secretariat that is responsible for assisting in the implementation of agreements with different recipient entities.[41]

The Kyoto Protocol is governed by the UNFCCC Conference of the Parties, which had voting and operational standing over implementation of Protocol, evaluation of activities and proposed future steps.[42] This included the ability of members to propose and create additional sub-organs within the Kyoto Protocol system.[43] Throughout the duration of the Kyoto Protocol's applicability, it was administered and overseen on a daily basis by the UNFCCC Secretariat.[44]

It was possible for the Kyoto Protocol's members to withdraw after providing official notice to the UN and waiting for one year.[45] However, withdrawal from the Kyoto Protocol would have been automatic in the event a UNFCCC member withdrew from the overarching Convention.[46]

Clean Development Mechanism

The Clean Development Mechanism (CDM) is a program through which a developed State can assist a developing State in creating and implementing a project aimed at reducing the developing State's carbon emissions.[47] This assistance is most typically in the form of providing financing and/or technical assistance for the project.[48] Given the importance of sovereignty, the assistance must of course be voluntary, meaning that a developed State could not decide to start a project in the developing State without the consent of the developing State.[49] Further, it is intended that CDM projects be created for long-term benefits and sustainability rather than for a short-term reduction in carbon emissions alone.[50] To avoid duplication or attempts to gain credits not properly attributable to a project, qualifying CDM projects are required to result in carbon reduction benefits beyond those which would otherwise occur in a particular area.[51]

The Kyoto Protocol does not simply allow developed and developing States to enter into these agreements and issue carbon credits on their own.[52] Instead, the Kyoto Protocol and the rules that have grown out of it have created an organizational mechanism to handle these projects and issue carbon credits. Indeed, these carbon credits are not free – in order to assist the UNFCCC organization with financing other projects, there is a 2 per cent tax placed on all issued carbon credits.[53]

Organizationally, the highest level of governance for the CDM is the Executive Board, which reports to the main UNFCCC Conference.[54] There are 10 full members of the Executive Board and then 10 alternative members, all of which must be States that have ratified the Kyoto Protocol.[55] There is a set quota of members from certain organizations and locations, specifically five members must be from UN associated regional groups, two members must be from developed States, two members must be from developing States and one member must be from a small island developing State.[56]

The Executive Board has a number of functions, such as: creating procedures and rules for the functioning of the CDM process; giving approval to new scientific methods that will be used for

CDM projects and that claim to reduce carbon emissions; giving ultimate recognition and approval to CDM projects; physically issuing the carbon credits at the end of a project; registering the CDM projects that have been completed or are ongoing; assisting in the location of interested investors and partner projects for proposed CDM measures; and providing the public with access to information on past, current and proposed CDM projects.[57] Additionally, the Executive Board has the power to create panels, committees and other subsidiary bodies as it deems necessary to assist in the development and implementation of meaningful CDM projects.[58]

Of course, the main work of the CDM project is conducted at the national and local level. At the national level, CDM projects are coordinated and overseen by designated national authorities.[59] The designated national authorities also act as liaisons with the CDM Executive Board in order to ensure that there will be issuance of the carbon credits at the end of the project.[60] To date, more than one billion carbon credits have been issued through the CDM system and there have been successful projects – from airports to ports to wind farms – created as a result.[61]

Joint Implementation

The Joint Implementation system is very similar to the CDM except that it technically involves only developed States. In the Joint Implementation system a developed State would be able to earn carbon credits for assisting with a qualifying project in another developed State that is deemed to be less fully developed.[62] There is an extensive series of guidelines for the use of the Joint Implementation system in order to ensure that projects are truly meeting the goal of reduced carbon emissions.[63]

The highest entity within the organizational structure of the Joint Implementation system is the Joint Implementation Supervisory Committee, which reports to the UNFCCC Conference of the Parties and is tasked with oversight of approved Joint Implementation projects.[64] The membership of the Supervisory Committee is decided by geography, with nine members coming from a combination of developed and developing States.[65] The tenth member of the Supervisory Committee is also a representative from a small island developing State.[66] Overall, the Supervisory Committee is a more consolidated entity than the CDM Executive Board, meaning that there are fewer established layers of organizational structure.[67]

Paris Agreement on climate action

After several years of negotiations, the international community eventually adopted the Paris Agreement on climate action in 2015 as the follow-up to the expired Kyoto Protocol. The Paris Agreement is notable for a many reasons, key among them the incorporation of sustainable development as a policy goal and the attempt to keep global temperature increases at no more than 1.5 degrees Celsius above pre-industrial levels.[68] In conjunction with attempts to ensure compliance, each Member State is required to file a nationally determined contributions Statement each year, broken down by carbon emissions, including the emissions from industries and other sources.[69]

Within the text of the Paris Agreement is the endorsement of a relatively new entity, the Warsaw International Mechanism for Loss and Damage associated with Climate Change Impacts.[70] The Warsaw Mechanism is intended to address issues associated with severe or unpredictable weather and other natural disasters that can be affected by climate change.[71] Included in the intended areas covered by the Warsaw Mechanism are emergency preparedness, creation of early warning systems, handling permanent and short-term damage from natural events, comprehensive risk assessment and management, risk insurance and financing methods, handling of non-economic losses, and addressing the environmental and other forms of damage caused.[72]

Additionally, there are new commitment requirements for developed States to provide financial assistance for developing States in terms of mitigation and adaptation efforts.[73] One further entity created through the Paris Agreement is the Technology Mechanism, which is intended to assist in facilitating technology transfers.[74] Finally, the Paris Agreement creates a framework for the implementation of transparency measures in climate change laws and regulations.[75]

United Nations Environment Programme

Background

The UN Environment Programme (UNEP) is a UN-affiliated international organization, the goal of which is to provide assistance in the creation and implementation of environmental protection and development while still protecting future generations.[76] Specifically, the UNEP is tasked with assisting in the creation and implementation of environmentally friendly laws and policies at the domestic and international level, generating scientific information on the environment and threats to it at the domestic, regional and international level, assisting in environmentally-focused technology transfer, and creating partnerships between civil society, governments, international organizations and NGOs.[77]

Structure and membership

As a UN-affiliated international organization, the UNEP is ultimately accountable to the UN General Assembly and must periodically report to ECOSOC.[78] The highest-level organ within the UNEP is the General Council, which is directly responsible to ECOSOC.[79] There are 58 members on the General Council, each of whom is elected by the Environment Assembly[80] and, within the 58 members, the Environment Assembly is required to keep the idea of a geographic balance in mind when electing members.[81] The General Council is responsible for oversight of the Secretariat equivalent within the UNEP, and also handles inter- and intra-organizational environmental issues.[82] As a part of this function, the General Council is charged with acting as the overall UN environmental advisory entity.[83]

The Environment Assembly is the plenary organ of UNEP, in which each Member State has a seat and a vote.[84] Key among its abilities is the power to create committees and sub-organs which are able to address the specific needs of the constituencies involved in and impacted by UNEP's work.[85]

The UNEP Secretariat exists as a standard secretariat entity for the UNEP organizational needs and structure as well as meeting the needs of the multilateral environmental agreements that has designated UNEP as the home of their secretariats.[86] It is headed by an Executive Director who is elected through the UNEP organs and is responsible for functions and duties as dictated by the Environment Assembly.[87]

The daily functions of the UNEP are handled by a senior management team and supported by a bureaucratic system that includes offices around the world.[88] Included in this bureaucratic system are functional programs, which handle specific issues of environmental policy involving science as well as law.[89] These programs are: early warning and assessment (for environmental disasters and environmental harm), environmental policy implementation, technology, industry and economics, regional cooperation, environmental law, Global Environmental Facility Coordination (this is a specialized funding program for environmental projects that is run in cooperation with the World Bank), and communications and information.[90]

In addition, the UNEP is host to secretariats that are created through a number of key international environmental law treaties such as the Convention on Biological Diversity, the Convention on International Trade in Endangered Species of Flora and Fauna and the Convention on Migratory Species.[91]

Functions

With the creation of the Sustainable Development Goals (SDGs), the UNEP has been tasked with further responsibilities regarding programming and assistance to bridge between the SDGs and environmental laws and policies at the domestic and international levels.[92] In addition, issues that have been identified as playing a specific role in climate change and associated harms, such as desertification and drought, are of particular importance to the UNEP structure.[93] It is also heavily involved with the implementation and evolution of the Paris Agreement.[94]

United Nations Development Programme

Background

The UN Development Programme (UNDP) is a UN-affiliated international organization that works in environmental programming and policy as well as health, labor and business development in order to encourage the sustainable growth and development of developing States throughout the world.[95] Through the nature of its work, the UNDP is also heavily involved in attempts to secure the implementation of the Sustainable Development Goals.[96]

Structure and membership

The highest organ within the UNDP is the Executive Board, which is elected by ECOSOC and reports to ECOSOC.[97] There are specific geographical requirements for the UNDP's Executive Board membership, namely eight members from Africa, seven members from Asia and the Pacific, four members from Eastern Europe, five members from Latin America and the Caribbean, and 12 members from Western Europe and "other States".[98] In addition, there is a President of the Executive Board, however that position rotates between Member States every year based loosely on geography.[99]

The daily work of the UNDP is overseen by a bureaucracy that is headed by an Administrator.[100] Underneath the Administrator is a series of regional offices and then individual Member State offices that are charged with implementing UNDP policy at the regional and local level, and providing the UNDP with information on policy effectiveness from these perspectives.[101] There are also many internal UNDP offices that handle the administration of UNDP projects and work with other entities such as international organizations and NGOs.[102]

Functions

Due to the multifaceted nature of the UNDP's mandate, it is not uncommon for it to merge many different policies – including those which relate to different aspects of environmental concerns – together in holistic policies and procedures.[103] This includes the incorporation of mandatory Social and Environmental Standards for every UNDP project or associated project in order to ensure that there is a balance between the potential impacts and benefits of the UNDP's actions.[104]

Additionally, the UNDP is extremely involved in ensuring accountability in its operations, and has evolved from working simply within the overarching UN system for accountability to generating its own apparatus.[105] An integral part of this is the Code of Ethics promulgated by the UNDP for its staff and associated personnel.[106] The UNDP also places a heavy emphasis on evaluation of its activities generally as well as for the purposes of ensuring accountability and anti-corruption.[107]

Conclusions

This chapter has discussed critical environmental organizations, many of which have been created under one another's auspices, or as elements of an overall plan for the implementation of a long-range-based international treaty regime. In itself, this sets the entities discussed here apart from many of the other international organizations profiled in this book, since other international organizations do not have the same tendency to function as nesting dolls of policy as their environmental counterparts.

At the same time, the environmental organizations have demonstrated the flexibility of the genre through the incorporation of newly emerging science, financing, and other methodologies in subsequent iterations of regulation and policy. This is a testament to the durability of environmental organizations in general, as they exist in an atmosphere of constant technical change accompanied by changes in the way that domestic and international laws and policies conceive of appropriate remedies and measures.

Notes

1 *See generally* United Nations Framework Convention on Climate Change (1992) art 2.
2 *See id.* at preamble.
3 *See generally* Kyoto Protocol to the UN Framework Convention on Climate Change (1992).
4 *Id.* at art 7.
5 *See id.*
6 *See id.*
7 *See id.*
8 *See id.*
9 *See id.*
10 *See id.*
11 *See id.*
12 *See id.*
13 *See id.*
14 *See id.*
15 *Id.* at art 7(4).
16 *Id.* at art 7(5).
17 *Id.* at art 7(6).
18 *Id.* at art 8.
19 *Id.*
20 *Id.* at art 9. For information on activities of the Subsidiary Body for Scientific and Technological Advice, *see, e.g.,* UNFCCC, Report of the Subsidiary Body for Scientific and Technological Advice on its forty-third session, FCCC/SBSTA/2016/2 (2016); UNFCCC, Report of the Subsidiary Body for Scientific and Technological Advice on its forty-second session, FCCC/SBSTA/2015/2 (2015); UNFCCC, Report of the Subsidiary Body for Scientific and Technological Advice on its thirty-eighth session, FCCC/SBSTA/2013/3 (2013); UNFCCC, Report of the Subsidiary Body for Scientific and Technological Advice on its thirtieth session, FCCC/SBSTA/2009/3 (2009); UNFCCC, Report of the Subsidiary Body for Scientific and Technological Advice on its twenty-sixth session, FCCC/SBSTA/2007/4 (2007); UNFCCC, Report of the Subsidiary Body for Scientific and Technological Advice on its sixteenth session, FCCC/SBSTA/2002/6 (2002); UNFCCC, Report of the Subsidiary Body for Scientific and Technological Advice on its twelfth session, FCCC/SBSTA/2000/5 (2000); UNFCCC, Report of the Subsidiary Body for Scientific and Technological Advice on its fifth session, FCCC/SBSTA/1997/4 (1997); UNFCCC, Report of the Subsidiary Body for Scientific and Technological Advice on its first session, FCCC/SBSTA/1995/3 (1995).
21 Kyoto Protocol, *supra* note 3 at art 10. For information on activities of the Subsidiary Body for Implementation, *see, e.g.,* UNFCCC, Report of the Subsidiary Body for Implementation, FCCC/SBI/2017/7 (2017); UNFCCC, Report of the Subsidiary Body for Implementation, FCCC/SBI/2016/8 (2016); UNFCCC, Report of the Subsidiary Body for Implementation, FCCC/SBI/2009/8 (2009); UNFCCC, Report of the Subsidiary Body for Implementation, FCCC/SBI/2003/8 (2003); UNFCCC, Report of the Subsidiary Body for Implementation, FCCC/SBI/2001/8 (2001).
22 Kyoto Protocol, *supra* note 3 at art 11. The purpose of this particular subsidiary body is to ensure that efforts for developed States to assist developing States in financing projects that promote the environment are properly implemented. *Id.*
23 UNFCCC, *supra* note 1 at art 9(1).
24 *Id.* at art 9(2).
25 *Id.* at art 10(10).
26 *Id.* at art 10(2).
27 *Id.* at art 11.
28 *Id.*
29 *Id.* at art 25.

30 Id. at art 4(1). Other essential principles in the UNFCCC are articulated as "The Parties should protect the climate system for the benefit of present and future generations of humankind, on the basis of equity and in accordance with their common but differentiated responsibilities and respective capabilities. Accordingly, the developed country Parties should take the lead in combating climate change and the adverse effects thereof . . . The Parties should take precautionary measures to anticipate, prevent or minimize the causes of climate change and mitigate its adverse effects. Where there are threats of serious or irreversible damage, lack of full scientific certainty should not be used as a reason for postponing such measures, taking into account that policies and measures to deal with climate change should be cost-effective so as to ensure global benefits at the lowest possible cost. To achieve this, such policies and measures should take into account different socio-economic contexts, be comprehensive, cover all relevant sources, sinks and reservoirs of greenhouse gases and adaptation, and comprise all economic sectors. Efforts to address climate change may be carried out cooperatively by interested Parties. The Parties have a right to, and should, promote sustainable development. Policies and measures to protect the climate system against human-induced change should be appropriate for the specific conditions of each Party and should be integrated with national development programmes, taking into account that economic development is essential for adopting measures to address climate change. The Parties should cooperate to promote a supportive and open international economic system that would lead to sustainable economic growth and development in all Parties, particularly developing country Parties, thus enabling them better to address the problems of climate change. Measures taken to combat climate change, including unilateral ones, should not constitute a means of arbitrary or unjustifiable discrimination or a disguised restriction on international trade."). Id. at art 3.
31 Id. at art 4(2), 4(3).
32 Id.
33 See Kyoto Protocol, supra note 3.
34 Id. at art 1.
35 See id. at art 2(1)(a).
36 See id. at art 2(1)(b).
37 Id. at art 17.
38 See European Union, The EU Emissions Trading System (EU ETS) (2016).
39 Adaptation Fund, Governance, https://www.adaptation-fund.org/about/governance/, last accessed 15 January 2018.
40 Id.
41 Id.
42 Kyoto Protocol, supra note 3 at art 13.
43 Id.
44 Id. at art 14.
45 Id. at art 27.
46 Id.
47 See id. at art.12.
48 Id.
49 Id.
50 Id. at art 12(5).
51 Id. at art 12(6).
52 Id.
53 About CDM, Clean Development Mechanism, http://cdm.unfccc.int/about/index.html, last accessed 15 January 2018.
54 Governance, Clean Development Mechanism, http://cdm.unfccc.int/about/index.html, last accessed 15 January 2018.
55 Id.
56 Id.
57 Id.
58 Id.
59 Designated National Authorities, Clean Development Mechanism, http://cdm.unfccc.int/DNA/index.html, last accessed 14 January 2018.
60 Id.
61 Id.
62 See Eligibility Requirements, Joint Implementation, http://ji.unfccc.int/Eligibility/index.html, last accessed 15 January 2018.
63 See Criteria for Baseline Setting and Monitoring, Joint Implementation, http://ji.unfccc.int/CritBasMon/index.html, last accessed 15 January 2018.
64 See Joint Implementation Supervisory Committee, Joint Implementation, http://ji.unfccc.int/Sup_Committee/index.html, last accessed 15 January 2018.
65 See id.
66 See id.
67 See id.

68 Paris Agreement on climate action (2015) art 2.
69 Id. at art 4.
70 Id. at art 8.
71 Id.
72 Id.
73 Id. at art 9.
74 Id. at art 10.
75 Id. at art 13.
76 About, UN Environment Programme, http://web.unep.org/about/, last accessed 15 January 2018.
77 Id.
78 Id.
79 Id.
80 Id.
81 Id. Specifically, according to decisions of the General Assembly, 16 seats are allotted to African States, 13 seats are allotted to Asian States, 6 seats are allotted to Eastern European States, 10 seats are allotted to Latin American States, and 13 seats are allotted to "Western European and other States." See UNGA, 2112th plenary meeting (1972).
82 See UNGA, 2112th plenary meeting, supra note 81.
83 See id.
84 See Rules of Procedure of the United Nations Environment Assembly of the Environment Programme, UNEP/EA.3/3 (2016) pt III.
85 See id. at rules 61–63.
86 See id. at pt V.
87 See id. at rules 25–27.
88 Id.
89 Id.
90 Id. UNEP, Medium Term Strategy 2014–2017 (2015); UNEP, Medium Term Strategy 2018–2021 (2016).
91 Rules of Procedure of the United Nations Environment Assembly of the Environment Programme, UNEP/EA.3/3 (2016) rules 25–27; UNEP, Medium Term Strategy 2014–2017 (2015); UNEP, Medium Term Strategy 2018–2021, supra note 90; United Nations Environment Assembly of the United Nations Environment Programme, Relationship between the United Nations Environment Programme and the multilateral environmental agreements for which it provides the secretariats, UNEP/EA.2/Res.18 (2016); United Nations Environment Assembly of the United Nations Environment Programme, Enhancing the work of the United Nations Environment Programme in facilitating cooperation, collaboration and synergies among biodiversity-related conventions, UNEP/EA.2/Res.17 (2016).
92 See United Nations Environment Assembly of the United Nations Environment Programme, Role, functions and modalities for United Nations Environment Programme implementation of the SAMOA Pathway as a means of facilitating achievement of the Sustainable Development Goals, UNEP/EA.2/Res.4 (2016); United Nations Environment Assembly of the United Nations Environment Programme, Delivering on the 2030 Agenda for Sustainable Development, UNEP/EA.2/Res.5 (2016); United Nations Environment Assembly of the United Nations Environment Programme, Sustainable management of natural capital for sustainable development and poverty eradication, UNEP/EA.2/Res.13 (2016).
93 See United Nations Environment Assembly of the United Nations Environment Programme, Combating desertification, land degradation and drought and promoting sustainable pastoralism and rangelands, UNEP/EA.2/Res.24 (2016).
94 United Nations Environment Assembly of the United Nations Environment Programme, Supporting the Paris Agreement, UNEP/EA.2/Res.6 (2016).
95 See About Us, UN Development Programme, http://www.undp.org/content/undp/en/home/operations/about_us.html, last accessed 15 January 2018.
96 See id.
97 Information note about the Executive Board, UN Development Programme, http://www.undp.org/content/undp/en/home/operations/executive_board/information_noteontheexecutiveboard/, last accessed 15 January 2018.
98 Id.
99 Id.
100 See Leadership, UN Development Programme, http://www.undp.org/content/undp/en/home/operations/leadership/administrator.html, last accessed 15 January 2018.
101 Id.
102 Id.
103 See, e.g., UNDP, UNDP strategic vision on assistance to crisis-affected countries, DP/2007/20/Rev.1 (2007); UNDP, UNDP strategic plan 2008–2011, DP/2007/43/Add.1 (2008); UNDP, Decisions adopted by the Executive Board in 2010, DP/2011/2 (2011); UNDP, Decisions adopted by the Executive Board in 2011, DP/2011/21 (2011); UNDP, UNDP Strategic Plan 2014–2017, DP/2013/40 (2013); UNDP, Multilateral Aid Review: United Nations Development Programme (2011).

104 *See* UNDP, Stakeholder Response Mechanism: Overview and Guidance (2014); UNDP, Investigation Guidelines: Social and Environmental Compliance Unit (2014).

105 *See* UNDP, The UNDP accountability system: Accountability framework and oversight policy, DP/2008/16/Rev.1 (2008).

106 UNDP, Code of Ethics: Operating with Unwavering Integrity (2017).

107 *See* UNDP, Annual report on evaluation in UNDP 2010, DP/2011/24 (2011); UNDP, Annual report on evaluation in UNDP 2011, DP/2012/20 (2012); UNDP, UNDP policy against fraud and other corrupt practices (2015); UNDP, Independent Evaluation Office: Evaluation Annual Report 2015 (2016); UNDP, Independent Evaluation Office: Evaluation Annual Report 2016 (2017).

Chapter 20

Conclusion

This book began with a seemingly innocuous question: what is an international organization? After reading the contents of the work and studying the general and specific aspects of international organizations, the answer should include elements of openness and flexibility, as well as an understanding of the laws and rules that are applicable to these organizations. In other words, the best answer to this question might focus on organizations that generally apply standard laws and rules but are also in a state of constant evolution.

Combining the certainty of law with the flexibility of evolution could perhaps seem counterintuitive, especially in the context of an organization tasked with creating and implementing international law and norms. However, the lessons of this book prove quite the contrary. Indeed, a quintessential aspect of the history and practice of international organizations is that they are durable and able to incorporate flexibility in everything from membership to function without losing the legitimacy they have gained in the international community.

This is not an easy feat, and indeed in the years before the creation of the United Nations very few attempted to use a system that would be recognized as an international organization and even fewer were successful in doing so. A primary example of this comes from the League of Nations, which was founded after World War I with many of the same intentions as the United Nations but was unable to sustain itself in the face of a constantly changing and increasingly hostile international legal and political community. This failure can be attributed to many factors; however, underlying most of them is an inherent inability of the organization to balance attempts at preserving legitimacy with the ability to adapt to the international climate in which it functioned. By contrast, the United Nations has been able to survive and grow as an international organization – and in many circles the international organization – because its members have been flexible when faced with difficult legal, political and societal problems.

The legitimacy of international organizations derives from the strengths of their foundational texts, the willingness of their members to be flexible in their application in order to realistically function, and their ability to address issues as neutral actors when it might be impossible for States themselves to do so. The nearly sacred place in which opinions of the International Court of Justice are held – even by those on the losing end of them – provide illustrations of this legitimacy.

And this type of legitimacy is what has provided the international community with a greater sense of openness and participation which has led to State formation and dialogue between States and private entities that would not have otherwise been possible. For example, the UN Trusteeship Council was an essential tool in ensuring the process of decolonization occurred and for providing assistance to those colonial holdings seeking to become independent States. Although it has finished work for the moment, the Trusteeship Council is a prime example of the ways in which an international organization may give a voice to those who are otherwise without power and access. In so doing, it emphasizes its legitimacy at the same time as it seeks to solve issues that plague the international community it is pledged to serve.

This book has used Part I as a vehicle to understanding the components of international organizations which have led to their rise, permanence and ability to exert legitimacy in the international and domestic spheres. In Chapter 2, the book provided the history necessary to appreciate how and why international organizations have developed in the way they have, including examples of international organizations which did not succeed in their early iterations. This was done as an expression of the belief that there are as many lessons for readers in the failure of entities such as the League of Nations as there are in the successes of entities such as the United Nations.

In addition, Chapter 2 provided insights into the standard UN structure and functions. More than simply necessary to an understanding of the UN as an organization, these insights provide an explanation of the basic system on which the majority of international organizations have developed in the past decades. This is essential to understanding how and where the balance between organizational law and flexibility might occur and methods for resolving it in a sustainable manner. It is for the same reason that the Vienna Conventions were included in that chapter; without understanding the gap-filling provisions for the construction of international law and organizations it is impossible to understand the terminology choices made by organizations themselves.

Chapter 3 focused on membership in international organizations and stressed the various dynamics involved in this from the perspective of the international organization and the State. For the international organization, membership laws and procedures are essential to ensuring that only those intent on following its rules are in fact admitted, while at the same time having to balance this against the potential benefit of including those who are in the process of becoming capable of following these rules. For the would-be Member States, especially those emerging from conflict or otherwise having newly gained their independence, the ability to join an international organization may be seen as a way of bolstering their legitimacy and credibility as a member of the international community as a whole. In both cases, there are losses and gains to be made in the membership process.

The focus of Chapter 4 was on voting rights within an international organization. As the examples demonstrated, it would be highly unusual for a State to join an international organization and yet have no voting rights at all. However, while there is typically one organ in which each State may have a vote, there are typically others in which a Member State will not be able to vote unless it is elected for a certain period of time or because of a particular status. A necessary evil, perhaps, given the size of the international community of States and the seriousness of some issues involved, yet still a method of imposing uneven status which must be balanced against the overall benefit of the organization for Member States which do not have a vote in all organs. Similar considerations must enter the discussion when there are organizations in which votes possessed are tied to an interest in the organization such as the number of shares held. Regardless the potential for inequality in these realities, they are borne by the impacted Member States because of the legitimacy of and potential benefits from the organization.

Function and structure are the centers of attention in Chapter 5 and demonstrate the many ways in which international organizations can be crafted to represent the needs of the constituencies they are meant to serve while still using similar structures. This reinforces the lessons of Chapter 2 in terms of the translatability of the UN's general structures and highlights their legitimacy across various fields and organization forms.

Acceptance of functions and structures within which to operate as an international organization must, in turn, come with attendant burdens for failure to comply with their strictures. Chapter 6 examines this balancing requirement in terms of available punishments in the context of international level and highlights the importance of having multiple options available in order to accomplish the goals of the organization while not causing severe harm to citizens of the errant Member State. This is a delicate determination, as the excessive use of punishments can lead to questions of legitimacy in the same way that the failure to use punishments may also generate questions as to the organization's abilities.

The rights and duties of international organizations, the international community and of host States to one another were discussed in Chapter 7 and Chapter 8 of the book in order to provide a necessary perspective on the practicalities of implementing agreements relating to international organizations. All of these relationships require the ceding and acquiring of certain levels of power and sovereignty, decisions which are not to be undertaken lightly in the international or domestic spheres and which can have significant consequences for perceived and actual legitimacy and durability. This is particularly so in the case of an international organization, as it will be rendered functionally meaningless if its actors and offices cannot be given the basic protections necessary to carry out their functions without interference from State or domestic actors.

Switching to the exercise of certain functions by international organizations, Chapter 9 examined the ability of an organization to negotiate an international instrument – binding or non-binding – under its offices. The chapter demonstrated the balance between the legitimacy of international organizations as honest brokers and sources of instrument negotiation forums at the same time as it discussed the limitations on organizations since they cannot ratify instruments or hold States accountable under them unless they have successfully completed the domestic ratification process.

As was noted in Chapter 1, disputes are a simple fact of life in any sphere and this is no less the case in the realm of international organizations. With this in mind, Chapter 10 reviewed the ways in which disputes can be settled at the international organization level, ranging from conciliation and mediation with the assistance of outside actors to the highly formalized systems used by the International Court of Justice and the World Trade Organization. The key points in this chapter are the ways in which flexibility in settling disputes can result in the durability that is necessary for international organizations to become entrenched members of the international community and hold legitimacy.

In some instances, however, it may be necessary for an international organization to cease its operations and ultimately terminate its operations as a matter of law and practice. Chapter 11 addressed these instances and the ways in which such actions are validly effected under international law and the law of international organizations. This emphasized that durability in international organizations does have boundaries and that, when these boundaries are reached, it is necessary for organizations to act through established methods in order to effect an orderly and equitable winding-up process.

From that point on, this book provided a number of examples of international organizations and how they function. These organizations were clustered by theme of activity and intended meaning, allowing the reader to compare and contrast them throughout. Regardless the theme or international organization discussed, what is evident is that those organizations which have exhibited longevity and which are regarded as legitimate in the international community have been able to demonstrate flexibility in their laws and application of them as necessary. To this end, the book examined international organizations relating to some of the most sensitive areas for statehood, such as military functions and economic practices, as well as some of the most beneficial areas of policy, such as joining together in regional organizations.

Understanding the answer to what an international organization is proves essential for current matters of international law and policy. Indeed, some of the most important questions of the moment are being debated and framed in the setting of international organizations and this is unlikely to change in a world that is increasingly globalized in its approaches to law as it is in its approaches to technology or trade.

At the same time, international organizations will doubtless be the site of much law and policy generation surrounding future issues that face the international and domestic communities. Emerging issues such as climate change and its impacts – from environmental to financial to issues of statehood and State identity – will require international answers in order to create uniform methods of implementation. This includes the growth and faceting of the Sustainable Development Goals, which have been embraced by the majority of international organizations at some level, although without a standard method of coordination for these efforts.

Issues of military and security threats to the international communities have, tragically, changed drastically since the time that NATO and the UN were founded in order to counter conflicts. Increasingly, the threats faced by the international community do not originate in one State or even one block of States but rather in an organization that spans borders and evades its unwilling host States as well as the States it victimizes. In this scenario, international organizations are vital to any potential responses to these threats as well as to post-conflict attempts at reconstructing domestic and international societies.

Financially, the international community is increasingly bound together through the merging of markets and consumers, which has become endemic of globalized trade and finance. The regulation of this requires States to work in concerted efforts rather than simply acting on their own to regulate an industry, and international organizations are the logical actors to fill the needs of States, producers, regulators and consumers.

Finally, Brexit – the word that seems to have changed the world – is an ongoing phenomenon that seems likely to continue to raise uncertainty in a variety of constituencies. It is also an occurrence framed within the confines of a unique international organization and will, as a result, find solutions only through the law of international organizations.

These represent only the tip of a large iceberg of issues facing the international community that will, doubtless, fall under the rubric of international organizations at some point in the future. Given the nature of these issues as existential challenges or opportunities to international law and the actors impacted by it, perhaps a follow-up question is necessary: what is the international community in the age of international organizations?

Index